to Claude BOWERS

Luis Quintanilla
1954

My Mission to Spain

WATCHING THE REHEARSAL

FOR WORLD WAR II

BY

Claude G. Bowers

Former United States Ambassador to Spain

SIMON AND SCHUSTER · NEW YORK · 1954

LIBRARY OF CONGRESS CATALOG CARD NUMBER: 54–6668
DEWEY DECIMAL CLASSIFICATION NUMBER: 92

MANUFACTURED IN THE UNITED STATES OF AMERICA

 66

Foreword

For six years, during the most dramatic period in Spanish history since the crusade against the Moors, I was accredited Ambassador to Spain by President Roosevelt. I loved Spain and had admiration and affection for the Spanish people. During the first three and a half years I traveled extensively into every section of that delectable country, partly to familiarize myself with the Spanish scene, but frequently to check personally on the ground absurd stories of anarchy and disorder put out by Fascist propagandists. No one can grasp the significance of what took place later without this background of political maneuvering, since the international conspiracy of the Fascist powers was quietly unfolding during the period of outward peace when covert conversations were going on in Berlin and Rome. The record of the political events during these years reveals the technique of the totalitarians, of both the Right and Left, in setting the stage for their attacks on democratic nations.

The manuscript was withheld from publication during the World War because its caustic treatment of Mr. Chamberlain might have been misinterpreted as an attack upon the English people; and later because I doubted the propriety of its publication while active in the foreign service of the United States. Now that I have retired it can be published after fourteen years.

The immediate menace just before the war was the Nazi and Fascist segment of the totalitarians; since the war the immediate menace has come from the communist segment, and the danger is that in fighting one we may lose sight of the antidemocratic ideology of the other, which is by no means dead. I prefer to think that we shall not return to the shoddy days just before the war when it was popular in high circles to believe that to oppose communism one must follow the Fascist line. The two segments of totalitarianism are equally bent on the extermination of democracy and the freedoms.

I hope I have been able to picture the lovely Spain of peace. In driving thousands of miles through this magic land I came to love its mountains looming on the horizon everywhere, enveloped in their blue or purple haze, the quaint old dusty villages soaked with history, the old cathedrals with their works of art, the romance of the aged cities, the laughing, happy people.

Across the stage will pass distinguished nonpolitical figures of international renown—Benavente, the dramatist; Unamuno, the philosopher; Madariaga, the historian and biographer; Belmonte, the famous matador; Zuloaga, the painter; Margarita Xirgu, the actress; Argentina, the dancer; and Ramón del Valle Inclán and Pérez de Ayala, the novelists.

The political leaders in the forefront behind whom the totalitarian conspiracy was hatching are all here as I knew them— Azaña, Lerroux, Gil Robles, Count Romanones, Martínez Barrio, Juan Negrin, Prieto, and all the others. I have tried to paint their portraits with fidelity to the truth.

Throughout the war in Spain, after the active participation of the Axis became notorious, my sympathy was with the Spanish republicans and their democratic ideology. Had the struggle been confined to Spaniards on the issue of monarchy or republic I could have viewed it with objectivity. My allegiance is to democracy, and there can be democratic monarchies as in England and Scandinavia and totalitarian republics as in Russia and prewar Germany. In the Spanish war my sympathies were enlisted on the side of democracy. As a Jeffersonian democrat I could not feel otherwise.

My official relations with the governments of both the Right and Left were equally cordial.

The manuscript is based upon my diary, personal contacts and conversations, and dispatches that are not quoted.

If we are to preserve the heritage of our fathers, we must be prepared to fight as the gallant loyalists of Spain fought and died, holding back with their bodies and their blood for two and a half years the flood of barbarism that swept over Europe until they succumbed to the strange indifference of democratic nations in whose defense they were valiantly fighting. World War II began in Spain in 1936.

New York, November 1953   CLAUDE G. BOWERS

Contents

I

THE PRISTINE REPUBLIC

Chapter I

Two Presidents and a Minister

O N THE first of June, 1933, I presented my credentials to President Alcalá Zamora, of Spain, accompanied to the palace by the Presidential Guard on spirited black horses and in colorful uniforms. The Introducer of Ambassadors, Lopez Largo, sat beside me in gloomy silence, and he was the only Spaniard I was to meet who realized the popular conception of the "melancholy Don." I was conducted into a large room on the ground floor of the palace where the President's Military Household stood about in groups; and in the foreground stood a small but handsome man—Alcalá Zamora. He was of medium height, and rather slender, and his white hair and mustache accentuated the gypsy swarthiness of his color, the pink of his cheeks, and the luminous eyes that gave distinction to his countenance and denoted Moorish blood. The eyes were beaming pleasantly, and I was to find that he smiled readily.

After the brief speeches, his and mine, both striking the keynote of democracy, he shook hands warmly and smilingly led me to a couch for a brief conversation, which, despite its brevity, impressed me with the very human qualities of the man. I had been prepared to like Alcalá Zamora, and nothing I had seen had altered my preconceived impression. He had attained distinction at the Madrid Bar, and as an orator, though, being an Andalusian, he was a bit too prone to emphasize unduly the value of the rounded phrase.

Born in a small town in the province of Córdoba, he had moved to Madrid to participate in the political life of the monarchy, and, more than once, to serve as a minister of the King. Not long before the advent of the Republic he had become a militant spokesman of the republican revolt. In the exciting twilight days of the dynasty he had figured as the stellar attraction in the revolutionary demonstrations, and, when the rising of December, 1930, failed, he had gone to prison. There, he and his associates held their crowded levees; and, literally, he passed from prison to the provisional presidency of the Republic, proclaimed from the balcony of the Ministry of the Interior in the Puerta del Sol where Spanish patriots had been massacred by Napoleon.

The suddenness of his conversion to republicanism had excited some suspicion as to its depth. There was jealousy among some of the republican leaders who had borne the brunt of the battle through the long lean years, and there was hatred among the monarchists who could never condone what they described as the "ingratitude" and "disloyalty" of Alcalá Zamora. From both sides I heard uncomplimentary things about him before I had been in Madrid ten days. "The white rat!" exclaimed the Duke of Alba when his name was mentioned in conversation.

Slender and of low stature, he did not seem a revolutionary orator capable of dominating a tumultuous crowd. He was meticulously careful in the composition of his speeches to give them literary flavor. He had the Andalusian love of words, the artist's feeling for the phrase. His voice, while pleasant, lacked the Dantonian qualities, and yet he had been able to stir great audiences through the transmission of his own emotions to the crowd.

Early in his provisional presidency some of his future troubles were foreshadowed. There were definite limitations to his revolutionary creed. More than any other leader of the revolution he was a devout Catholic, and almost immediately he found himself embarrassed by measures touching on religion, favored by a majority of the Constituent Assembly, and his unhappiness became acute. On the fall of the monarchy, Cardinal Segura, Archbishop of Toledo, rendered no service to the church by the violence of his attacks on the Republic. Salvador de Madariaga believes that had his conduct been as temperate as that of Cardinal Vidal, Archbishop of Tarragona, the bitter resentment incurred by the Cardinal of Toledo might not have dominated the Constituent Assembly as it did. It not only separated the church and state, but it shocked Catholicity throughout the world by forbidding teaching by religious orders. When I asked why this was done I was reminded of Segura's fanatic attacks on the Republic and was asked if I doubted that religious orders would instill hatred of the Republic into the minds of children. Finally, in an attempt to stem the tide, Alcalá Zamora tendered his resignation. Azaña sprang into the breach with a powerful speech and he was chosen his successor. The Assembly continued its work and wrote into the fundamental law the provisions that had wrung from the tortured man his resignation.

And then he was elected President of the Republic.

In the clash of scruples and ambition, he yielded to the latter and took a solemn oath to put into effect the provisions that warred with his nature. Meanwhile, his resignation of the provisional presidency had made him an object of suspicion.

Quite soon, too, he was to alienate most of the political leaders of both the Right and Left. An erudite lawyer, with a passion for polemics, able, even brilliant, and convinced of his intellectual superiority, he had his full share of vanity. Soon he was seeking to circumvent the constitutional limitations of his office. More and more he was to annoy his ministers by his persistent interference with their program. The length of his speeches before the Council of Ministers, trying to divert them from their purpose, became the subject of jests in the cafés. It was less at the substance of the speeches that the jokers smiled than at the length of the reprimand, and the disposition to treat the ministers as schoolboys to be instructed.

Then, too, his manner was not conciliatory. A certain condescension in his smile did not endear him to his co-workers. When I arrived in Madrid I was amazed at the absurdity of the stories set afloat about him through malice. That he was a decent and honest man, his critics generally conceded. He had exceptional executive ability and a truly marvelous memory. He was so conscientious that he studied routine decrees of his ministers, and in this concentration on details he lost perspective.

Maintaining offices on the ground floor of the palace, he declined to live there, and he continued to reside in his own house,
quite near my own, distinguished from the houses of private citizens solely by the sentinels at his gate. His friends ascribed this to
his innate simplicity; his enemies, among the monarchists, assured
the stranger that he was ashamed to move into the house of the
King whom he had served and against whom he had turned. The
gossips intensified their whispering campaign until he seemed
utterly alone.

2

Even before I presented my credentials a ministerial crisis was
in the offing. The Catalan politicians were making demands. The
bill prohibiting teaching by religious orders was in the hands of
Alcalá Zamora, who writhed in an agony of spirit. One day the
rumor spread that all the ministers had been excommunicated by
the Pope, and while this was a canard, it fanned the smoldering fire.
Rex Smith of the Associated Press had arranged for us to lunch
with Fernando de los Ríos, Minister of Justice, who had hesitated
to fix a date, with the explanation that very soon he might be plain
"Mr. de los Ríos." At length it was arranged for us to lunch in
Alcalá de Henares, and we were to meet at the embassy. Smith had
arrived and we were chatting, waiting for the minister, when I was
called to the telephone.

"I thought you might be interested to know," said Jay Allen of
the Chicago *Tribune*, "that the entire government has resigned."

Smith rushed into another room to notify his office, and, in his
absence, a black-bearded man, with keen, laughing eyes, came in.
It was the minister. Coming directly from the Council of Ministers,
he told me what had happened. The filling of a vacancy created by
the death of the Minister of Finance was up, along with the designation of a minister for a newly created department. Alcalá Zamora
agreed to Azaña's choice for Minister of Finance but insisted that
he would name the minister of the new department. Azaña did not
misinterpret the significance of this unusual demand.

"That implies," he said coldly, "that you have withdrawn your
confidence."

"If you interpret it that way, yes," said the President.

Instantly, Azaña tendered the resignation of the government.

It was assumed at the moment that Alcalá Zamora's action was motivated by his bitter resentment of the measure prohibiting teaching by religious orders. He had been savagely lashed by some churchmen as a renegade of the church, to which, in truth, he was almost fanatically devoted. That he was in a highly emotional state there can be no doubt. It was whispered about that he was suffering from a persecution complex, and it became fashionable in certain quarters to question his sanity. I had never credited these malicious stories, though some of my colleagues did. One day at an art exhibit at the Casa Velázquez, the ambassador of a South American Republic, who could not abide republics, said to me in a whisper: "Isn't it dreadful about the President?" "What about the President?" I asked, glancing at Alcalá Zamora discussing a picture with the French Ambassador a few feet away. "Why, night before last he was in such a state of hysteria that he crawled under the bed and said they were trying to kill him," was the astonishing reply. There stood the President, calm, serene, smiling, talking with animation with the French Ambassador. It was absurd. He was sane enough—no doubt of that. But his spirit was tortured by the knowledge that churchmen with zeal equal to his own were looking upon him as a renegade. The Madrid gossips had it that he had gone to his confessor for guidance, to be advised to consult some higher ecclesiastic authority, who had told him to sign the education bill and then resign. He signed, but he did not resign, and the tale is probably imaginary.

But he hated Azaña—no doubt of that. His vanity had been touched by the overshadowing of a more imposing personality and a greater intellect.

Acting on Azaña's resignation, the President invited Prieto, the socialist orator, to form a government, but he stumbled and fell over the obstacle put in his way—the insistence of the President that he include a member of Lerroux' party of opposition. When Prieto failed, Lerroux expected to be summoned to the palace. Had he formed a government it would not have survived a vote of confidence, and this would have meant elections the President wished to avoid. That night Lerroux retired early to gather strength for the work of the morrow; but at midnight Azaña was called to the

palace. With some shifting of positions, the new Azaña government was of the same political complexion as the last. The day it
was announced, Fernando de los Ríos called upon me in his new
role of Minister of Foreign Affairs.

3

I made my first visit to the Cortes to hear Azaña announce his
program and to witness the debate on Lerroux' motion of no
confidence. The lawmakers of Spain legislated in a beautiful
chamber, but little smaller than the United States Senate. The
benches of the deputies were in a crescent facing the President's
desk, each row a little higher than the one below. On one side, close
to the tribune, was the Blue Bench of the ministers. Behind the
President's desk was an alcove, shut off by a curtain, in which had
stood the throne. At a small table immediately before the tribune
sat the official reporters. On the walls were marble tablets bearing
the names of old leaders, most of whom had died a violent death—
Cánovas, Prim, Sagasta, and Galán and García Hernández, the
two young officers executed after the unsuccessful rising at Jaca
four months before the fall of the throne.

The chamber was lighted from the ceiling, which was painted
with historical pictures. In front of the rostrum was the speaker's
tribune, though only once was I to see it used. The press gallery
was small and always packed; and the diplomatic gallery was
smaller, but with a lounge room behind it. The public galleries
were always packed to capacity.

The sessions were usually scheduled for four o'clock, and at that
hour the street was patrolled by police, mounted and on foot. The
members appeared on time but lingered in the lobbies, and sometimes the galleries were filled almost an hour before a single deputy
appeared on the floor. At length, with the entrance of the President,
a gong sounded in the lobbies, and the members rushed in pell-
mell, laughing and talking like schoolboys after a recess. But once
in their seats, the deputies listened intently to the speakers. Now
and then, especially just before the rebellion of the generals, and the
invasion of the armed forces of the Axis, there were many stormy
scenes. On these occasions, the President vigorously rang his bell

and shouted through an amplifier, usually making a mighty but futile noise.

4

Azaña was speaking when I reached the gallery. Behind him sat the socialists and his own small party. The opposition, under Lerroux, sat directly facing the Blue Bench. It was my first view of Azaña, and it was evident at a glance that he had been grossly maligned by the cartoonists. He was speaking conversationally, fluently, with few gestures. Occasionally there was a spreading of the fingers, and a laying of the hand over the heart. Jean Herbette, the French Ambassador beside me, commented admiringly on his perfect Castilian. "No one speaks so purely," he said, and I was to find this the opinion of friend and foe alike. He was cheered lustily.

Then there was a stir in the chamber when Lerroux rose. It was also my first view of this picturesque, colorful figure. After seventy years of strenuous life, and in earlier years of robustious living, he stood erect as a ramrod. Short, sturdily built, and bald, he resembled Azaña in these features, but the resemblance ended there. He lacked Azaña's economy of words, his abhorrence of redundancy, his precision of diction, his closely knit reasoning. Fluency Lerroux had, and his voice was good, but the oratorical tricks of the stump speaker were too much in evidence, though, to do him justice, he did not saw the air.

The burden of his attack was less on Azaña than on the socialists, whom he attacked fiercely and loosely, calling forth bitter protests from the socialist benches, until Julián Besteiro, the scholarly President, had to resort to the gavel and the bell. When Lerroux falsely accused the socialists of fomenting trouble, a frail consumptive rose from the Blue Bench and said calmly: "That is a lie." The storm broke. The bell could not be heard as Lerroux' followers clamored that their chief had been insulted; but the old man, cynical from long experience, and probably knowing he had drawn on his imagination, and impervious to insult, waved them to silence.

The roll was called, and Azaña had his vote of confidence.

He was to have two months more. He had been Prime Minister from the forming of the Republic, but the accumulated grievances and disappointments of a long tenure were telling against him, and the opposition was complaining that on the completion of the constitution the Constituent Assembly should have been dissolved and elections called. The government was contending that until measures had been taken to give substance to the fundamental principles of the constitution, its work was unfinished.

Meanwhile, a young man named Gil Robles was going about the country organizing the opposition and arranging some incongruous combinations for the election.

5

Manuel Azaña spent most of his time in the palace of Buena Vista, but he received his ministers and diplomats at the Presidencia on the Castellana in a large brick mansion with stone trimmings, once the palace of one of the infantas. I found him standing in the middle of his private room—a short, sturdily built man in a gray-blue suit. It was my first close-up of the man described in those days by the London *Times* and *The New York Times* as "the strong man of Spain," and without one exception this estimate was accepted by every member of the diplomatic corps, including Raffaele Guariglia, the Italian Ambassador. But this diplomat, a short, good-looking man of mild manner, astonished me when he said to me: "Azaña is the ablest man, but there are not enough like him, and, under democratic forms, he can do nothing. The world is gravely ill and a major operation will be necessary."

Azaña's personality dominated the room. I got less an impression of charm than of intellectual power. There was nothing in his appearance to justify the cruelty of the cartoons which gave to his face a grossness that was not there. The sensuous lips existed solely in the malice of the artist, for, while full, they were firm, and his mouth denoted strength and character. His complexion, described by his detractors as looking like damp clay, was certainly not florid, and in the artificial light of the Cortes it seemed unusually pallid. His head, while bald on top, had an abundance of iron-gray hair. His voice was good, confident, sincere, masculine. His genius revealed itself when, in speaking, his face lit up amazingly. His eyes were keen, expressive, changing with the mood of the moment. His manner was serene, and yet, busy as he was, he appeared to miss nothing.

"You evidently like Spain, judging from the amount of traveling you have done," he said.

I had motored quietly, unofficially, calling on no functionaries, keeping out of the newspapers, but he knew everywhere I had been. When I asked how he managed with his multitudinous duties, he replied, with a wry smile: "By working all the time."

It is impossible to understand the Spanish scene under the Republic without a visualization and comprehension of Azaña, who, whatever else may be said, unquestionably was the bulwark of the Republic before the war. He was hated but not despised by the beneficiaries of feudalistic privileges, because they recognized in him the greatest obstacle to the restoration of the old regime. Their hatred of him was fantastic, and yet no man in public life in Spain was less a demagogue or less given to vituperation. Their hatred was a tribute to his intellect.

Born in Alcalá de Henares, the charming little city of Cervantes' nativity, he was fifty-three years old when I reached Spain. His family was of the middle class. His early youth found him in the Jesuit college of María Cristina in the Escorial, studying under the monks. His life there was to make an indelible impression upon him, and later he was to relive it in his beautifully composed autobiographical novel, *The Garden of the Monks*.

On leaving college, he went to Madrid to attend the lectures of Francisco Giner de los Ríos, one of the noblest thinkers and reformers produced by Spanish culture and aspirations, a liberal and a humanist, a torchbearer of liberty and democracy, a courageous crusader for popular education, and under the eloquence of this rare soul, Azaña may have imbided the political philosophy that was to shape his career.

Francisco Giner was the teacher and inspirer of many of the choicest Spanish men of his age—among them Antonio Machado, the great poet, who on his master's death wrote: "Yes, carry his body to the hills of the blue peaks of the wide Guadarramas. There are deep gulches of green pines where the wind sings. There is the rest for his spirit under a cold live oak, in loam full of thyme where play golden butterflies. There the master one day dreamed new flowerings for Spain."

So dreamed Azaña, too.

On receiving his Doctorate of Law, he found a position in the office of the Director-General of Registers, and it seemed he would be indefinitely buried behind a bureaucratic desk in the Ministry of Justice. He then had no powerful friends but he had time, and assiduously he dedicated it to study. He read and wrote. In his twenty-fourth year he spent a year in Paris writing penetrating articles for *La Correspondencia de España* of Madrid over the signature of "Martín Pinel." Meanwhile, he had joined the Ateneo in Madrid, famous as a club of the liberals and intellectuals for a century, and in a series of brilliant addresses in defense of the memory of Segismundo Moret, he established his reputation as a scholar and orator. He had attained celebrity in a circle which, while limited, was more distinguished than any other in the country. In a society composed mostly of Spaniards of international renown, such as Unamuno, he had won his spurs. But being accorded a place among the aristocrats of mind and spirit did not give him recognition among politicians, nor among the followers of the Court.

Then, in 1914, came Armageddon. When the greater part of the Spanish aristocracy and nobility arrayed themselves with the Central Powers, and Juan March laid the foundation of his fortune, which was to play its mighty part against the Republic, young Azaña, a thorough democrat, took his stand with the Allies. He thus became one of the little group of liberals and democrats that organized the pro-Ally rallies, culminating in a great demonstration in the bull ring in Madrid, where his eloquence extended his reputation. In the cause of the allied democracies, he visited the French and Italian fronts and reported what he saw for *El Liberal* at home. At the close of the war he returned to Paris for another year of study and observation and to write his *Studies in French Contemporary Politics*, the first volume of which appeared under the title *Military Policy*.

Returning to Madrid, he and Rivas Cherif founded a monthly literary review, *La Pluma*, which was abandoned after two years, when Azaña became editor of a weekly periodical of opinion, *España*. This inevitably fell under the frown of Primo de Rivera in

1925, though Azaña wrote little on politics. During these early post-war years he seemed destined for a purely literary career. It was during this fecund period that he wrote *The Garden of the Monks*, and his brilliant biography of Juan Valera, the Spanish novelist and diplomat, which brought him the first prize in national literature, and a dramatic work called *The Crown*. He made translations of George Borrow's *Bible in Spain*, Prosper Mérimée's novel, *His Holiness's Coach*, and Gilbert Chesterton's *The Orb and the Cross*.

6

Meanwhile, a liberal and a democrat by instinct, and a disciple of Giner, he was turning to politics as the only medium for the achievement of the social and political reforms he thought necessary for the conversion of Spain into a modern European state. He was a reformer rather than a revolutionist, and he hoped for reforms of the monarchy within the framework of the law. In his twenty-sixth year he enlisted under the banner of Melquíades Álvarez, aiming not at the overthrow but the liberalization of the monarchy. He soon found the party a mere drawing-room protest which was heard with a tolerant yawn. It was only then that he abandoned the monarchy, and, with a small group of friends, founded the Republican Acción party, though it was scarcely noticed.

On the fall of the monarchy, he was elected to the Constituent Assembly and the Republic found a leader. As Minister of War he made drastic reforms. Hundreds of idle officers made to adorn drawing rooms were retired on pensions, though all these were enemies of the Republic. The proportion of officers to men in the Spanish army had been fantastic. Very soon he was Prime Minister, and from the beginning he moved in his new role with the confident skill of a veteran parliamentarian.

An ardent democrat, he was bent on economic and social reforms. He ruled through a general appreciation of his mental qualities, a statesman more than a politician.

Cold, a bit aloof, too proud to bend to the petty devices of the demagogue, his was not the personality for the leadership of a mob. His mental processes were those of the French logicians. He was incapable of the emotional inebriation of the Spaniard, though he was all Spanish. Despite these disadvantages, he was accorded leadership, and though he had but a small party of his own, he became the leader of the leaders of all the truly republican parties.

Salvador de Madariaga, who knew him well, has described him as "a proud intellectual, and something of a recluse, of delicate tastes in ethical and artistic matters," as a "man of great intellectual distinction, moral elevation and pride, with a certain feminine aspect in his character to which was due his excessive sensibility." (Madariaga's *Spain*, Editorial Sudamericano, Buenos Aires, 1942.)

Passionately bent on reforms, a few thought he had some of the qualities of a dictator. One of his friends surprised me by insisting on a resemblance to Robespierre "in some ways," and on his being "a typical French Jacobin." This calls for reservations. He was a French Jacobin of the years 1789–1791, but not of the later period of the demagogy and extremism of Robespierre and Marat. He may have resembled Robespierre in the intensity of his adherence to his ideology, but the fanaticism that precipitated the Reign of Terror was foreign to his nature. In truth, it was his toleration toward his enemies that was to be his undoing. Among the French Revolutionary leaders he resembled Vergniaud, not Robespierre.

His worst enemies conceded the superiority of his oratory. The purity of his Spanish, the distinction of his diction, the melody of his phrasing, the irresistibility of his reasoning, his power of condensation, the profundity of his thought, made all his major speeches national events. Álvarez del Vayo, one of his most severe critics, has recently (1950) said that "as an orator and lecturer he had no equal"; that he "chose each word with such precision that nobody could have found one more exactly fitted to the idea he had to express"; that "his addresses have become the model for the new style of speaking, free from the artifice and baroque of most contemporary Spanish and Latin-American oratory. His oratory was addressed exclusively to the intellect." Thus this critic concludes that "with an ability that penetrated to the bottom—the past, the present, and the future of his country, Azaña gave the exact measure of his analytic temperament and his incapacity for enthusiasm" (*The Last Optimist*, page 173)—which merely means that his great speeches were more analytic than emotional.

Whatever storms might rage without, he invariably was serene in appearance. When General Sanjurjo led his insurrection, easily put down in 1932, Azaña stood at the window of the palace of Buena Vista nonchalantly smoking a cigarette and watching the street fighting; and when Seville was taken for a few days, and the government in Madrid was expected to be in a state of panic, the Cortes met, and Azaña called up an agricultural bill for the discussion of an amendment. He was a good psychologist.

7

Fernando de los Ríos was the first of the foreign ministers with whom I dealt. Later he was the most cultured diplomat Spain had sent to Washington since Juan Valera was there. His was a background of culture and high public service in both politics and education. It was his uncle, Francisco Giner, who molded his mind. He had been a professor at the University of Granada and later at the University of Madrid, of which he was the Rector. Intensely interested in education, a scholar and an orator, he naturally was a liberal in politics. He became a socialist, and later a republican.

In time, came the premature revolt of December, 1930, its failure, and the arrest of the principals. Don Fernando's experience during the first week, though not generally known, reads like an episode from a Dumas novel. He took refuge in the home of Pérez de Ayala, the novelist, but his host was then a republican, and his house was almost certain to be searched. The friends of Don Fernando put their heads together to find a safer refuge. Not far from Madrid, Juan Belmonte, the famous and beloved matador, had a farm and he was in residence there. Perfect!—but how get Don Fernando there? The soldiers were stopping all cars on the highways. Belmonte found a way.

Thus, one bitterly cold morning, Belmonte drove his car to the house of Pérez de Ayala. A large man, covered with a Spanish shawl against the cold, wrapped up to his eyes to conceal his beard, entered the back seat and Belmonte took the wheel. The car sped into the country, but scarcely had it reached the outskirts of the town when soldiers, lining the highway, stopped it. The door flew open. The familiar face of Belmonte, with its protruding chin, registered indignation. The soldiers fell back, humiliated by their blunder—more a blunder than if they had stopped the car of the

King. A muttered apology, and a smiling wave of dismissal. The car sped on, and thus Belmonte's car ran the blockade of the soldiers of Alfonso.

At Belmonte's farm, Don Fernando lingered in safety for a week, and then he returned voluntarily to Madrid to join his fellow conspirators in cells filled with the flowers of their followers. Soon the King was speeding through the night to Cartagena to begin his travels, the populace was pouring in festive mood into the streets and packing the Puerta del Sol, and from the balcony of the Ministry of the Interior, the Republic was being proclaimed. Don Fernando was a colorful part of the drama of the day, since he and Lerroux were the first of the provisional government to reach the Ministry and take possession. He became Minister of Justice, wrote the judicial statute for the provisional period, and another document, still unpublished, setting forth the agreement of the political parties on the social and military measures of the transition period.

Occasionally I saw him at his home. He lived modestly in an apartment house, and the rooms revealed the scholar. His cultivated wife made regular excursions into the country as a volunteer teacher among the peasants.

8

The day after presenting my credentials we moved into the palace of the Duke of Montellano, which I had taken. The grounds of the palace occupied a full city block. The large garden, facing the Castellana, was surrounded by a high iron picket fence, and the landscape gardener had so placed trees and shrubbery that one could walk or sit in the garden without being seen from the street, and have dinner on the terrace in private. Ena Victoria, the Queen, loved this garden. The palace had been designed by a French architect. In one room, especially designed for them, hung four of Goya's famous panels. The marble dining room, the ceiling decorated by an Italian painter, was both beautiful and distinguished. When Mexico sent President Díaz upon his travels and he appeared in Madrid, the King could not entertain him in the royal palace for political reasons, but he gave a dinner in his honor in the Montellano dining room. In the Red Salon were four large Guardis, again fashionable after a long period of eclipse; and on the walls of the ballroom, unmatched in any other embassy, hung Zuloaga's portrait of the Duchess of Arion, mother of the young Duchess of Montellano, and Boldini's portrait of the Duchess Dowager looking like a Christy girl—for it was painted in the days when girls patterned themselves thus.

Both the ballroom at one end of the house and the dining room at the other opened on a wide marble terrace with steps leading down into the garden with its flowers, its handsome fountain, and its many pine, plane, and horse-chestnut trees. Facing the terrace was a charming little stone house for tea or cards. One of Franco's shells crashed into it during the war. Hidden from the terrace by shrubbery and trees were three stone houses for servants, cars, and coaches, and behind these was a brick stable for nine horses, with the names of Montellano's polo ponies painted over the stalls.

In the quiet section of the city, one could sit under the trees in summer and imagine oneself in the heart of the country.

The atmosphere and some of the physical aspects of Madrid reminded me of Washington. The tree-lined streets, the circles with their monuments, the absence of the smoke of factories, the easy official air, were all suggestive of the American capital I knew in the first decade of the century.

Fond as we became of Madrid in these early days, it was a wholesome relief from tiresome ceremonial calls to drive into the country, so accessible. I had heard so much disparagement of the "dull, drab Castilian plains." They fascinated me from the beginning, and my affection for them was constantly to grow. The brown fields, spotted here and there with the dusty greenery of the olive orchards, and all shut in by the not-far-distant mountains, draped in a blue or purple haze—these were never to become monotonous to me. And they never seemed the same, because of the play of light and shadows. I came to love these plains, especially toward evening, and from them I have seen the most entrancing sunsets. And over all, all the time, brooded a perfect peace. Only a little distance away was Toledo, on which four civilizations had left their imprint; and the Escorial, through whose coldly austere corridors so much pageantry had passed; and the palace of El Pardo, which was my favorite; and the fascinating and delectable little town of Alcalá de Henares, where, for centuries, princes and philosophers were disciples at the feet of famous scholars.

That first summer we motored all over Spain, checking what I saw with what I had heard. In July, 1931, three months after the fall of the monarchy, my wife and daughter motored over Spain, meeting nothing but courtesy and seeing nothing of disorder. In July, two years later, the gossips of the drawing rooms were busy spreading the story that the country was in a state of disorder verging on anarchy. I determined to see for myself.

Chapter II

Meanderings in a Magic Land

IN EARLY JUNE we drove to Gibraltar to meet Patricia. Thus did we see La Mancha and salute the windmills against which Don Quixote had tilted, and rode into the colorful opulence of Andalusia, so different from the austerity of Castile. In this summer excursion I was to find that Spanish roads are excellent, and the best hotels clean and comfortable. In charm, in color, in the diversity of beauty, in the courtesy and cordiality of the people, in the scenes of historical significance, and in the artistic treasures of the churches, I know of no European country more delightful. Primo de Rivera has his monument in the superb roads he built. The *turismo* had conducted a campaign among the tavern keepers against the use of oil and, especially, rancid oil in cooking for the foreigner. To make provision for meals and lodging, in the absence of cities with adequate hotel facilities, the government had built *paradores* to meet the need. Most of these delightful little taverns in miniature are on the outskirts of villages, gay with color inside and out, with all the reasonable comforts of a big hotel. Our first contact with one of these was at Manzanares, and the memory of the many meals I have had there in an atmosphere of homey hospitality will last.

Soon after leaving Manzanares, we were in the midst of the rich fecundity of Andalusia. Olive orchards dotted the landscape. Peasants were threshing in the yellow fields, tramping out the grain like Biblical figures, or extracting it with drags driven by girls or women holding the lines on the patient horse or mule. Occasionally, American agricultural machinery could be seen, but the amount permitted is limited by law, since the general use would deprive the peasants of a means of livelihood. In other fields we saw horses hitched to poles going round and round drawing water for the stock. Along the highway we passed donkeys bearing young girls and old women and panniers filled with vegetables. Now and then we met a short procession of these patient, lovable burden-bearers of the poor, only their heads visible as they bore upon their backs great forests of small twigs from the woods for the baking of bread. A weather-beaten peasant usually walked beside them.

2

He who once said that "the real nobility of Spain is the peasantry" knew his Spain. Patient, picturesque, courteous, industrious, rising at dawn to work to dark for a pittance on the great estates, they dwell in poverty in the dusty, yellow, ancient villages. Few own the implements of their toil. In most regions, especially in the south, the peasant who owns a mule or plow is rare. Their very existence depends on the will or whim of the absentee landlords of the huge estates. The old patriarchal days when the nobleman lived a portion of the year on his estate and personally looked after his peasants ended long ago. He now lives luxuriously in Madrid, Paris, and London, leaving his land and the humanity dependent on it to the none-too-considerate ministrations of overseers whose sole intent is to make a financial showing to the master. The peasant women share in the struggle for existence, sowing, plowing, pitching hay, helping in the gardening and the threshing. Never have I motored through the country that I have not found a group of peasant women bending on the banks of streams washing clothes and using a smooth stone for a washboard. The clothing, hanging on near-by bushes to dry in the sun, was always white as snow.

Observing an old peasant trudging with bowed head along the road, we call him to us for information. Bronzed by the sun, his skin wrinkled from exposure, the old man approaches, and, with a courtly gesture, removes his hat. We look into his eyes and know that he uncovers, not as an admission of inferiority, but as one gentleman to another. If he is illiterate, his eyes denote character and intelligence. He gives directions with precision, and there is an innate dignity in his bearing. The Spanish peasant is a gentleman by instinct. If elementary education has been denied him, that is his tragedy and not his fault. He is apt to confuse education with good manners. When a drunken gypsy in an Andalusian café poured forth unprovoked abuse upon a foreigner, the peasant girl, waiting on the table, thought to make amends. "You must not mind him," she said. "He has no education." And she could neither read nor write.

3

We drove into the ancient Moorish capital of Córdoba toward evening. The air was heavy with the fragrance of flowers, and the streets swarmed with shouting children. A dozen smiling urchins tried to jump on the running board, eagerly offering their services as guides to the Hotel Regina. Pepe, the chauffeur, angrily tried to shoo them away, but it was like reasoning with a swarm of bees. The real masters of Spain are the children, and they rule by charm.

Aside from the mosque, few monuments of the Moorish occupation remain. Without interfering with the cathedral, literally built within the walls of the old temple of Mohammed, the government has been restoring and preserving the old Moorish art. But in Córdoba I was to find it easier to recapture the atmosphere of Moorish days in the palace of the Marquis de Viana, formerly the King's Master of the Horse, with its numerous patios with their cypress trees and fountains, with oranges clinging to the walls, to make life more endurable through an Andalusian summer.

The road to Seville was always pleasing, but never more so, I am sure, than when I saw it first. In the fields were enormous droves of sheep, tended by serene shepherds and alert sheep dogs that Landseer would have loved. Donkeys passed us nonchalantly on the roadside. A pretty peasant girl smiled from one, and an old woman whose leathery face had been much scratched by time brooded on another. "Good day," chirped the girl. "Go with God," muttered the old woman.

A hurried lunch at Seville, and the early afternoon found us at Jerez, "the home of sherry," whence so many tourists, sampling too many brands of the wine sheds, have gone forth a little tipsy. The life of this proud little city revolves around the wine houses. Here Primo de Rivera was born, and in the plaza he haughtily surveys his town from his prancing horse, for the people here are partial to the old regime.

It was late in the afternoon when we drove on to Algeciras over the winding mountain road, and often beside the blue sea, marveling at the beauty of the vistas.

4

On the main road between Seville and Algeciras one cannot but notice Cádiz, a sparkling white city by the sea. Its avenue of palms by the ocean front proclaims the tropics. Its streets are clean and narrow. We lingered long enough to visit the old chapel of the Capuchins, and to see Murillo's famous painting of St. Francis, with its rapt expression, and another of his pictures, which he was painting from a ladder when he had his fatal fall.

Feeling that diplomatic immunity imposes a special obligation, we stopped the car for sheep and cattle, dodged chickens and dogs, and slowed down so as not to ruffle the dignity of a haughty duck waddling across the road. I was to find the Spaniard himself a greater problem because of his passion for feeling the breeze of a passing car. "Did you notice the men we literally grazed?" asked a companion who knew his Spain. "That," explained my friend, "is the matador complex. They like the matadors to graze the bull, and half the people want to be matadors."

5

The sun was setting when we drove back to Seville. In the old part of the town in a labyrinth of narrow streets, we found the Hotel Madrid, once the palace of a nobleman. I came to love it more than any other hotel in Spain. The walls were in Spanish colors, bright blue, red, and yellow, and on the walls were many paintings, and in the patio were oranges and palms and fountains that sang one to sleep at night. One breakfasts there before an open French door in the sunshine, the air sweet with the fragrance of the oranges clinging to the walls.

One does not describe Seville, one feels it. More than Paris,

it is "a woman's town with roses in her hair." It is the town of
Carmen, and the matadors, of narrow streets, latticed windows,
and balconies whence romance peers down; the town of the music
of guitars in shadows, of *flamenco* singing, of merry laughter and
dancing, of sidewalk cafés with the tables reaching from curb to
curb.

I found that the Andalusian differs from the Castilian as the
Bavarian once differed from the Prussian. They live at ease,
drowsing in the sun. They are the Gascons of the Peninsula—expansive, flamboyant, given to gasconading, softer and more pliable
than the Castilians. I was disappointed to find that there were no
cafés where one could see gypsy or Spanish dancing. Why not? I
asked a Spaniard. I was told that cafés would not pay, since the
men would not take their wives. "Not," my informant hastened to
add, "that they do not trust their wives; it is their friends they do
not trust."

The Alcázar, palace of the Moorish kings and their successors,
dreaming in its matchless garden, with its maze of boxwood walks,
its orange, date, pepper, and cypress trees, seemed sad that summer, its tapestries removed. There was something rather touching
in one of the smaller rooms where Kodak pictures of Alfonso's
daughters had not been disturbed by the Republic.

But it is the superb cathedral that dominates the city, always
beautiful, always changing with the lights and shadows, always the
same. Dignity, grandeur, romance, tragedy, history, are caught
and held in that massive mountain of stone. Some pretty young girls
hurried by us as we entered and went directly to a shrine and
knelt—it was the shrine of the saint that lures back straying lovers.
At the door was a congestion of beggars, and their whining pleas
mingled with the chant of the priests inside the church.

6

As we drove thence through the province of Badajoz there was
the thrill of strange, sad beauty in the winding mountain road with
its vivid views. It was not easy to associate so much beauty with so
much human misery, for in this province of vast estates, the poverty
of the underpaid peasantry was pitiful. The fields were enclosed
with fences of stone and cactus. At noon we drove over the old

Roman bridge into Mérida, whose ancient Roman amphitheater
is still used at times for the classic drama. We lunched there at a
pleasant *parador*, and that afternoon we drove straight into the
heart of the Middle Ages.

Never shall I forget that afternoon's drive to the old monastery
of Guadalupe. In many fields, men, women, horses, and mules
were busy with the threshing. Across the road at times strutted
lordly chickens at their leisure, forcing us to stop. Men on mules,
and dark-eyed girls on donkeys, rode by, returning from the fields.
The scenery was relaxing, and the scenes seemed scarcely of the
modern world, though this may have been due to the magic of the
evening. At length we drove into the ancient and decrepit village
that sprawls about the fourteenth-century monastery where we
were to stay the night.

Centuries ago, this monastery in the mountains, and off the
beaten path, gave refuge to the traveler, and the custom has continued on a more comfortable scale. An old woman carried our
luggage into the reception room where we were joined by the
Director-General, Father Julio Florza, distinctly youthful despite
his baldness. He bubbled with good humor. We were taken to the
old cloisters, recently restored for the entertainment of travelers.
We ascended to the second floor and walked along a wide stone
balcony overlooking the patio to a huge, lofty room with three
beds, simple as a monk's cell. It was so arranged that with the aid of
curtains each bed could have its privacy. A French door, which was
open, looked out over parts of the sorry village to the neighboring
mountains.

That night we dined with Father Florza on simple but wholesome fare. And then we went out into the village street by twilight.
A few old men sat gossiping before a wine shop. But for these, the
village was as a dead town. Suddenly, from a narrow winding alley,
a pathetic procession moved down the street, a priest leading, all
walking or shuffling, and bearing a rough coffin. It was a funeral by
twilight. One short and simple annal of the poor was written. So it
has been for hundreds of years in the shadow of the monastery.

The dark church and monastery reeked with age. Famous as a
religious shrine centuries ago, monarchs and men have made their
way, through the generations, over the rough mountain paths to

these shrines and altars. The monarchs had gone bearing gifts I was to be shown on the morrow. There Cortes, returning from the conquest of Mexico, had lingered for the sake of his soul. Generations of peasants had been born within its shadow, had lived their simple and laborious lives, and been borne to their graves and forgotten, but the monastery has not changed.

The twilight deepened. The old men before the wine shop were a blur. Nothing stirred in the primitive streets. Somewhere a dog was barking. Beyond that, it was literally a village of the dead.

Father Julio had said at dinner that there would be a procession by torchlight to the various shrines after the midnight mass, and that we might find it interesting. Noting my hesitation, the young priest smiled knowingly. "You go to bed, and at one o'clock I will knock on your door," he said. And so, fully dressed, we threw ourselves upon the beds, leaving the French door open, and the moonlight cast eerie shadows, and a murmur came up from the mountain forest, and we slept. Then came the clamor of the heavy iron knocker, and the sound of voices on the balcony. We rose, and passed from the balcony to the patio. The night was strangely beautiful. The sky seemed thick with stars that appeared larger and closer to earth than usual, and the air was fragrant. We entered the dimly lit church.

It was almost two in the morning, but wide-awake children were playing in the aisles. The mass was not yet over. I was fascinated by the Virgin of Guadalupe above the altar. The mass over, we followed the monks, bearing torches, as they went from shrine to shrine. It had been a memorable experience in this sweet retreat, so remote from the hurly-burly of the modern world. We asked for the bill. "Whatever you please to give," was the answer. For thus it has always been in Guadalupe.

7

After a few days in Madrid, we set forth one sunny morning under a blue sky for the famous fiesta at Pamplona. Having touched the southern extremity of Spain and found no semblance of disorder or popular discontent, we were now going to the extreme north. The road as far as Burgos ran like a ribbon through a pleasing countryside. Near that city we lunched by the roadside under

the trees and could see the exquisite towers of the cathedral outlined against the sky. An old peasant woman, brown and wrinkled,
slowly rode by us on a donkey, greeting us with the ceremonial manner of a queen. Thence onward, the road to Pamplona was more
beautiful. Old Moorish watchtowers whence flaming signals
flashed centuries ago from many a hilltop looked down upon us.
Again we were in a green country, as in Andalusia, but how different the people! These sons and daughters of Navarre still think and
feel in terms of the sixteenth century. These are the Carlists, who
include everything in the words "God and King." I found this inscribed at the top of the newspaper they read.

It was evening when, from the windows of the Grand Hotel, we
looked down upon the Plaza de San Francisco, dominated from the
center by a statue of the saint. The streets and hotel lobbies seethed
with visitors. The villas of San Sebastián, Biarritz, and Saint-Jean-
de-Luz poured a festive crowd into Pamplona, but these were not
drawn by the religious fervor of the Carlists, since these came for the
bullfight, the feast, the frolic. That night we threaded our way
through the congested Plaza de la Republica, where gay parties
frolicked and flirted, and found a resting place near the hotel made
famous by Ernest Hemingway in *The Sun Also Rises*. The air
throbbed with the music of guitars and the songs of the region.
Scarcely did the natives seem to walk—they danced through their
fiesta. One was dancing on unsteady feet, hugging to his breast a
goat's skin filled with wine as he approached us on our homeward
journey, his face aglow with ribald mirth as he proffered the nozzle
of the skin bag. When we drank, he smiled approval and lurched on,
dancing as he went.

The next morning at the ungodly hour of six, we witnessed the
driving of the fighting bulls to the bull pen for the battles of the
afternoon and saw the amusing "bullfight" of well-padded young
men with very young bulls. In the grandstand the girls flirted and
the boys sang the songs of Navarre.

And now we hurried back for a little sleep. Consciousness was
fading when the laughing and shouting of children hurried us to
the window. The Plaza of San Francisco swarmed with children in
party dresses, running, dodging, screaming, pursued by huge
monsters on stilts with gargoyle faces applying air-filled bladders to

the heads of the youngsters with a resounding noise. Presto, change!
Now the children are dancing, the Plaza swirling with the steps of
the "Navarre"—and now they are singing, and now the pursuit of
the monsters begins again. We go back to bed.

8

I had seen my first bullfight under a burning Madrid sky one
day in June. The scene itself was thrilling—the bluest of blue skies,
the scorching sun rays accentuating the blue, green, red, and yellow dresses and parasols of the women in the stand. Twenty thousand people, tense, expectant. The murmur of so many voices beat
upon the eardrums like the pounding of the sea. From the moment
the two horsemen in the garb of the time of Philip II rode, to the
sound of bugles, into the arena for the key to the bull ring, my emotions were acutely aroused, but confused. The color, gusto, bravado,
of the procession lead by the strutting matadors in gorgeous uniforms, the first breath-taking charge of the bull, the grace and daring of the cape work, the skill and valor of the matadors, the brilliance and audacity of the *banderilleros*, the knowledge that death
hovered in the air close to the bloodstained sand, would quicken
the pulse of a statue. And out of it all, in the end, emerged one
dominant feeling—a profound admiration and pity for the courageous, magnificent fighting bull. My sympathies ever after were to be
enlisted on his side.

"But it is not a sport," explains the Spaniard. "It is a tragedy."
Do the English think it cruel? They are asked to explain the hunting
down of the little fox that cannot defend itself. "It seems so cruel,"
said an American woman, without tact. "Perhaps," replied a
Spanish woman who did not care for bullfights, "perhaps, and yet
we do not have to have Societies for the Prevention of Cruelty to
Children."

That afternoon in Pamplona I saw Ortega and Armillita Chico,
the Mexican, both graceful, daring, and skillful, at their best.

9

Back in Madrid for two months. The city swelters in the burning sun. We close the offices at two, and after lunch we lounge till
five. Tea at six-thirty, dinner at nine on the terrace, which is cool

after the garden has been sprayed and the breeze comes down from the Guadarramas. Ever memorable to me the nights that summer when a full moon flooded the garden, the trees stirring in a gentle, refreshing wind. The horse chestnuts, the planes, the pines, were beautiful in the light of the moon. Madrid is charming even in the heat.

We now set forth for San Sebastián and the Pyrenees. Then, for the first of many nights, we were to sleep in a comfortable hotel in Burgos until at dawn the thunderous bells of the ancient church across the street made sleep impossible. That morning the air was chilly, and we ran into rain in the mountains. We rode through the lovely mountains of the Basques, all garbed in vivid green. The trees were thick and stately, and we wound over roads as good as any in the world. Far up, from a veritable shelf on the mountainside, we looked down upon the sea where the blue water foamed white against the rocks. Then we reached San Sebastián and the Continental Hotel, looking out upon the Concha, where the tide surged in with a boom upon the sands.

10

That afternoon, at a tea dance in the villa of a friend, I met an interesting youth destined for a tragic end. José Primo de Rivera, eldest son of the Dictator, was young and darkly handsome. His coal-black hair shone glossily. His eyes were dark and keenly intelligent. His face was slender and of Andalusian hue. His manner was courtly, modest, deferential. The passion of his life was the vindication of his father. The old Dictator who had prolonged the life of the monarchy in a crisis had been given a curt dismissal when his work was done; and, neglected, broken in health, he had hurried across the border with a satchel, to die in Paris a little later, deserted. The memory rankled in the heart of José. When I met him that day he had begun the organization of the Fascist party. Some hundreds of the young, a daring and noisy group, had enlisted under his banner, and their dashing leader had set the pace. He hurried about the country organizing his meager forces and making fervent speeches. Seriously, as I know, he set himself to the task of mastering the art of oratory, and in time he was to become a good speaker, his speeches rich in substance, well phrased, but with an irrepressible Andalusian weakness for floridity. Soon he would be elected to the Cortes, where he would become a thorn in the sides of many hypocrites with whom he was allied. Incapable of dissimulation, with a gift for the barbed phrase, he was to arouse the bitter enmity of many, and to live dangerously, going about with a reckless abandon that was the despair of his friends. He loved the crowds and refused to shun them. One night when riding in Madrid he was fired upon from the shadows. Stopping his car, he sprang out in pursuit, alone, unarmed, heedless of the possible enemies lurking in the dark. A little later he appeared smiling and jubilant at the Bakanik, where fashion went for cocktails, and those to whom he told the story found him as delighted as a child. He was of the breed of Dumas' Musketeers. I shall always remember him as I saw him first, young, boyish, courteous, smiling and dancing that afternoon in the villa in San Sebastián.

11

Two mornings later, we drove on to Bilbao over a scenic highway that wound gracefully through the mountains, and that afternoon we sat in a sweltering mass to see Ortega and Chico fight the largest and fiercest bulls in Spain. Young Franklin Roosevelt was with us, boyishly delighted when a matador dedicated a bull to him. As we were leaving the hotel for the bull ring, we found ourselves in a milling mass at the entrance, tossed about like dry leaves in a storm. Noting the spot on which the crowd converged, we found the explanation—men in heavily encrusted uniforms were pushing out. Ortega and his men were going to the fight, and the great man was in a haughty mood. Though he condescended to shake hands with his idolaters, he did it with a yawn. But he was brilliant in the arena that day.

The next morning found us in Santander, the seat of the modern and favorite palace of the King, standing on a promontory beside the sea, and looking, from a distance, like a fairy palace silhouetted against the sky. After the establishment of the Republic, Fernando de los Ríos took it over for the summer sessions of the national university. As we drove through the grounds, the silk stockings of American students were drying in the sun at the open windows of the palace of a king.

12

The six-hour drive through the mountains to Gijón, in the Asturias, is an experience easily remembered. Beautiful, these wild majestic mountains and peaceful little valleys, and the interesting Asturian villages drowsing in the shade. The Asturian mountaineers are stouthearted, robust, and proudly independent. When the Moorish invasion swept up triumphantly from the south, it plunged against the stone wall of these Asturian mountaineers—and stopped. During the seven centuries of Moorish occupation this was one of the two spots the foot of the invader never trod. A peaceful, happy land—and yet, somewhere in these mountains are the coal mines where the workers live in misery and darkness.

That night at Gijón, Patricia and I, under the guidance of a native, sauntered forth near midnight into the streets. Soon we were wandering through an ugly section near the sea in search of the fish market. The deserted quarter, with its shadows, seemed sinister. Now and then we passed a human derelict, not pleasant to look upon. Finally we reached a low wooden building, the stock exchange of the fishmongers. About it were grouped grim-looking men with glowering and brown, seamed faces—the fishermen and the sailors. A large pile of fresh fish glistened on the floor in the middle of the small room. Beside it stood the auctioneer.

Every evening, fishermen, returning from the sea, unloaded their hauls on the floor of the old shack. On one side of the low room was a balcony, with a long table, and behind this crude wooden table was a row of women with the most arresting faces I have ever seen. This was the stock market of the women who dealt in fish. Their chairs were the seats they had bought. Not one young or pretty face among them. All were old, with hard, bronzed faces. The hair of some was plastered to their heads, while that of others was blowsy. Their mouths were hard and stern, and their bold eyes cold and cynical. One old crone was smoking a cigar.

And then the auctioneer began the sale; a gruff voice from the balcony growled an offer; a sharp voice at the table raised the bid; and then another, and finally the auctioneer announced a sale. The successful bidder pressed a button, which rang a bell and released a ball bearing her name, and this shot down a groove to the bill clerk, who prepared the bill of sale. And the old women went out into the night with their purchases in huge baskets on their heads. These fierce old women had their stock market, their seats upon it, their rules and regulations.

13

The next morning, we turned through the mountains for Galicia. This is the land of the Celts, where, some insist, the Irish race was cradled. The drive to Lugo in the late afternoon was delightful. The scene was breath-taking in its beauty. Charming little Galician villages nestled in narrow valleys, and near these, and along the road, we passed women and young girls with the glowing cheeks and sparkling eyes of robust health, bearing baskets of provisions or jugs on their heads. So perfect was their carriage that their hands did not touch the burdens they bore. Travelers for centuries have commented on the incomparable poise and carriage of Spanish women from the princess to the peasant. The air was sweetly fragrant with the breath of the mountains, and everywhere was Scotland's purple heather.

14

The path of Spanish lovers in the past has not been without its hurdles. The problem of the girl in modest circumstances was in making contact with the male. But Cupid long ago devised a cunning plan, and with its dart, pointed the young men to the *paseo* as the happy hunting ground for lovers. And so it came about that in the evening before dinner in every city and hamlet, one could see them promenading back and forth for an hour or so on some chosen streets. The girls walked in groups, as did the boys, and, as they passed, eyes flashed their messages, and the girl knew from the persistence of the young man's pursuit the measure of his admiration; and the young man knew by subtle signs whether his attentions were interesting or not. The smitten youth did not intrude, but bided his time. Quite soon, perhaps, the mother received a note requesting permission to call upon her daughter. The young man called, the mother hovering near as chaperon, and he took the charmer to the cinema with her sister; and so, in time, romance blossomed into marriage. While Spanish girls today are breaking away from the shackles of tradition, the *paseo* continues everywhere.

That evening at Lugo, I found the street of the *paseo*. A mass of the young reached from curb to curb and moved slowly back and forth. Because the *paseo* has its privileges, no vehicular traffic is permitted in the street. Along the sidewalk by the curb were many tables where one might have tea or coffee or wine, or read his paper by the light of the great arc lamp. I was reading, when suddenly the light grew dim, and, glancing up, I found the *paseo* was over, and the street was empty. The electric light in the middle of the block was turned off. An automobile swung into the street.

I remember Lugo for its clean, narrow streets, its thirteenth-century church, black with age and loaded with charm.

15

Thence onward into Santiago de Compostela, we were on historic ground, sacred to the pious pilgrims of dead centuries who laboriously made their way to the alleged tomb of St. James. One day, the story runs, a body was washed up by the sea and a miraculous light proclaimed it the body of the apostle. They gave him a tomb in the splendid old cathedral, and from all parts of Christendom, through the Middle Ages, thousands constantly were tramping or riding on mules or horses to their devotions at the shrine. They beat the paths that were to become the present arteries of travel, and many died and were buried by the roadside, and taverns sprang up to accommodate both man and beast. And the pilgrims who survived the hardships of the journey and reached Santiago de Compostela went directly to the cathedral and with their bare hands made the deep impression on the hard stone of the great column just inside the entrance.

Seen from the street, this church is tremendously impressive, and within, it has the mellowness of age and the dignity of history, but it has no special beauty. We climbed to the top just as the great bronze bells, the gifts of kings, began to peal, and the noise was maddening. Far up, we stepped out upon what in a castle would be called the battlement and we were startled to find at that great height, beyond the view of the street, large statues of the saints, black with age and weather. In the chapel we saw the alleged tomb of St. James. An awe-inspiring cathedral, saturated with the romantic stories of the pilgrims of an age of fanatic faith.

The next day was Sunday, with a brilliant sun. I went out for a stroll through the very narrow medieval streets, and for an hour meandered through these charming lanes between houses hoary with age. Many were strolling with me. Some were going to the cathedral with their prayer books in their hands. Many women passed, bearing incredible burdens on their heads. At the wide-open window of a wine shop men sat drinking beer and amusing themselves with the passing pedestrians. The cathedral bells seemed very near in the Sabbath quiet.

Suddenly the weird notes of the bagpipe.

Down the lanelike street marched men in kilts, bare knees showing, playing on the pipes. Others gave no heed, as though bagpipe music were no novelty in Santiago. And so for hours I strolled through the clean streets, paved with great stone slabs worn smooth as marble. Now and then an unexpected opening in the street disclosed a plaza with an exquisite medieval stone structure in the rear—perhaps a thirteenth-century church, a hospital, or college. The unique city comes down from the mystic Middle Ages, but there is no evidence of decay.

In the afternoon we drove on to León for the night, and the next day we stopped at Valladolid, ancient seat of the kings, to see where burned the fires of the Inquisition, and the remains of the palace where Charles V fought and killed his bull in celebration of the birth of an heir.

We had traveled from one end of Spain to the other in search of the disorders "bordering on anarchy" of which we had heard in the drawing rooms in Madrid and had found nothing of the sort. We found partisans of the monarchy, but among them a disposition quietly to await developments. In Pamplona, as we expected, the people, the Carlists, were as always passionately devoted to "God and King," and they made no secret about it. Perhaps the disorders of which we had heard were on the Mediterranean coast somewhere between Barcelona and Málaga. We planned to make a survey in that quarter.

Chapter III

Politics, Politicians, and Picnics

WHILE we had found no disorder, there was much whispering about a possible military *coup d'état*, but nothing definite on which to base it. However, Azaña's position was far from comfortable during the hot summer of 1933. For more than two years he had run the parliamentary machinery at high speed, pressing and passing measures of reform. Behind him was his own party, more impressive in quality than in quantity, but his socialist allies were growing restive. The conversion of Spain, economically and socially, into a thoroughly modern twentieth-century state could not instantly be accomplished by the waving of a magic wand, but not a few of the workers in the political vineyard were complaining over the delay. Among the reform laws passed not one was really socialistic, and Julián Besteiro, the scholarly socialist President of the Cortes, was urging that his party should not take office until it could take power as well, through three socialist-held ministerial posts. The opposition was bitterly contending that the Constituent Assembly was illegally converting itself into a legislative Cortes and was demanding a dissolution and elections.

2

In the elections of members of the Court of Constitutional Guarantees, the first Sunday in September, 1933, the governing coalition lost heavily. Juan March, reputed to be the richest man in Spain, was elected by the enemies of the regime. On this pretext,

Lerroux raised the question of confidence in the Cortes, and I heard the debate in a scant chamber. Lerroux attacked, and Azaña replied with vigor and was sustained with a majority of one hundred and twenty-seven, but the next day, in the Council of Ministers, Azaña tendered the resignation of his government. Dissembling his delight, Alcalá Zamora requested the government to continue until the ratification of the pending Uruguayan treaty, but at the same time propounded three questions to Azaña. Fernando de los Ròos gave them to me at the time:

First, whether the government coalition was broken; second, whether Azaña thought the continuance of the existing government would be good or bad for the republican electorate; and third, whether he felt the existing government best for the conduct of the municipal elections.

Azaña replied that while the coalition was not broken, it was disintegrating and that the President was the person to answer the other two questions. He insisted on his resignation. At this time Fernando de los Ríos told me that the drift was away from the Leftists, and that the more conservative element should be permitted to try its hand. The socialists, he said, would be content to go along, provided there was no proscription or persecution.

Lerroux, entrusted with the forming of a government, knew that Azaña would not co-operate, and that the socialists would oppose any government formed. He was not then ready to enter into a coalition with parties notoriously hostile to the regime. There was but one solution—the formation of a government composed exclusively of his own party, and a recessing of the Cortes to escape a vote of confidence. It was during this thirty-day recess that I had my first contact with Lerroux.

3

He had given me an appointment for five o'clock. The scenes in the Presidencia were in striking contrast with those in Azaña's time. After some confusion and jostling in the corridors, I was ushered upstairs to a room beyond the reception room of the Prime Minister, and, in passing the open door of this room, I was amazed by the scene within. The room hummed, buzzed, rumbled, and roared with vociferous, gesticulating men, flushed and excited, all eager for the boss's ear. I waited in an elegant anteroom which was hung with blue silk, with a golden table in the center and golden chairs with blue upholstering. An ornate clock on the mantel ticked loudly in the silence. I waited and wondered, seemingly forgotten. When the confused usher returned, he led me into the packed reception room, where, with vigorous jabs of the elbows, he forced a path to Lerroux' door. There, to my astonishment, he left me in charge of the door guard. It would have been offensive but for the manifest confusion of the usher, and I did not mind. It gave me an opportunity to study Spanish spoilsmen in a hungry moment. How many times had I witnessed just such scenes in the waiting room of a political boss at home in the hour of the distribution of the loaves and fishes! Then I knew the difference between Azaña and Lerroux—one was a statesman, and the other was a boss.

When at length the door opened, I found myself facing a short, stockily built man with a twinkling, friendly eye, who did not look his seventy years. His ruddy face was full and he seemed robust, though I knew he retired each night at nine and refused most dinners. The impish upward twist of his mustache proclaimed him of the breed of the Gascons. His hair was almost white, the dome of his head was bald but for the few hairs, standing aloof and in proud disdain of their neighbors in the true Spanish fashion. His brown eyes twinkled benevolently, betraying a rich sense of humor, and in their depths I could read craftiness, cunning, worldly wisdom, and not a little cynicism. Indeed, life had little to teach Lerroux.

He was born in the sleepy Andalusian village of La Rambia in the province of Córdoba. His father was an army veterinarian, and the family was poor. Lerroux served a short apprenticeship in a cobbler's shop, and, at times, he tended the altar of his uncle's church in the dusty village of Benavente in Castile. He enlisted in the army and then deserted; and then he wrote and published a cookbook! But clever and ambitious, he aspired to higher things, and when he was offered a secretarial position in Madrid at nine duros a month, he eagerly accepted, and ate at taverns on a peseta or so a day. But the gusty Andalusian youth of powerful frame and abundant courage was not content with small things, and when a gambling house in the Puerta del Sol needed a croupier, it found one in Lerroux, but soon lost him to a republican paper which needed a bouncer, since publishing a republican paper was an invitation to violence. Strong as a bull, arrogant as a Gascon, vain as a peacock, he swaggered possessively among the loungers of the Puerta del Sol, both admired and feared. He became a colorful personality in the capital as he swaggered through the streets dressed like a dandy, twisting his great black mustache, and wearing a bowler hat set rakishly on his head.

Having vicariously had a taste of politics, he went to Barcelona, and to this day his enemies insist that he was sent by the monarchists to organize a harmless republican party to divide the separatists. Exit the dandy; enter the champion of the proletariat in a flannel shirt open at the neck, displaying hair on his chest. He founded the Casa del Pueblo and developed a mob style of eloquence in which moderation had no part. Soon he was a dominant figure in Barcelona, known as the "Emperor of the Paralelo"— which is to the Catalan capital what Montmartre, the Bowery, the Barbary Coast once were in other cities. Under the banner of republicanism, he perfected a political machine that would have reflected credit on the ingenuity of the most consummate of American city bosses, entrenched himself in the municipal government, with his tentacles reaching wide. Meanwhile, he had studied law and been admitted to the Bar. In time, this clever, practical politician extended his organization throughout the country, and, with the passing of the giants, he seized the scepter of party leadership. He had charm of manner and fluency of speech. By the time he assumed the leadership of the republican party in the Cortes, he had begun to take on the dignity of a steel engraving. His enemies were skeptical of his sincerity and doubted the fiber of his republicanism, though, for the most part, his party was composed of sincere republicans, and he was one at heart. Madariaga describes him as "a domesticated lion in the garden of the Monarchy."

When, on the establishment of the Republic, Azaña shot above him, his hatred of the intruder was not unnatural. Thus his party was to become, first, an ally, and then the tool, of the enemies of republicanism. Human nature explains much, but not all. There were irreconcilable differences in the two men's concepts of the mission of the new regime.

To Lerroux, it meant political change; to Azaña, it meant a

drastic economic and social change. Lerroux would have exchanged a King for a President and called it a day; to Azaña that meant nothing. He proposed to create a new Spain, with greater opportunities for the masses, more rights and dignity for labor, land for peasants, the extermination of feudalistic privileges.

Interested primarily in power and patronage, Lerroux unconsciously, I am sure, was to lead his party into a close alliance with the enemies of the liberalism he had once preached and the Republic he had championed. Unwittingly, he was helping to prepare the soil for Fascism. I am sure history will indict him for having permitted pique and personal ambition to divide the republican forces at a critical juncture.

And yet, as I sat that day with the old veteran, I felt the appeal of his personality. The mellowing years had touched him with a certain dignity. As I looked into his twinkling eyes, he seemed to me a benevolent and easy boss who knew that "the constitution is nothing between friends." Time had cured him of his illusions, and he had sobered into a smiling cynic, no end amused by the clamor of ideologies. I had called upon him in the interest of imprisoned Americans who had struck a Civil Guard, and he was graciousness itself. "I will do everything I can within the law," he said, and then, with a twinkle in his eye, "and outside it, if necessary." He kept his word.

But Lerroux had to face the music when the Cortes met. The diplomatic gallery was packed for the debate. The gong sounded, the deputies rushed in, laughing, jesting. New faces were on the Blue Bench. And Lerroux rose, calm, cynical, to face his foe and the vote of confidence. "We who are about to die, salute you," he began. His not unmelodious voice flowed on smoothly, the sentences like long ribbons in a breeze, illustrating perfectly Talleyrand's definition of the purpose of words. On the whole, a bromidic speech. He was heard in silence, and when he closed, only his own party cheered.

4

Then rose Indalecio Prieto, premier orator of the socialists, short, corpulent, bald but for a rim of hair around the lower head and neck. His dynamic oratory was felt immediately. I had observed him on the Blue Bench as an Azaña minister, when his huge fat face, double chin, and surplus flesh at the back of his neck gave an impression of grossness, but the moment he rose there was an astonishing transformation. His face lighted with animation. His voice, clear and flexible, was like a bugle call. His oratorical mannerisms reminded me of Burke Cockran, the great American—the same gesticulation, the same swell of the voice as he approached the end of a glowing period, with a resounding boom of the clenched fist on the chest, or the noisy slap of a fat hand on the thigh. His was a devastating attack.

No man in Spain had a more vivid or powerful personality, with more genius for political life. His eloquence was of nature, not of the academy. Press correspondents, who easily penetrate the disguise of pretense, assured me that he was a man of generous impulses, jovial, an amusing companion, witty, humorous, intensely human in his virtues and vices. Even his most virulent enemies would not have accused him of being more bloodthirsty than a lamb. He had the conservatism of balance, and he was a master of mass psychology. One of the most cultivated of Spaniards told me that he had "never known another man" with "more natural talent" or with "a more enormous capacity for understanding." To illustrate, he cited the opinion of a distinguished expert in financial matters Prieto had consulted on a very technical question. The expert had given him a complicated explanation, and the next day in a speech Prieto had made an explanation as lucid as the expert could have done. The latter had said that he had "never known a man of such comprehension."

He had educated himself while selling papers in the streets of Bilbao from his eleventh year. He had devoured and assimilated everything written by Pablo Iglesias, the brilliant founder of the socialist party in Spain. From him he had learned the art of clarity, directness, and simplicity.

He was speaking now on the resolution of confidence, and as he threw all the artillery of his rich oratorical equipment into action— wit, irony, sarcasm, humor, invective, mimicry—the chamber rocked with laughter and applause. I thought more and more of Danton as he spoke. "A tremendous personality," whispered Señora Pérez de Ayala beside me.

Azaña was to close after the recess. During the speeches of
Lerroux and Prieto he had sat unmoved, seemingly remote, and
white as chalk since he had risen from a sickbed. He rose in an intense silence. Lerroux leaned forward, cupping his ear with his
hand. Azaña's tone was conversational, but eloquent and artful.
He was a master of the effective pause and could put dynamite into
the inflection of a word. Time and again his irony brought storms
of applause. Lerroux, with flushed face, stared unceasingly at him,
until finally he angrily interrupted to challenge the speaker to say
when, as charged, Lerroux had said the people had lost confidence
in the Cortes. Azaña furnished book, chapter, and verse in a bored
tone, and went on. On the roll call, only Lerroux' party voted with
him. Lerroux was out.

5

Three days later, I took General Fuqua to the palace for his
initial call on the President. Reporters and photographers crowded
the entrance, for Alcalá Zamora, in search of a government, was
still sending for leaders. A soldier, stiff as a ramrod, wearing a gray
uniform and steel helmet, admitted us to the President's room,
where we found him in a happy mood, promising a speedy ending of
the crisis. A private secretary, accompanying us to the outer door,
indicated two men in the reception room and whispered that one
of them would probably be the next Prime Minister. He referred to
Sánchez Román, a leader of the Madrid Bar, a staunch republican,
and a conservative. But Román had called to decline, and in the
end a government was formed under Martínez Barrio, then the
first lieutenant of Lerroux.

The campaign was on.

6

A banquet of the American Chamber of Commerce took me to
Barcelona in October. Though the visit was made "unofficial" to
escape certain embarrassment in protocol, I called immediately
upon Colonel Maciá, President of the autonomous state and symbol of Catalan autonomy. Despite his acknowledgment of the in-
formal nature of the call, when we entered the court of the beautiful

fifteenth-century palace, then the Presidencia, smart soldiers in dress uniforms were waiting. They marched ahead, and fell behind, and such was the informality of my presentation to this fascinating old man in the reception hall. He led me into a charming room with small pane windows of colored glass.

Maciá had passionately dedicated himself to the historic Catalan movement and had won the lasting affection of the masses. One glance, and I was under the spell of his rare charm. Of medium height, and elegant slenderness, his seventy-odd years rested upon him serenely. His abundant hair and neat mustache were snow white, his features were small and refined, his large, luminous brown eyes were kindly. He was dressed nattily in gray, his tie the color of his suit and socks. A silk handkerchief protruded coquettishly from his upper coat pocket. Here was Beau Brummell, grown gray. His voice was low, musical, perfectly modulated. If he was the "leader of the rabble," as his enemies said, he was nevertheless an exquisite and a gentleman. On returning to the residence of Claude Dawson, our Consul General, we found a huge willow basket filled with yellow roses for my wife and bearing the card of Maciá, though her presence in Barcelona had not been mentioned. He knew everything. Soon he made his return call, and we exchanged toasts and shook hands, and as the venerable figure with a poet's face retired, I knew I had been in contact with the raw material of history.

7

Barcelona is a beautiful modern city, throbbing with energy and enterprise. The Catalan is as different from the Castilian, as the Galician is different from the Basque. The Catalans and the Basques are the Yankees of Spain, dynamic, pushing, acquisitive, progressive in a material way, a bit turbulent at times. They are happiest in the factory, the counting room, or the emporium. But Barcelona is not typically Spanish.

One day we had a picnic lunch with the Consul General and his wife far up on the sides of Montserrat, crowned by the ancient monastery associated with the legend of Tristram and Isolde. There, among trees and flowers, with a magnificent vista spread out before us, we lunched in the shade of giant trees before visiting the monastery whose origin goes back to the early centuries of Christianity. There, too, is the church, where we were shown the treasures of which the churches had not been robbed by the Republic as so many were led to believe outside Spain, and we mounted the ladder to get a closer view of the famous Black Virgin. But more impressive, as a church, was the cathedral in the heart of the old part of the city where the streets are narrow and the surrounding buildings throw the interior into a religious twilight even when the sun is bright. And the cloister—there was the charm and thrill, for there lie the Catalan patriots murdered by Napoleon. The front door of the cathedral opens on a street so narrow that three steps suffice to cross; and this was convenient to Ferdinand and Isabella, who lived in the ancient palace across the lanelike passage. One day, centuries ago, a curious procession marched down this narrow lane behind some sailors and Indians, with Columbus in the lead. The Discoverer, just returned from his great achievement, was going to the palace to report to the Catholic monarchs. This was the first Columbus Day parade in history. The old palace is filled with moldering manuscript today.

I found and heard of no disorders in Barcelona.

8

The election campaign was proceeding quietly. Toward the close of October, I drove with Fernando de los Ríos to lunch in the unique restaurant in the deserted University of Alcalá de Henares. He talked freely of the approaching elections and said the Rightists would win, but that the victory would be disastrous to the victors, who would wipe out the reforms of the Azaña regime and bring a reaction that would be "terrible." I was to remember this later. He had just returned from his constituency of Granada. The Rightists were telling the peasants there that the retention of their new rights, granted by the Leftists, depended on their voting for the Rightists. Don Fernando smiled through his beard. "These peasants are not fools," he said, "and the stupidity of the threat has made them bitter." But that which impressed me most was his admission of defeat.

9

The campaign, judged by the American standard, seemed ab-
normally quiet. The most significant republican demonstration was
not advertised as political at all. One October day, a French warship anchored in the harbor of Valencia, bearing the ashes of
Blasco-Ibáñez from France, where he had died in exile. His novels
depicting the lives of the miners, fishermen, and peasants meant
more to the Spaniards than his *Four Horsemen* that had gripped the
world during the First World War. In his home town of Valencia,
he was the idol of the republicans, who had built a splendid tomb
for his ashes.

In driving to Valencia with Rex Smith of the Associated Press,
a miscalculation found us at lunchtime remote from a *parador* and in
a small village. We were reconciled to a hunk of bread and cheese
but we had not reckoned on the resourcefulness of Pepe. After
speaking to a native, he drove us down a side street to a barnlike
structure. The room we entered was large, cold, dreary, poorly
furnished, with many cheap, bare tables surrounded by poorly
dressed peasants and a priest. They were drinking coffee. It was the
village clubhouse of the poor.

The proprietor, pleased but shy, approached, and we ordered
eggs, to be on the safe side. Yes, he could give us eggs, and a pig
was killed in the village that morning, and perhaps he could give us
pig meat too? We ordered pig. Shivering in the cold air after the
drive, we asked for brandy. Our host seemed a bit embarrassed, but
he disappeared and soon returned with cognac. Meanwhile, the
room was clearing. Soon we were led into the family sitting room,
simply furnished but immaculately clean. A snow-white cloth covered the table. From my place on a worn but comfortable couch
against the wall, I could drop my right hand into the cradle of a
baby, and my left on the head of a wistful dog waiting for crumbs
from the rich man's table. Two neat, wholesome women, like those
of American farms, busied themselves about the room and smiled
pleasantly as they placed a huge platter with a dozen fresh eggs
and rice before us, with homemade bread, and the wine of the vicinity; and as we gluttonously cleaned the platter, luxuriating in
the warmth of the brazier beneath the table, the two women were

kneeling before the wood fire of the grate frying pig meat, and the mingled odor of the frying meat and the burning wood was sweet. Soon they brought a huge platter piled high with pig meat. Indulgently the women smiled as I sneakingly slipped bits to the grateful dog, and when we were through, there was nothing on the platter. When our host presented the bill he seemed embarrassed about its size, explaining that he had no brandy in the house and had been forced to buy a bottle. I glanced at the bill. We were paying the equivalent of a dollar and a quarter for the three of us—including the dog. I doubled the amount. As we drove away, the two women and the man were in the street smiling and waving, and the dog was barking a farewell. I had felt the simple, warmhearted hospitality of a Spanish villager and had had an experience I shall never forget.

10

We arrived in Valencia toward evening, and that night the French warship entered the harbor with the ashes of Ibáñez. The next morning when I joined the presidential party at the City Hall in the reception room opening on a balcony looking down on a vast multitude, I found, in addition to Alcalá Zamora, Colonel Maciá and Lerroux. The street scene was one of color and animation. A dark-eyed woman standing beside me on the balcony spoke to me of Ibáñez' great admiration for American institutions. It was the widow of Ibáñez, a Chilean. Some years later, in Santiago, she was to give me some luscious *paella* feasts at her home. The Italian Fascists had driven her from the novelist's home in Mentone and had destroyed his choice library.

At length, from far down the street, came the blare of a band, and the procession came in sight, led by many horsemen. Thousands of marchers followed more bands. A forest of flags made the street a mass of moving colors. The procession moved slowly, and it was long before the large casket of the famous novelist passed beneath the balcony, borne on the shoulders of many men. At frequent intervals there was a pause as the heavy burden was shifted to fresh shoulders. The band was playing a funeral dirge. Ibáñez was home again, and he was home to stay.

It was late afternoon when we sat down to an official luncheon in honor of Alcalá Zamora—a small luncheon of twenty-six. The President sat directly across the table, with Maciá beside him, and I observed that the latter, slender and starry-eyed, was the more elegant of the two and more at ease. A deadly luncheon, long drawn out, and silent as a sepulcher. The silence was uncomfortable. Lerroux caught my eye and lifted his champagne goblet, and we drank a silent toast.

11

The next morning we started for the rice fields where friends had promised me a *paella* feast. As we drove through a small village on the way, the impassioned voice of Lerroux thundered across the road. A radio from the Nautical Club in Valencia was carrying his message to his partisans throughout the province. We stopped on the way at the popular duck-hunting grounds among the rice fields. Concessions for the privilege of shooting were sold for seven thousand pesetas, and this money was the chief revenue of a number of small villages.

And then another reminder that an election campaign was on. Before lunch, we had started to a pavilion on an enormous beach for cocktails when we noticed a small party ascending the steps before us, with Maciá among them. "We don't want to run into these Catalans," said one of my party of Valencians. I ascribed the ill-natured remark to regional antipathies until I learned later that my companions were Rightists in politics. It was my last view of this charming old man, for within a few months he was dead, sincerely mourned by the Catalonian masses.

12

Outdoors, under an autumn sun that baked my back, I sat facing a Valencian highway and gorged on *paella* while enjoying a picturesque procession of wagons, piled high with green shrubbery for the home fires, with happy children perched on top, eating melons. After lunch, we inspected the pleasant home of the peasant foreman of the rice fields. It was strange but most attractive, spotlessly white, with bright blue trimmings, and with dried vegetables hanging from the rafters. Later the peasant foreman took us in a motorboat on the old canal, dug hundreds of years ago during the Moorish occupation. It was a memorable ride to me, since the mixed company disclosed the instinctive democracy of the Spanish people. The old peasant and the young one who operated the boat were treated by the lawyer, the aviator, and the aristocrat as equals, and they accepted the treatment with dignity as their due. They were divided in politics, but politics was adjourned on a social occasion. As we rode back, all were laughing, jesting, singing, and darkness fell, and the moon threw a shimmering light on the old Moorish canal and the rice fields soaked in water like a swamp.

13

That night I had a premonition of the Spanish tragedy ahead. We were having refreshments at the Vodka, a favorite bar, when the peril to the democracy in Spain was impressed upon me forcibly. Some officers of the Aviation Corps, very snappy in dress uniforms, for they had been ordered from Madrid for the homecoming of Ibáñez, burst into the room in a high state of elation, eagerly passing a newspaper from hand to hand. It contained a statement from José Primo de Rivera announcing that his Fascists would fight their battles "in the street" and not at the polls. These officers of the army, sworn to fidelity to democratic institutions, were delighted. Thus early did coming events cast their shadows before.

We returned to Madrid in time for the elections.

2

PERIOD OF THE SAPPERS

Chapter IV

Liquidation of the Republic Begins

THE campaign itself no more indicated a crisis for the regime than one in the United States. The most significant feature was the alliance of the republican party of Lerroux with other parties secretly hostile, not only to republicanism, but to democracy.

The Azaña parties entered the campaign bearing the burden of the usual accumulated grievances of their enemies and dissensions among their friends. Azaña had given the nation two and a half years of normal stability under democratic processes, but his enemies made his liberalism a liability. The monarchists' hatred of the regime was natural, since the nobility had been deprived of its erstwhile privileges. The Carlists were bitter against it because of the curtailment of the political power of the hierarchy. The great landowners with their immense wealth feared it because of its projected agrarian reforms. The big industrialists resented its labor laws, such as had been on the statutes in the United States for many years; and the financiers reflected the hostility of the industrialists and the landlords. The hierarchy of the church was arrayed against it primarily because of the separation of church and state, and though there was no interference with religious worship, there was a prohibition against teaching by religious orders. Thus the richest and most powerful elements made common cause against Azaña and the democracy he symbolized, and he could count only on the middle class, writers, professional men, intellectuals, peasants, and industrial workers. His government had moved with such feverish haste that some of its reforms were still on paper only, and there was some resentment and disillusionment even among those whose interests he sought to serve.

Azaña told me that his agrarian reforms were motivated by his conviction that the poverty and misery of the peasants, comprising eighty-five per cent of the country, would inevitably make for social disorders and communism unless their economic and social status could be raised. A well-known English writer called on me at the beginning of Azaña's second Ministry and astonished me with his bitterness against Azaña's land reforms. When I expressed my astonishment, since he wrote for a famous liberal magazine, he explained: "It will hold back the revolution." I learned later that this man was a communist. Thus the communists knew that Azaña's land program was aimed at communism, but the great landowners were not so wise. When the landowners were restricted in their exportation of grain and agricultural products to keep prices within reach of the masses, the landowners called it "communism."

Agrarian reform was especially imperative in Andalusia and Estremadura, where more than five hundred huge estates owned by very rich men were not under cultivation. The law enacted confiscated without compensation the old feudal *fundos*. Uncultivated land and enclosed common land was assigned to the farm workers, but compensation was provided at the rate of five per cent. Nothing more was proposed in Spain than had been done in France, but the French Revolution, aimed at feudalism, had made no impression on Spain. Thus the agrarian reforms were a challenge to the persistent feudalistic society of the Spanish state. From early in the nineteenth century, Spain had been dominated by the landowners. There was no possible solution of a grave social problem without this reform. The landowners, naturally, were hostile, but the peasants themselves were not satisfied with the slow legal process. The Azaña government had moved so rapidly over so much ground that it had not had time to consolidate its position anywhere.

The labor laws enacted were not even socialistic, but to the industrialists they were revolutionary and "communistic." They provided a legal status for labor, gave it a contractual relation with the employers, and, as in other countries, for the first time fixed the legal hours of labor, provided insurance against unemployment and for accidents, and maternity care. Under the Azaña regime, the status of labor had been raised, but in the settlement of disputes by a commission composed equally of representatives of both labor and capital, with the deciding vote in case of a tie by the Minister of Labor, Largo Caballero, the deciding vote invariably went to labor even in cases where labor was clearly wrong, and this alienated some of the middle class.

In the field of popular education, the Azaña regime had acted enthusiastically, since the need was pressing in a country with an appalling percentage of illiteracy; where more than nine thousand communities were without a teacher and hundreds of thousands of children were without schools. But the task was colossal and meant an enormous building program. Under the Ministry of Marcelino Domingo much progress was made, and under that of Fernando de los Ríos ten thousand schools were established. But for the public schools there was a dearth of teachers and little time for their training. Under the brief Ministry of Salvador de Madariaga, later, a serious attempt was made to provide training for teachers. Even so, when church schools were unhappily closed the state was not prepared completely to assume the obligation. The laws against religious teaching mobilized the more devout Catholics against the liberal regime. There was no interference with religious worship; the great wealth in gold and silver in the treasure rooms of cathedrals remained to be shown by the priests to tourists, but the parish priests no longer were paid out of the public treasury, the maintenance of the machinery of the church was no longer the obligation of the state. The Jesuits had been expelled, on paper, though Catholic monarchs had done as much, but the suppression of what may be described in American terms as parochial, or church, schools aroused the fury of the devout, and the full force of the intensive organization of the hierarchy was turned against Azaña and his allies.

2

Thus while the legislative machinery ground day and night far into the torrid summer, a comparatively obscure young man was feverishly active in the organization of a clerical party to be known as the CEDA (Confederación Española de Derechos Autónomos). Its primary concern, it said, was the church. It entered the campaign with a proclamation of indifference as between monarchy and Republic, and with the announced purpose of restoring the ancient political status of the church. Throughout the campaign it was to be disturbingly reticent regarding its attitude toward the Republic, but it was generally assumed to be monarchistic at heart. Some thought of it as contemplating such a mission as that of the old Catholic Center party of Germany, with its young leader cast for the role of Windthorst; others wondered if the young man aspired to a role similar to that of Hitler and Mussolini.

This young leader had disclosed a certain genius as an organizer, and his fervent declamations evoked the fanatic emotions of the days of the crusades. Thus, with amazing rapidity, he mobilized a strong party, responding as unquestioningly to his every nod, as the Italian Fascists and the German Nazis to their chiefs.

Thus Gil Robles emerged from the shadows of the wings into the spotlight on the stage.

But, with the creation of his party, he was by no means finished. His organizing genius and a certain talent for intrigue, found more to do. He found both the Rightist and the Leftist enrolled in various parties, each jealous of its entity. If he could but form a solid front of all the parties of the Right, including the monarchists and the few Fascists, it would prevail over the divided parties of the Left. Soon he was conferring in quiet corners with the leaders of the monarchists and the Carlists, sworn enemies of the Republic; with the agrarians, sworn enemies of agrarian reforms; with the Rightists of Catalonia, loyal champions of economic privilege; and with the veteran Lerroux and his Radical-Republican party. Everything depended on a combination with the notoriously anticlerical Lerroux. To him, the combination promised the premiership; to the semi-republicans, it offered a republican façade. And out of these conditions and necessities the solid Right front was formed—an incongruous combination of incompatible and irreconcilable elements; a combination that was to make inevitable the formation of the Popular Front parties in the next election. But, for the purpose of this election, it would serve. Lerroux, the sly old fox, smiled behind his hand at the young man's naïveté and began counting his chickens before they were hatched. He was confident that his party of practical politicians of experience would lead the poll and that he would at length become Prime Minister.

3

A few weeks before the election, all Spain was chuckling over the bizarre "escape" from prison of the immensely wealthy Juan March, familiarly known as "the contrabandist." No one had profited so richly through the dictatorship, which had given him a monopoly in tobacco. The prison, facing the old Archbishop's Palace in Alcalá de Henares, with its iron-barred windows, had seemed secure enough. And there, for eighteen months, the little old man with an odorous reputation, but so perfumed with his enormous wealth that even the pure of heart found his presence sweet, had meditated on his sins. Often I looked through the little windowpanes of the natal room of Catherine of Aragon in the Archbishop's Palace, across the little court to the barred windows, and wondered if Juan March was satisfied with the service. One evening, when the night guard came, the old man said: "A great injustice has been done me. You should open the door and let me out into the street." And the sensitive guard, tender beneath his rough exterior, and touched by the persecution of the good gray man, did as he was told. In the cynical, ribald laughter of the cafés, men told this story and roared with the joy of it, but there were cynics to suggest that the supersensitive guard had been less moved by the good man's wrongs than by the bank notes in his hand. However, so deep was the guard's devotion to his charge that they made their escape together.

A bitter enemy of the Republic, and no friend of democracy, powerful because of his immense fortune, was now at large.

But Madrid buzzed with other rumors, and soon March was forgotten. It was whispered that Largo Caballero, left-wing socialist leader, was meddling with the army in the preparation of a rebellion if the Leftists were swept from power. The Council of Ministers sat in solemn conclave. Mounted soldiers pranced their horses in the streets, police on motorcycles with gun attachments whizzed by, and others patrolled with rifles on their shoulders. But this was mostly due to rumors of a military *coup d'état* in preparation if the Rightists should lose, and the eyes of the reactionaries sparkled. But on the whole, order and decorum marked the political meetings, and the few disturbances that occurred were mostly the work of the Rightist provocateurs. They howled Prieto from the platform in Cádiz, and at Bilbao they threw gas bombs into a meeting of Azaña and Prieto and broke up the meeting. Prieto said quietly: "They make us weep water now; but we will make them weep blood."

A few days before the election I lunched as the guest of officers of the Aviation School and met Ramón Franco, famous for his flight to South America and for the fierceness of his republicanism when, just before the passing of the King, he had flown over the palace dropping revolutionary leaflets. He was a handsome man, short but compactly built, with black hair, a dark complexion, and extraordinarily dark eyes that twinkled on the verge of laughter. The next day he sent me one of the few volumes containing the Constitution of the Republic, printed in colors, bound in leather, with the silver seal of the Republic on the back. It is with laughter that I now read the inscription to me in the book: "*Al gran periodista, ilustre escritor, y Republicano, el bien amigo*—Ramón Franco." When three years later this ardent republican joined his brother in the attack on the Republic, I placed the volume under lock and key and reflected on the mockeries of history and the fickleness of man.

The campaign passed serenely. Even so, there was rejoicing when the day before the election dawned dark and rainy. Spanish insurrections, I was told, do not flourish in wet weather. The next day was Sunday, election day. People having no pressing business out, remained indoors, and even the British church abandoned the morning service lest rioters roam the streets. The election in Madrid was as quiet as an election in Indianapolis, with fewer incidents than mark an election in Kentucky.

The unification of all the parties of the Right on a single ticket, together with the huge campaign fund of the monarchists, the landowners, the industrialists, and Juan March, was easily successful, as foreseen. Throughout the campaign I heard many things, but never once did anyone express interest or concern about the communists. In the elections immediately following the fall of the monarchy, grotesquely ascribed to the communists at a later day, the communists had elected but one member of the Cortes out of more than four hundred and seventy members, and he was a man of substance and a parlor communist at whom people smiled. In the election of 1933 they lost this one seat.

It was the party of Gil Robles that led all the rest.

4

For two years Gil Robles was to be the master of the immediate destiny of Spain, if not the ostensible head of the government. As the organizer of the victory and leader of the most numerous party in the Cortes, normally he would have been Prime Minister. But he was in a quandary, and for the time he preferred the power to the responsibility. And then, too, there was an obstacle in Alcalá Zamora, who had not failed to note that throughout the campaign Gil Robles had refrained from pledging allegiance to the Republic. Stoutly, Alcalá Zamora declared that he would never turn the government over to a leader who refused publicly to make the pledge. Then again, while Gil Robles' party was more numerous than the others, it numbered no more than twenty-five per cent of the members of the Cortes. It was a minority party.

But the young leader's concern was scarcely greater than that of the monarchists, who, with unprecedented lavishness, had poured their money into the campaign coffers. If Gil Robles had not uttered a word for the Republic, he had made no open pledge to the monarchy, and when they asked him when the King was coming back, he turned upon them the face of a poker player.

Thus, at once, Gil Robles was tasting the fruit of an impossible alliance of incongruous elements, and the taste was bitter.

The monarchists wanted the King—*at once*.

The agrarians wanted the few peasants driven from their land —*at once*.

The industrialists and financiers insisted on wiping out the labor laws—*at once*.

And none of this was possible. But the party of Lerroux, which moved suavely about the lobby of the Palace Hotel, was far more reasonable. All it asked was power—*at once;* and this not only was possible but convenient. Lerroux became the Minister, Gil Robles the Master, and thus began the partnership between the old church baiter and the young church champion.

The father of Gil Robles had been a militantly reactionary professor at Salamanca, with a fierce hatred of liberalism. The son had distinguished himself at Salamanca by leading a small group of students in bitter attacks on the great Spanish philosopher, Unamuno, who gave distinction to the university. He hated Unamuno because he was a liberal, since, in his lexicon, a liberal is subversive of society and religion. He was born a conservative. When his father died, leaving little property, he became a lecturer in law while living in Madrid, and he served as a police-court magistrate while practicing law. His ability and zeal attracted the attention of Ángel Herrera.

This remarkable man had founded *El Debate*, a newspaper dedicated solely to the interest of the church. He manned his staff with men of zeal and capacity, acquired the best news service, and the most modern mechanical equipment, and he presented both news and views in a style dignified and interesting. On the occasion of my visit, a beautiful tea was served in a large, tastefully furnished reading and reception room, and I was introduced to the paper's own school of journalism. Herrera was a power within himself, but he had retired, entrusting the management of the paper to his brother Francisco.

When Gil Robles became a writer on *El Debate* he was taken under the wing of Ángel Herrera, and this gave him prestige and power from the beginning.

5

For a moment, after the election, Madrid was dull, and we made a pilgrimage to Ávila, associated with so much that was inspiring in Catholic history. The sun was shining brightly as we drove through the Guadarramas, but we had gone but a little way into the mountains when the sky was darkened by threatening clouds that threw the wooded road into a semitwilight. The scene was one of magic, with the dark shadows under the black clouds, and with brilliant spots of light where the sun shone through. But, when high in the mountains it began to rain, and we drove through clouds impenetrable for ten feet, the adventure had its alloy. The forest was banked with snow. The sun glistening on great wet rocks made them sparkle like huge diamonds. The rain increased in intensity. The shepherds in the fields, wrapped in their Spanish shawls, were picturesque but chilly. We were glad to drive through the medieval gates of the walls of Ávila, built nine hundred years ago and still in a state of perfect preservation, with their eighty-odd towers almost as good as new. We had been to Carcassonne, where much had been restored for the tourists; Ávila was the real thing.

Our hotel room looked down on the Plaza de Catedral, and through our window loomed the entrance to the great gray church not half a block away. The two figures of warriors in armor carved on either side of the entrance, the fact that the apse of the church was built into and beyond the city walls as part of the military defense proclaimed the war preoccupation of the militant religion of the eleventh century. I saw this fortresslike temple of worship in the dim light of a cloudy day, to take away the memory of the alabaster carvings of the nave, and the feeling that I had touched the Middle Ages.

But more fascinating was the monastery of San Tomás, founded by Isabella and Ferdinand. On the death of their son, Juan, in his nineteenth year, he was buried in the monastery, and the genius of Fancelli, the Florentine sculptor, was summoned to make the tomb. It is a magnificent sarcophagus of alabaster, exquisitely carved, and I thought the recumbent figure of the young prince the most beautiful I had seen. The features of the prince bore a rapt expression. There, before the altar, through the centuries, lies the young man who "died for love." Very frail, and married to a robust young princess, the doctors advised a separation until his health improved, but Isabella, remembering the scriptural admonition, "let no man put asunder," vetoed the advice, and in a little while the delicate youth was dead.

We emerged into a white world. Huge snowflakes were falling, and the next morning we looked out on a dreary scene in the Plaza de Catedral. The ground was deeply covered, and the flakes still fell. A patient little donkey, with milk cans for panniers, stood patiently in front of a door waiting for its master, bending its head against the wind and snow. Some monks in cowls crossed the plaza cautiously on their way to church. Troops of young girls in gay colors picked their way toward the cathedral. The streets were slushy and almost deserted, and Ávila seemed more than ever like something beautiful and dead under a white mantle.

Meanwhile, Pepe announced that the roads were being cleared and that by leaving early we might make the journey to Madrid in safety. Workers had begun operations at the walls of Ávila, and we drove several miles into the mountains over hard-bottom roads swept clean. All about us, miles and miles of whiteness. The damp, glistening snow clung to each little twig of the mountain forest. Peasants, red-faced and laughing, were enjoying the discomfiture of those who impatiently tried to pass other cars by driving into the snowdrifts beside the highway. Twelve large oxen hitched to a snow plow were hard at work. We reached the peak without difficulty and from the height we surveyed a scene like fairyland. This height is well known to the young Madrileños who drive there regularly throughout the winter for the skiing. Soon we were descending on the other side and rolling into the warm sunshine of the plain.

Ávila is more than a medieval city—it is a symbol, the symbol of a Spain that is mystical, medieval, almost fanatically religious. To know Ávila is to understand many things political.

6

And Martínez Barrio still was Prime Minister.

The usual rumors were afloat. The foreign press, so grossly unfair to republican Spain, luridly described the "terror and tension" in Madrid one Sunday morning because of "fears of an anarchist or syndicalist rising." There was no suggestion, even in sensational foreign papers, of a communist danger. On that day of "terror" when a London paper had us all behind locked doors, I drove for more than an hour in the Retiro, a huge park in the heart of the city, and found thousands of young men and women promenading and flirting cheerfully in the sunshine. Madrid was as serene that morning as New York or London.

Nothing more serious had occurred than a waiters' strike! The next day in the Cortes, Prieto interrogated the government on the strike. In its reply, its spokesman charged that the trouble had been inspired by the campaign speeches of the socialists. This was patently untrue. The trouble had come from anarchists and syndicalists, and the government's denunciation of their preference for violence paled before the lurid attack of the socialist orator. He reminded the Rightist that during the Azaña regime a rising of anarchists had been sternly suppressed and in consequence the Rightists had attacked Azaña for his sternness.

"What caused the unrest?" he thundered.

"Why the unholy alliance of the party of Lerroux with the avowed enemies of the Republic."

And that was partly true.

7

A month later, as the Cortes met, Martínez Barrio resigned and Lerroux became Prime Minister. But behind the scenes all was not serene. Barrio, a robust republican with a democratic ideology, who would not compromise for power, was looking askance upon his chief's alliance with the enemies of the republican regime. It was generally understood that Lerroux had promised to wipe out the army reforms of Azaña and restore hundreds of anti-republican officers to their commissions. When Lerroux proposed to give himself the Ministry of Defense, the rumor began to take on the semblance of truth. The connection was not lost on Barrio, who made his displeasure felt, and since Lerroux dared not break with his ablest lieutenant, to whom he referred in public as "my spiritual child," he yielded.

But Barrio was not easily reconciled to his chief's strange bed-fellows. Before leaving the Presidencia to make room for Lerroux, he gave a luncheon for the reporters who had covered it during his tenure, and it brought a sensation. The first lieutenant of Lerroux paid tribute to Azaña as the ablest statesman in Spain with whom he might, in the future, co-operate. The cafés buzzed with excited conversation.

That day, in a packed Cortes, Lerroux monotonously read a short, insipid speech, to be cheered by his own party and to be heard in silence by the other parties in his coalition.

Then Gil Robles rose.

The young man was master of Spain's immediate destiny. With

the votes and power, he could, by a nod of his head, tumble Lerroux from the pedestal in a moment. There was something of the arrogance of conscious power in his manner. His physical appearance was not impressive. He was of medium height and a slight paunch protruded from beneath his vest. Like almost all the Spanish leaders, he was bald. No single feature would attract attention, and he would have passed in a crowd unnoticed. His eyes, betraying no sense of humor, but much of suspicion, seemed brooding on distant things. I have watched him for hours from the diplomatic gallery without seeing him smile. His general expression suggested anger, suspicion, disapproval, petulance. He worked incessantly and showed the effect in a nervous manner and tired eyes. He was high-strung, and his constant fidgeting with his tie, and the peculiar jerks of his head, as though trying to relieve his neck of the friction of a collar, revealed his constant tension.

But there could be no denying his eloquence. It was the eloquence of intense feeling, of passionate fervor for a cause, or scornful hatred of a foe. He had a way of leading up to a climax by increasing the rapidity of his utterance and the volume of his high-pitched voice; and while his faithful followers roared approval, he would sip a glass of water. There was no wit, no humor, no real irony, and he depended for effect on the intensity of his partisan declamation. His admirers proclaimed him a twentieth-century Peter the Hermit who would preach a crusade and lead one.

That day he annoyed his monarchist allies with the reminder that being a Rightist did not necessarily imply being a monarchist. And it must have wounded the pride of Lerroux to note how generally all looked to Gil Robles for a foreshadowing of governmental policies, rather than to the Prime Minister.

That day none of the leaders of the opposition spoke. There was an undefinable undercurrent of bitterness painfully discernible, and Goicoechea, the monarchist leader, prodded Prieto into an attack on the telephone contract and into an uncomplimentary reference to Primo de Rivera, the Dictator. The latter's son, now the sole Fascist member of the Cortes, furiously rushed toward the speaker, but deputies intervened, and the gossips had it later that more than one hand grasped a pistol. But the most significant feature of this clash came in the attempt of Gil Robles to pour oil on the troubled waters. It was not time, he said, to discuss the disputed contract. But, he added, authoritatively, it would soon be taken up.

Lerroux, on the Blue Bench, blinked. Already the young man was taking upon himself the right to speak for the government.

8

Christmas came, and its spirit rested momentarily upon the politicians, and, for a time, there was peace. Along the country roads, peasants with long rods patiently were driving droves of turkeys to the market; close to the curb in congested streets these droves of strutting turkeys, under the peasants' watchful eyes, moved close together with a strange docility, ignoring the noise of the traffic and their impending doom. Curious and amused spectators paused to survey the scene and to pick their turkey for the Christmas feast. On one of the narrow streets open markets for children's toys stridently advertised themselves by brisk and noisy bargaining. And friends, meeting in the street, jested merrily on their chances in the Christmas lottery.

9

On a rainy day in late December, my wife and I started by car to Granada as guests of honor in a three-day fiesta arranged by the Centro Artístico in honor of Washington Irving. For no foreign author do the Spaniards have a greater affection, since, as the Duke of Alba told me, none other had done so much for Spain. We drove to the old romantic city through a deluge of rain that gave to the day and scenery a strange, weird beauty, with great black clouds broken here and there with patches of blue. The wind howled, water splashed against the windows of the car, and the wind and rain fairly rippled across the great expanse of brown fields. The mountains in their distant draperies of mist loomed through the gloom, mysterious and unreal. From Manzanares, where we lunched, the road to Bailén winds around hills, and we reached the historic scene of the Spaniards' triumph over Napoleon in the light of a half moon.

There, at the edge of the town, little more than a village, we found the *parador*, and we stepped from the chill into a lounge furnished in blue, where the flames of a wood fire were leaping cheerfully in a big fireplace. Nothing could have been cosier, with the rain pelting against the house, and the wind howling around the corners. There was a large red brick fireplace, set on a raised brick platform, with benches covered by soft blue cushions on either side, and with big easy chairs on the platform facing the fire. The odor of the burning wood was pleasing, and, after an excellent dinner, we sat drowsing until bedtime. The bedrooms were small, impeccably clean, compact, with almost every convenience, as in a modern Pullman coach. This was typical of all the *paradores*.

The morning drive to Granada, over a charming countryside with its rolling hills and mountains, recalling centuries of dramatic history, was thrilling. It was easy to imagine the forays of the Moorish cavalry, and the army of Isabella marching with banners. For some miles we rode between rows of green olive trees. Out in a field, a mere mite of a girl, dressed in light summer clothing, was herding pigs, and rubbing her poor red hands together to keep them warm. On a steep hillside, an enormous drove of sheep was grazing from the base to the summit. We reached the Alhambra Palace hotel in time for lunch.

Under the guidance of a delightful group of young men and women, we had our first view of the Alhambra under lowering skies, with a heavy rain splashing on the stone pavement of the Court of the Lions. And that night we were taken to the gypsy caves.

These gypsies are not of the nomad type. There for generations they have lived in the caves on the hillside on the narrow road leading to Monte Sacramento. The entertainment committee had scoured all the caves for the prettiest and most artistic of the dancers, who had been assembled in one cave for our amusement. I had heard that these caves were dirty, but I did not find them so. The front room was spotlessly clean, the walls perfectly white and hung with old copper pans burnished bright. Around the walls sat the gypsy women, pretty, graceful, picturesque, and at the entrance sat the gypsy men with the guitars. The dancers appeared singly or in couples, throwing themselves into their expressive dance with utter abandon, and without a suggestion of indelicacy. Beautiful and voluptuous, whirling faster and faster, eyes sparkling, smiles flashing, they were encouraged by the others around the wall with the rhythmic clapping of hands and with cries of approval. When wine was served, the gypsy girls drank little. When a press photographer appeared at the entrance, the effect was magical, for the gypsies are as children in their eagerness to be photographed. They moved in my direction on the assumption that I was certain to be in the picture, and in a moment I was surrounded, some grouped behind my chair standing, others gracefully seated on the floor in front, and Ziegfeld could not have arranged a more charming ensemble than did these gypsy girls naturally. The result, however, was to crowd all my party out of the picture, and it appeared in the press with but one man in the center surrounded by his harem.

I wondered why these exquisite dancers did not exploit their art in Paris and New York and I was told that they soon became homesick for the caves, for the drowsy atmosphere of Granada, for the old narrow road to Monte Sacramento, and hurry back. Some, however, have become famous. "Pepita's" story has been delightfully told by Victoria Sackville-West.

The next morning we visited the Generalife, and in the afternoon, in the Alhambra woods, Sybil unveiled the tablet which gave the principal road the name of Irving; and we visited the Pantheon of the Catholic monarchs, more impressive to me than the tomb of Napoleon. On the last night of the fiesta, a play written for the occasion around the life of the Granada that Irving knew was presented by a company of professional players. As we entered the box draped with the American flag held in place by a huge bronze eagle, the orchestra played "America," and the entire audience rose. Then the consular corps entered the box, and the German Consul, as *doyen*, extended a formal welcome, and a group of pretty young girls appeared and Marie Louise Hernández read a pleasant little speech in perfect English. And then the play went on.

Returning to Madrid, we stayed the night again in the *parador* at Bailén.

Chapter V

Reaction Begins: Personalities

THE President's dinner for the diplomatic corps in early January formally opened the season for official entertainment. We drove between scores of officers in the courtyard of the palace and ascended the broad, beautiful marble stairway, receiving salutes at every third step from the Presidential Guard in uniforms of blue, red, and white, with gold helmets and plumes, and greeted Alcalá Zamora and his attractive wife in one of the salons of the magnificent palace.

We had been warned that our blood would congeal in the frigid atmosphere of that huge mountain of masonry, but this year great log fires were blazing in all the rooms. We dined in the long banquet hall at an enormous table with large silver candelabra at close intervals, and with islands of flowers in the center. The menu was worthy of the traditions of the hall, but my cynical neighbor, a monarchist at heart, commented sourly on the use of the royal silver. After coffee, liqueurs, and cigars, in an adjoining salon, we filed into the throne room for the entertainment, and I sat just behind Alzalá Zamora, opposite the vacant throne, interesting then as a museum piece.

The entertainer was the incomparable Argentina. Entirely alone, without music, she danced that night with her usual brilliance—danced the "Serenata," the "Danza de la Ópera," the "Nida Brava," the "Tango-Flamenco," the "Navarre," and closed with "La Corrida," the passionate, tempestuous dance of the bull ring. The musical accompaniment was her castanets, and she never missed a note, and never was there a click that was not of the precise tone. With Argentina, castanets were both music and eloquence. The lightning changes of expression with every variation of the dance were fascinating. And she was ageless, though her girlish slenderness symbolized the spirit of jocund youth. Summoned by the President at the conclusion of the program, she appeared, smiling, blushing, and shy. It was a pleasant evening with no suggestion of the political tensity of the time, and when we left at two in the morning, there still stood the guardsmen on the steps, immobile as statues.

2

A few days later, Pita Romero, Minister of Foreign Affairs, gave his first dinner for the chiefs of missions in the ministry, so grim and austere without, so rich in unexpected possibilities within. We went up the broad, carpeted stairs to the balcony of the patio for cocktails in the ministers' room. The dinner was served at a great horseshoe table in the patio, with the balconies around hung with priceless old tapestries, and the indirect lighting gave the impression of daylight. The surprise of the menu was the serving of vodka with the caviar course. Lest this be misunderstood, it may be stated that Pita Romero was of the Center if not of the Right and certainly he was a devout Catholic. After dinner, coffee and liqueurs were served on the balcony, which was a mass of animated colors, until early morning, for the old dining room opening on the balcony was given over to the dancers.

Pita Romero was very young, of fine build, with a shapely head, black hair, large, expressive dark eyes, and graceful manner. There was much mystification over the miracle of his rapid rise, for he was not the type to appeal to the spoilsmen around Lerroux, and he was more an independent than a partisan, but he was a personal favorite of Alcalá Zamora. He thought rapidly, decided quickly, acted speedily, and always in good faith. All thought of his political character was lost in the charm of his personality. He impressed me as a devout Catholic and a staunch republican.

From the presidential dinner into June, there was a succession of diplomatic functions that soon became enervating. Among the diplomats there were some real personalities who had played historic parts in the transition from monarchy to republic.

My first contact with the corps came on the first night of our arrival when Princess Elizabeth Bibesco, wife of the Rumanian Minister and daughter of Asquith, the English statesman, telephoned an invitation to lunch the following day. I knew her as the author of clever, epigrammatic novels and I had heard that when her husband was stationed in Washington she had a reputation for snubbing bores. Petite, pretty, brilliant, scintillatingly clever in conversation, I found her the most fascinating woman of the corps. Reared in the political atmosphere of her father's home, under the influence of her remarkable mother, she had a penetrating insight into politics. One day she showed me a scrapbook filled with articles she had written anonymously on American politics for a London paper. She was a friend of Azaña's, who admired her, and she played the *enfant terrible* with him, criticizing him to his face; but she was also a friend of José Primo de Rivera's, and after his death she wrote a novel dedicated to his memory. Unhappily, a political turn in Rumania resulted in the recall of her husband soon after I reached Madrid. She frequently acted as hostess for the British Ambassador, Sir George Graham, who was a bachelor.

Sir George, who was to be my best friend among the ambassadors, had ascended the diplomatic ladder almost rung by rung in Paris. Though a favorite of Curzon's, he never was to be forgiven by him for refusing the embassy in Germany when it was the most important post to the British. Though unmarried, he had excellent taste in women's wear, and when in Paris he often shopped for Lady Curzon. Very tall, slightly stooped, a bit shy, I found him invariably charming, interesting, very human. Observing an attractive landscape on the wall, I inquired the name of the artist. He said, with a blush, that it was his work. He wrote short stories for his own amusement, and occasionally showed them to his intimates, and they were very clever, but he was horrified at the thought of publishing. Impressive to me was his political prescience and penetration, which I was to find singularly lacking in most career diplomats. His position as the ambassador of the country of the Spanish Queen could not have been an easy one on the fall of the monarchy, but in his every move he had been meticulously correct. Though a conservative by tradition, his observations and experience had liberalized his outlook. A more stimulating and profitable companion before the fire I have never known. He had an open mind, a sense of humor, and a disposition to "talk it out." After his retirement we continued in contact through correspondence, and on his death he left me some of his choice old silver.

The Nuncio, Monsignor Tedeschini, an Italian, now Cardinal and Archpriest of St. Peter's, lived in the oldest part of town in a crumbling palace that had been old when taken by the Vatican generations before. So narrow was the street that a large car had to move warily. Tedeschini was tall, elegantly slender and graceful, with fine features sharply chiseled as in a cameo, with eyes remarkably expressive and eloquent. His voice was vibrant with cordiality and his manner warmly friendly. His presence would be felt in any crowd. Very artful, with a genius for the right word and tone, he impressed me as a diplomat in the grand manner of the old school. He had shown consummate diplomacy in the transition from monarchy to republic. A monarchist, no doubt, he was also a realist, and his primary object was the interest of the church. When he figured among the three leading cardinals in the election of the present Pope, the *Manchester Guardian* reported hostility to him in some quarters because of his alleged advice not to commit the church irrevocably to Franco. I always remember him in his red robes at dinners, and, as I have often seen him walking alone in the more remote quarters of the Casa de Campo, reading as he walked, and followed by his car to pick him up for the return journey to the old palace.

Count Welczeck, the German Ambassador, had been an intimate friend and hunting companion of the King's. He had entered the diplomatic service reluctantly on the insistence of his father. "I always wanted to be a farmer," he told me. Belonging to an old landowning Junker family, he was a thorough aristocrat, a man of the world, devoted to pleasure and tireless in the dance. He seemed a casual observer, little concerned with political or diplomatic problems, but this affectation of frivolity was a mask. He was a German diplomat of the days of the Emperor, and a friend of Hindenburg's, and he found the Nazis distasteful and Hitler dan-

gerous. One day in the garden of my house, he talked frankly, and I
knew his real feeling. Transferred after eight years to Paris, he
resigned before World War II began. Years later I knew him in
Chile. His great estates were to be confiscated by the communists
and his income reduced to nothing.

Jean Herbette, the French Ambassador, presumably a socialist,
and a clever journalist, had been anathema to the Spanish aristocracy because of his socialism and his diplomatic mission in Moscow,
but he was the prime favorite of the Leftist parties. Cold, distant,
personally unprepossessing, he was not popular generally. After the
fall of Irún in the early days of the Fascist war, he abandoned his
old friends with cynical indifference and assiduously cultivated the
Fascist commander in Irún. "Was he a socialist?" I asked a French
diplomat years later. "No, he was a Herbettist."

I was fond of Robert Everts, the Belgian Ambassador, and Jean
Perlowski, the Polish Minister, who was a man of great charm and
culture, interested in books and pictures. Associated with Paderewski in the years when the great pianist abandoned his art for his
country, Perlowski was rich in reminiscences of his brilliant coun-
tryman. Once when seated with him at a conference table the
artist observed his assistant running his fingers over the table and
asked if he played the piano. "I did a little when I was young,"
Perlowski replied. An expression of ineffable sadness appeared on
Paderewski's face. "So did I," he said, "so did I."

3

The municipal elections of January, 1934, in Catalonia resulted
in a sweeping victory for the Leftists. Azaña and Prieto had cam-
paigned there on the issue of saving the Republic. The reversal
of the trend of the preceding November brought some uneasiness
to those in power. And Lerroux was still worried over the disaffec-
tion of Martínez Barrio because of the close affiliation of his party
with the enemies of democracy and the Republic. The air was full
of rumors. To dramatize the denial of these rumors, the radicals
arranged a dinner at the Ritz in honor of their leader, where he
and Barrio exchanged compliments, and Lerroux announced that
the party never would accept the chains of the Rightists and that
he would die for the Republic. It was assumed that this declaration

was the price exacted by Barrio for remaining within the fold. But this family reconciliation scene did not deter the ruling coalition from increasing its efforts to separate them, and thus further to isolate Lerroux.

In early February, Barrio, in an interview, disapproved a part of the program of the ruling coalition, and the next day the Cortes was packed in expectation of a dramatic scene. Lerroux seemed very old and tired that day as he entered the chamber.

Gil Robles launched his attack on Lerroux' chief lieutenant in a domineering mood and manner, demanding an explanation of the interview. He demanded to know if Barrio, as minister, would enforce law and order. If so, Gil Robles and his party would continue to support the government. Barrio lifted his large body from the Blue Bench. A powerfully built man, physically impressive, he added to the impression of force by his forthright manner of speaking. That day he was in no contrite spirit, and he neither hedged nor sought to soften the resentment of his supercilious foes. Certainly, he said, he did not agree with all of the program of the government, and in his ministerial duties he would not tolerate any interference from his colleagues within, nor from his enemies without. Maintain order? He would, against "all the enemies of the Republic, whether they be of the Right or the Left, socialists, monarchists, or Fascists."

It was not at all what Gil Robles wanted, and he appealed to Lerroux. The weary old man, hard pressed, replied that the government stood for law and order, and that he would favor an even stronger law for their maintenance.

Manifestly, two acts were planned for that day's drama. One was to drive the democratic Barrio from the government, and the other was to stigmatize the socialists as public enemies to be suppressed. Prieto, with the rage of an angry bull, charged at the conspirators, and, despite the jeering, he soon struck his stride and was hurling defiance at his enemies. Had the coalition in power united for the persecution of the socialists? Did they want a fight? Then let it come, he shouted. Deprive the socialists of one of their parliamentary or constitutional rights and they would make their answer in the streets.

Two historic events were foreshadowed that day—the driving of the democratic Barrio from the government, and the rising of October.

4

The following Sunday in a Madrid theater I attended my first
political mass meeting in Spain to hear Azaña. When I arrived,
Azaña had been speaking for an hour. The doors had been closed
against congestion, but an officer admitted me upon a scene tremendously impressive. The theater was packed to the second
gallery, and the aisles on the ground floor were crowded with
standing men. Azaña was talking conversationally, but with artful
inflections that brought laughter, and at times storms of applause.
He was warning that under the domination of Gil Robles the
Lerroux government was moving to the extreme Right. Though
he did not agree with the whole of the socialist program, the preservation of the Republic called for the unification of all the republican
and democratic parties of the Left. A statesman's speech, moder-
ately phrased, free from demagogy, continuing more than two
hours, without one man leaving the room, with absolute silence
despite the hundreds standing in the aisles. Never in my country
have I seen a political meeting conducted with more decorum
or pitched on a higher plane.

*Azaña had foreshadowed another historic event, though many months
ahead—the creation of the Popular Front.*

5

The next day the government was uneasy. Rumors were afloat
of a rising, not of communists, who had not yet been discovered as
a menace, but of syndicalists. Lerroux, who habitually retired at
nine, was passing between the Ministry of War and the Interior at
midnight. The army was under suspicion, and government agents
had been sent to the barracks to take over the telephones. The
water supply was put under guard.

Meanwhile, Lerroux' party was dividing. The real democrats
and republicans were moving toward Barrio; the others, political
soldiers of fortune, were joining Gil Robles in assailing Barrio in
the party caucus. Lerroux, in a highly emotional state, rose to
announce his complete approval of Barrio's action, to declare his
party more to the Left than to the Right, and to reiterate his

devotion to the Republic. In referring to the charge that he was disloyal to it, or too weak to defend it, his voice broke and he was unable to go on. A moment of wonderment, and then the entire meeting rose to give the tearful old man a prolonged ovation. Again the crisis passed.

But the Rightist extremists were riding hard, putting Lerroux more and more under their dictation; and then, on a cold, damp day in April, Barrio, who had had enough, resigned. Lerroux informed Alcalá Zamora, who, exercising his presidential preroga-tive, suggested the resignation of the entire Ministry. It was said that Lerroux had been asked to include in his new government a greater representation of the reactionary agrarians and some of the party of Gil Robles. But the new government differed scarcely at all from the old. The one surprise was the recall of Salvador de Madariaga from his Embassy in Paris to become Minister of Education. It seemed a demotion, but some assumed that he would speedily be transferred to the Foreign Office.

6

Salvador de Madariaga had called upon me soon after I reached Madrid. I was familiar with some of his brilliant books and with his well-earned international reputation as an intellectual. He was very partisan to England, where he had lectured at Oxford, and very prejudiced against the United States, because of its failure to enter the League of Nations.

He is a rather small, slender man, with the keenly intelligent face of a professor. That day I formed the impression of a charming, scintillating, witty, humorous human being, more idealist than realist, a dreamer, but a personality. At Geneva, where he repre-sented Spain in the League of Nations, he had set an example in fidelity to the Covenant that must have been embarrassing to some of his colleagues. He was universally liked and admired. But he impressed me as an outsider in domestic politics. Azaña had been his friend and admirer, but Lerroux continued him in office. He had no party affiliations that went deep. He had a capacity for righteous wrath that shocked the diplomatic world, and when he denounced ammunition makers as manufacturers of wars, the reactionaries of the kept press of Paris, from motives not disinterested, demanded his recall. I was to find him a brilliant, invigorating human being, entertaining, and delightful. But the Rightists were speedily to put an end to the ministerial career.

7

Madrid, at this time, was rich in personalities remote from politics, and at a luncheon for Catalina Barcena, the Spanish actress, and Martínez Sierra, dramatist, author of *The Cradle Song*, I first met Benavente, world-famous dramatist, winner of the Nobel Prize, who, despite his advancing years, regularly produced one or two sprightly comedies a season. A rather tiny man with a great bald dome, a close-cropped gray mustache, a beard not extending below the chin, and with mocking eyes—such was Benavente. Something in his appearance suggested D'Annunzio—perhaps a similarity in frame and dome, possibly the fastidiousness of their attire, for no young blade could have been more considerate of it than Benavente. I noticed especially his tiny, well-shaped hands and the exotic ring that fairly screamed from one of his fingers. I saw him often thereafter, frequently in summer in front of his favorite outdoor café in San Sebastián. He was a courtly man and invariably he rose and bowed.

And that spring I saw much of Pérez de Ayala, the novelist, then Ambassador in London, at home on leave. He was a slender man, impeccably attired, and looking younger than his years. He had made his mastery of the art of the novelist tell heavily against the old regime. He was one of the younger intellectuals who, in the fading days of the monarchy, had made republicanism fashionable in artistic circles. He was keen on bullfights and was a close friend of Belmonte, the famous matador. One afternoon I went with him and Sir George Graham to a fight. He was an ideal companion for the occasion since he knew all the finer points of the art of the matador, and he commented intelligently on the quality of the bulls, bubbling with boyish enthusiasm. I expressed regret that Belmonte, then long in retirement, had decided to fight again, since he had become a legend, and now that he was older he might easily dim the legend or be killed. "But Belmonte is as good as ever," he snapped. "But not so young," I suggested. "Ah, but Belmonte's legs never have been good and never has he depended on them. He brings the bull to him and does his work with his arms, and they are not old. He will not be hurt."

8

The government of Lerroux was moving rapidly, if unconsciously, toward the liquidation of the Republic. A bill for the resumption of the payment of salaries to parish priests was being hurried through. True, these priests had been miserably underpaid under the old regime, but the constitution was a barrier to the resumption of payment since this would imply the restoration of the combination of church and state. While I know some staunch republicans thought it a mistake to have deprived the parish priests of their meager pay, their restoration to the government pay roll would be a precedent for the violation of all other provisions of the constitution.

Smiling cynically and mischievously through his mustache, Lerroux declared, with a poker face, that the payment was not to be made to priests, but to "public servants out of work" and without means of support. The socialists made a bitter protest in the Cortes, but the large Rightist majority moved toward its goal clumsily, but inevitably, like a tank.

It was during this debate that Martínez Barrio made political history by entering the chamber and seating himself among the deputies of the Left. The schism in the party of Lerroux could no longer be camouflaged. The preceding Sunday, in Seville, Barrio had called for a unification of all the real republican parties for the defense of the Republic. The Lerroux party, he said, was logically a party of the Left, and under no obligations to take orders from the Rightists, as it was doing.

And the next day, Lerroux took more orders.

A bill granting amnesty to political prisoners was under discussion, but republicans involved in labor disputes were excluded from the benefits, while those who had drawn their swords against the constituted authority were included.

In August, 1932, General Sanjurjo had led a revolt which speedily petered out, and he was captured, condemned to death, and saved through Azaña's commutation of the sentence. Under the proposed amnesty, Sanjurjo would return to hobnob with his fellow conspirators; Juan March, who had bribed his way from prison, would return to resume his old activities; and Calvo Sotelo, Finance Minister under the Dictator, would begin to pack for home.

Prieto thundered in the Cortes against a measure so deliberately designed to serve the deadly enemies of the regime, but his was as a voice crying in the wilderness. Sanjurjo emerged from prison and hastened to Lisbon to weave the web of new conspiracies. Juan March sneaked back to his intrigues, and Calvo Sotelo would soon stalk into the Cortes with supreme impudence in his manner.

The amnesty bill was an open scandal and scarcely less than treason. It had been defended by a stupid minister as in accord with the mandate of the people, but when Prieto proposed to submit the bill to a referendum of the people, Gil Robles and Lerroux rejected the proposal. The bill was hurried to its passage.

9

Meanwhile, reactionary leaders were making mysterious pilgrimages to Germany and Italy, presumably seeking military assistance from Hitler and Mussolini in their plan for the extermination of democracy in Spain. Though Gil Robles attended the Nazi Congress in Germany, there is no indication that he negotiated with the Nazi chiefs.

I did not believe, and do not now believe, that Gil Robles was Fascistic, though the trend of his party tended toward totalitarianism, and his juveniles, who were Fascistic, created a bad impression by their demands for "all power to the chief." Certain it is that after the insurrection of October, 1934, he sternly rejected the proposals of the army for the establishment of a dictatorship. During the Spanish War his most virulent foes were the Fascists and militarists, and he was not permitted by the Franco regime to return to Spain from Portugal, where he had exiled himself. I am persuaded that he favored the parliamentary system, as well he might, since his was a major party and might easily have returned to power.

In March, Goicoechea, leader of the meager monarchist party in the Cortes, accompanied by Rafael Olazabal, sat down in Rome with Mussolini and Marshal Balbo, and a preliminary agreement was made for the active military participation of Fascist Italy in a "civil war" that was to be arranged in Spain. This was to become the technique of the Axis. About this time José Primo de Rivera appeared in Berlin as a guest of the Nazi government and was accorded every honor.

The Spanish Ambassador in Berlin, Luis de Zulueta, holding over from the Azaña regime, and gravely concerned over these visits, warned the Lerroux government, but no reply reached him from Madrid. He therefore tendered his resignation. He was succeeded by Sr. Agramonte, who had been Minister in Prague, and who was notoriously contemptuous of the democratic regime in his own country. Soon he was cheek by jowl with the delectable Ribbentrop.

The Lerroux government had been in power but two months, and the work of liquidating the regime and exterminating democracy was going on outside as well as within the country.

10

But the conspiracy was not ripe for rebellion, and the conspirators wore the mask of loyalty. In the midst of these secret negotiations the government staged a brilliant demonstration for the anniversary of the Republic. Madariaga, Minister of Education, had planned a striking series of spectacles. In the Plaza de Toros, under a flaming sun, twenty thousand people crowded to see *El Alcalde de Zalamea*, by Calderón, performed by a company headed by Margarita Xirgu. The scene was colorful, the sky a spotless blue, the air warm and fragrant, and the gay colors of the women's dresses gave a festive air. As the band blared forth the "Hymn of Riego" thousands stood as the President entered his box, and Lerroux, looking the worse for wear, bowed soberly.

The next day thousands crowded the court of the royal palace, where men and women sang the songs and danced the dances of the provinces of their origin in regional costumes, and vendors sold pictures of the republican martyrs of Jaca. That evening, driving in the Casa de Campo, we passed a long procession of young men marching to fife and drum.

11

There could be no misunderstanding of the enthusiasm of the multitude celebrating the third anniversary, but behind the scenes politicians hostile to the democratic regime were pressing on with their work of destruction. Lerroux, however, was having trouble at the palace. Alcalá Zamora understood perfectly the significance of the law of amnesty. If he signed the bill, it would be with the publication of a devastating protest. While the storm raged without, he sat with his head very close to the paper on which he was writing.

Soon Lerroux was summoned to the palace. Alcalá Zamora, looking very grave, produced his protest with the comment that it amounted to his resignation. Lerroux simulated mystification. Under the law, the President could not publish his protest unless countersigned by members of the Ministry. Lerroux refused to sign any paper that amounted to a condemnation of his own official action. He tendered his resignation—and Alcalá Zamora published his protest. Gil Robles muttered something about impeachment and making Lerroux President—but the old man, wise with years, was not impressed.

Already a reaction was setting in against the Rightists in power. They wanted nothing less and feared nothing more than a dissolution of the Cortes and elections, five months after their electoral triumph. The real friends of the regime were now convinced that the Republic was in peril and the working class was already girding for the struggle. But they would give fair warning first.

Gabino, my butler, wakened me one morning with a lugubrious face and the announcement that there would be no bread for breakfast, since a twenty-four-hour strike had been declared and the city was closed tight. So, following the idea of Marie Antoinette, we had griddle cakes instead. I looked out the windows on deserted streets. Not a taxi was in sight. The blinds of the stores were drawn, and there was an ominous silence. The reason? Lerroux had refused permission for the socialists to hold a meeting, while granting permission for Gil Robles, and the answer was—silence in the streets.

12

But during these really critical days all was quiet. No one was molested on the streets and the country highways were serene, as I found in a drive to the palace of El Pardo and to the famous old town of Guadalajara. The palace of El Pardo was my favorite.

Built in 1547, in the days of Charles V, it had been actually lived in by every succeeding monarch. The village of El Pardo is drab enough, but just beyond is the hunting park of the kings, where royalty has shot game for centuries. It is a rolling country, with stunted green oak trees against a yellow background. From the elevations, the view of the distant capital is superb.

But it was the palace itself that appealed to my imagination. The court, with its great, worn flagstones, the dormer windows of the old edifice, the wide, austere granite stairs, all spoke of age, but the smaller rooms gave to the palace the charm of simplicity and the feeling that an intimate family life had been lived there. Except for the furnishing, it had been little changed by the centuries. History sprawled familiarly in its cosy corners. The little theater, built by Isabella, whose rough boards had been trod by some of the greatest histrionic artists of the age, illuminated the court of that gay lady. From this old palace, María Cristina and Victoria had ridden into Madrid for their marriages; here Zita, unhappy Empress of Austria, found refuge with her court of forty attendants; here Otto, her son and heir, came for his convalescence; and within these walls the unfortunate Prince of the Asturias spent lonesome days.

13

Back in Madrid, Lerroux no longer was Prime Minister—except by proxy. When Ricardo Samper was substituted, it was merely an exchange of man for master. He was a provincial politician, of meager ability and utterly without distinction or achievements. A less attractive person it would have been difficult to find. He was a short, ugly man, whose bulging eyes and large nose gave him the appearance of a bullfrog. He carried himself with grotesque solemnity. Of wit, charm, or eloquence, he had none. It was assumed that he would be a stopgap for a month when Lerroux would resume his old post. But in times so critical, it seemed incredible that one so incompetent should be put at the head of the government, unless the Rightist coalition sought to make it ridiculous for a purpose. It seemed like poking fun at the Republic.

The effect of the amnesty was soon apparent when the bitter

enemies of a democratic Republic, who had financed insurrections and drawn their swords against it, came trailing back to plunge anew into the old conspiracies. Again the mean, meager figure of Juan March was seen lounging in the lobby of the Palace Hotel, and Calvo Sotelo resumed his place in the Cortes with the condescension of a conqueror and amused himself with sneers at democracy and open jibes at the regime.

Calvo Sotelo was still in his thirties when he became Finance Minister under the Dictator, and the legend had been created that he had shown genius in his post. The state of the finances on the advent of the Republic did not explain the legend, but it had taken root. He was a handsome, slender man with sleek black hair, with strong aristocratic features, and he bore himself with grace and some distinction. His hatred of the Republic, his contempt for democracy, his impatience with social reforms, his obsequious devotion to the highly placed, made him particularly obnoxious to the democrats. He was, in fact, a Fascist. He was an able and audacious man, though capable of ruthless methods in putting down "newfangled ideas." He unquestionably had great gifts for action, and his personal courage was undoubted. Despite his intense activity, he was studious. He was the pride and agent of the plutocracy that set up Hitler in Germany and Mussolini in Italy.

He lost no time in asserting himself on his return. In a debate on the budget, he found his opening, and the audacity of his action, the arrogance of his manner, stamped him at once as, by odds, the most dangerous, and the ablest, of the enemies of a democratic regime.

But looking down upon the scene from the gallery of the Cortes, it was clear to me that there was something wrong with the picture. He, the ablest of the Rightists, in a chamber packed with Rightists, was being snubbed. His reception was frigid. His mannerisms were not endearing and his supercilious condescension toward his colleagues was not appealing, but there was something deeper in the mystery.

This mystery was all the more intriguing when Prieto rose to reply, and the Cortes on both sides gave the first socialist Finance Minister an amazingly sympathetic hearing. Forced to reply without preparation, he exposed the financial condition left by Calvo

Sotelo as he had found it, and the Rightists that day joined in the ovation he received. When the session ended, the ovation was repeated in the street, where Calvo Sotelo was greeted with shouts of "back to Paris." Even the Rightist press the next day conceded the popularity of Prieto's reply.

The incident was the topic of general speculation. Unquestionably he had returned with the determination to seize the leadership of the movement against the democratic regime, and this conflicted with the plans of Gil Robles and his party. Calvo Sotelo could not be "put in his place" too soon.

14

Then, for a moment, all was serene again on the surface, and Alcalá Zamora was smiling and happy at the dinner I gave him at the embassy. He was well protected, as the King had been on similar occasions, with the Paseo de Cisne swarming with mounted soldiers, and soldiers on foot with rifles. Armed men were also stationed in the garden facing the Castellana. That afternoon, the police called to inquire on which side of the house the dining room was situated. An American guest, turning into the Paseo de Cisne, was so startled by the military array that he almost turned back. I was to find that the more elaborate the precautions of the police, the better pleased were the hosts on such occasions. A little before, at a luncheon of the British Ambassador for the ministers, I found the street of the embassy so congested with armed men that I asked Sir George Graham if there was any special reason. "Well," said Sir George, "I have practically the entire government here, and one bomb would wipe it out." Then, with a smile, "Besides, I am here." He had asked for the protection.

That night, at my house, Alcalá Zamora was in fine fettle, smiling, laughing, joking, talking, seemingly fearless of the political future. He did ascribe his troubles to me that night to the single-chamber system and lamented the absence of a senate. But that night he showed no concern over the political crisis. I asked one of my guests, a cynical old diplomat, many years in the service, what was going to happen. "Nothing—nothing at all," he said. "Nothing ever happens in Spain."

Chapter VI

Portraits and Pageantry

IN THE MIDST of the crisis, a brilliant pro-American fiesta in Toledo produced a miracle in Spain—a momentary social mingling of opposing parties. To me, Toledo is the most fascinating city in Spain. The granite palace of the Alcázar first commands the attention of the approaching visitor. Its façade was interesting, its stone-paved court with its balconies was picturesque, but never was I to be moved emotionally by this great granite pile, and its destruction in the Fascist war failed to shock me. Entering the town through the old Moorish gate, and ascending the hill road, one drives into the historic plaza. A fierce sun beats upon it in the morning, but every evening from early spring until late autumn, a goodly portion of the population swarms about the tables before the cafés and bars of the plaza for gossip and refreshments. In the twilight, the imagination easily stirs to the scene. There is the Bloody Gate, the great stone entrance to the plaza, through which the victims of the Inquisition made their death march to their funeral pyres in the center under the cold eyes of civil and ecclesiastical dignitaries in the balcony above. Times without number have I passed under the arch of the Bloody Gate to descend the age-worn steps to the tiny street where stood the colorful old inn, reeking with the atmosphere of the far-off times when Don Quixote spurred Rosinante on her travels; for this old inn that offered refreshment to men and beasts in the time of Philip II was serving its original purpose still. The little patio, with its decrepit, sagging balconies on which the guests' rooms opened, was redolent of the sixteenth century. Thence Cervantes once looked down on animated scenes—the gay cavalier, the sweating peasant, the itinerant courtesan, the chickens scratching for crumbs—and caught, as now, the mingled odors of the kitchen and the stable. The chickens still were scratching and clucking in the patio, and on market days, the stalls of the stable were filled with donkeys, and peasants were there eating their homemade lunch. Alas, the savage bombing of Toledo would soon wreck this precious tavern of Cervantes—a far greater loss to me than the destruction of the Alcázar.

Always I would go through the narrow, crooked streets to the old parish church of Santo Tomé, to sit in silence before the El Greco masterpiece, the *Burial of Count Orgaz.* Here this rich and powerful nobleman had been buried long before El Greco gave him immortality. The church is small and drab, and, but for the incomparable canvas, which draws lovers of the beautiful from every quarter, it would not be worth a visit.

The house called El Greco's may or may not have been his abode, but it unquestionably was the house of Samuel Levy, an enormously rich Jew on whose fabulous store of gold kings drew for their necessities, until Pedro the Cruel found it better business to steal the vast hordes of gold in the underground passages than to pay principal and interest. Near by this house of Levy is the old Jewish synagogue that he presented to his coreligionists. The Moors tolerated it, but the less liberal Christians expelled the Jews to use it for a church, and the Hebrew decorations and inscriptions were plastered over, and the beauty hidden, but the defacing plaster has been removed. This is the monument to Levy, the Jew who put his faith in kings.

But the glory of Toledo is the cathedral, though this magnificent, imposing edifice is so hemmed in by lanelike streets that one must drive into the country beyond the Tagus to see it silhouetted in its true grandeur against the sky. Hence, for centuries, cardinals have directed both the spiritual and temporal life of the realm; here a score or more of them have found their tombs and their hats hang from the ceiling. In the chapter room are the numerous portraits of these dignitaries of the centuries, and, in another room, are El

Greco's vividly illuminative portraits of the Disciples. In the treasure room one looks through glass on untold wealth in gold, silver, precious stones, ancient bishops' robes encrusted with jewels, and on a large cross made with the first gold brought by Columbus from the New World. Three locks protect these treasures from intrusion, and the three keys necessary for the opening of the heavy door are held by three priests.

No one can stand within this beautiful cathedral with its stained glass windows, its superbly carved procession of the Cross in marble, without an emotion of reverence. "More impressive to me than St. Peter's," said Dr. Harry Garfield of Williams College when I showed him through.

But Toledo is never so charming as at night when one meanders through the narrow, winding streets by moonlight, under the mysterious balconies whence come the tinkle of guitars, the peal of laughter, the plaintive strains of *flamenco* singing. If the houses seem austere without, the initiated know of the beauty, taste, and charm within, and behind the stark stone walls are hidden patios with murmuring fountains and with orange and palm trees.

2

A commission from Toledo, Ohio, on a pilgrimage to Toledo, Spain, was given a colorful reception. The locomotive of the train bearing them, flying the stars and stripes, drew into the station while a military band played our national anthem, and a fleet of airplanes flew low. Across the old Roman bridge the keys of the city were presented as pretty girls in gay costumes pelted the visitors with red roses from a balcony. In the plaza, packed with cheering people, we reviewed the soldiers swinging by; and then, through the narrow street, with tapestries hanging from every window, with ticker tape of every color fluttering down from curb to curb, with laughing girls raining rose petals from the balconies, we made our way to the municipal building, where, from the balcony, we faced a multitude packed into the plaza of the cathedral.

The next day we viewed the procession of Corpus Christi from the balcony of an apartment, noting that many knelt, though some did not, as the Host went by. At the palace of the cardinal we presented an album to Cardinal Gomá in the throne room with its

velvet throne and canopy of red, with its portraits of bishops in attendance on the portrait of Isabella II in her youth and beauty.
Cardinal Gomá was of medium height and rather heavy, a Catalan
with a strong face and keen, intelligent gray-blue eyes that denoted
a militant leader. Two years later, he would play his part in the
dreadful tragedy of the rebellion.

3

One afternoon, we were entertained at the country home of
Dr. Marañón. Twenty years before, he had bought an abandoned
convent on a hill, whence, across a deep valley, loomed, like an
El Greco picture, the ancient city. Dr. Gregorio Marañón was both
brilliant and versatile, a famous physician, author of some clever
books, and a speaker of some grace and substance. In the days of
the monarchy he was an avowed academic republican, but because
of his charm and professional brilliance he remained the physician
of the Court and the aristocracy. When Primo de Rivera put him
in prison his cell was banked with flowers from lofty stations, and
grandees visited him in the jail. On the establishment of the Republic he abandoned politics, but when a political crisis came and
Alcalá Zamora, in accordance with custom, summoned the leaders
of political parties, Marañón invariably was called. In appearance,
he was a real Apollo, of medium height, slender and graceful, with
handsome features, coal-black hair and dark eyes. I was to know
him personally and professionally and was to find him interesting
and charming.

We were all on the lawn when a disreputable old machine drove
into the grounds, and a hand extended from the window, dangling
birds.

The man with the birds evidently was a friend of Marañón's
returning from a successful hunt. Marañón took me by the arm
and, leading me toward the car, astonished me by saying: "I want
you to meet Count Romanones."

4

Romanones was one of the few Spaniards with whose career I
was reasonably familiar before going to Spain. Frequently he had
been Prime Minister and Minister of Foreign Affairs under the

King. As one of the Ministry, he had inducted Alfonso, the boy, into kingship, and he was the one to whom the King turned, too late, to save the toppling throne. With the people growling ominously before the palace, Alcalá Zamora had hurried to the home of Marañón, and the two had summoned Romanones to warn him that unless the King left that night they could not assume responsibility for the consequences. Facing grim realities, Romanones had advised the King's departure, and when, the next morning, the Queen and children took the train for exile in the deserted station at Escorial, Romanones sat on a truck and wept. He was to incur the enmity of the nobility for advising the departure. When taken to task in the street a few days later, the old man replied that had the King remained, he would probably have lost his life and that "the rest of us would have had our throats slit." As it turned out, not a drop of blood was shed. Two months after the King's departure, Marañón wrote that the monarchists who did so little to save the monarchy, and afterward insulted Romanones, would blush with shame could they have heard with what desperate persistency he strove to save the regime. The critics of Romanones ignored the fact that after his advice was given, General Sanjurjo was summoned to the palace and asked by the King if the soldiers could be counted on to protect him. When Sanjurjo hung his head in silence, Alfonso asked if they could be depended upon to protect the Queen and children. The answer was they could.

But Romanones frequently found himself at cross-purposes with a large segment of his class. During the First World War, when the nobility and aristocracy mostly sympathized with Germany, Romanones was a stout champion of the Allies. He believed in constitutional monarchy; the others in autocracy. He wanted a constitutional monarchy; they clung to the ideas of the eighteenth century.

When, in the midst of the revolutionary ferment, elections were called, Romanones, in his seventies, had the temerity to announce his candidacy as a monarchist, and he was elected. When, in his absence, the King was tried in the Cortes for treason, Romanones had the courage to stand alone in his defense. Press correspondents have told me an amusing story of this act of daring. On the afternoon of the day he was to speak for the King at night, they found the old man at his house in the Castellana, swearing violently as he hobbled back and forth in the room. "Excuse me a moment, gentlemen," he said, as he resumed his walk and his sulphurous observations. "I am going to the Cortes tonight to defend my King against a rabble," he said. "Great as is my dislike for the enemies of the King, they are admirable compared to his fair-weather friends. Everyone knows that, singlehanded, I am to defend the King tonight, but not one soul has had the courage to so much as leave a card."

Later, when less courage was required and the monarchists formed a party, Romanones, though the only one among them with political sagacity and capacity, remained aloof, and sat alone in the Cortes as an independent monarchist. He favored a limited constitutional monarchy similar to that of England. The republicans, even the socialists in the Cortes, respected and admired the grim old man, and this accentuated the distrust of his own people. "A clever old fox," they murmured. Meanwhile, he attended the sessions of the Cortes, wrote his valuable memoirs, his biographies of María Cristina and Espartero, superintended his large estates, and hunted in the mountains.

5

"I want you to meet Romanones," said Marañón.

The old man was getting out of his disreputable car as we approached. He had been hunting in the mountains, and there was a three-days' growth of beard on his roughly hewn face. A gray flannel shirt, open at the neck, was screaming for the laundry, and his rough boots, caked with mud, were overrun at the heels. Crippled in one leg from childhood, he always carried a cane. As press photographers approached, he hobbled toward them, shaking his cane with simulated fury. Even the bristly beard could not conceal the strength of his features—a strong, masterful, clever face, with a protruding chin, a cynical, mocking mouth, and eyes to match.

He hobbled over the lawn to join the party from Toledo, most of whom were his political enemies, republicans, socialists, labor unionists, but he sat down among them with the nonchalance of a host among old friends. His foes, who nevertheless respected him, grouped themselves around him. The old fox looked mockingly at the waistline of the governor of Toledo, and made an ironic comment. The governor appeared resentful, and the old man grinned impishly. "You should not be irritated by compliments," he said. Then he asked me to accompany the Americans to his country place near Toledo the next afternoon; and, turning to the working-class mayor of Toledo, invited him and all his friends. Political foes did not mingle socially in Spain—but they were there. The American visitors had performed a miracle.

The Romanones country place of Buena Vista was reminiscent of feudal days. A servant stood at the crossroads to direct us, and we drove through a stone gate and to the impressive, low-lying house, where, on the lawn, the count and countess, with daughters and granddaughters greeted us with the familiarity of old friends. Romanones led me to a garden behind the house and asked why, at a moment of discord in Cuba, the United States should abrogate the Platt Amendment. I told him the effect of the amendment on our relations with South America had not been happy, and that, in case of necessity, we would join with South American countries in preventing anarchy. The old man's features lighted with an ironic smile. "They have none too much order themselves," he said.

The house was mostly of the fourteenth century and was once the home of the great cardinal referred to by Cervantes in the preface to the second edition of *Don Quixote*. Over one of the doors the cardinal had placed a Latin inscription proclaiming this the most beautiful spot in the world. We sat down, and the old statesman asked questions about Franklin D. Roosevelt. He thought that Woodrow Wilson would grow greater with time. One of his questions impressed me as curious—whether a Negro can be named for the Cabinet in the United States. I explained that there is no legal prohibition, but that prejudice might prevent it. Again the enigmatic smile. "I am the only liberal left in Spain," he said, apropos of nothing. A fascinating conversationalist and a charming host.

A long table on the lawn was loaded with food, and I noticed that Romanones knew Americans—he was serving whisky and soda instead of wine. Here again I marveled at his familiar mingling with his political and class enemies. The photographer caught him seated on a coping in conversation with the working-class mayor of Toledo. A clever novelist, an Azaña republican, chatted with him wickedly. "I am putting you in a novel," he said. "Why me?" asked Romanones. "Because you are too clever," replied the novelist. "You manage to stay on top, but you are undermining the Republic." The old man smiled mockingly, without comment.

6

Before leaving, I gave a reception at the embassy for the delegation from Ohio, and that afternoon it was whispered about that a military *coup d'état* was prepared for the kidnaping of Alcalá Zamora, and the imposition of a military dictatorship. A socialist told me that his people were prepared for action, day and night. I overheard Roca, the Foreign Minister, telling Romanones about it. The old man maintained a poker face.

Politically, all was outwardly serene. Samper seemed likely to drowse through the summer and until the Cortes met in October. But there were disturbing portents. A committee of the Cortes had recommended the expulsion of a socialist member in whose house arms had been found. Prieto attacked the legality of the proceedings on the ground that the report had not first been submitted to the accused; and amazingly enough, Gil Robles rose to declare Prieto right. The socialist orator bowed his thanks, and the Chamber roared with mirth. A few days later, with the rules observed, the committee repeated its recommendation but added a recommendation for the expulsion of José Primo de Rivera, who had assumed responsibility for arms found in the house of one of his Fascist followers. When the case of the socialist was called, Prieto brilliantly evoked parliamentary immunity, which was to have been expected, but when the case of the Fascist leader was called, Prieto, with as much vigor and eloquence, protested against the proceedings. The Chamber gasped as Primo de Rivera rushed to grasp Prieto's hand and praise him for his "sporting action." Such courtly courtesies of toleration were sensationally rare.

The next day, Madariaga called, in a happy, mocking mood, in no sense cast down by his drop from the Ministry, for he retained his post as spokesman of Spain in Geneva, which meant more to him than any place in the government, but he was pessimistic over the domestic situation. He thought Azaña an able statesman but feared that "the magnitude of his fall, measured by the meager reasons for it" had crushed his spirit.

Within a few days the "crushed spirit" of Azaña was manifest in the reorganization of the revolutionary committee that had sponsored the Pact of San Sebastián of 1930. The original signers were on again with two exceptions. Alcalá Zamora was excluded by his office, and Lerroux, if unwittingly, had gone over bag and baggage to the Rightist extremists who were conspiring against the regime, and was not asked. At this time, Azaña was thought to have regained control of the newspapers *El Sol* and *La Voz*. Gil Robles' organ, *El Debate*, was slashing at the Catalan policy of his colleagues. Lerroux was said to be planning an organ of his own. The *A.B.C.*, the monarchist organ, no longer fearful of a governmental frown, was vehemently demanding the recall of the King.

7

But, with so much gossip, politics was not taken seriously by the public. Lerroux had retired to his little villa in the pleasant mountain village of San Rafael, and Samper and Rightist leaders were beating a pathway to his door, but nothing seemed stirring. Madrid was deserted by the diplomatic corps when funeral services for Hindenburg were held in the Lutheran church on the grounds of the German Embassy. That afternoon I was in the garden turning the pages of a Conrad novel while awaiting a call from Count Welczeck, the German Ambassador, when Perlowski, the Polish Minister, appeared. I pointed to the novel, expecting an appreciative smile. "I hate Conrad," he said passionately. "I hate him. I do not like his novels and I do not like the man."

Perlowski and Conrad had been boyhood friends when the uncle of the diplomat was the guardian of the future novelist. Perlowski could not forgive Conrad for writing in English, and for contributing nothing to his country's struggle for independence. "He did not lift a finger or write a line for Poland," he said. "The last time I saw him was at my uncle's funeral and he talked in English. I asked him if he had forgotten his native tongue. He seemed embarrassed."

8

The first of August, 1934, we left Madrid for the summer capital in San Sebastián, spending the night at Burgos, visiting the cathedral to see the exterior in a dim light. It was enchanting, and even the beggars who swarmed about us were tolerable. The next morning we visited the ancient church and monastery of Las Huelgas, passing through the twelfth-century walls to the Middle Ages, where the Black Prince had been admitted for a time in an atmosphere of piety, and we stood beside the altar where Edward I of England had been made a knight in 1284. The cloister, overrun with flowers, could not have changed much in seven hundred years. We visited the sixteenth-century monastery of Milaflores, where we were conducted by a witty monk. Tourists should not ignore this monastery because of the magnificent tomb of Juan II and Isabella, his wife. The lace on the dress of the Queen and the embroidery on the uniform of the King were uncannily realistic. As we admired this brilliant masterpiece, the monk remarked that Gil de Siloë, the sculptor, had worked four years and four months on the achievement; and then, with a sly dig at the labor laws of the Republic, he added: "He must have worked more than eight hours a day." With a whimsical smile, he pointed to the exquisitely carved choir stalls and told the story of their creation. An unconverted Jew, a consummate artist, was sentenced to death for his religion, and Queen Isabella had promised him his life if he would do the choir stalls well. "He did them most beautifully and artistically," said the monk, "but most profanely, for there is not a religious motif in all the work."

San Sebastián is a beautiful city, far more attractive than Biarritz, with smart shops along the Alameda, and with sidewalk cafés where hundreds sit beneath gay-colored umbrellas, gossiping and inspecting the promenaders. The drives about the foothills and beside the sea are picturesque. At Rentería we could sit in the garden of a tavern beneath the sycamores and gorge on Spanish chocolate and *churros*, but more interesting to me was the fishing village of Passejas, whose stone steps leading down to the water suggest Venice, and where one pauses before a house on the edge

of the sea, with a stone balcony overhanging the water, where
Victor Hugo lived and wrote his Spanish play. One day we drove
over a winding road to Loyola to visit the birthplace of the founder
of the Jesuit order. I was disappointed, since the rooms most intimately associated with Loyola have been so loaded with gold and
silver, with marble and precious stones, that nothing now remotely
suggests the palace that Loyola knew.

9

It was in San Sebastián that I had my first view of Belmonte in
the sanded arena. Traffic congestion had delayed us, and we
reached our seats just in time to see the master matador killing his
first bull with one thrust of the sword. His first bull had been
"good," and Belmonte's work was brilliant, but the second was
dangerously erratic, and even the idol did not escape some grum-
bling when he showed a disposition to cut the cape work short.

It was later that summer at Aranjuez that I saw Belmonte at
greater advantage. We started early to escape the congestion, but
not early enough, for as we approached Aranjuez we moved at a
snail's pace, the cars in a solid stream. When one car bumped another, doing no harm, the driver sprang out to estimate the damage
and fix the responsibility, and immediately three men in a wild
state of excitement were shouting, shaking fists, gesticulating extravagantly, seeming on the verge of a stroke, with the veins standing out dangerously on neck and brow. At length, an agreement
was reached, and the most violent of the trio leaped into a van—
since he was not concerned with either car in the collision. But,
being Spanish and unable to resist the opportunity for a stout verbal
combat in the grand manner, he had sprung from the van and
plunged into the glorious strife for its own sake.

And then to the bull ring and Belmonte. With a perfect bull he
was superb. Once, fighting very close, as was his wont, the bull's
hoof struck his leg, and he started walking toward the barrier with
a limp. The crowd was painfully concerned lest its idol had been
hurt badly. In a moment Belmonte ceased to limp, and with a
nonchalant air, bowed reassuringly to his worshipers. Another time,
he fought so close he was pushed over, and again one could feel
the tremor running through the crowd. But Belmonte sprang to

his feet, spreading his hands as a token that all was well. Then followed the most thrilling exhibition with the cape I have ever seen, as Belmonte took the bull around him, against his body, and then turned the enraged animal in the opposite direction, and all so rapidly that it was impossible to tell what was happening. Again his second bull was a "bad one," refusing to charge the cape, standing stock still gazing at the red cape curiously. At length, in despair of the bull, Belmonte prepared to make the kill, and a howl of disapproval roared from the crowd. Belmonte paused, looked at the crowd, and then, with a smile, tried again with the cape and with no better success. Once, when the bull was close to the barrier, Belmonte plunged with the sword, and, with an angry toss of the head, the bull sent it flying. Belmonte cringed and scowled. That season another of Belmonte's bulls had sent his sword flying into the grandstand, wounding a spectator, and that day the matador cried like a baby. This time he coaxed the bull from the barrier before he tried again.

<h2 style="text-align:center">10</h2>

Three days after the Belmonte fight, a general strike paralyzed Madrid. It was a protest against the government's attitude toward Catalonia. That day again we had no bread. It was a peaceful strike, with no disturbance. For more than an hour I walked through the streets without seeing so much as a frown. There had been no preliminary notice of the strike. Orders had gone out at two in the morning, and instantly all work ceased for twenty-four hours. There was no excitement—except in the foreign press.

But we were verging on serious trouble. There were rumors of a tampering with the military barracks in Catalonia and Aragon, and whisperings about a military *coup d'état*. Arrangements had been made for the burial under the Arch of Charles III in Madrid of Galán and García Hernández, the officers who died before a firing squad in December, 1930, after the unsuccessful rising at Jaca. These had become republican martyrs, and their names were inscribed on marble plaques in the Cortes. An elaborate ceremony had been planned. The graves under the arch were ready. The date had long been set for September 15, 1934. Consequently, when, without explanation, the government, thought by the masses to be hostile to the Republic, withdrew its permission, there was an ominous growling. Why this withdrawal of permission? Was it because the fifteenth was the anniversary of the *coup d'état* of Primo de Rivera? Why not the twenty-third? asked the government. Was it because on that day the Rightists were giving a complimentary dinner to Lerroux and presenting him with the house of his birth? No one appeared to know, but it all seemed most peculiar. The bodies of Galán and García Hernández still lay in the cemetery where they fell, and it was said that soldiers had been sent to prevent their removal. The gossips stirred expectation with the story that republican groups would forcibly take the bodies to Madrid for burial, as planned.

But there was no ceremony on the fifteenth or the twenty-third, and it was clear that the government of Lerroux had no intention of doing homage to the martyrs of the Republic.

Meanwhile, the enemies of the regime were riding hard. The brilliant editor of *La Presse* of San Sebastián, Manuel Andrés, a staunch republican who had been Azaña's first Director of General Security, had been shot in the back on leaving his office. Since he was a formidable figure among the republicans, he had been "liquidated" in the classic Fascist way. Azaña, who attended the funeral of his friend, was so overcome with emotion that he fainted.

A crisis was approaching. Many, if not most, thought the country on the verge of bloody events. But it was a military, not a Fascist *coup d'état* that was expected. *I never once heard anyone suggest the faintest possibility of an attempt at a* coup d'état *by communists who were so insignificant in numbers that I seldom heard them mentioned at the time. All suggestions of a* coup d'état *by the Leftists contemplated a rising of organized labor.*

Chapter VII

The Moors Come Back

Two weeks before the deluge, Mallory Browne, of the Paris Bureau of the *Christian Science Monitor*, sent to Spain to clarify the Spanish situation for his paper, asked my advice as to contacts he would do well to make, and I advised him to see Azaña, Lerroux, Gil Robles, Count Romanones, José Primo de Rivera, Largo Caballero, and Fernando de los Ríos and gave him letters to some of them. Assuming that they might speak more frankly for publication three thousand miles away, I gratefully accepted Browne's offer to report to me on his conversations.

For some time, Largo Caballero, left-wing socialist, had been making almost daily threats of revolution, and Browne found him in a state of great excitement. A number of his assistants in the socialists' headquarters had just been imprisoned. He was bitter. No longer, he said, could the socialists, now subjected to open persecution, hope to advance along evolutionary lines. Force alone could now solve their problem of existence. He freely admitted that a rebellion against Gil Robles' policies was in incubation, and that with the exception of Julián Besteiro, all socialist leaders favored such a course.

The next day Browne saw Fernando de los Ríos and was much impressed by his dignity and intellectual charm. He made it clear that while, temperamentally, he opposed force, he would yield to party discipline. He admitted that the leaders who had signed the

Pact of San Sebastián had signed a new agreement on collaboration, but that later the socialists had determined upon independent
action. I assumed from this that the rebellion possibly in preparation would be a purely socialist movement, in which the other
republican parties would not be involved.

Two days later, nothing had developed and it was apparent
that the socialists and the Rightists were maneuvering for advantage, each bent on forcing upon the other the onus of precipitating
the conflict. From a source I respected, I heard that Caballero's
purpose in making open threats was to prod Salazar Alonzo,
Minister of the Interior, into some violent unconstitutional measure
that would justify the socialists in claiming that they had struck in
self-defense. It was significant that such left-wing socialists as Juan
Negrín and Álvarez del Vayo had not been taken into the confidence of Caballero because he thought they had "spent too much
time abroad and did not understand the Spanish temperament."

Browne thought Azaña the ablest of the Spanish statesmen. His
report to me on his conversation was positive proof to me that
Azaña was opposed to a resort to force. As a human being and a
democrat, he said, he sympathized with the irritation of the
socialists who were being persecuted, but he thought an armed
rising tactically suicidal. He doubted the ability of the socialists to
carry off a *coup d'état*, and even if they scored a momentary success,
he doubted their ability to carry on, because of the almost certain
sabotage of the civil service. The result, in any event, he thought,
would be defeat, and an inevitable reaction that might sweep away
the foundations of the Republic. I was to remember this interview
a very little later when Azaña would be accused of having organized and directed the rebellion.

José Primo de Rivera charmed Browne without convincing him
of the young man's ability for the role to which he was aspiring,
and Count Romanones, on his estate in Guadalajara, was gracious
and amusing, but the old fox was cagey about the threatened
rebellion.

Browne had found Gil Robles uncannily elusive, but at length
he was received in the leader's study. His apartment house on the
Velázquez was guarded by armed men, though he had no official
position. The correspondent was impressed by his fanatic partisan-

ship and the bitterness of his comments on his political opponents. He was astonished to hear that the CEDA leader, no less than Azaña, wanted a dissolution and elections, since sentiment was shifting rapidly to the Left. But the country was jittery, overfed on Fascist tales of "communist plots," and fantastic lies about the "arrival of Trotsky in Barcelona." Did Gil Robles feel that the hour was psychologically favorable to the Rightists? Or, infuriated by his continued exclusion from full power, was he ready to risk the verdict of the polls? When asked if his party would go to the electorate as a republican party, he evaded a simple, direct answer.

"We will be judged by what we say in the campaign," he said.

"But your opponents say you are an enemy of the Republic," he was told.

"I am the only friend of the Republic," was the astonishing answer.

Browne left with the distinct impression that Gil Robles was no friend of a democratic Republic. When asked if it were possible for his party to work in collaboration with liberals, like Azaña, the young leader snapped:

"Azaña is no liberal; he is a despot."

Which recalled Azaña's comment on him: "He is not an individual; he is a tool."

2

Four days later the Cortes met after a four-months' recess, and Gil Robles struck for power. Samper that day was to give an account of his stewardship as Prime Minister. It had not been brilliant, but his constant pilgrimages to the villa of Lerroux at San Rafael had created the impression that his every official act was dictated by his chief. It was confidently expected that on the meeting of the Cortes he would resign and make way for the restoration of Lerroux, but there had been a hitch somewhere.

The galleries were packed when the deputies stamped into the Chamber on the ringing of the bell. The socialists, out in force, were crowded just beneath the diplomatic gallery. Prieto seemed glum and grave, though occasionally some of his witticisms brought smiles to the lips of the deputy beside him. But he was clearly nervous.

The party of Lerroux was also there in force . . . Romanones hobbled to his seat on the center aisle, shaking hands on the way . . . Samper took his place on the Blue Bench, then left the Chamber . . . Gil Robles whispered to Santiago Alba in the chair, presumably on the day's program. Returning to his seat, he shook hands with Romanones, patting him repeatedly on the back . . . Samper returned to the Blue Bench . . . Lerroux entered, quiet as a mouse, and found a seat three rows behind Samper. The mountain air of San Rafael had given him color.

Samper, no orator, began to speak, and the CEDA to interrupt. He fought his way awkwardly through the confusion in the Chamber. Gil Robles followed with a bitter attack on the government's timid handling of the Catalan question, speaking angrily, and his party dutifully chimed in with murmurs of approval, like old men in the Amen Corner. Angered by some statements, Samper noisily opened his desk and took out a pad for notes, and his foes glowered at the impertinence of the intent. When he asked that all the party leaders be heard on the subject, a storm of indignation swept over the Rightist benches. Romanones, from his seat, was making violent gestures with his cane and shouting at Samper. Alba rang his bell and shouted "order," but Romanones repeated his gestures and his words.

"You are making fun of us—resign," shouted Romanones. "You are making fun of us—go away."

Just then, as though by prearrangement, after adequate rehearsals, the corpulent Cid, one of Samper's ministers, notoriously far to the Right, simulating disgust, and foreshadowing resignation, rose and began wriggling his way from the Blue Bench, with some of his colleagues clinging to his coattails.

Deserted by everyone, even by Lerroux, Samper now asked for a recess to consider the situation, and after twenty minutes, when the session was resumed, and before all the deputies could reach their seats, Santiago Alba was reading the Prime Minister's announcement of a crisis.

Lerroux was entrusted with the formation of a government, but two days later, he was having unexpected trouble. Gil Robles demanding either the portfolio of war or of the interior for his party—these representing armed forces. Lerroux refused. He was running back and forth to the palace, where Alcalá Zamora, much excited, was lamenting that "my friend Largo Caballero wants to cut off my head"—a fantastic notion.

Meanwhile, rumors were thick that if Gil Robles' men entered the Ministry there would be a revolutionary strike; and Martínez Barrio, sane and reasonably conservative, was telling an audience in Seville that a military dictatorship was planned and that this meant war. Prieto had given the same warning in the Cortes.

The next day, Lerroux announced his government, with CEDA men as Ministers of Labor, Agriculture, and Justice. The naming of Dr. de Sujo as Minister of Labor was like pouring oil on flames. As Governor of Barcelona he had aroused the hatred of the workers by the severity of his regime. Though reputed to be a strong, stern, ruthless man, there was nothing to denote it in his appearance, for he was slight and frail, with the pinched face of the ascetic. He dressed soberly in black, and because of the cut of his coat, he could easily have been mistaken for a priest. When he spoke, his voice and manner were those of an old man. But he symbolized the opposition to ameliorative measures for the workers.

3

To the republicans, the admission of the CEDA men into the government meant peril, and after events were to justify this fear. In expectation of these events, the socialists, on their own, had been preparing for revolution. Nothing could have been more amusing than the ease with which the socialists had bought a great amount of arms for their labor unions from the government itself. These had been loaded on the ship *Turquesa* in the presence of an officer of the General Staff of the Army, and the stupid Samper, then Prime Minister, had ordered the cargo cleared "urgently" in a telegram. The arms were to be delivered in the Asturias, and in the Basque country, and in the end all were delivered in Asturias under the personal supervision of Prieto. Thirty trucks going back and forth in the process attracted attention.

The directors of the rising, Caballero and Prieto, had established headquarters in the Madrid home of one of their followers. This was the studio of Luis Quintanilla, the painter. The neighbors were used to seeing and hearing all sorts of men going and coming from the studio at all hours. The room was large and it had the advantage of a terrace. The republican parties were not asked to join in the rising, nor, in the event of success, were they to be asked to participate in the government. It was to be a purely socialist insurrection. The leaders counted on the support of a number of officers in command of regiments and battalions in Madrid and the provinces—a reliance that was to fail them. The rising was conditioned on the admission of the CEDA men into the Ministry, and Largo Caballero clung to the belief that Alcalá Zamora would continue to oppose their admission. However, a revolutionary Ministry had been named, which held itself in readiness in the studio of Quintanilla.

The extremists and the separatists in Barcelona had planned to take advantage of the situation to declare their province an independent state. Meanwhile, Azaña, then in Barcelona to attend the funeral of Jaime Carner, his former Minister of Finance, learning of the plan, decided to remain to prevent its consummation.

The CEDA entered the Ministry. The hour struck. At midnight I was informed that the revolution would break at four in the morning, with the railroads involved, and with all the socialists in the street. The next morning we breakfasted without bread—the strike was on. No papers appeared except the organs of the monarchists and the CEDA—the *A.B.C.* and *El Debate*, which were nonunion papers. The streetcars and taxicabs were stationary. When some small shops opened in the residential section, their owners took one look at the stern-faced men who appeared to protest and hurriedly closed their doors. The railroads, while operating, were short of men.

But in Barcelona all was quiet. It was understood that Azaña had persuaded Luis Companys, head of the autonomous state, rigidly to maintain order, and not to disturb the status quo unless Madrid imposed martial law. Order was maintained, and Madrid was not eager to declare martial law, as Azaña knew. But, gravely concerned, he telegraphed leaders in Madrid to join him in Barcelona. None responded. Companys appealed to the people over the radio to maintain order and to trust the local government for the protection of their interests. But that very night, Consul General Dawson telephoned me that arms were being distributed. It had been observed, he said, that Azaña had been very active with the functionaries entrusted with the maintenance of order.

In Madrid, all was serene on the surface. The people on the streets were in good humor, more curious than alarmed, but at ten o'clock that night the correspondent of an American paper telephoned me to hold my hat on during the next two hours—just that and nothing more. Thinking it possible that the *A.B.C.*, on the Castellana, near my garden, was to be bombed, we closed the steel shutters on that side of the house and waited—but nothing happened. I learned later that the object of the bombing was to have been the Fascist headquarters a few blocks away, but something interfered.

The next morning the *A.B.C.* and *El Debate* reported the strike crushed, but their equally positive assertion that Madrid had been entirely normal discredited the accuracy of their report. From a reliable source I received different information. The trouble in the Asturias was spreading, the socialists had taken La Carolina in the south, the railroads had all but ceased operation, and trains had neither entered nor left the Atoche station. A courier from Paris, expected at the embassy in the morning, did not arrive—caught in the country by the stopping of the train. In the Tetuán section of Madrid, its *St. Antoine*, street fighting was beginning.

But in the evening the situation was more ominous. Lester Ziffern, of the United Press, telephoned me that Catalonia would declare its independence in an hour. A few minutes later, Consul General Dawson telephoned me a confirmation—the declaration had been made. Azaña had lost his fight.

Meanwhile, shooting had become general in the streets of Madrid. Machine guns were rattling in the Puerta del Sol, where, in the Heidelberg restaurant, press reporters were lying flat on the floor to escape bullets. I asked Captain Logan Rock, of the Telephone Company, to get me quick connection with Washington, and a moment later, after he left his office for the purpose, the room was literally sprayed with bullets from snipers on neighboring roofs. My call had probably saved his life. That night I talked with

Cordell Hull, reporting the safety of the Americans and the closing of the frontiers. There was no assurance that a cable would have reached the State Department, which would be importuned for news by relatives of Americans in Spain.

From the balcony of the Ministry of the Interior, Lerroux denounced the Catalans and declared the entire country under martial law. That night we closed the steel shutters and had candles taken to each room as a precaution against the cutting of the electric wires. An infantry regiment patrolled the streets. Pedestrians walked awkwardly, holding their hands high above their heads.

And then, on Sunday, came the collapse of the rebellion in Catalonia. It was a day of sunshine and invigorating air. A servant returning from church reported many soldiers guarding the house of Alcalá Zamora near the embassy. All pedestrians were now forced to hold their hands above their heads. From the direction of the Fascist headquarters came the sound of cheering—cheering for José Primo de Rivera.

In the demonstrations for the government, Lerroux and his ministers took the Fascist salute! The enemies of democracy had not forgotten their compact with Hitler and Mussolini. Thus the enemies of the regime and of democracy were out in the open.

4

Meanwhile, there was much needless killing. Soldiers entered the crowded Puerta del Sol with a machine gun, lost their heads, and, without provocation, fired. Inexperienced and jittery young soldiers were prone to pull the trigger because of their nervous tension. Firing hysterically at imaginary foes on roofs, they occasionally shot into the apartments of inoffensive people. Drivers and passengers in cars became hardened to seeing a shaking musket poked through the window and into their faces by frightened young soldiers.

One night, the beautiful Alcalá presented a weird, sinister aspect. Lights were on only at every third street intersection, and the broad thoroughfare was in semidarkness. Soldiers paced the sidewalks, while pedestrians walked on the car tracks in the middle of the street, holding their hands high. On every street, pedestrians, on hearing a shot, threw themselves prone upon the ground until the danger of a fusillade was over.

But the next day the rebellion entered a new phase. Machine guns appeared in crowded streets in Madrid and Barcelona, and again press correspondents telephoned me that they were marooned in the Heidelberg restaurant with the street outside swept by bullets.

That day I was startled by the unexpected appearance of Samper at the embassy on his ceremonial call as the new Minister of Foreign Affairs. Evidently he had slept well, and he appeared unworried. The only reasonable explanation of his venturing out, a target for bullets, was to show the serenity of the government by a dramatic gesture. I accompanied him to the door and noticed that he had no armed men in his car.

But not everyone felt so serene. That day Jay Allen, of the Chicago *Tribune*, returned to his apartment on the Alcalá to find police had ransacked the place. He telephoned me that he was puzzled, though the explanation was not far to seek, since the dispersion of the revolutionary Ministry from the studio of Quintanilla had led Negrín and Del Vayo to seek news in Jay's apartment. Then a second call from Allen—the police had returned, and with drawn guns had forced Allen, Leland Stowe, and Edward Taylor, the journalists, to throw up their hands. When, indignantly, they protested, the police said someone had fired from the balcony of Jay's apartment—which was not true. The police apologized, pleading in extenuation that the sniping had driven them to distraction. After a whisky and soda, they left in good humor—but only to return on the morrow. Allen telephoned me that they were with him again, and that, in the event they took him, Leland Stowe would inform me at once. Scarcely had he hung up when Stowe called to say they had taken Allen away. I protested vigorously to the Foreign Office, and Allen was instantly released.

An hour later, Allen was on the phone again, and I assumed he was calling to thank me, but he did not mention the incident, now, after an hour, ancient history: "Here is some real news," he said. "The King of Yugoslavia, Barthou, and a French general have all been murdered in Marseille"—and he hung up.

The Second World War was in preparation.

5

Because of the rigid military censorship, Madrid for days knew almost nothing of what was transpiring in the Asturias. That the insurrection was over in Barcelona and Madrid was clear. Largo Caballero and Prieto were still in hiding. But for days the fate of Azaña remained a mystery. With all the republican papers suppressed, the papers of the ruling coalition made the most of their opportunity to assail him with unscrupulous abandon. He had "fled to France," he had "escaped through a sewer," he was the "instigator of the rebellion," and he was a "Christ killer." His enemies spewed forth their spleen with such insane fury that a reaction was inevitable.

The truth is that Azaña had opposed the rebellion. En route to Barcelona to attend the funeral of his former minister, he occupied a seat on the train with Largo Caballero and sought to persuade the firebrand that the insurrection planned would play into the hands of the enemy, but this only elicited an insult. "I have prestige," shouted Caballero, "and the fact that I have talked with you so long will lower my prestige." Astonished, Azaña calmly replied: "Then you will need all the prestige you can get."

Certain it is that in Barcelona he continued his attempt to prevent the desperate enterprise of separationists. Reviewing his conduct there, Madariaga finds that it was "impeccable" and that "he gave the Catalans, who were entirely disoriented, advice worthy of a statesman, which they would have done well to heed and which they did not listen to, mainly because Companys was not brave enough to be prudent." (Madariaga's *Spain*, page 529.) Failing in his attempt, Azaña had retired to his room in a hotel in the center of the danger zone. Pressed by his friends to seek safer quarters, he arranged to go to a hotel in the country, not far away. But the taxi driver who was to meet him on the outskirts of the city failed to appear, and he returned to town and took refuge in the apartment of a friend. He lost his liberty through a cup of coffee! Soldiers had made a futile search of the apartment and were on the point of leaving when they noticed an untouched cup of coffee on the table. "Who is that cup of coffee for?" they demanded. There was a strained silence. The soldiers renewed the search. Azaña had stepped out on a balcony, and there he was found; but the normality of the capture did not satisfy the hysteria of the times, and so the enemy press reported that he was found "under a bed," and had been found "trembling like a leaf," and "with a gun in his hand." One of the Madrid papers bitterly criticized the soldiers for not having shot him on the spot to save future trouble, and this gentle statement, so reminiscent of the Berlin and Rome of Hitler and Mussolini, passed the military censor.

He was at first confined to a small cabin on a boat in the harbor with Luis Bello, who, after a long life of distinguished service to education, was in the last stages of consumption. He was refused permission to make a statement, the papers of his supporters were suppressed, and thus gagged, his enemies were to deluge him with unthinkable abuse.

After five years, most of the founders of the Republic were dead, in jail, or in hiding. From his mysterious refuge, Prieto smuggled an interview to the foreign press through Jay Allen, denouncing the savagery of the Moors and the Foreign Legion in the Asturias and warning that this had left ineradicable scars and that Spain would never be the same again. Allen showed it to me before sending it out, disregarding my suggestion that I could not keep him out of jail forever.

6

The abuse of Azaña gained momentum, finally becoming fantastic. The *A.B.C.* howled with mirth because he had put a cigarette in his mouth when arrested and did not light it. It called him "a wild Iberian boor." When soldiers on guard at the police station where he was first taken treated him with the respect due a former chief of government, they were denounced; and when soldiers on guard at the prison ship, knowing discretion to be the better part of valor, did not salute, the *A.B.C.* gloated over the incident.

But the government was far from happy, and at the funeral services for Barthou, I noticed the pasty complexion of the ministers and the dark rings under their eyes. Meanwhile, the military censor was guarding the secret of the cruel events in the Asturias. It was leaking out that Moors and Legionnaires had been brought over from Africa and turned loose against the Asturian miners, but there was no mention of their presence in the press. As a topic of conversation it was tabooed. In diplomatic circles it was mentioned in whispers. During the seven centuries of Moorish occupation, the infidels had found the province of Asturias impenetrable, and for centuries Christians were to refer with pride to the valor of the hardy mountaineers. Many thought it incredible that the Spanish government had brought back the Moors to take their revenge by slaughtering Spaniards. But the truth could not be suppressed. More Moorish troops had landed in Cádiz, and two trainloads had passed through Madrid to the Asturias, where the army was making little progress. The drama there was continuing too long for comfort in official circles, since sympathy might turn to the Asturians fighting behind their barricades.

7

Meanwhile, all over Spain, opponents of the government's policies were being arrested wholesale—socialists, of course, but also Azaña liberals, Barrio republicans, democrats generally, labor leaders in particular—and thrown into prison without a charge. A few months later I noticed from a balcony of the Alhambra in Granada a large modern building and I inquired its purpose. "That is the women's prison," I was told, "but it is now packed with men. The men's prison could not hold all who were arrested in the October trouble." But, I said, there was no trouble in Granada. "No," was the answer, "but there were a lot of democrats and republicans." That was quite enough; and so the dragnet drew in the liberals until more than thirty thousand were in jail, most of them to remain without trial, or even a charge, for eighteen months. At that moment there were no more civil rights in Spain than in Germany, Italy, or Russia.

One night it occurred to the military to look for Largo Caballero in his home, and there they found him. He was sent to the Model prison. But Prieto remained elusive and increasingly maddening to the police. One day the editor of *A.B.C.*, who editorially had charged the socialist orator with an offense he had not committed, received a dignified denial, signed, "Prieto." Such impertinence! But the editor was sporting enough to publish the denial, and Madrid laughed heartily and surmised that Prieto would not be taken. He was prejudiced against prisons and was one of the few leaders who had escaped capture after the failure of the rising of 1930, and the gossips had it that he had crossed the frontier disguised as a jolly, fat friar. Just where he was hidden in 1934 I have never heard. Many tales were told of his escape to France, but the truth is that he was driven across by Ignacio Hidalgo Cisneros, head of the loyalist air force during the Fascist war. The stories of Prieto's escapes would have delighted Dumas.

8

Meanwhile, the government papers were publishing ghastly stories of the "atrocities" of the Asturian miners that were to influence public opinion outside Spain. And seeping into Madrid through subterranean channels came stories of the thievery, the rapes, the assassinations, and the tortures by the Moors. Drumhead court-martials were certainly killing freely, and public sentiment began to veer.

With the usual stupidity of arbitrary governments, a rigid censorship was enforced, and whisperings ran like the murmuring of wind through a wheat field and made matters worse. The foreign press, curious about the silence in the Asturias, began to print strange tales. The theaters rumbled from the pit with politics. When the newsreels showed General Ochoa leading his troops into Oviedo, the government supporters cheered passionately; and when Raquel Meller, in fervent song, proclaimed that Spaniards never would wear the Fascist chains of slavery, the Leftists screamed their approval. And Hate was in the saddle, and Hate had become the order of the day. The press of the Right ran riot with lurid fabrications designed to feed the blood lust. Priests had been "crucified," in the Asturias, they said. "Twenty nuns had been hanged." The children of Civil Guards had had their eyes put out—monstrous lies patterned on the technique of Goebbels. But when the appetite for horror was still unsatisfied, the preposterous story was put out that a priest had been murdered, stripped, and hung on a meat hook in front of a butcher shop. This was Goebbels propaganda at its worst. The air was quivering with hymns of hate against the democrats whether implicated in the rebellion or not, for public opinion was being prepared for wholesale executions of political prisoners.

9

It was on this issue that the victors turned on each other. The persecuting spirit had come to stay awhile. Even that early, the stupid were being impressed with the Fascist propaganda that to be a democrat was to be a "red." Had not Hitler said so?—and Mussolini? On two succeeding days the Council of Ministers deliberated on the situation, but the silence imposed by censorship left the public in the dark as to the precise point of cleavage between Alcalá Zamora and the politicians of the Right. The President was opposed to the trial of political prisoners by military tribunals, but it was not known whether he opposed the execution of the two army officers condemned in Barcelona. Lerroux, in his old-age wisdom, knew it was unprofitable to make martyrs. It was known that the Ministry was divided and that the three Gil Robles ministers were demanding death sentences.

On the third day, the ministers assembled in council under the chairmanship of Alcalá Zamora at the palace—assembled at eleven, lunched at two, and continued deliberations until five. For a long time the President spoke, demanding that the death sentences of the military tribunals should be reviewed by the Supreme Court. It was a fighting speech. He compared the treason of the two Catalan officers, sentenced to death, with the treason of General Sanjurjo, who led the rebellion against the regime in 1932. The Catalan officers, he said, were under compulsion to obey the orders of the Generalidad of Catalonia, recognized as an autonomous state; but Sanjurjo was an officer of the general government only, and he had turned his sword against his government, against the Republic, and "against the sovereign people." And where, he asked, did the ministers before him stand on clemency for Sanjurjo? Turning to some papers on his desk, he took up a telegram pleading for clemency—and signed by Manuel Jimenez Fernández, the CEDA Minister of Agriculture, who was insisting on the death penalty for the Catalans. And then, turning to Lerroux:

"At that time, and at the time of the Amnesty Bill which started all this trouble, you were fond of quoting, 'the quality of mercy is not strained.' Is it strained, Sr. Lerroux, only when it operates in the interest of republicans?"

Then, abruptly, he shifted to a vigorous attack on military officers presuming to dictate to the civil government. Turning to Hidalgo, Minister of War, he asked if it were true that there were committees among officers presuming to intimidate the state. Hidalgo admitted it was true and quoted two colonels as threatening a military rebellion if the executions were not carried out.

"I have a right to assume that these colonels were promptly placed under arrest?" he asked in an ironical tone.

There was no reply.

The President went on to say that he had reason to know that everything he said would immediately be known to some of the generals.

"What generals?" asked Hidalgo.

"The generals with whom you are conspiring," snapped the President, referring to Franco and Goded.

Under the law, the speech of the President could not be published without the consent of the ministers. Fearing the preparation of a military *coup d'état*, he was determined that it should reach the public. After the ministers had gone, he dictated his speech with the view to its clandestine publication. I was told that one copy was sent to Paris for safekeeping; another was given to a certain minister, a personal friend. But with the acceptance of his plan for a review of the death sentences of military tribunals by the Supreme Court, there was no need for publication.

However, the indignation of the extreme Right and the army officers knew no bounds, and the town was buzzing with rumors of a *coup d'état*. In the War Office sat Generals Franco and Goded, directing the fight against the Asturians. Popular surmise made Franco the prospective Dictator, though many questioned his capacity for the role. It was agreed that Goded—ruthless, unscrupulous, treacherous—would fit it better. He had betrayed the King, then Primo de Rivera, then Azaña and Lerroux, but it was agreed that he was too unpopular with the other generals. Strangely enough, at this time I did not hear Sanjurjo mentioned for the part.

10

On the surface there was a temporary lull. Never had I seen Madrid so gay and charming. The rebellion was over. There was a golden autumn sunshine, and the air was fresh and fragrant with the odors of the fall. Along the Castellana, promenaders walked so close together that, seen from a car, they appeared to move as a mass. In the beautiful Retiro many cars were parked, the walks were crowded as on the Castellana, and many were strolling along the cosy wooded paths.

While waiting for the meeting of the Cortes, I made another of many sentimental journeys to Alcalá de Henares, the sweetest, most charming small town in old Castile. Its glory, which illuminated generations, departed when the famous university was moved to Madrid. All the glory was gone, but there remained the monuments, the stout buildings now converted into barracks. The choicest of these was reserved for the enjoyment of the public. Driving along a narrow street, bordered by the buildings of the old university, one comes suddenly upon the hostelry of Estudiente. We entered the courtyard, paved with boulders, and passed an ancient well whose stone coping is cut deep with the ropes of generations, to enter the room reserved in olden times as the dining room of the famous professors and star students. In the center, on one side, is a huge stone fireplace on a slight elevation. Here the wild game was cooked for the young men with swords and ruffles who were dining by candlelight. Frequently I arrived there in the winter, when one was glad to mount the platform, one step up, and sit on a stool covered with goatskin, and let the blaze draw out the sting of the mountain wind. About the tables are saddleback chairs, and others more designed for comfort. In a corner of the room is a big pigskin, fat with the juice of the grape. It was delightful to sit before the leaping flames partaking of a many-course dinner.

From the dining room one may pass into the loveliest patio surrounded by two-story stone buildings colored a pale pink by the centuries. Nothing is changed, though the gargoyles have been worn a bit by rain and hail. In the center is an old well with a bucket, merely ornamental now, though centuries ago the savants there slaked their thirst. Opening from the patio is a lecture room, so awe-inspiring in its associations and beauty that a guest of mine from Oxford University instinctively removed his hat with the exclamation: "There is nothing at Oxford more inspiring than this." The great height of the ceiling, itself a work of art, is impressive, as is the lecture tribune and the raised platform around the walls on which are set the marble plaques recording the names of the scholars and philosophers of former centuries who have lectured here. After the tumult and the shouting of the politicians and the military conspirators of Madrid, a few minutes in this hall seemed like a spiritual bath—a cleansing of the spirit.

Always I stopped just inside the medieval stone gate of the former walls of the old town at the principal church, memorable in its austere simplicity, and its memories. Usually we found ourselves alone. Beneath a tomb of extraordinary beauty, a gem of the Renaissance, in front of the altar, slept the great Cardinal Cisneros, of the golden days of Isabella the Catholic. How serene, majestic, masterful he seemed in the recumbent figure. Later, this masterpiece was to be smashed by the bombs of foreign Fascist aviators.

Always fascinating to me, the old Archbishop's Palace, built centuries ago when the cardinals competed openly with the King for temporal power. Neglected until recently, there is something very sad in the present state of this magnificent building. We enter the great court, which reeks of death and desertion, and ascend the wide stairway to the broad stone balcony that surrounds the court, and thence pass through the many rooms, now filled from floor to ceiling with yellow crumbling documents that hold the secrets of history. We note, with respect for the archbishops' love of beauty, the ornate wood carvings of the ceilings of the rooms, the design changing with each apartment; and then on until we reach the two great halls where cardinals and kings once determined the destiny of Spain, and where Isabella the Catholic gave birth to Catherine of Aragon, who was the first unhappy wife of Henry VIII of England. The ceilings are beautiful still, but the small panes of colored glass in the long windows have suffered from the rocks of young rowdies. We look through these windows across the way to where a modern building with iron-barred windows frowns upon the grounds.

"It is the prison," says the guide. "Juan March is over there"— and he smiles with satisfaction.

A little later, we peer through the same windows on the prison.

"Juan March bribed the jailor and got away," says the guide sourly.

And now Juan March is sitting in a corner of the rotunda of the Palace Hotel in Madrid, and people bow respectfully, for he has great possessions. With the passing of the Azaña regime, his importance is growing by leaps and bounds. He has become a great "patriot" and has resumed his place in the Cortes, which is meeting now.

It is time for us to cross the street and observe proceedings in that quarter.

Chapter VIII

Sowing the Wind

WITH the antidemocratic press flooding the country with lurid tales of the "atrocities" of the Asturian miners, news began to seep into Madrid that there were more than enough atrocities on the other side. One night a press correspondent, who had made a house-to-house canvass in Oviedo along the road traversed by the Moors and the Foreign Legion in entering the city, brought me his report, and it was revolting. Thus the story of robbery, rape, and murder reached the capital. Very soon the Lerroux-Gil Robles government's desperate device of *ordering a censorship of words spoken in debate* in the Cortes gave proof that it had something to conceal.

Denouncing parliamentary proceedings under a censorship as a mockery, the socialists and many republicans refused to attend the opening session of the Cortes in early November, 1934. The streets about the Cortes swarmed with soldiers, but the government supporters had the Cortes to themselves. Lerroux spoke calmly, promising to end the cruelty of punishment and reiterating his allegiance to the Rightists. He had reversed his declaration at the Barrio dinner of allegiance to the Leftists. Gil Robles clapped his hands discreetly and then spoke with great vehemence, while his party responded with a series of ovations. His complete mastery of the government was evident.

But the next day his mastery was challenged by Calvo Sotelo, the beneficiary of the armistice, in an abusive attack on republicanism and democracy, and a laudatory reference to the Fascist concept of society. He was known to favor Fascism with a puppet King, and to be reaching for the leadership of the Rightist coalition. His arrogance was intimidative.

When Gil Robles sprang to his feet with a surprising denunciation of the superstate, everyone knew that the contest was less one of democracy against Fascism than of Gil Robles against Calvo Sotelo. Even so, it was a notable debate. Then, for a week, the proceedings in the Cortes were dull routine, and I responded to the call of the road again.

2

One clear November day we drove an American Ursuline nun, a tall woman with an expressive Irish face lighted by keenly intelligent, mirthful eyes, to the interesting medieval castle of Oropesa. She was engaged on a book on colonial Peru. During the October troubles, she had lived in the Irish convent in Madrid, going back and forth to the library in her nun's uniform at a time when the London *Mail* had the streets running with blood, and nuns being shot on sight.

The castle of Oropesa had been the home of the fifth viceroy of Peru, in which Charles V had found refuge while awaiting the completion of preparations for his reception in a neighboring monastery where he was to spend the remainder of his days. Saint Theresa had rested a few days at Oropesa on one of her journeys. Misfortune having fallen on the owner of the castle, it had been converted into a charming *parador*, its windows commanding a marvelous view for miles. A scraggly little village sprawled about it. That day we went to the fourteenth-century tower and ramparts, over the loose rocks that were once steps but now offered a perilous footing. Long ago the balconies surrounding the court had been gay with men and women in silks and frills looking down on tournaments. Now the court has a small stone amphitheater for the accommodation of villagers at bullfights. Children were playing about in the court that day, for a public school had been opened in part of the castle. Just off the main court, we found a little room where work peculiar to the region could be bought. A man, an old woman, and two younger ones were grouped about a glowing brazier. The women were busy with their knitting, the man with his newspaper. We made some purchases under the keen eyes of the old woman, and, on leaving, the entire family bade us a ceremonious farewell.

A few days later, we drove over the mountains to Segovia to see the Knight Templar's church of Vera Cruz. I knew the Segovia of the Alcázar where the Catholic monarchs were crowned, and the perfectly preserved aqueduct of Roman days in the heart of the city, but the little church of Vera Cruz I had seen but faintly through a mist from the ramparts of the medieval castle. It stands outside the city in a lonely and deserted spot, and there it has stood unchanged since it was built in 1209. Entering through a fine Romanesque door, we found ourselves in a cold, lonesome, strangely constructed room, the center dominated by a tiny church within a tiny church—a structure with two floors. In the room below, the Knights donned their uniforms and swords before going forth to battle for the tomb of Christ. In the room above they prayed all night, looking down through a window on the altar. In a small room beside the entrance to the church, where the Knights received their uniforms and swords, tradition says there once was a section of the Cross. What a romantic age of flaming faith this little church revived! On a white stone wall I found some scribbling covered with a pane of glass. More than half a century ago that incomparable Spanish orator and republican, Emilio Castelar, on a sentimental pilgrimage, emotionally had written on the wall the feeling the church evoked in him.

As we were leaving, a gust of rain drove us back into the ancient doorway, and as we looked out on the lonely valley, misty with the driving rain, it seemed it could not have been greatly different in the days of the Crusaders.

3

In the Cortes, Gil Robles was now ready to strike for power.

It was not until six o'clock that the fight began. The socialists and many of the republicans were still absent. Martínez Barrio and Miguel Maura were in their seats, but as attentive listeners only. On the Blue Bench sat Samper, Hidalgo, Minister of War, and Roca, all under attack from the coalition masters—and they sat alone, deserted. Clearly, Lerroux was prepared to throw them to the sharks. They all looked sober, hurt, indignant. Gil Robles was not to speak. Lerroux was to hold his peace. An obscure monarchist was put forth to stab the victims in the house of their friends lest they turn on the leaders with an "*et tu, Brute.*"

Hidalgo met the attack with a spirited denunciation of the misrepresentation of the facts, but with Samper, who had his intellectual and oratorical limitations, it was different. When the little man with the frog face flung the epithet "liar" at his tormentor, and Santiago Alba, a party colleague and president of the Cortes, demanded an apology, Samper was left alone. Others joined in the attack, but none of the leaders. Shame exacts its toll. And none of the leaders whom Samper had served as a dog serves its master uttered a word in his defense.

Two days later, Samper and Hidalgo went out, since Lerroux no longer had the spirit or capacity to defend his own. He was in chains and reconciled. But if Gil Robles thought to get the Ministry of War for his party, he was disappointed. Lerroux took that post himself and transferred his friend Roca from the navy to the Foreign Office.

4

Meanwhile, the Right coalition was not entirely happy. Azaña remained in his prison ship with his consumptive companion, in a small cabin, viciously assailed each day, and refused permission to reply. The inevitable reaction for fair play came, when, defying the military censorship, a circular, "*El Caso de Manuel Azaña,*" was scattered broadcast in Madrid, signed by many of the most luminous names in Spain. It denounced the persistent misrepresentations of hate and the brazen lie that Azaña had inspired the rebellion, when it said, "It is well known, not only to us, but to his detractors, that it is false." It charged that the purpose of his enemies was to "annihilate" him and "to arm an assassin."

"With him," it said, "we have more or less ideological concurrences, but we are not of the same political belief or bound to him by interests of any kind. What is being done against Señor Azaña has perhaps no precedent in our history, and if it has, it will be better not to remember. It is not an opposition that is being exercised against him, but a persecution. He is not being criticized, but denounced, slandered, and threatened. They are not trying to defeat him but to destroy him. In order to harm him, they have used all manner of insults. He is made to appear as his country's enemy, as the cause of all its misfortunes, as being a monster unworthy of living.

"We all know, his worse detractors included, that this is not true, that Azaña's ideas and his conduct are absolutely opposed to the sad events that have recently afflicted our country, and that he has followed, in power and in opposition, a policy of the people's welfare, honesty, and integrity, and which give him a mental and moral worth which anyone may oppose, but none can cheapen.

"Our protest is taken merely against the manner of the attacks which have reached such a blind malevolence, which seem intended to prevent fair action by the state—to provoke a blind revolt or to put weapons in the hands of an assassin."

The distinction in literature, art, politics, and science of the signers drove the government to action, and a committee from the Cortes was sent to Barcelona to take Azaña's deposition. But even his replies were refused publication by the government papers, and the Leftists' press was silenced by the censor.

Infuriated to stupidity by the possibility of Azaña's release, Gil Robles' Minister of Justice hurried in a bill for the reorganization of the Supreme Court before it could pass upon his case, and to pack it for his conviction. But the court, anticipating the trick and acting quickly, held there was no evidence to warrant either the trial or the detention of Azaña. Released at once, Azaña went to the home of Margarita Xirgu, the actress, near Barcelona, where his wife awaited him. The fury of the government and the Rightist press flamed with bitter attacks upon the court.

5

But the coalition was having difficulties, too. Manuel Jiménez Fernández, the most conspicuous member of the CEDA after Gil Robles, and Minister of Agriculture, was distressing the agrarians. A tall, athletic man with black mustache and hair, and with a pleasant, boyish manner, he was attractive-looking. Unlike those of his chief, his speeches were unemotional, factual, argumentative. He had no sense of drama. He was deeply and intelligently interested in the plight of the peasants, and he had theories and visions of his own, not dissimilar to those of the Christian Socialists, which the Hierarchy itself had mildly fostered once. He astonished not a few of his coreligionists by taking seriously the famous labor pronouncement of Leo XIII.

But, like all the other parties in the incongruous Rightist combination, the agrarians placed their own interpretation on the electoral triumph. To them, it meant the scrapping of all plans for the amelioration of the pitiful condition of the peasantry, the immediate expulsion of the peasants the Azaña regime had put on some land, and the squeezing from them of the utmost work for the least possible pay.

When, on assuming his post, Fernández warned the old feudalistic landlords over the radio that they should not assume the right to reduce the already miserable pay of the peasants, the agrarians cheerfully absorbed the shock with the reflection that this was the device of a politician to gain time. But, as time went on, there was no little growling when the peasants remained upon the land.

At length, Fernández made his position clear, speaking with moderation but with emphasis on his purpose. Azaña had established peasants, if possessing a mule or plow, on the land of absentee landlords. These, warned Fernández, would not be evicted for at least a year, and not even then, unless, in the meantime, a sound substitute policy could be devised. The landlords, who lived on and cultivated their land, he said, would be pleased to have their labor problem thus reduced; and as to the "absentee landlords living in Paris and Madrid, and interested only in profits"— these did not matter.

The agrarians were startled, and Velasco, their leader, a lawyer of Madrid, with no real connection with the soil, made angry protest. Fernández replied that if his views did not suit the government, it knew what it could do.

And then the agrarians had their second shock when, in defending his minister, Gil Robles said that the great landlords who ignored their social obligations had "not learned the lesson of the revolution." The gossips began to wonder about the CEDA leader. The agrarians were furious, pretending to have been deceived.

But, as it turned out, something was transpiring behind the scenes, and very soon thereafter Fernández resigned—thrown to the agrarian wolves. *The fate of the peasantry under the Rightist coalition was thus sealed.* The incident was not lost on the peasants. Fernando de los Ríos' prophecy was coming true. Reaction was in the saddle, booted and spurred. Was Gil Robles in the hands of forces stronger than himself? The extreme reactionaries of the Right no longer trusted him.

6

Then, about this time, Roya Villanueva, a Rightist near the Center, and Minister of Education, a gentleman of excellent ability and charm, with a round, pink face framed by a snow-white beard that invited confidence, submitted to the Cortes a plan for public instruction that Gil Robles bitterly attacked. Villanueva replied with dignity that he was merely acting in conformity with the Constitution—which was true. When the monarchy fell, there were ninety thousand children without school facilities, and the Azaña regime had planned to remedy this wrong. After the fall of the Azaña regime, the building of schoolhouses had all but ceased. Villanueva hotly accused Gil Robles of the determination to scrap the public schools and go back to the old system, with its enormous illiteracy among the masses. When Gil Robles replied contemptuously that Villanueva was "trying to raise a tempest in a teapot," Martínez Barrio cried out:

"Señor Azaña's exact words!"—and sat chuckling.

Villanueva offered his resignation, but Lerroux persuaded him to withhold it, thus furnishing food for the gossips, but four days later, Villanueva was insisting on his resignation, and thus one of the soundest and most conservative of Spaniards passed from office.

And with his passing, the fate of the public schools under the Right coalition was sealed. The "liquidation" of reforms was an essential part of the liquidation of democracy in Spain.

7

Meanwhile, the fight between Gil Robles and Calvo Sotelo for the domination of the Rightists was increasing in virulence. A contemptuous and avowed enemy of democracy, Calvo Sotelo appealed more and more to the extremists of the ruling coalition, dreaming of a military *coup d'état*. The clashing ambitions of the two men shook the air. The monarchists' organ was printing Calvo Sotelo's open letter to his rival, accusing him of using the censorship to prevent the monarchists from reaching the public, and Gil Robles replied that the sole mission of the monarchist press was to attack him, but that he would "join" in an effort to lift the censorship. Calvo Sotelo retorted, and with point, that since Gil Robles *was* the government, there was no need for anyone to join him to end the censorship.

But it was a sham battle in an atmosphere of hypocrisy, for the censorship was aimed, not at the monarchists, whose organ daily thundered against the Republic, but at the socialists and the followers of Azaña; and the primary purpose of the censorship was to prevent publicity for the charge of atrocities in the Asturias made against the Moors and the Foreign Legion. For terrible tales were now seeping into the city—tales of miners castrated, kept in cold water, and tortured for "confessions" until physicians rebelled against signing certificates that murdered men had died a natural death, and judges refused to convict on evidence secured through torture.

8

With rumors of a total crisis rife, I called one day on Sr. Roca, Minister of Foreign Affairs, and an intimate of Lerroux', and found him much depressed. Sadly, he said that the next day would be his last in the Foreign Office, and that it would be better to postpone business discussions until his successor could receive me a few days later. He had issued invitations for a tea at the ministry the next night, and, with a wistful grin, he said the tea had been planned as a farewell to the old year (1934), but it was turning out to be a farewell to himself. But the next night at the tea no one was happier, for Velasco had declined the post, and Roca remained.

Sr. Roca was neither brilliant nor ornamental, but he was friendly, and very human. He reveled in the luncheons and dinners of the diplomatic corps, and I suspect he would have missed these most. He was an excellent storyteller, and I liked him. He was standing beside Alcalá Zamora still, as Minister of Foreign Affairs, when the President gave his dinner for the heads of the diplomatic missions.

That night, Alcalá Zamora seemed happy and carefree, smiling constantly beside his slender, gray-haired wife. Lerroux was there, a picture of complacency despite his troubles, and, contrary to custom, his wife appeared. As Lerroux meandered about the palace in a careful inspection, Sir George Graham whispered to me that "he acts like a man who has taken a lease and is calculating just what he will do with the house when he moves in." No longer was it a secret that he expected the Presidency from the Gil Robles coalition as a reward for his complacency.

And Santiago Alba, President of the Cortes, smiling and chatty, was mingling with the guests. He had been a minister of the King, and a strange tale was told of Alfonso's alleged attempt to trick him into prison. On the day of Primo de Rivera's *coup d'état*, he was in San Sebastián, and, knowing of his intention to return to Madrid by train, the King persuaded Alba to drive with him into the country. They reached the station barely in time to catch the train. As Alba was mounting the steps, a friend whispered that there was a military *coup d'état* in Madrid and that his enemies were in power. Had the King known? Alba was sure he had. He turned from the station and drove across the frontier into France, and there he was to remain until after the passing of the King, practicing law in the French courts with success for some years. After the fall of the Dictator and the establishment of the Republic, he had returned and had cast his fortunes with the party of Lerroux; and on his accession to power, Alba was made president of the Cortes. He was a short, stockily built man with a mustache and goatee, with a finely shaped head, and eyes that revealed both intelligence and cunning. His enemies charged him with being unscrupulous and with having a grasping disposition, but more disinterested critics thought his greatest vice was his timidity. "Had he possessed moral and physical courage commensurate with his ability, he would have been a great man," they told me. At any rate, with Barrio gone, he was by odds the greatest figure now left in the party of Lerroux.

9

The Gil Robles coalition had been in power for fifteen months without a single constructive achievement to its credit. There was disgust among the monarchists, anger among the agrarians, resentment among the industrialists, and ill feeling between the leaders of the coalition. Rumors of an impending crisis were spreading in the cafés and hotel lobbies. The parties being unable to agree on policies, nothing was done. Embittered by the release of Azaña, his enemies were exerting their ingenuity in seeking some pretext for his arrest and ruin. Much was being said about arms smuggling some time before, but no one thought Azaña implicated in anything criminal or discreditable.

But to proceed against Azaña in the courts, the permission of the Cortes would be necessary; and that would mean giving Azaña an opportunity to defend himself from a tribunal where he was a master and where all could see and hear. Lerroux, wise in his generation, had no desire thus to play into Azaña's hands. It was said that the agrarians would vote with Lerroux against it.

At this time, Lerroux and Gil Robles had a two-hour conference. Some thought the reason was the political complications; others were sure it was because the nation's business was at a standstill. *El Debate* was complaining and insisting it might be necessary to choose between "efficiency and democracy," which meant, from it, between Fascism and democracy. El Debate *must have known at the time that arrangements had been made with Mussolini to give material aid to a rebellion in Spain.*

It is significant that at this time in the reassignment of high officers in the army, every vital and strategic spot was put under the command of a general hostile to the democratic regime. The army was already in possession of antidemocratic forces.

Still, all was not serene within the camp of the enemies—they could not agree on their objective.

10

"A truce to Spanish politics," said General Fuqua one February day, "I want you to drive with me to a fine medieval castle." He did not know the name of the castle but he knew where to find it. Soon we were speeding over a perfect highway, and when we reached a dirt road, branching off, Fuqua stopped and drew out his inevitable map. "Yes," he said, "this road will take us to the castle. Yonder are the mountains mentioned by the man who gave me directions, and there is the little stream." We turned from the perfect highway into the little dirt road, evidently abandoned years before, and we seemed to be jolting through a field. A cold, bitter wind descended from the snow-capped mountains and whipped us savagely in the face. Black clouds were scurrying across the sky, threatening a momentary deluge. The road became more impassable with each turning of the wheels, and it felt as though we were riding over the rocky bottom of a dried-up creek—and nowhere could we see the castle. After a long time, we emerged upon a perfect road—the very one we had left for this mad excursion—and there before us loomed the castle—which I had visited months before.

I had seen it one August day when lunching near by at a country house. It had been built in the sixteenth century as a residence and fortress combined. That afternoon we wandered alone through the romantic ruins associated with a romantic age when a nobleman who lived there, of the famous family of Mendoza, had kidnaped the lady of his choice and taken her beside him on his horse to the castle. The court of the castle was desolate indeed, filled with fallen blocks and rocks, but from the outside it seemed in a perfect state of preservation. We had found our way to the great ornate gallery, with its delicately carved balustrades and slender pillars, whence one could see for many miles over a lovely landscape.

I had occasionally heard the story of that castle, which illustrates one of the reasons for the social unrest in Spain. The owner, a grandee, with a vast fortune and high intelligence, had been urged to restore the castle and present it to the nation as a monument of sixteenth-century culture. The work began. But because the work was backbreaking, with the lifting and shifting of enormous stones, the workmen, receiving the merest pittance for their labor, asked for one or two pesetas more a day—less than a quarter. Enraged by the "extravagant notions" of the workers, the owner indignantly declared that he would not stand for such presumption from "communists," and so he abandoned the project. Several times I was told that story by charming women, who sat back at the conclusion with a light of triumph in their eyes, as much as to say: "What can you do with communists such as these?"

The court still was a junk heap of stones and rocks. The maintenance of the medieval status of the workers demanded that rather than pay a few cents more a day, this priceless monument of a romantic age should ultimately perish.

Chapter IX

The Right Coalition Cracks

O UTWARDLY there was a lull in political activity, and it would be a month before Azaña would defend himself against his maligners in the Cortes. Propaganda, however, was active, and systematically the story was put out that the country was in a state of disorder bordering on anarchy, and it was to satisfy myself as to the truth that in February, in the company of General Fuqua and Biddle Garrison, I drove south. Though a serious-minded soldier, Fuqua was always as gay and eager as a boy on these excursions, witty, jovial, adjustable. The professional habit of years had made him a slave of the map, and out it would come with every change of scenery, and along with it, from some mysterious hiding place, would appear a book with full information about every village we touched.

We stayed the night at Córdoba, watched the workmen in the old mosque, peered again into the fourteen patios of the palace of Viana with their richly laden orange trees and murmuring fountains, and drove on to Seville in time for lunch. To a remarkable degree, the old Moorish influence lingered in Seville, where there were rigid rules of propriety for women. Though famous for their charm and beauty, one seldom sees a beautiful woman of the upper strata on the street. They are restrained behind the curtained windows. The daughter of a diplomat told me an amazing story of her experience as the guest of a girl friend in Seville. Prepared, as she was, for strict chaperonage, she was astonished to find that her friend dare not enter the high-walled garden behind the house without a chaperon. Could not one flirt from the garden, shut in by high brick walls, with a person at the upper window of a neighboring house?

And so in Seville there were no cabarets where one could see Spanish or gypsy dancing because, I was told, the Sevillian would not take his wife or daughter to such places. We decided on a sentimental journey to Palos, whence Columbus sailed on his immortal voyage, and to La Rabida, the monastery where he pled for help. We were accompanied by Emily Wright, long the representative of the Congressional Library in the archives of the Indies. Knowing we would find no *parador* on this neglected road, we had a lunch prepared to take along. The good road stretched through a lonesome countryside into a section strangely ignored by the tourist. At length we came to Palos. This fishing village numbered but four hundred souls when Washington Irving saw it a century before, but today the population has increased six fold. I wished especially to see the little church of San Jorge de Palos, where Columbus attended mass, and whence his crew marched directly to his ships after mass that fifteenth-century morning. As we drove along, Miss Wright recalled her last visit to the little church and told me an illuminating story.

For centuries, the greatest treasure of San Jorge has been a small, beautifully wrought figure of the Virgin in ivory. Long years ago, some members of the parish reverently dressed the figure in a red velvet gown, concealing the beauty and artistry of the carving, since only the head remained uncovered. Each succeeding year added its layer of dust and dirt to the velvet gown, which began to fade. At length, not long before, a new priest appeared in the parish who had a sense of beauty and a reverence for it. The desecration of the Virgin with the filthy red gown distressed him, and his fingers itched to remove the covering, but he wondered if the simple fisherfolk, who loved it as they had always known it, would understand. Then one day when Miss Wright and some friends were visiting the church, he suddenly determined to remove the robe at once and suited the action to the thought. Just then a murmur at the open door revealed the presence of a large group of villagers in suspicious and ugly mood. Taking the precaution to notify the Civil Guard, the priest went to the door and explained that no treasure was being taken away, that the ugly gown of the Virgin had been removed because it concealed a fine work of art in which the parishioners should take pride. He then invited the peasants and fishermen to satisfy themselves that the figure still was there. They went away partly mollified, but disturbed and distressed.

I heard similar stories of the ardent devotion of peasants to works of art in the village churches. When, not so long ago, it was found that a fine old painting in a village church was seriously in need of a restoration, arrangements were made to remove it for the purpose to the Prado in Madrid. But when the strangers from the capital appeared, peasants with clubs and pitchforks met them, prepared to defend their picture with their lives. No reasoning or persuading could reconcile them to its removal, but they agreed to the retouching by an expert from Madrid in the village. A studio was improvised, and there the expert worked under the unblinking eyes of a vigilance committee, a peasant, a schoolteacher, and a village tradesman.

This was typically Spanish, and when, during the Fascist rebellion I was to hear that the peasants and workers were bent on selling their art works to other countries, I knew it to be a lie.

2

Palos seemed pathetic in its loneliness. The little church of San Jorge, seated between the sea and a hill, fully looked its age. It was cold, small, decaying, and lonesome. There was the little iron pulpit with its winding steps whence the King's messenger had read the authorization for the expedition to the Indies. Here the heroic crew for the last time heard mass before embarking on their immortal voyage. Sacred as the church should be to two rich continents, it is falling to ruin from neglect. We could not enter the little chapel where the Pinzóns were christened, since a large part of the ceiling had fallen, and the rest was loose. The hill behind the church, and pressing upon it, ultimately will push it over and destroy it. Only a small amount of money would be required to preserve the chapel of the Pinsons and to level the hill. The curate,

Cristóbal Escribane Olivia, a young priest with a pleasant, intelligent countenance, talked feelingly of the difficulty of getting money. Considering the enormous revenue of the hierarchy, I could not understand why nothing had been done.

3

Hence on to the monastery of La Rabida.

Pine trees were about it, though the great pine forest that Columbus knew had long since fallen before the artillery of the French. It is a low-lying monastery, unimpressive exteriorly but for its association. Only four monks kept vigil there, and, but for the tourists, the monastery would have been closed, as it had been when Irving visited it a century ago.

Arriving at noon, we asked a pleasant monk if we could eat our lunch there, and, with a warm smile, he led us into a small room where the five monks ate. He spread a clean cloth and brought us knives and forks, spoons and glasses, and all we could pay was for a bottle of wine. As we ate, with the kind monk hovering over us, I noticed a sudden smile of inspiration light his countenance as he went to a table by the wall where a small box sat and pressed a button. And thus it was that in the monastery in which Columbus pled his cause, and where Cortes rested from his labors, we sat in the presence of the smiling monk, listening to the strains of *Carmen* floating in to us from Seville. Never shall I forget that monastery, the lunch in the tiny room to the strains of *Carmen*, and the gracious monk who was so friendly in the charming Spanish way.

It was raining when we passed the ancient town of Niebla, which has perched upon its hill of rock since the Stone Age, and we merely drove through the gates into the plaza, paved with uneven cobblestones. The rain splashed fiercely upon the pavement. Here desertion brooded in the rain with no one visible—no one but a solitary beggar, who emerged suddenly from some doorway to solicit alms. It was uncanny. It was here that the tablets bearing precisely the same mysterious inscriptions as those unearthed in Guatemala were uncovered—proof positive, some think, of the existence of the lost Atlantis.

4

Resuming our journey, we lingered at Jerez, "the home of sherry," long enough for lunch and a visit to the wine sheds of the Gonzales. There we met the venerable head of the famous house, a real patriarch in his eighty-sixth year, handsome, virile, vigorous, bubbling with humor, keenly interested in contemporary life. I found him interesting as a political symbol. He confessed to sadness over the political conditions in Spain, and I saw his meaning. To test him, I asked if conditions were not better now that the Rightists were in. He shook his white head. "Property is still in danger," he said. It was the viewpoint of the leading families of Jerez, who are monarchistic, with a special partiality for the dictatorship of Primo de Rivera, whose statue is in the plaza.

The drive from Jerez to Cádiz is fascinating, with the great salt marshes and huge piles of salt glistening in the sun, with the canals to let in the salt water of the ocean. At intervals these canals are drained, and the remaining salt is shoveled into pyramids to be dried and cleaned.

We reached Cádiz in the early evening. With preparations made for the Easter Carnival, the Calle Anoche, the favorite evening *paseo*, was thronged from curb to curb. It is a long, narrow street with excellent shops. That evening we saw more pretty women than during days in Seville. The Moorish influence, once so strong, has faded.

Another night at the María Cristina in Algeciras, and then on to Málaga along an enchanting coast road, the hills on one side, the surging sea upon the other.

That night Málaga was lovely, the Collete Palace, where we stayed, crowded with gay men and women for the carnival, dance, and dinner. Though many were in costumes, masks were not allowed. The scene was colorful, and the dancing, dining, drinking lasted until dawn.

From Málaga we drove to the picturesque, charming fishing village of Torremolines, as yet unspoiled by tourists, old and typical of the region. High on a hill, many years ago the customs guards dwelt in small stone cottages, long since abandoned for that purpose. Years ago these passed into the possession of a Span-

iard, but with financial losses, the cottages were leased to an Englishman with the provision that the old Spaniard, now gone queer,
should live upon the hill. In time the daughter of the Englishman
married an American architect who loved the town so much that
he pitched his tent and stayed. The cottages are now part of the
hostelry of Santa Clara. From the shadowed lawn, one looks down
upon the sea and over the mountains. No vista could be more
beautiful—the indigo blue sea, the deep blue sky, the snow on the
mountain-tops, the white surge of the waters on the beach far below.
We sat on the hill that afternoon sipping wine and enjoying the
prospect.

On our way to Granada we lunched in a village in the mountains on ham and eggs. Though the restaurant had been highly
recommended, the approach was so unprepossessing and un-
appetizing, that we decided on ham and eggs as the least likely to be
tainted. But the tables in the dining room were spotless, and, as we
observed the sumptuous fare of our neighbors, we regretted our
caution. We reached Granada in the evening, and in the morning
we revisited the Alhambra, whence we looked down on the crowded
prison filled with political prisoners guilty of the crime of liberality
and democracy. That night we slept in the *parador* of Manzanares,
and we reached Madrid at noon.

We had seen nothing of disorder, but the foreign press was spreading
the Fascist propaganda that the nation was in the throes of anarchy.

5

Returning to Madrid, I immediately visited Lerroux. A characteristically stupid censorship had forbidden the United Press to
serve its Spanish clients with the story about a new military con-
scription in Germany, though the Fabre Agency, which is French,
was permitted to send the story out. Then, too, the young son of a
messenger who had served the embassy for years, had been arrested,
ostensibly for having a gun, but probably for thinking himself a
socialist. I was eager to know why the American press agency had
suffered this discrimination, and whether the incarceration of the
boy without a trial was to have no ending.

At the Presidencia that evening, Lerroux looked blooming. It was whispered that he was failing and looked droopy, but that evening he was dapper as a dandy, his handkerchief with blue edges peeking coquettishly out of his upper pocket, the Order of the Republic in his buttonhole, and he wore a blue striped shirt and a tie to match. His complexion was ruddy, healthy, youthful, and his keen, cunning brown eyes were sparkling. He was cordiality itself, and when I commented on his birthday, he spoke glowingly of the little dusty Andalusian village where he was born.

"But why the censorship on news from Germany?" he asked, clearly puzzled. I told him I shared his curiosity, and he promised to investigate and to receive the United Press representative on the morrow. He listened sympathetically to the story of the boy and he promised to take action—and he did. Again he impressed me with his age-old cunning, his mellowness, his political sagacity. Nothing in his carefree manner indicated the impending crisis that figured in the gossip. True, Gil Robles was insisting on the execution of González Pena, leader of the Asturian miners in the late troubles, and Alcalá Zamora, supported by Lerroux, was reported as opposing. Many predicted that the CEDA leader would withdraw his representatives from the Ministry and force a crisis, though no one knew exactly why. He and his party had thus far monopolized the fruits of the coalition victory, and the monarchists and agrarians had been left out.

Then, too, Lerroux was thought to be impatient with the insistence of his young co-leader on bringing Azaña to trial on a trumped-up charge. The old warrior, wise from many battles, preferred to let sleeping dogs lie, and it was said that Gil Robles saw the point but was unable to control his impulsive and impetuous followers. These demanded the trial of Azaña.

6

Two days later I drove through the rain to the Cortes for the debate on the trumped-up charges. The diplomatic gallery was packed. Salvador de Madariaga was there, keenly interested. A little before five the Chamber filled. Azaña entered, walking with quick, short steps, and found a seat immediately below us, with his own small party and a little group of Martínez Barrio's. The socialists were absent, not having returned since the censorship on debate was imposed. Azaña was surrounded by enemies who hated him.

An unimportant member of the CEDA presented the charges and maintained them poorly. Goicoechea, the monarchist leader, followed with little simpering gestures which Miguel Maura mimicked from his seat, to the amusement of the Chamber. A Carlist followed with a performance as poor. The attack was utterly unimpressive.

Azaña rose, and there was the usual hush that invariably paid tribute to the remarkable little man with the bald head. Every eye was turned to him and never shifted throughout his speech. Lerroux on the Blue Bench sat cupping his ear with his hand. Crouched in his aisle seat, Count Romanones sat in a similar attitude listening.

Azaña was in excellent voice and coldly calm, almost contemptuous, though he had his customary pallor. Soon he was in the full sweep of a brilliant speech. Referring to the charges, he read them, section by section, with ironic comments that wrung reluctant laughter from his foes. He spoke with vigor, occasionally with passion, and with an amazing rapidity of utterance. There was manifest disquiet on the faces of his enemies, though I thought the old parliamentarians, Lerroux and Romanones, admired him for the cleverness of his performance.

For Azaña's defense was a vigorous counterattack, with satire, sarcasm, irony, wit, and eloquence. Occasionally, when his fire became too hot, someone would interrupt, and Samper, now high up on the mountain behind the Blue Bench, lost his temper and blurted out a comment that Azaña caught and deftly tossed back to the amusement of even Samper's associates. Goicoechea occasionally interjected a remark which Azaña paused to get and then pulverized it in a sentence. When he had spoken two and half hours, and Gil Robles began to interrupt, there was no parliamentary expression on his face, and he was as ineffectual as the rest.

When the time allotted expired and Santiago Alba announced that Azaña could continue only with the consent of the Chamber, Gil Robles proposed that he be permitted to proceed after a recess, and Azaña announced that he would continue after dinner. Then an amazing thing happened—the Chamber, packed with his enemies, resounded with cheers. Madariaga beside me whispered: "A great speech."

When after dinner I arrived for the finish, the diplomatic gallery was all but deserted, though Madariaga was there again. Even the benches of the deputies were not filled. Lerroux and Romanones had gone to bed. When Azaña resumed, the effect of the punishment inflicted was manifest in the crudely offensive interruptions, accompanied by jeers. After another hour, Azaña finished. It was after midnight when I left.

While obscure members were talking, Azaña sat in his seat correcting the stenographic report of his speech. That night, I stopped at the office of the United Press and learned that the censor had forbidden the transmission of portions of the speech to the United States. All favorable comments on the speech had been blue-penciled by the censor. The next morning, the opposition papers abused the speaker—but suppressed the speech.

The conclusion of the debate the next afternoon was deadly dull. Azaña sat in his place listening as if bored. In the end, the vote was taken and a committee was agreed upon for drawing up the formal charges.

Two days before, Lerroux had told press correspondents that there was no evidence against Azaña and that nothing was involved but politics. He was disgusted.

7

One week later, the Lerroux government faced a crisis. The Supreme Court's having held that there were grounds for the commutation of the sentence of González Pena, the opinion was passed on to the Council of Ministers, and Gil Robles was threatening Lerroux with the resignation of the three CEDA ministers. The wily and experienced old fox in the Presidencia merely smiled. He knew his young ally wanted no dissolution and elections.

About this time, there was much merriment in a small circle over the irritating experience of the Nuncio, Monsignor Tedeschini, which shed light on the strategy and expectations of the CEDA. In reporting to the Vatican, it was Tedeschini's custom, on occasions, to report by telephone. One day, at his request, the line was cleared for one of his conversations. It was when Pita Romero, the

Foreign Minister, had been named to negotiate a concordat with
the Vatican. He was a devout Catholic, but, being a robust republican, he was suspected. The Nuncio asked for an official at the
Vatican. The military attaché of the Spanish Embassy in Rome
bore the same name, and the operator in Rome put the Nuncio in
communication with the embassy. The attaché was astonished to
hear the soft voice of the Nuncio pouring into his ears the secrets of
the strategy of the CEDA, but realizing the importance of the
revelations, he held his peace and carefully took notes. Toward the
close, he found the revelations piquant. The Nuncio was discussing
the early arrival in Rome of Romero and was advising that he be
treated with the greatest suavity and respect, but should not be
permitted to consummate his mission. He was to be nursed along,
encouraged, delayed some weeks or months, until the CEDA, in
full power, would be complete master. When the Spanish Ambassador was informed, he, in turn, informed Pita Romero, who was
still Foreign Minister in Madrid. When, a little later, the Minister
met the Nuncio and smilingly observed that he understood the
latter had recently enjoyed a conversation with Rome, Tedeschini,
in his most ingratiating tone, replied that he had been glad to
prepare the way for the young envoy's reception through a personal
conversation rather than through the more stilted form of correspondence. Tedeschini beamed on Pita Romero, who smiled
sweetly on the Nuncio.

8

Meanwhile, as the conferences of the ministers continued, *El
Debate* created a mild sensation with an editorial opinion that
there could be no justification for a crisis over the death penalty for
González Pena and twenty others. This, interpreted the gossips,
was clearly the voice of Ángel Herrera, the patron and sponsor of
Gil Robles. Many wondered if Herrera, the master, was breaking
with Gil Robles, the man.

But when the Council of Ministers convened to make a decision,
the mystery deepened, since the three CEDA ministers and the
agrarians voted for the execution of the twenty-one men. Lerroux
and the others voted for commutation and won.

Lerroux thereupon hurried to the palace with his resignation, and Alcalá Zamora entrusted him with the forming of a new government. The schism on the death penalty seemed complete.

And again one heard, "quite confidentially," from many quarters, of a military *coup d'état* in preparation.

After two days of vain endeavor to persuade the CEDA and the agrarians to co-operate, Lerroux reported his failure, and Martínez Velasco, leader of the agrarians, was invited to try his hand. But he was to find Gil Robles as uncompromising as Lerroux had found him. The CEDA leader had demanded six places, including the Ministry of War, for which, significantly enough, he had a constant yearning.

Thus, in the end, Lerroux again was summoned and he responded with a government composed entirely of members of his own party and technicians. A general became Minister of War; an admiral, Minister of Marine; and the governor of the Bank of Spain, Minister of Finance. In expert knowledge in vital posts it was a Ministry of respectability, but its political domination was impossible, and it dared not submit itself to a hostile Chamber.

So Alcalá Zamora recessed the Cortes for thirty days. The purpose was transparent. A desperate effort was being made by Alcalá Zamora and the Rightist leaders to prevent the necessity for elections. It was hoped that in thirty days the leaders of the parties of the Right might reconcile their differences and agree upon a government that could carry on without an electoral test of public sentiment. But it seemed that the Rightist coalition was navigating in a stream that had more rocks than water.

9

Fernando de los Ríos came to see me on the evening of the day of the stopgap government, in high good humor over the political outlook, but realistic and reasonable. He thought the attempt of the Rightist coalitionists doomed to failure, and that in May there would be a dissolution of the Cortes and elections. The tragedy of Lerroux, he thought, was in his hesitation and vacillation, and in his belated realization that he had been whittling the Republic away. He was sure Lerroux had lost sight of the central theme of the Republic, else he never would have consented to the violation of parts of the Constitution.

"But the elections," I said, "how will they go?"

"The Lefts will win easily," he replied.

To get an amplification of his views, I told him that was not the opinion of the people with whom I had talked.

"Naturally," he replied. "In a diplomatic post you are thrown mostly into the company of financiers, industrialists, the aristocracy and its toadies and parasites. I am thinking of what the people are thinking and saying. We know that in all the small towns and villages the people are bitter against the reactionary government they are getting. We know, since we have taken a perfect poll. The incredible savagery of the Moors and the Foreign Legion in the Asturias has been suppressed by the press censors and even in the Cortes, but in every village the people have the complete story, which has reached them by word of mouth and in pamphlets distributed by hand."

I was to remember that conversation ten months later when the elections came.

The Right coalition had lost the confidence of the people, and the leaders were suspecting each other, and saying so.

But for thirty days at least, nothing would happen publicly while a temporary truce was being worked out behind closed doors, and we made plans to visit Seville during Holy Week. The impression had been created outside Spain that the church was being persecuted, and while a case could be made against the suppression of parochial schools, I had seen no interference with religious worship. The treasures were still in the churches under lock and key, with the keys in possession of the clergy. But I thought the real test would come when religious ceremonies were held in the streets, as in Seville. I would go and see.

Chapter X

Holy Week in Seville, 1935

THE skies were a fleckless blue, the distant mountains beautiful in their purple haze, and the air was balmy as we rolled over the fine roads of Andalusia to Seville. When we reached Córdoba in the evening, the air was sweet with the fragrance of blossoming flowers. That the fiesta would be more brilliant than usual was evident when we found the Hotel Regina so crowded with guests on their way that we had to take rooms on the ground floor just off the lobby, which buzzed with talk and laughter far into the night. Again the famous images of the churches were to be taken into the streets to be shown to the people, and it seemed that all of Spain was on the highway.

On the way from Córdoba, we passed a picturesque procession. From a distance, it resembled an approaching cavalry spreading entirely across the road, but as we got nearer, the horsemen drew off, single file on one side. And then, at the head of the procession we saw strapped on the back of a sturdy mule the casket. Behind it rode twenty or thirty men on mules and horses, and, as the mourners passed, they smiled and gaily shouted greetings.

Such was our introduction to Holy Week in Seville.

We found that romantic city overcrowded. The huge Andalusian Palace Hotel, closed since the flight of the King, was reopened for the occasion, but long before the beginning of the week all hotel accommodations had been exhausted, and some of the hardier spirits were content to sleep on mattresses in bathtubs.

Never had Seville seemed softer, sweeter, more fragrant, or feminine. The streets were packed with men and women in holiday mood, and the lobbies of the hotels swarmed. The city hummed and sang—sang, literally, for almost always one could hear from afar the plaintive chanting of *flamenco* singers. Happily, we took possession of the ambassador's quarters in the beautiful consulate set back in a garden, with a high iron picket fence and a locked gate to guarantee against invasion; with its tiled patio, murmurous with the playing of the fountain designed by Gertrude Vanderbilt Whitney. There it was possible to sleep at night.

2

The processions began to move on Monday and continued until Friday, reaching a climax of the picturesque on Thursday. Every parish church has its cherished image, its favorite Virgin, its figures of the crucifixion, its march to Calvary. The figures are exquisitely beautiful in themselves, but they are garbed in the richest of rich robes, with gold embroidery, and some shimmer with precious stones. They are carried on *paseos*, much like floats, and many are of silver and most are covered with a gorgeous and costly canopy. These are the property of the brotherhoods of the various churches, and whenever they are taken into the street, they are accompanied by members of the brotherhoods, their identity concealed by hoods. Among the anonymous marchers always there are some men of distinction and from all classes. This year Juan Belmonte marched unnoticed beneath his concealing hood, though the multitude adored him. Once a year, these figures are carried from their churches along the entire line of march to the cathedral, and into the church, and before the huge altar; and then, out again and back to their parish home. Thousands gather before the parish churches to see the emergence of the images into the sunlight and to greet them with acclamations of affection.

Nothing could realize one's concept of beauty more completely than these *paseos* with their burdens. The image alone is a work of art; the richness of the embroidered and jeweled robes beggars description; the silver floats, with elaborate candelabra in the rear, and with the front flickering and flaming with scores of huge lighted candles by night, delight the eye.

And so the procession moves. The burdens borne are of enormous weight, and human shoulders bear the burden, though the bearers are concealed from view by the draperies of the *paseos*. At intervals, the bearers are forced to set their burdens down to rest, and often, in these intervals, they refresh themselves with wine. This method of conveyance is traditional, and the suggestion that motorcars be substituted for human labor is covered with derision. Because of the great strength required, the burden bearers are recruited mostly from among the workers on the wharfs, and many of these are syndicalists, enemies of the church. Religion, borne on backs of unbelievers!

Often a band precedes or follows. In front, the hooded members of the brotherhoods sweep along. Behind, trudge the penitents in black, in bare feet, bearing their heavy black crosses. Now and then one cuts his foot on glass. He wraps a cloth around it and trudges on. On balconies along the line of march, men, and sometimes women, emerge to sing to the passing images.

3

Our first view of the procession was from the balcony of the Anglo-South American Bank, the marchers moving from the narrow and historic Sierpe, now a thoroughfare of fashionable shops and clubs. First we see a great number of huge flaming candles on the *paseo* in front of the image. The music of bands—the thrilling cadence of *flamenco* singers—the movement of white- and black-robed men—the penitents with their crosses—a masterpiece in color, a pageant rich in drama, all redolent of medieval and mystic times. The next night we occupied our box in the reviewing stand. But preferring to mingle with the people in the street, we paced the narrow Sierpe the following afternoon. This ancient passage, from which vehicles are excluded, was lined with chairs for rent at ridiculously low prices, but we had been warned of the danger of being trampled by horses or crushed by the surging crowd. The procession had not yet appeared. From building to building humanity was packed. We stood at an intersection, near the site of the old prison of Cervantes' incarceration, where he wrote the greater part of *Don Quixote*, and we felt the spell. The rare genius of Cervantes cast a halo on the scene.

And then—a restless movement of the crowd, which began to draw back against the buildings, or to form groups at the intersections. Far down the street could be seen the head of the procession, and, as it moved along, there was an excited clatter of tongues, gasps of admiration, some pushing and shoving for position. Tiring of the spectacle, many withdrew into the intersecting streets to sit at tables in the open and sip wine. And then, an intaking of breath at the beauty of an approaching *paseo* sounded like a gust of wind, and the tables were deserted. Beggars finished the wine. The *paseo* stopped to rest the bearers directly in front of us. At tables at the open window of a café on the second floor across the street, we saw men lunching. As the image was set down, we saw one of the party push back his chair and emerge through the window upon a balcony, holding his napkin in his hand. He threw back his head, extended his hands toward the Virgin, and, in *flamenco*, sang to her. In the great crowd there was utter silence. One could hear his neighbor breathing. When at the close, the singer backed off the balcony and resumed his place at the café table, the Sierpe and the intersecting streets rang with applause. The bearers of the *paseo* took up their burden, and the procession moved slowly toward the cathedral. From far down the street we could hear others singing to the images.

<h2 style="text-align:center">4</h2>

Thursday was to be the great day. The favorite figure of the masses was to be taken on its leisurely march. At one o'clock in the morning the Macarena would emerge from the little church of San Gil in Triana, surrounded by her guard of Roman soldiers. So after lunch, we drove to Triana to see the Macarena in her home. For centuries Triana has been the home of men who go out upon the sea in ships, and, more recently, of gypsies. It was there that Rodrigo was to join Columbus and to be the first to sight the New World. But few know about Rodrigo today, while everyone knows about Juan Belmonte, who was born in Triana. It was from this ancient town that he, as a boy, was wont to steal forth to swim the river to reach the pasture of the bulls to try his prowess. Perhaps it is because so many bullfighters come from there that the Macarena is known as "the Virgin of the matadors."

We made our way through a labyrinth of narrow streets to the front of the little parish church with its Romanesque entrance. Crowds were going in and out. There was nothing remarkable about the church itself, though, no doubt, it has its history, its romances and tragedies. But there we saw the Macarena close at hand.

It stood on its *paseo*, a shining silver platform with heavy silver poles at the four corners supporting the canopy. It is easy to accept the popular opinion that among all the images seen in the streets during Holy Week, she is the most beautiful. She stands, leaning slightly forward, one hand on her breast, the other held downward in a gesture of supplication. The face is beautiful and ineffably sweet, and the teardrops on her cheeks are pearls. On her head rests a large golden ornament, and her robes are of gorgeous green, heavily embroidered with gold, and sparkling with jewels. Humble folk stand looking at her reverently, and the simple people of the parish keenly observe the stranger to catch his expression of admiration. Then they smile.

The head of the brotherhood came to act as my guide. Having heard that on his death, Joselito, the brilliant matador, once rival of Belmonte, had bequeathed a ring to the Macarena, I asked for the story. I was told that it was the custom of Joselito to give a ring to the Virgin each year, and that the silver candelabra in the rear of the *paseo* was his gift. Into the red robe spread out over the back of the *paseo*, a small portion of the cape of the great matador had been woven.

5

Fortunate the spectator invited as we were to view the procession from a balcony on the Sierpe, for here one gets the full emotional effect and color of Holy Week. Thence we looked down upon a mass of humanity, seated in chairs on the pavement or pressed against the buildings, through which slowly moved the images and marchers. From a balcony apartment across the narrow street, a pretty woman with coal-black hair and lustrous eyes, and with a red rose in her hair, smiled upon us. She personified Seville. Between the passing of the *paseos*, the guests in her apartment made merry at the table with wine and food, but when a *paseo* approached, they rushed to the window again. Up from the crowd came murmurs of admiration, from an adjoining balcony a *flamenco* singer poured forth a tremulous, chanting song, and when the cheers died down we could hear others singing far down the street. Here in the Sierpe was the soul of Holy Week—the mass of humanity, the balconies with their tapestries, the murmurs and exclamations of the people, the moving, melancholy chanting of the singers. On moved the procession, the marchers concealed beneath their hoods and cloaks, the penitents trudging painfully in bare feet under their heavy cross.

Then suddenly came an expectant surging of the crowd, and from far up the street came lusty, gusty cheering that registered nothing of religious emotion, but in its militant, exultant tone suggested something more earthy. The mystery soon was solved. On prancing horses, mounted members of the Guardia Civile came clattering along, receiving the homage of the crowd. And then the enthusiasm reached hysteria. Behind the mounted men marched the young orphans of this famous military organization, small boys in the uniforms of the Guards, superbly military in their bearing, marching with a gusto and precision that would have done credit to the Old Guard of Napoleon, their eyes fixed straight ahead, heads up and never once diverted by the curiosity of the crowd. A woman reached over and affectionately patted one of the small boys on the cheek. He marched on with supercilious indifference, his expression as immobile as that of a marble bust, without a glance at his admirer.

But all the while one is tempted to smile at the ironical situation, with many nonreligious workers from the wharfs bearing the priceless images. To most of these, it was merely another job with good pay. But armed soldiers marched in front and beside the richest of the *paseos*, and it was said that beneath each *paseo*, with the bearers of the burden, were one or two of the brotherhoods, ready to give the alarm should any disposition to damage the image be observed.

6

This procession ended at ten o'clock; at midnight, the other for which we were waiting would begin. At one o'clock in the morning, the Macarena would emerge from its little church, and we proposed to witness the emergence. The streets in the vicinity of San Gil are narrow, and we parked our car some distance off and went on foot, fighting our way through the dense crowd toward the church door, but a block away we had to take our stand. Backed against the building, we surveyed the scene. All the balconies were jammed, and not a few had mounted to the roofs and held their precarious position merrily. There we stood, jostled by the amiable crowd.

Then a nervous tremor of the crowd, a gasp from many hundreds, a glare up the narrow street toward the church, and we knew the Macarena had just emerged into the night. And then the clatter of horses' hoofs upon the pavement—the procession of the Macarena was approaching. We pressed back tightly against the wall to escape the trampling of the horses. And then the horsemen appeared—passed. And just behind, in a great glare of candle-light from innumerable large candles flaming red, came the Macarena—the beautiful, tender face of the Virgin, with pearls for tears, to look upon her people. And all about her the glitter of the silver armor and helmets of the Roman soldiers who are her invariable companions and protectors when she ventures into the street. The scene was entrancing, memorable, thus seen in Triana in the night, in the narrow street through which so much history has passed.

7

On the reviewing stand of the Aéreo Club we sat for four hours watching the mystic glow of candles bobbing up and down the street. Here we were in the midst of the fiesta, a social scene, with friends chatting, laughing, commenting on the procession—all waiting for the Macarena, slowly working its way toward the cathedral. From an upper balcony of the club a man and woman sang *flamenco* songs to the holy images as they passed. The night was cold, but waiters circulated constantly, serving cognac.

A great rumble far off heralded the approach of the Macarena. It was six o'clock, and a gray dawn had come. A gasp of admiration swept through the stand, and there, immediately before us, rested the favorite image of Seville. Stiff and cold, we rose on the passing of the Macarena and drove to a roadhouse near the city for hot drinks, and then, at seven-thirty, to bed.

So the Macarena finished her pilgrimage to the cathedral in Holy Week in 1935.

8

Friday night saw the last of the processions. The purely religious phase would end with the ceremony in the cathedral on Sunday morning, and the thoughts of the people now turned to the bull-fight for Sunday afternoon, which, for generations, has been the gala occasion of the week.

On Saturday afternoon, Juan Belmonte invited his friends to his near-by ranch for the testing of the year-old bulls. Hundreds of people were clinging to the fence of the great enclosure when we drove into the field and parked our car among the others in the center. Three antique farm wagons had been drawn together and converted into a platform for the ladies. A number of horsemen were riding about, and as we approached the center, one of these, a short man with legs a little bowed, and with the protruding chin of the Hapsburgs, sprang from his horse to bid us welcome with the luminous smile that has thrilled millions in the arena of blood and sand. It was the great Belmonte.

The purpose of the testing of the bulls is to determine from their reactions which possess the fighting spirit and which do not. Those that give promise are given special care for another year, when there is another testing and further eliminations.

Suddenly the shouting of men and the beating of hoofs on the hard, dry ground draw our attention far across the field, where a single young bull has been admitted. Horsemen are riding beside it, behind it, and in front, exciting it, seeking to arouse its anger. The riders carry long poles, and, in making sharp turns, they lean over and, catching the bull off balance, topple it over with a push. Now comes the test. Does the bull lose confidence and fighting spirit and slink away? It is marked for elimination. Does it rise and charge at the horses with increased fury? It qualifies thus far.

And now a padded horse is introduced into the drama. Will the young bull charge the horse? He charges, and charges again, and then he makes for an unpadded horse, whose rider puts spur to escape the young horns.

That day two gallant young bulls charged with such violence

that they snapped their spinal cords and fell in their tracks. This was the sensation of the afternoon. The death of the bulls meant a monetary loss to Belmonte, since it is illegal to sell bulls, thus killed, for meat, the law having been designed to encourage all possible precautions against casualties. I was told that it was most unusual for so many bulls to be killed in the testing. But that year there had been a long drought, leaving the animals comparatively weak, and, together with the cement hardness of the baked ground, this accounted for the disasters of the afternoon.

After the testing we all repaired to a huge barnlike structure for refreshments. The guests crowding the large room were representative of the nobility, the aristocracy, the intelligentsia, with women outnumbering the men. A long table all but sagged beneath the weight of food—sea food of all sorts, chicken, ham, sausages, cheese, olives, pickles, cakes—and there was wine enough for an army. Everyone crowded about the table, serving themselves, and then backed off to stand in groups and chat about the proceedings of the afternoon. Belmonte, wearing his eyeglasses, his chin stuck out, his eyes sparkling, enjoyed the role of host. When I introduced Ruth Chatterton, and she apologized for appearing without an invitation, he bowed with the courtliness of a courtier, smiled his broadest, and replied: "Madame, a lady with your beauty needs no invitation anywhere." After the feasting, came gypsy dancing and *flamenco* singing.

9

Thus, gradually, we were approaching the bullfight of Sunday afternoon. We had seen the testing of the young bulls, and that night we went a short distance from Seville to witness "the boxing of the bulls" that were destined for the fight on the morrow. In a field was a platform that looked down on the drama of the deception of the bulls. From this point of vantage we could see the play of Judas, with steers in the title role. For some reason, the bulls have confidence in the steers. Looking down, we saw a wicked drama. A door opened, a steer entered, followed by an unsuspecting bull, and just as the steer passed through the second door into another room, the door was slammed in the face of the bull, which found itself shut off. Clearly mystified, the bull turned around, only to find that the door through which he had followed the steer was closed. He stood for a moment undecided, and then, noting a third door on the side, he charged with a great noise through it and found himself on the truck that was to convey him to his death in the arena. None of the bulls that day seemed in the least ferocious; none sought, as might be thought, to butt their way to freedom. They seemed quite helpless and pitiful to me—these bulls for the gala fight.

And indeed the fight was memorable because so wretched, and I am sure the great throng that sat in the sunshine that Sunday suffered boredom through the inadequacy of the performance. In other days, the management had mobilized the greatest of the matadors along with the best of the fighting bulls, but human greed had intervened, and the management was more interested in profits than in presenting a great performance. None of the matadors was of consequence except Palma, who was no longer young, and the bulls were the cheapest that could be bought.

10

My impressions of Holy Week in the fourth year of the Republic were varied. Nowhere may one see a more colorful spectacle. The animation of the gay throngs in the streets, the balconies hung with red damask and tapestries, the processions flaming with great candles, the mystic aspect, the mystery of the robed marchers, the strange mingling of the sacred and profane, the pretty women with mantillas and high combs, combined to make a spectacle of unforgettable beauty. In other times, far back, there was a more reverential attitude of the crowd, I am told, and men and women dropped more easily to their knees when the images went by. The religious phase was then predominant, but now one gets the feeling of being a spectator at a magnificent pageant, a splendid artistic drama, with thousands of actors on a huge stage. Against the background of the interesting old houses in the narrow streets, the effect is thrilling, but only in the cathedral does one get a reverential reaction now, only there does the profound religious significance of the festival stand out.

However, there was not one irreligious gesture throughout the week; and, mingling with the crowds, I did not hear one cynical or

disrespectful expression, and if any special military or police precaution had been taken, it was nowhere visible.

On the whole, Holy Week in Seville is a *feria*, a festival, a
brilliant social function, and thousands flock there as to the Derby
in England for amusement and the show. No doubt some of the
devout went on a religious pilgrimage, but between the processions
the hotels were packed with merry parties eating and drinking, and
the lobbies rang with laughter. The wineshops of the poor were
also crowded, but there was little drunkenness, and this confined to
foreigners. No one could have mingled with the people in the
streets without a realization of innate courtesy and kindliness of the
Spanish people.

At Córdoba, on our return, we found no hotel accommodations,
so we drove on to the familiar *parador* at Bailén, and there we stayed
the night.

Meanwhile, in Madrid, politics were seething.

Chapter XI

Straws in the Wind

FOR generations the members of the Spanish nobility had shirked the duties and responsibilities of public life. They made a virtue of their indifference to political affairs, so unlike the English, and in consequence they were politically inept and ignorant, and when the King's dark days came, there were few among them capable of service to the Crown. But there were two exceptions. The most notable was Count Romanones, the wisest, cleverest, most experienced of them all. The other was the Duke of Alba, who had offered his services and acted as Minister of State and of Education, and who was to be Franco's "Ambassador" in London during the Spanish war. The fortunes of his house go back to the days when the famous Duke of Alba led his armies a bit ruthlessly over the fields of Flanders, and the late duke is reputed to have been one of the richest men in Spain, and certainly one of the greatest landowners. His palace in Madrid, with its priceless treasures in art and history, was the most famous in the capital, and that in Seville one of the most magnificent in Spain. He was a man of culture and he had interested himself advantageously in the encouragement of art and letters with his money.

I met him the first time in his palace of Liria, in the heart of the old section, not far from the royal palace. I had gone to ask his assistance in identifying some of the personalities and places in the Spain of the days of Washington Irving. He was in close touch with the scholars, was head of the Academy of History, and the social and political story of the country could have been written from his archives. The palace of Liria stood in large grounds, shut in from the sordid ugliness around. His office opened upon the spacious entrance hall in which could be seen the sedan chair in which the celebrated duchess of the days of Goya was carried on her calls.

The duke was of average height, slender, but of athletic build, with a bronze complexion, a lean face, black hair, a mustache which was a mere streak above the lip, and with a strong nose and keen and intelligent eyes. A beautiful yellow dog stood watching him intently as he talked, and whenever its master glanced its way, it sprang forward eagerly for a stroke. A little girl of six or seven was presented and gravely took the introduction, though plainly bored. Being the only child, she would become Duchess of Alba in her own right unless her father remarried and had a son.

He talked with animation and much humor. That day we talked history, and politics were not mentioned. He made a note of everything I wished to know, and in each instance mentioned the expert at his disposal who would be able to furnish the information. On a matter touching on the church he said: "My monk will get that"—referring to a monk in the Escorial, a brilliant scholar.

A few days later he came to my house with the replies to my questions all typed out. This time, under my probing, he was not so chary about politics. When I asked if he expected any trouble, he replied in the negative, but added that no one could tell, since Wellington was right when he said that Spain is the only country where two and two do not necessarily mean four. When I asked if General Goded, an ambitious and unscrupulous soldier, thought to favor a military dictatorship, had really been made Chief of Staff by Gil Robles, as I had heard, I was impressed with his reply. "Has he been appointed *yet?*" he asked. Taking note of the word "yet," I knew Alba had heard such an appointment possible. But when I asked whom he thought the best officer in the army, he said it was General Franco, whom he described as a "brilliant strategist." Like all the great landowners, he was bitterly opposed to land reform.

Later, I was shown through the palace of Liria, a veritable gallery of art, an archive, and museum of history, with paintings of the old masters, relics of the great duke, Zuloaga's striking portrait of the late duchess in a red gown, impressive salons. I was shown the apartment in which the Empress Eugénie, the duke's aunt, died. Her physicians had denied her a certain food of which she was fond, and when the duke left for London, the servants were instructed that under no circumstances was it to be served. But taking advantage of the absence of her host, and the inability of the servants to deny the imperative demands of an empress, she disobeyed the doctor's orders and died in consequence—or so runs the story.

This was the treasure house the bombs of Italian aviators destroyed in the Fascist rebellion.

2

Because of the general uneasiness systematically fostered by dark forces, some fears of trouble on May Day were entertained, but throughout the whole of Spain that day there was perfect peace, without an incident. It was a beautiful day, sweet with the fragrance of spring, and we sat in the garden as the workers swept by on the Castellana.

Two days later, Lerroux' government resigned, but it was perfectly understood that during the month of secret conferences the leaders of the parties of the coalition had accommodated their differences and agreed upon the personnel of the new government.

With the announcement of the new Ministry, the enemies of the democratic regime entered into full power.

Gil Robles received the six portfolios he sought, including the War Ministry for himself. Among the foes of the regime there was open jubilation over the expected shifting of monarchistic or Fascist-minded generals to the strategic positions, and the relegation of the more robust republican generals to inferior posts. So assured were his own people of this purpose that they proposed to induct Gil Robles into office with a demonstration, which he wisely frowned upon. However, in taking office, he made the significant statement that *the future of Spain was in the hands of the army.*

For the increasingly important portfolio of Finance, Sr. Chap‐
prieta, of the Bank of Spain, was chosen. He was a member of th
Cortes, though not a professional politician, and soon he was t
shock his Rightist colleagues with a realistic attitude toward gov
ernmental sinecures and taxes.

*With this new government of Lerroux' the history of the Republic en‐
tered upon a new phase which boded no good to democracy or reform.*

Alcalá Zamora, having held out against the inclusion of Gil
Robles' party in the government until it appeared before the
electorate as a republican party, had surrendered. The night after
the new government was announced, I met the President at a
dinner at the German Embassy, where he was so lively that a col‐
league suggested he felt the humiliation so keenly that he simu‐
lated joy to conceal his grief. His enmity toward Gil Robles had
interested me. He was an ardent Catholic, almost superstitious in
his religion, and it seemed surprising that he so heartily disliked
the young leader of the party dedicated wholly to the political
interests of the church. The dislike was mutual. It must have
rested more on personal than on political grounds, and on per‐
sonal grounds there was a simple explanation in human nature.
Alcalá Zamora was exceedingly vain, and Gil Robles was no
shrinking violet. The President thought that his age, experience,
and position entitled him to the deference of the younger man. He
had been a prominent figure in public life when the younger man
was a boy. But the rapid rise of Gil Robles had had the inevitable
effect on his equilibrium and perspective, and he carried himself
as though conscious of his superiority. He did not consult with
Alcalá Zamora; he met him to lay down the law—and that was
the speciality of the President. They were destined to clash.

Thus, when Gil Robles entered the War Office, Alcalá Zamora
suffered an eclipse—but he did not know it. At the dinner I gave
him at this time, he was in exuberant spirits and he showed no
signs of worry. After dinner he sat until midnight in the ballroom
chatting pleasantly and in the best of humor.

More interesting to me at that dinner was General Batet, the
officer who so vigorously suppressed the separatist insurrection in
Barcelona. He looked every inch the soldier. His round face was
bronzed, his features strong, his eyes implied the habit of com‐

a-
e
o

ium height and compactly built, he wore his uni-
odel. That night he spent much of his time in the
tudying the pictures. In a little more than a year he
ot on the orders of fellow officers because of his refusal
is oath of allegiance to the constitutional regime, given
or of a soldier.

3

at July and August of 1935 we spent mostly in Madrid.
igh those burning months all was politically tranquil on the
ce. Gil Robles had summoned to his side as Chief of Staff the
eral Franco that everyone implied might lead a military *coup
at*. Whatever plans and changes were being made behind the
es in the old palace of Buena Vista were guarded from pub-
city. Some strange movements and shifting of troops were noted
by General Fuqua, my military attaché, and high officers were
being changed about, but little was said about it, and few knew of
the understanding with Hitler and Mussolini. *But there were reasons
to believe that the government was less interested in political, social, and
economic problems than in military matters.*

4

This was evident in July, when the Cortes was called upon to
act on the recommendation of its packed committee that Azaña
should be dragged before the courts on a trumped-up charge. There
was not a scintilla of evidence to sustain it, and Lerroux had said
as much. Roya Villanueva, agrarian member of the government,
had declared in the Cortes that since there was no evidence
against Azaña, the charges should be dropped. It was generally
believed that Gil Robles shared this view but dared not affront his
own extremists by so admitting.

The Chamber that afternoon was not filled, and I noted an
abnormal number of absentees among the party of Lerroux, and it
was said that he had inspired their absence to prevent the polling
of enough votes for action. I saw Gil Robles on the Blue Bench the
first time that afternoon. Lerroux was there, looking like a statue
of placidity. Villanueva, with his white beard and colored glasses,

sat on the Blue Bench with folded arms, looking ineffably bored. Roca, Minister of State, noticing my daughter, Patricia, in the gallery, sent up a box of chocolates. Only one speech stood out— that of Augusto Barcia, leader of the Azaña party, who demanded action. A man of good appearance and much culture, with a handsome and keenly intelligent face, he spoke with vigor and with some distinction. Now and then Lerroux interrupted perfunctorily.

Then came the vote, and the announcement was made that the charges against Azaña were dropped. That travesty was over.

5

July and August in Madrid were bearable. The evenings were cool in the garden when the wind came down from the mountains, and in the late afternoon there was tea to be had at the two country clubs and, better still, at the Fuente de la Reina, located on a hill near town. For many years the hilltop had been the property of the King, and members of the Court in other times were wont to spread their picnic lunches there. Some years before, the King gave the property to a favorite servant, who opened a restaurant and served lunches and dinners. In the winter the guests would gather about the fireplace in a cosy corner; in the summer, when it was most in fashion, the tables were placed outdoors under the trees, from which were strung electric lights for dinners. But to me, it was most charming in the late afternoon when gracious breezes fanned the trees, when sounds of pastoral life came up from the deep valley, and many miles of country were spread out in all directions. I often watched a shepherd far below who almost always sat propped up against a tree, his eyes on a book, as the sheep grazed about him. But it was at night when the hilltop was merriest, for the dinners served were excellent, the wines were of the best, and the tables were crowded. I have felt the chill of the breeze on that hill near Madrid in early August.

6

And that August when Patricia and I drove to Hendaye to meet one of her college friends, I saw, at greater leisure than before, the Burgos that was to be Franco's capital during the rebellion. The weather was ideal. Peasants were busy threshing in the fields, working in the primitive manner. In the yellow fields were many threshers with donkeys, mules, and oxen. Young girls, scarcely more than children, rode on the drags that were patiently drawn over the wheat to extract the kernel. Though we saw many threshing scenes that day, only once did we note the use of modern machinery. Oxen appeared favored as beasts of burden and they made their rounds with patience and toleration, as blasé veterans of the threshing field.

But that which impressed me most was the town itself, since it has a personality. For centuries its citizens of property have been unswerving in their fidelity to church and King, the town dominated in its higher strata by the philosophy and ideals of the sixteenth century. The smoke of factories does not dull the greenery of its gardens, for it is in the center of a purely agricultural country. Nowhere, I think, is the conservative element more devoted to the aristocratic or reactionary concept of the social structure. And its special glory is the cathedral.

It was on this journey in the fall of 1935 that I first saw the cathedral illuminated in the night. The effect is that of magic, the picture memorable and entrancing. Great searchlights on the tops of surrounding buildings played on the magnificent structure from the ground to the highest peak and brought out, with a vividness impossible in the sunlight, the minute details of the delicate carving of the sculptors. Against the background of the sky, this flaming thing of beauty seemed scarcely real, the illuminated spires rising toward the sky like sheets of white fire touched by the genius of an artist. It seemed to me that nothing could symbolize so perfectly the spirit of the ancient city.

But it had its rebels. One Sunday morning I went out for a walk when everyone in town seemed afoot, going to or returning from church. There was a delightful serenity in the narrow streets. I paused on one side of the church of San Lorenzo, with its huge coat of arms, and in front of the fish market, crowded with housewives on the morning marketing. Women alone presided at the counters, and great was the gesticulation and chatter of the women bargaining bitterly. One ancient crone emerged in high dudgeon, to be followed in hot pursuit by one of the women butchers, her eyes flashing indignation and disgust. The argument was continued, with much shaking of heads and hands, and, in the end, the old woman evidently won, for she turned with a triumphant swagger and followed the fish vender back into the shop.

I sat one sunny morning at the open window of my hotel looking out on the Calle de Lain Carvo, and the four-story buildings with the little iron balconies and sun porches of the living apartments. It was between nine and ten. Now and then, a woman, drawing her dressing gown about her breast, stepped out on the balcony to survey the street and catch a glimpse of an acquaintance. She stood in lazy contemplation for a moment and then returned to her breakfast or her work . . . A cart, drawn by mules and laden with small bells, went tinkling by . . . A soldier in smart uniform went swaggering down the street . . . Women sauntered by with black veils over their heads on their way to church, full-breasted women with ample hips . . . Soon children were swarming in the street, and at the windows of the apartments women were sitting knitting . . . From the doorway across from the hotel a woman appeared with two children, one tiny and cute but solemn as a philosopher, and, noticing the woman cross herself, I wondered if it was for protection against the evil eye at my window . . . In one of the windows a bird was singing rapturously in its cage.

And then it was marketing time, and women passed with bags and baskets and with bundles in their arms . . . Just across the street at an open window a woman was hanging clothes upon the line to dry . . . And such are the simple scenes I associate with Burgos.

Of course, Burgos has its reminders of the Cid, the little church of San Gil, before which the horse of the hero is supposed to have knelt centuries ago, and the medieval little church of San Gadea, where the Cid is said to have forced Alfonso VI to swear that he had not been implicated in the murder of his brother. This small Gothic structure, with its stone steps worn deep by the centuries, smells of time.

Such was the Burgos in which, during the rebellion, German Nazi and Italian Fascist officers strutted possessively and impudently in the streets.

7

By the middle of September, 1935, the political pot was boiling. Lerroux was spending some days in Barcelona, receiving the homage of the governing coalition, and Azaña and leaders of the Left were preparing a manifesto, which was awaited with much anxiety and curiosity. But more threatening than Lerroux' ovations and Azaña's manifesto was the insistence of Joaquín Chapaprieta, Minister of Finance, on the abolishing of some ministries for the sake of economy. The financial situation was unsound, and the problem of exchange was reaching serious proportions. It was clearly necessary to spend less money and to raise more revenue through new taxes, and the Minister, more financier than politician, proposed to face realities. Lerroux and Gil Robles did not dare disagree, but they could not agree between themselves on their proportionate sacrifice of the loaves and fishes. Lerroux' reported negotiations with Sr. Cambó, the reactionary Catalan Rightist leader, for representation of his party in the government, was drawing from Roya Villanueva a threat of resignation, since he "would not serve with a Catalan."

More important was the increasing fear concerning the plan of Mussolini to drag Abyssinia under the chariot wheels of a new Roman imperialism, made manifest in flamboyant gestures of defiance and contempt before the League of Nations. It seemed a brutal and immoral piece of business—this flaunting of international law and of the covenant of the League, this making a mockery of the plighted word.

But the amusing spectacle was presented of the dictator of a bankrupt state bullying the whole of Europe.

England's demand for the application of sanctions under the covenant of the League was embarrassing to France, for had not the infamous Laval assured Mussolini of the blessings of France on any undertaking against the independence of an unoffending little nation that believed in the honor of the League of Nations?

And Spain was jittery. Time and again, I was pumped by Aguinaga, the clever Sub-Minister of Foreign Affairs, regarding the attitude of the United States. It seemed strange that Spain should be so reluctant to take a stand, since no nation had given more sincere support to the organization at Geneva, and Salvador de Madariaga, her spokesman there, was said to favor sanctions. A high official said to me that Mussolini was a "madman." I reached the conclusion from conversations with government officials that Spain was eager to support the British. Meanwhile, Madariaga, as chairman of the committee dealing with the Abyssinian crisis, was more and more conspicuous.

And then the cat was out of the bag—Gil Robles and his party were with Mussolini and against England. Long before, the enemies of Spanish democracy had been conspiring in Rome for co-operative action in the wiping out of democracy in Spain.

Despite the popular sympathy in Spain for Abyssinia, *El Debate* and *Ya*, the organs of the CEDA, took a pronounced stand for Mussolini; and Gil Robles had the Spanish government at his mercy. *El Liberal* cited the position of *El Debate* and *Ya* as proof that Gil Robles and his party were against democracy. And at this very moment the young members of the party were publicly denouncing "Nineteenth-century democracy" and demanding a return to the governmental theories of the sixteenth century.

These ardent youths were running amuck at a critical moment in an issue of their organ, the *J.P.M.*, that was a masterpiece of indiscretion and political stupidity. They plastered their paper with tiresome reiterations of the phrases, "All power to the Chief" and "The Chief is always right." Their posters and banners bore similar inscriptions, implying a demand for dictatorial power for their leader. One issue of their paper reached the climax of ineptitude in assailing all the other parties in the Right coalition, jeering at the agrarians, attacking the one democrat in the ministry for "teaching infidelity with the money of Catholics"—meaning that the Minister of Education was making a bromidic pretense of carrying out the constitutional provision for public schools. And the attacks on Mussolini? Unpardonable, said the young fanatics. And the League of Nations? A rotten organization "dominated by Protestant nations."

This issue was too much for "the Chief," who ordered it called in.

8

In the midst of the international complications, the government resigned. This was necessitated by Chapaprieta's demand for a reduction in the pay roll, and by Roya Villanueva's resignation in protest against concessions to the Catalans. Alcalá Zamora pled with the ministers to reconcile their differences at least during the international crisis, but he pled in vain. Lerroux was out—and out for good.

Two days later, on a Sunday morning, Santiago Alba set to work to form a government with a representation of all the parties, including the socialists, to create a national front to meet an international crisis. To this end, he invited Julián Besteiro, most conservative and academic of the socialists, to a conference, only to learn that he could not accept office unless designated by his party. One evening it was rumored that Gil Robles had agreed to serve in a government with a moderate socialist. For a brief moment it seemed that Spain was girding its loins for whatever might betide as a result of the buccaneering of Mussolini, but when Santiago Alba found that not he, but the political parties, would name their representatives in the Ministry, he confessed failure.

Azaña had just published his book, *My Rebellion in Barcelona*, a masterpiece of irony, in his usual brilliant style, and the first edition instantly was sold out, and another run. It was a crushing answer to the absurd charge that had besmeared him so long. The Left press praised it enthusiastically and the Right press paid it the tribute of its silence.

With Santiago Alba's failure, Chapaprieta was asked to form a government. He whose insistence on higher taxes and on reductions in the pay roll had precipitated the crisis actually was asked to head a government! The Rightist coalition manifestly was in desperate straits. That evening I walked down the Castellana, where hundreds sat under the trees blissfully indifferent to the distress of the politicians, and visited the office of the United Press. There I learned that the situation of the Rightist parties was so desperate, and their fear of an electoral test of sentiment so acute, that they had assured Chapaprieta of their party and personal support and pledged him a free hand in naming his ministers.

The next day he announced his government. He, as Prime Minister, retained the Ministry of Finance. Gil Robles remained Minister of War, Lerroux became Minister of Foreign Affairs. Martínez Velasco, the agrarian leader, became Minister of Agriculture. There was nothing in the complexion of the new government to relieve the anxieties of the Left. Chapaprieta was an able and cautious banker, and honest, but in the very nature of his training and environment, he was not concerned with the material interests of the masses. Short of stature, he seemed mostly head when seen from the gallery. He had a huge head and a large face with strong features. With Velasco as Minister of Agriculture, all hope for agricultural reforms went glimmering. His party existed precisely to prevent that. *And Gil Robles, significantly enough, remained Minister of War, with Franco as his Chief of Staff, in position to manipulate the army to serve whatever end he might have in view. Few longer doubted that he looked forward to the use of the army in the determination of the destiny of the country. He remained the real master of the game. He could overturn the government with a nod.*

Meanwhile, the English were increasingly concerned lest Spain, on Gil Robles' orders, refuse to support them on sanctions against the Italian adventure in Abyssinia. At this time someone said to Lerroux that "we must remain neutral," and he was reported to have replied: "You are wrong. We must follow England at any cost." But Spain remained mysteriously coy, and many thought they knew the reason. Even so, few realized that at that very hour an understanding had been reached that if the Right extremists forced a civil war, they could count on Mussolini's, if not Hitler's, participation in a military intervention to end democracy in Spain.

When I returned Lerroux' call as Minister of State, I found him standing in the middle of the room with a whimsical smile in his cunning eyes and exuding charm and cordiality. But he was cagey on the subject of sanctions, and on the Italian situation generally. He was "optimistic" about preventing war, or of limiting it if it came. He thought Mussolini "a little more reasonable" and hoped that "if Italian honor were vindicated by a victory in some small skirmish, he might be willing to negotiate." Spain's attitude on sanctions? That would be determined at the proper time in a Council of Ministers.

But just the day before, Antonio Goicoechea, the monarchist leader in the Cortes, bringing the Italian dispute into the discussion, squarely put his party behind Italy and Fascism. He had made his deal with Mussolini a full year before.

The very day Goicoechea made his declaration, the Italians crossed the frontier into Abyssinia, and Mussolini's war of conquest had begun. The Abyssinian Emperor had withdrawn his troops thirty kilometers back from the frontier on the request of the League of Nations, which seemed determined to make its betrayal of Abyssinia as flagrant as possible. In this, and in this alone, it was to be conspicuously successful.

If the Spanish people realized that the crossing of the Abyssinian frontier was the beginning of the march of the Axis Powers against Spanish democracy, they gave no sign.

Chapter XII

"Viva Straperlo"; Rotten Fruit

WITH sore distress among the leaders of the governing coalition because of their intensifying dissensions, a luncheon, or love feast, in honor of Lerroux, was arranged. Allied now with the enemies of the republican regime as he was, Lerroux asserted that his purpose was the consolidation of the Republic. Gil Robles was lyrical in praise of him, and the diners drank toasts and cheered. Lerroux had become a "grand old man," the savior of the nation, and almost a child of the church. It had become a social error to mention the famous manifesto. Every possible concession was made to maintain the governing coalition for the now inevitable elections.

But the prospects were not brilliant. Without organization or regimentation, fifty thousand people had swarmed to hear Azaña in Valencia, and seventy-five thousand in Bilbao. When a request was made for the use of the bull ring in Madrid for an Azaña meeting, the government foolishly denied it; and arrangements were made for the use of a large field just outside the city beyond the Toledo bridge. To meet the cost of the temporary stadium, an admittance fee was charged. When it was learned that multitudes were flocking from all classes and quarters of the country, that they would come by train and truck, on mules and donkeys and on foot, there was real alarm. Some days before the meeting, these were pouring into the city.

2

The floodgates seemed to open the day before the meeting when thousands entered the city with the rush and roar of a Niagara. There were special trains and chartered trucks, many came on mules and some afoot, and they swept into the city bearing banners; and as this enthusiastic throng surged through the streets, there was some fear that these strangers would get out of hand and attack persons and property. Nazi- and Fascist-inspired provocateurs, then in Spain, encouraged this alarm. The women of the aristocracy shut themselves in their houses and drew the blinds, but there was perfect order. Only where the parties of the Right flung provocative banners to the breeze was there any clamor or disturbance. The banners were ordered down by the police, and the night passed peaceably.

In the morning, the entire city seemed moving toward the bridge that spanned the Manzanares on the Toledo road. It was an awe-inspiring demonstration of the numerical power of the people. Thousands worked their way across the bridge into the field and as near as possible to the platform, where they stood still. Observers thought attempts were made by officers to provoke disturbances—the Fascist technique—for mounted troops harassed the crowd crossing the bridge. Amplifiers were provided to carry the speakers' words to the outer rim of the crowd of a quarter of a million people assembled to hear Azaña. During his two-hour speech there was perfect order.

O'Connell swayed vast multitudes, but he was of commanding stature, while Azaña was short; and O'Connell played artfully on the emotions, while Azaña appealed solely to their reason. His speech that day was that of a statesman that might have been delivered before a senate or an academy, and while not without its irony, it was singularly free of invective. The speech was a demand for the restoration of the Republic to its pristine purpose, and for elections to test the public will. Coldly, the orator pointed to the government's dearth of achievement, and to its reactionary trend.

The silence that was unbroken during the enunciation of his program was ascribed by some to disappointment over his moderation. In that vast throng, there were liberals, democrats, republicans, socialists, but there, too, were communists, syndicalists, and anarchists. But if the extremists preferred an incitation to revolution, they nevertheless paid the speaker the tribute of their silence.

One historic thing Azaña did that day—he laid the foundation for a coalition of the parties of the Left for the elections that could not much longer be denied.

At the conclusion of the speech, the multitude turned toward the city, soberly and in good order, and by evening they were speeding home by bus or train, or riding slowly toward the mountains, or trudging wearily along the highway. The immensity of the meeting created consternation among the coalition leaders of the Right, but they found some consolation in the fact that the speech had ended without the realization of their worst fears. Rumor was bruiting it abroad that leading members of the government group had been caught red-handed in a gambling scandal. A day or so before the meeting, everyone was puzzling over a cryptic statement from the government regarding charges by "an irresponsible Cuban gambler" against government officials. It was announced that the Attorney General had been instructed to investigate. Why had the government thus accused itself? It had discovered that Prieto, in exile in Paris, coming into possession of proof of the turpitude, had sent the evidence to Azaña, who might use it in his speech. Since Azaña had the evidence, the government could not but anticipate an attack.

But there was no attack. Azaña merely squinted at "immorality." But the enormous success of the meeting had given new hope to the opposition, and Prieto, who had been in the depths of depression, hurried home to organize the right wing of the socialists for the elections.

3

Madrileños are a fun-loving people, and soon they were chortling over the droll story of the panhandling of a professional gambler by some of the leaders of the Right coalition. Though public gambling was forbidden, a Cuban adventurer had approached public officials with an offer for a monopoly on gambling. He had a gambling device called "Straperlo," and this word was to enter for weeks into the vocabulary of the streets. The story ran that public officials had sold the monopoly on gambling and that part payment had been made. Unhappily, the gambler had blundered in advertising in the papers the opening of the Casino in San Sebastián, and when *El Sol* and *La Voz* refused the advertisement and made pointed editorial observations, and an attempt was made to bribe them, and the gambler was ejected from their offices, the bizarre tale was public property. The politicians involved advised the gambler to cross the frontier for a while, but he crossed without the money that remained in the pockets of the politicians.

In Paris, Prieto heard the story, and, touched by the sorrows of the stranger, he placed his ingenuity at the service of the victim. He advised that a pathetic note be sent to the politicians with the bribe money begging for its return to save the Cuban from utter ruin. Incredibly, it seems, he got some replies. The too-sympathetic Prieto thereupon had photostatic copies made and sent them to Alcalá Zamora. The charges involved a ward of Lerroux, Lerroux' mayor of Madrid, his governor of Catalonia, and the leader of his party in Valencia. Indirectly they touched Lerroux as well.

The town rocked with laughter, the loungers in the cafés and wineshops shaking with the joy of it, and the drawing rooms were all smiles and giggles. Many marveled that Lerroux, having approached deification in his old age, should have endangered his historic status with the petty pilfering of his subordinates.

Instantly he tendered his resignation, which Chapaprieta brushed aside. There was indignation and consternation in Lerroux' party, with Santiago Alba demanding a full exposure and the purging of the radicals. There were rumors of wholesale desertions from the party Lerroux so long had led. The Rightist coalition was threatened with disintegration, and the leaders of the Azaña parties were silent and happy, as they could afford to be. Interrogated in the Cortes, Chapaprieta refused to discuss the scandal until the Attorney General had reported. Gil Robles proposed a parliamentary inquiry. Lerroux lamely complained that the Leftists sought publicity for the tale.

There was intense anxiety within the governing coalition over what the investigation would reveal. Then *El Debate* and *El Liberal* rushed extras into the streets with the full report of the parliamentary commission, and great was the sensation. No one thereafter dared to doubt that there was substance in the gambler's story, for leaders of the party of Lerroux were all too clearly involved.

The charge against the dapper mayor of Madrid was that of tampering with official documents in an effort to conceal the crime. The governor was charged with having cashed one of the gambler's checks for thirty thousand pesetas, and, according to the gambler's story, this was to be divided between Lerroux and Roca. Count Romanones, disgusted with the sordid mess, was snarling that this was "graft in small change."

The superstructure of the Right coalition was trembling, and rumors flew that Lerroux and Roca would resign on Monday. On the Saturday before, there had been a stormy party conference, with some clamoring for the purging of the radical party, and the opportunists proposing to sustain Lerroux at any cost. The once-proud party of Lerroux, so recently in the odor of sanctity, was passing to oblivion in a stench.

4

The Cortes was packed in anticipation of a sensational debate. Lerroux, though quite calm, was serious, and looked pitiful. Chapaprieta entered soon and sat beside him in complete silence. Gil Robles, with an annoyed expression, sat on the other side of Lerroux. Roca, now miserably misplaced as Minister of Education, was the last to find his place on the far end of the Blue Bench.

The spokesman of the party of Miguel Maura presented the report of the committee. There was dead silence in the Chamber. Lerroux sat with folded arms, looking straight ahead, apparently unmoved. The meticulously attired Alonzo, mayor of Madrid, spoke emotionally in his own defense and was heard with manifest sympathy. Then Lerroux rose in a deathlike silence, speaking disjointedly, almost incoherently. Conscious of his incoherence, he referred to it himself, assuming the role of the tired old man worn out in the service of the Republic. He was heard in a cynical silence, and his own party appeared staggered by the weakness of his defense. When he closed, without a single handclap, he folded his arms and stared unseeingly into space. Once it was clear that his seeming indifference was a mask, an impetuous young man of his party demanded recognition of the chair, and Lerroux, instantly alert, glanced behind him furiously, caught the young man's eye, and, pounding the back of the Blue Bench, ordered him into his seat.

And then José Primo de Rivera plunged the Chamber into turmoil with a blunt protest against hypocrisy and corruption. Maura followed, speaking softly; Gil Robles rose to defend Lerroux. He could not see that morality was involved. Nothing was involved but an attempt of the Left to split the Right coalition. He touched neither on the charges nor the evidence. As he sat down, he turned to Lerroux, engaging him in a long and earnest conversation.

The Left parties wisely refrained from participating in the debate. It was not their dirty baby, and if the nurses quarreled over its cleansing, it was none of their concern.

When Alonzo was vindicated with a margin of three votes, after a complete exoneration of Lerroux, the deputies were startled by a shrill cry:

"*Viva Straperlo!*"

And all eyes turned on the impish face of José Primo de Rivera. He smiled with the irrepressibility of youth on the scowling faces of his elders.

5

But Lerroux and Roca resigned; Chapaprieta tendered the resignation of his government and was asked to form a new one. He was prepared for instant action. Martínez Velasco was made Minister of State; Gil Robles clung to the Ministry of War; and Lerroux announced a journey to Portugal to take a cure. In an effort to make his departure graceful, Santiago Alba said the old warrior certainly had earned a rest. But his position was tragic. Only yesterday, he had been pictured by the Rightists as the savior of the country, the champion of Christianity, and the custodian of public morals, and, after being anathema for more than forty years among the elite, he had been taken to their bosoms. And now, at seventy-two, loaded down with honors, he was being toppled from his pedestal. But when it was reported that he had abandoned the leadership of his party, the old man came vigorously to life again. So long as he lived, he said, he would remain the leader of the radicals. And leave the country for Portugal? No, he would remain in Spain, and might have much to say if the spirit moved him. The happy smile on the faces of the leaders of the Right seemed strained.

Meanwhile, Gil Robles was usurping the functions of his colleagues. When Paramount Films produced the picture *The Devil Was a Woman*, with Marlene Dietrich in the role of a courtesan making a fool of a pompous old Spanish general, Gil Robles peremptorily demanded its withdrawal, throughout the world, with the threat to ban all Paramount pictures in Spain otherwise. The grievance seemed farfetched. Was it an offering to Hitler, who had banned the Jewish actress in Germany? Or was he making the army sacrosanct, since "the destiny of Spain is in the army"? One thing was certain—he was playing the Dictator before the *coup d'état*.

And all the while the drift to the Left was gaining in momentum . . . The *A Hora*, more Right than Left, in reviewing a book on politics, was making ugly observations on corruption, and the increasing unpopularity of the Rightists, on the certainty of a Leftist triumph at the polls . . . In the leading bookstore in Madrid, etchings of Azaña were on sale . . . Beneath the surface there were uneasy stirrings, but Madrid was unchanged. It was in the golden sunshine of All Saints' Day that, driving aimlessly in the outskirts of the city, we found ourselves in the vicinity of the cemetery. The streets were congested with cars, and the sidewalks packed with men, women, and children watching the procession of people with flowers. All along the curb there was an unbroken string of stands offering sausages and chicken for the hungry, and flowers for those going to the graves. Hawkers shrilly cried their wares.

6

Taking advantage of another lull in the political crisis, we made a hurried trip to Santander. The countryside was bleak in a downpour of rain, though many peasants were working in the fields.

Under the black skies, flowers were blooming everywhere, magnolia trees were blossoming, and the grass of Santander was green. The next day Sybil and I drove to Santiago del Mar to see the unique caves of Altamira. An hour's drive over the wet roads brought us to the cave which scientists agree was inhabited fifteen thousand years ago when much of Europe was covered with ice. In the remote past, some upheaval of nature had closed the entrance to the cave, and for some centuries its existence was not suspected. One day in 1868, the dog of a hunter, becoming lost in the underbrush, was found to have entered a small underground passage between two huge rocks. It was not long after this that the cave was opened and explored, and, long after that, that the Duke of Alba and others made adequate provision for its preservation.

We entered first the huge room that was the caveman's kitchen, with a great hole in the center for the cooking of the game, and with the bones of wild animals, extinct for centuries, around the rim. Just off the kitchen is the smaller room called the "Sistine Chapel of the Cavemen." On the roof of smooth rock were painted large pictures of the wild animals of thousands of years ago. The drawing was perfect, the lines as true as those of any modern artist. The paintings, entirely in red and black, are said to have been painted with charcoal and cork with animal grease. So fresh and vivid are the colors after many centuries that we marveled in the presence of another lost art. Here, before us, was the proof that there was a civilization with a sense of beauty and a feeling for art of which we are in utter ignorance.

The little town of Santiago del Mar, near by, is fascinating. In the old days, when it was the capital of Eastern Asturias and the favorite residence of the nobility, its streets were lined with fine palaces, now occupied as tenements by the poor. But the coats of arms of famous families still are visible. We stood before the house of the Borgias—a stern, dour, powerfully built fortress and palace.

Feeling our way over the slippery cobblestones that rang with the clatter of the wooden overshoes of the natives, we reached the Collegiate Church, which occupies the site of a monastery of the sixth century. The present church was built in the twelfth century. As we entered, Sybil called attention to many wooden overshoes by the door. These last a lifetime, and in these parts, rubber is too

much of a luxury for the poor. The cloisters charmed me most—
cloisters that have known no other use for eight hundred years.
Between the flagstone of the court ragged grass was growing. The
columns were crudely carved, and yet each column had a different
design. Here was the past. One felt it—felt it all the more because
the day was gloomy and the rain was splashing on the stones.

7

Within two weeks the Chapaprieta government was trembling
under the blows of its pretended friends. A resentful follower of
Lerroux was charging that the Prime Minister was increasing the
rates on electricity to gouge the consumer and swell the profits of
the corporation . . . Gordón Ordás, republican, was denouncing
Gil Robles as an enemy of democracy, aiming at a dictatorship.
Had he not made a secret visit to the King at Fontainebleau?
What effrontery to demand a place in the government he was
planning to betray! . . . There was an ugly stir among the deputies when, touching on the suppression of the Asturian revolt,
Orgas cited the case of the thirty men, made prisoners, whose
bodies were found in a field riddled with bullets. He demanded an
investigation.

With the attack increasing and the defense weakening, Chapaprieta, noting the cold reception of this speech, was placing his
own interpretation on it. If there was a disposition to oppose his
fiscal policies, he said, he was ready to resign.

But the reactionary leaders of the Right wanted no resignation,
no election; Gil Robles, with a straight face, paid an extravagant
tribute to the Rightist Cortes that had accomplished nothing and
could not even maintain a quorum. The thing to do, he said, was
for the Cortes to remain and amend the Constitution in accordance
with his designs. He closed with a glowing tribute to Lerroux.

Meanwhile, with the parties of the Left very active in small
towns and villages, another scandal, involving leaders of the governing coalition, broke like a clap of thunder.

8

On the morning of November 29, 1935, the Madrid press announced under lurid headlines another scandal, and Miguel

Maura gave notice of an interpolation and a demand for a parliamentary inquiry. That morning I passed the Presidencia, where the Council of Ministers was in session, and noticed crowds standing in sullen silence in the street, with an unusual number of Civil Guards among them.

The new scandal story spread like wildfire on a prairie after a drought. Some time before, the government had contracted with a shipowner for two ships for service in Spanish Guinea. The ships furnished were so rotten that one sank in the still water at the wharf, and the government agent canceled the contract. The seller sued for five hundred thousand pesetas damages. The claim had gone to Lerroux, a friend of the seller's, and was turned over to his secretary for investigation. According to the story current, the latter was astonished at the moderation of the claim. "Why, ridiculous! The amount is too small. We must make it at least three million pesetas." And so it was made at first—on the insistence of the sued party. Then, so the story ran, the amount was raised to seven million; but, intimidated by their own audacity, it was restored to three. Thereupon, Lerroux instructed the agent in Spanish Guinea to pay the money, leaving the impression that the order came from the Council of Ministers. But the agent, an honest man, refused, and was summarily discharged. Returning, in hot haste to Madrid, the agent saw the other ministers, who denied any knowledge of the transaction, though one distinguished minister, noted for his piety, thought it less dangerous to pay the money than to risk the political consequences of an exposure.

As the story spread and it became clear that Lerroux' old shoulders were to bear the burden, his resentment flamed. His deputies were not appearing in their seats; and one day Lerroux, passing his co-leaders of the Right, gave them the cut direct. They were considerably concerned over the gesture. Lerroux appeared before the committee and insisted that the other ministers had been consulted.

Behind the scenes, the Rightist leaders were feverishly trying to manipulate the report. Maura, the chairman, resigned in protest. The CEDA, insisting on the pristine purity of Lerroux, was pouring forth its scorn on the humble secretary, selected as the sacrifice. The monarchists wished to pronounce both master and man guilty, but only of an "administrative error." The Left republicans were ready to report as guilty, not only the master and the man, but also Gil Robles as accessory after the fact.

9

The committee had been unable to agree, and a whitewash report of only nine of the twenty-one members was submitted by the CEDA as "the report of the committee," and the dissenting reports of the monarchists and the Left republicans were not even read. From the "report of the committee," Lerroux emerged "pure as light and stainless as a star," the innocent victim of a wicked secretary, who was excoriated with righteous wrath.

Disgusted with the mockery and hypocrisy of it all, José Primo de Rivera was like a bull with St. Vitus's dance in a china shop. He smashed hypocrisy with the evidence, and his robust denunciation of corruption caused uneasiness. Knowing that Lerroux could be exonerated only on the orders of Gil Robles, he turned dramatically to him, addressing him by name, imploring him not to make himself the habitual defender of those guilty of fraud against the state. The object of the appeal, with flushed, angry face, squirmed and twisted in his seat, and once seemed about to rise, but changed his mind. Lerroux sat immobile, with folded arms.

A violent debate, but meaningless. It was a sham battle. At ten the Cortes recessed until one-thirty in the morning. At six A.M. the vote was taken. Lerroux was exonerated, his obscure secretary condemned, on the theory that the better the day the better the deed—for it was Sunday morning. But scarcely was the result announced when a shrill voice rang from the deserted diplomatic gallery:

"*Viva Straperlo!*"

The deputies glared up into the impish face of José Primo de Rivera, who, with the exuberance of a mischievous child, was smiling down upon his elders. The deputies scowled angrily and filed out into the deserted street.

10

Meanwhile, the indifference of the ruling coalition to the Republic was apparent. In an amazing manifesto, the juvenile

members of the CEDA declared that the one important thing was
"to smash the revolution and forever exclude the Leftists from
power"—something impossible under a democracy. It dismissed
Chapaprieta's fiscal reforms as worthless because of the "bankruptcy of the state." And it demanded a new Constitution with "all
power to the Chief"—meaning Gil Robles.

Meanwhile, it was common gossip that Gil Robles and Franco
in the War Office were conspiring for a *coup d'état*. The mysterious
moving of troops, and the placing of antirepublican generals in
key positions, was not lost on the observer. The government was
more interested in guns than in laws, policies, or butter. But clearly,
it was crumbling. More than half of Lerroux' deputies, disgusted
by their leader's silence, had deserted and announced the formation
of other ties.

And just then, Chapaprieta resigned. He resigned because the
CEDA and the agrarians had not kept their pledge of wholehearted support when he proposed the reduction of salaries, with an
increase on the taxes of the rich.

With the ruling coalition in bankruptcy, torn by internal dissensions, dominated by sordid class interest and personal ambitions, Chapaprieta was urged to form a government of his personal
choice, with the promise of support for his fiscal policies. But when
he called on Gil Robles, he found him in a fury, breathing fire and
damnation, and demanding practically all the ministerial posts.
Chapaprieta abandoned his effort in disgust.

11

It was out of this chaos of the Rightists that Manuel Portela
emerged in a bit of comedy.

It was understood that the President's friend, Miguel Maura,
had been asked to form a government, and, according to his
version, he had promised to report his list of ministers on the
morrow. When he appeared at the palace, he was chagrined to
find Portela in the waiting room. His amazement grew when,
together, they were ushered into the presence of Alcalá Zamora,
and even more it grew when the President greeted them as his
two good friends whom he wished to form a government. "But
which one?" gasped Maura. The President hedged; and when

Maura said he had his list, as promised, he was told that conditions had changed overnight. Would not Maura and Portela talk it over? He himself would retire until they reached an agreement. With Maura protesting, Alcalá Zamora backed firmly out of the room, with little bobs and bows. Then Maura flew into a fury, with Portela sitting in silence, his two hands together, his pointed fingers in front like one in prayer. At length, Maura pounded on the door through which the President had disappeared. Alcalá Zamora appeared, rubbing his hands and smiling. "And so, you have agreed?" he asked. Maura flew into another rage and stalked out of the room slamming the door, and Portela remained to form a government. Such is the story told me at the time by a friend of one of the principals, who had described the scene.

Portela looked the part of a grim fighter and was reputed to be a strong man. Tall, a bit loose-jointed and Lincolnesque, slender, with a lean, purposeful face, and a great mass of perfectly white hair brushed back, he bore a striking resemblance to Sully's portrait of Andrew Jackson. He took the Ministry of the Interior himself, continued Chapaprieta as Minister of Finance, made Velasco Minister of State, and not a single member of the parties of Lerroux and Gil Robles was included.

This was an announcement of elections.

Two deserters from Lerroux' group, Pablo Blasco and Rafael del Río, were made Ministers of Agriculture and Public Works, and for the portfolios of War and Marine, Portela went outside the parties and appointed General Molero and Vice Admiral Francisco Salas. When Maura was selecting members of the government he thought he had been asked to form, Alcalá Zamora suggested Molero for War, and summoned him to Madrid to confer with Maura. Having seen Maura after his arrival, he made his call of courtesy on the then Minister of War, Gil Robles. "What are you doing here?" angrily demanded the minister. Molero explained. It must have been apparent that he had the approval of the President, his Commander in Chief, but he was ordered under arrest. Gil Robles was not without excuse for his nervous tension. He had either underplayed or overplayed his hand, and power rapidly was drifting from him, with nothing really accomplished during his more than two years of authority. Even so, he made an emotional and melodramatic exit from the War Office he so long had coveted. On taking office, he had moved into the palace of Buena Vista, set among the great trees of the grounds, surrounded by a high iron picket fence, and guarded constantly by soldiers. It was a beautiful place to live. It had been the home of Godoy, lover of María Luisa, in the days of his power, and it was through its open windows that the annoying cries of the venders of scurrilous pamphlets on the romance of the Queen and the "Prince of Peace" beat painfully upon the eardrums of the favorite. History brooded over the palace and beauty surrounded it, but almost in a huff, Gil Robles moved out two days before he had to, melodramatically promising to return.

12

In the midst of the excitement, the Pope gave the red cap of a cardinal to the Nuncio, Tedeschini.

In those days I loved to drive toward evening through the Casa de Campo, for centuries denied to all but the royal family and the Court, and destined to be the Madrid battleground for more than two years of the rebellion. A few minutes from the entrance to the palace one is in real country and on a country road. Often I would see a tall figure in a black robe approaching on foot in the middle of the highway, reading a book, and with a car following to pick him up when he had exercised enough. It was Tedeschini. Thus I met him a week before the ceremony at the palace when the President put the red cap on his head. It had been the privilege of Spanish kings, and though there was now a separation of church and state, and no state church, I am quite sure the devout Alcalá Zamora never quite realized it. At any rate, he stoutly insisted on the right to place the cap. The more cynical of the diplomatic corps thought this childish.

It was a ceremonious occasion, guards in brilliant uniform lining the stairway, the diplomats in their glittering full dress. We passed through cold rooms to the banquet hall for the ceremony. At length, through a side door, the wife of the President, in a black satin dress, glided in and bowed to the corps. Then, through a door at the end of the room emerged Alcalá Zamora in evening dress and all his decorations, flanked by Martínez Velasco, Minister of

State, and Portela. They advanced and paused at the end of the two lines facing the aisle between. Then, from the opposite end of the room came one of the Pope's noble guards, resplendent in gold braid, and wearing a silver helmet. A priest read a paper; Alcalá Zamora replied at length, as one chanting, with a speech carefully prepared and burnished, and even his meanest enemies agreed that few Spaniards in public life could have met the requirements more gracefully, or so much in the spirit of tradition. The Pope's messenger then deposited the red cap on the table and retired.

Soon he returned with Tedeschini, dressed in purple and wearing a red skullcap. He advanced to within a few feet of the President and bowed. Whereupon, Alcalá Zamora launched into another long speech, and Tedeschini, so long immovable, seemed weary.

The President concluded, and Tedeschini took up the red cap and passed it to him to have it placed upon his head. But the President was short; Tedeschini was very tall, and it was not an easy task, since Tedeschini did not kneel. As Alcalá Zamora stepped forward, cap in hand, his hands were trembling. It was his only moment of nervousness, but he succeeded without a mishap. Thereupon, Tedeschini removed his cap and, holding it in his hand, began reading his reply. I could see that it was written with a lead pencil and that parts had been scratched out and rewritten.

Meanwhile, everyone was suffering, standing still for much more than an hour. The ceremony over, the cardinal turned and retired through the door whence he had emerged, and the President and the ministers went in the opposite direction to their exit. The corps then passed through an adjoining salon to shake the hand of the new Prince of the Church, or to kiss his ring.

I both liked and admired Tedeschini, and I was glad to "assist" in the ceremony at the palace. Three years later he was to be one of the three cardinals leading in the balloting in the conclave in the election of the successor of St. Peter.

13

Now, with elections inevitable, and with the electorate divided into two hostile camps, Alcalá Zamora was eager to have a Center party to act as a buffer between the extremes. That, it was commonly understood, was to be the mission of Portela.

One day a leading journalist intimately identified with Gil Robles asked for an appointment. I knew and liked him. He spent more than an hour with me, and the interview was both illuminating and mystifying. He opened with the startling statement that Gil Robles expected the Azaña combination to win and to "precipitate a revolution bloodier than that of Russia"; though just why the Leftists, having won, should precipitate a revolution, was a mystery. It occurred to me that if the Leftists won, their opponents might be contemplating a revolution, as was indeed the case. He said a spy of Gil Robles' had reported on a secret meeting in Brussels between Azaña and Prieto when an agreement had been reached for a solid front of the Leftist parties to face the solid front of the Rightists, and that after the elections there would be a nationalization of the banks and all major industries. This, in part, was manifestly untrue.

I asked him to explain the pessimism of Gil Robles. He replied that it was based, first, on the solid front of the Left parties, including the syndicalists, not included before, and, second, on the efforts of Alcalá Zamora to form a Center party which would draw almost entirely from the conservatives of the Right.

More and more puzzled by the strange course of the conversation, I asked for Gil Robles' analysis of the election prospects. He replied that the Right combination would win north of the Guadarramas, where there were small farms, but that the Left combination would sweep Catalonia, Bilbao, Saragossa and Madrid, and "all south of Madrid." When I expressed surprise about Andalusia, he reminded me that the Leftists had won most of the seats there in 1931 without the aid of the syndicalists, and that with their support the majority would be large. And then he added: "If we have money enough, we can buy the syndicalists, for they are purchasable."

I asked his explanation of the Leftist trend of Andalusian peasants, and I was deeply impressed with the reply, coming from him.

"The peasants of the North, where they have small farms, are conservative," he said, in substance. "But in Andalusia, where there are no small holdings and only large estates, the peasants do not live on the estates, but in the villages. In the old days they were devoted to the landlords, but that was when these lived at least a portion of the year on the estates, had personal contacts with the peasants, and recognized their social obligations to them. Now they live mostly in Madrid, Paris, London, and Switzerland and leave their estates in the hands of supervisors who rob, cheat, and abuse the peasants. The contact is broken, and the peasant no longer looks upon the landlord as a protector and friend, but rather as a natural enemy."

He paused, and then he asked: "Do you realize what many of these peasants get? Two or three pesetas a day for work from dawn to dark."

I asked why, with so much involved, the landlords did not supervise the supervisors.

"Most of them are very rich," he replied, "and live much of their time abroad. They have heavy investments abroad and are not dependent on their Spanish income. So, you see, Spain can be ruined, and these men not be."

More and more astonished by the frankness of my visitor, and puzzled over his motive, I could think of nothing but a possible military *coup d'état* in preparation. So I asked him about the army. He replied that the leading officers in key positions were monarchists, but that these would be displaced by Leftist officers after the election. He said that while General Franco had not been displaced as Chief of Staff, he expected Portela to transfer him at any moment.

Becoming more confidential, he said the leaders of the Rightist parties in the Portela government were preparing to desert. He himself had arranged a secret meeting between Gil Robles and Chapaprieta in a private house, when the former was assured that the latter would not support Portela in the formation of a Center party, but would resign at the proper moment, along with Martínez Velasco.

"Of course," concluded my visitor as he was leaving, "if there is a common front of the Left, Gil Robles will have to make an alliance with the monarchists"—which is precisely what he had done in 1933 when there was no common front of the Lefts.

When he left, I was still in the dark as to the motives for these remarkable revelations, since he had made no request of me, but he said he was telling the same story to the British and German ambassadors, and to us alone. He did not see them for two weeks, and then he told the identical story, with one exception—Gil Robles did not then think the election prospects so hopeless. One of my colleagues bluntly inquired why he was being told. The reply was amazing: "Because England, Germany, and the United States have large investments in Spain, and I thought you might want to warn the President against encouraging the formation of a Center party." The ambassador was stunned to silence. To the other colleague, the direct request was made, and the emissary was told that it would be gravely improper for a diplomat thus to interfere in the internal politics of the country to which he was accredited.

14

Five days after this interview it was common knowledge that Chapaprieta and Velasco were not loyal to Portela and would resign. Gil Robles had declared that he would make no electoral alliance with any party represented in the government.

The first Portela government ended in a dramatic episode. Many tales were told, many born of fancy; but that the meeting of the Council of Ministers was stormy there can be no doubt. Grimly, Portela took the offensive with the assertion that some of his ministers had been holding secret meetings with Gil Robles, and that no man could remain in his government and conspire with the leader of the opposition. Pablo Blasco, pounding the table, shouted that no one could tell him with whom he could and could not confer, and Chapaprieta joined in. Whereupon, Portela contemptuously called the Minister of Finance a "double-crosser." "There are three ministers before me who have three faces," he snapped. "One for me, one for the President, and another for the public." It was said that an exchange of blows was imminent. When the excitement died down, Portela secured an agreement on the budget and an order for the dissolution of the Cortes. Then, facing the ministers, he said:

"Gentlemen, I hope there are no hard feelings. I thank you for transacting this business. I shall now go to the palace and resign."

With that he stalked out of the room, leaving his little audience flabbergasted.

That was at noon; at ten o'clock that night he had formed a new government. Neither the Right nor Left parties were represented. Most of the new ministers were independents. A few former Radicals who had left Lerroux on the scandals entered. The election was to be held in an atmosphere of bitterness, and Portela would conduct them.

15

Meanwhile, the enemies of a democratic regime were not relying on the elections and were pushing their preparations to take possession of the state by force.

The Italian Embassy was feverishly busy, and the black-shirt ambassador, Orazio Pedrazzi, recently sent by the impatient Mussolini to hasten a Fascist revolution, was not a stranger to Calvo Sotelo and Goicoechea, on whom the Duce apparently relied.

And the German Embassy was not drowsing behind the high fence enclosure. Long before, General Sanjurjo, who owed his life to the misplaced generosity of Azaña, would be in Germany, ostensibly to see the winter Olympic games, visiting the munition plants, conferring with the Nazi leaders. For Hitler's Germany, as well as Mussolini's Italy, was in the conspiracy to destroy democracy in Spain. Hitler got an agreement that he should get the iron ore of Spain for his war factories, working day and night in preparation for the World War to exterminate democracy throughout Europe. From behind the ugly high wall enclosure of the German Embassy, where a large supply of arms was stored, and from all German consulates, went forth propaganda, and the press campaign conducted publicly by "Gustav Reder" did not have to be imagined, since it slapped the least observant in the face. As early as September, 1935, the chief Nazi propagandist was boasting that Spanish papers had published one hundred and forty-five articles in glorification of Hitler. The paper *Informaciónes*, owned by Juan March, was looked upon as the organ of Germany; just as *El Debate* and *Ya* were considered the mouthpieces of Mussolini.

More significant, Spanish military men were being provided with a German military periodical known as *Ejército, Marina, Aviación*. Significantly enough, it was issued from the press that printed the official organ of the German General Staff, and it was founded by General Wilhelm Faupel, an intimate of Hindenburg's, who, some months after the war began, would appear as the German Ambassador to General Franco in Burgos and settle down there for a while as a military adviser. German and Italian spies were prying into military possibilities, and Gestapo agents were in the field.

At this time a new night club was opened by a German which attained an instantaneous popularity in fashionable circles hostile to the democratic regime. The club of Mayer's was small and stuffy, but the patrons were of the aristocracy, and as Jimmy Campbell, a unique entertainer, coaxed real melody from the piano, with a bottle of whisky on the stool beside him, the patrons squirmed about on the crowded dance floor. In the last months before the Fascist revolution broke, Mayer's was the most famous place for play in Madrid after midnight. So notoriously was it the meeting place of the enemies of the Republic that I heard men making wagers that it would be wrecked by a bomb. After the war began, and the staff of the German Embassy left Madrid, it was Mayer who moved in as custodian.

Such were the conditions and the atmosphere in which preparations were being made for the elections that the Rightist extremists already were discounting.

Chapter XIII

The Battle of the Ballots

AT THE beginning of the electoral campaign, intellectual and artistic Spain was moved by the death of Ramón del Valle Inclán in the rain-drenched, delicious city of Santiago de Compostela. This head of the Spanish Academy in Rome, popularly described as the "Anatole France of Spain," was a fascinating weaver of tales, with a gift for irony, and his novels descriptive of the Court of Isabella II had contributed not a little to undermining the popularity of the dynasty. Frequently I had seen this tall, frail man, with the long, narrow beard at a sidewalk café surrounded by admiring disciples. He wore glasses with large rims, and his eyes were both sharp and brooding. One arm was missing, and he liked to make a mystery of the reason to strangers, offering the most absurd explanations. His favorite among these was that when alone on the desert, and pursued by a lion, he had cut off his arm and thrown it to the beast as a peace offering. This tendency to fictionalize himself was characteristic. Occasionally he would shock those who did not know him well by casual references to murders he had committed. Even in his autobiography he wrote: "I remember with pride that there on the Deliah, I brutally murdered Sir Robert Jones. It was a stroke of revenge worthy of Benvenuto Cellini. I will tell you about it, though I consider you incapable of appreciating its beauty—but, then, on second thought —perhaps, I had best not tell you about it at all, since you might be shocked." On one occasion, going to his favorite café and finding a stranger in his usual seat, he promptly brushed over the intruder and took possession of the chair, and, with grave nonchalance, resumed his conversation with his companions. Though a republican in politics, he was no politician, and, except for the signing of the protest against the imprisonment and persecution of Azaña, I had not heard of him politically.

He was a native of Galicia, where he died, in the delightful city of St. James, to which unbroken processions of the faithful had moved through the centuries on pilgrimages to the fine old cathedral that allegedly holds the apostle's tomb. It rains frequently in Santiago de Compostela, and he was buried in the rain.

2

Portela launched his campaign with a surprise attack that left Gil Robles and his allies gasping. Assuming that the elections would be called for April, they were preparing for a leisurely approach to the perfecting of their organization and alliances, but the white-haired Prime Minister suddenly dissolved the Cortes and called elections for the middle of February, 1936. Gil Robles had not arranged his coalition. It was reported that he had rejected the demand of Calvo Sotelo that, as a price for the co-operation of the monarchists and the Fascist-minded, the King should be recalled in the event of a Rightist victory. The bitterness of the campaign was foreshadowed when the CEDA leader, speaking in Galicia in denunciation of Alcalá Zamora, was stoned. The reports trickled into Madrid that most of his audiences were composed of women. When, a little later, he discontinued his attacks on the President, it was assumed that pressure had been brought by the church.

Meanwhile, the Popular Front had been formed. This was nothing more sinister than a coalition, for the election, of all the parties of the Left. With all the parties of the Right in combination, it would have been stupid for the parties of the Left not to have combined. This meant the inclusion of the small communist party, just as the Rightist combination had meant the inclusion of the monarchists and the Fascists. Azaña, who was an uncompromising foe of communism, favored the combination as a matter of necessity, imposed by the action of the Rightists.

With the lifting of the censorship, it was immediately evident that quarter would be neither asked nor given. Prieto's paper in Bilbao printed eighteen pages of affidavits on the savagery of the Moors and the Foreign Legion in the Asturias. Brushing the Constitution aside, the government ordered the papers seized. It did not matter. The paper had been distributed throughout the country before it was put upon the street.

On Sunday morning, four days after the calling of the elections, when strolling through the fashionable residential section of the city, I marveled at the speed with which Gil Robles had plastered the walls with lurid posters. It was understood that he planned the printing of a vast number, and this meant a huge campaign fund.

But he was having trouble with his juveniles. One morning, politicians gasped on seeing posters denouncing the party of Lerroux as an organization for corruption. This was the work of young-men-in-a-hurry. Lerroux indignantly protested to his ally, only to be told, with a poker face, that since the propaganda was in the hands of the young men, there was nothing Gil Robles could do about it. Recalling the young men's monotonous reiteration of the cry, "All power to the Chief," Lerroux smiled wearily. Soon he was to find that he had ceased to be an asset and would be abandoned to his fate. The orange had been squeezed dry.

Two weeks after the calling of elections, the Rightists announced their solid front, including the monarchists. This meant the identical combination of incongruous and incompatible elements that had been successful in 1933.

But the Rightists took no chances with a manifesto setting forth their program. Despite this plan to blow hot and cold and play fast and loose, *Calvo Sotelo, ablest of the Rightists, a Fascist and a monarchist, campaigning tirelessly, courageously declared that a Right victory would mean the end of the Republic.*

Rightist politicians shivered when he publicly implied that under an agreement with Gil Robles, the new Cortes would be called a Constituent Assembly and would order a referendum on the restoration of the King, with the country under the dictatorial domination of General Sanjurjo during the interval and for the elections. This would have meant elections conducted under the directing swords of the generals. At this time, high officers of the army were going back and forth to Portugal, where Sanjurjo lived in voluntary exile. An attempt was made to challenge Calvo Sotelo's right to act as spokesman for the Rightists, but the superiority of his talents left no doubt of his pre-eminence in the combination.

Meanwhile, Gil Robles' poster factory was working day and night, with new posters appearing daily. In the fashionable section of Madrid, private mansions were plastered over with these lurid sheets. One, particularly amusing, declared that while there had been "no tuberculosis under the monarchy," thousands of cases had appeared under the Republic. For generations, tuberculosis had been the scourge of the Spanish poor, and the Republic, through free clinics for children, had lowered the death rate. The people read, and chuckled, and the jeering Leftists irreverently offered a shibboleth to the CEDA leaders—"Fight cancer; vote Right."

As late as two weeks before the elections, there was scarcely a Leftist poster to be seen. Meanwhile, Gil Robles' trucks were rushing his posters to all parts of the country.

The reactionaries had an enormous slush fund, ladies of the aristocracy went about distributing blankets and mattresses among the newly discovered poor. But more open bribery was indulged in. An agent, canvassing the apartment house in which Constancia de la Maura, a republican, though a daughter of the King's greatest Prime Minister, lived, thought he had bought her Andalusian maid for twenty-five pesetas, but she promptly reported to her mistress. On election day, a lady of the aristocracy drove this maid, and eleven others, to the polls. They thanked the lady, pocketed the pesetas, and voted with the Azaña group.

The Leftists had meager funds. The story, à la Goebbels, of the "Russian gold" was pure canard. Since the labor unions had exhausted their funds in caring for the families of their imprisoned members, they had little for the campaign.

In the middle of the campaign, El Sol again deserted Azaña. The paper was the property of a rich industrialist of Barcelona, and Chapaprieta was his lawyer. To meet the loss, the friends of Azaña launched Política, taking over the more liberal members of the *El Sol* staff. It was ably edited, dignified in style and tone, but it was handicapped by a lack of funds, and members of the staff worked at a sacrifice.

3

The Leftists announced their program in a meticulously prepared manifesto. Each affiliated party had submitted its desires; each draft was carefully studied, and the proposals in some instances were rejected. The socialists had asked for the nationalization of banks and the disbandment of the Civil Guards, but these proposals were denied. The clear purport of the manifesto was to pledge the restoration of the Republic of 1931. It provided for drastic agrarian reforms, for the betterment of the condition of labor, for the repeal of measures of the Rightist regime violative of the Constitution, and it promised immediate amnesty for the thirty thousand political prisoners caught in the dragnet of 1934.

The Rightists presented no program and made no definite promise to the public. They dared promise nothing to the peasants after ditching the mild program of Fernández; and nothing to the workers, for that would have alienated the industrialists and financiers. They could not declare for the Republic and hold the monarchists, nor promise the restoration of the monarchy and hold the republicans. They could not ask a new lease on power on their record, which was singularly barren of constructive achievement and was corrupt. And so they took refuge in mere abuse, denouncing all Leftists as "anarchists," "communists," and enemies of society. And they made the most of their contention that local autonomy in Catalonia and for the Basques would mean the disintegration of the nation.

Thus, in broad lines, we have the division of the Rightists and Leftists.

And then, two weeks before the election, Cardinal Gomá of Toledo issued a militant manifesto of intemperate denunciation of the parties under the leadership of Azaña. Many wondered. Not a few devout Catholics thought the Cardinal had made a mistake.

Then, at this time Portela issued his manifesto, pointing out the peril of dividing the country into two camps of extremists and urging the necessity of a Center party to serve as a buffer between the two extremes. It was a wise manifesto, but Spain was in no mood for moderation.

4

Meanwhile, the leaders were searching feverishly for safe constituencies. In the initial balloting of the socialists in Madrid, the failure of Julián Besteiro to win a place was a shock to the more conservative republicans. No public man had a higher reputation for probity, ability, and conservatism. He was an evolutionary socialist, with no patience with appeals to force. The Republic had taken him from the quiet of the academy to make him President of the Constituent Assembly, where for two and a half years he was to distinguish himself by his fairness, gentleness, and gentility. Everyone, including the monarchists, respected him as a scholar. He was tall, slender, a bit bowed, with a student's stoop, and with a lean, scholar's face. His cordial manner invited confidence at a glance. The fact that one of his distinction in his party had failed of nomination was pounced upon by the Fascist propagandists as verification of their contention that the Leftists were bent on government by violence.

The fact that Largo Caballero led the poll and was nominated on the initial ballot strengthened the contention. It was impossible to doubt the honesty and sincerity of this pet aversion of the conservatives. He was a plasterer by trade, and he had taken his socialism seriously. He had held a minor office under the monarchy. Azaña had made him Minister of Labor, and in cases involving employers and employees, his invariable decision for the latter, even in cases where they were clearly wrong, made an unpleasant impression. I do not believe that he was consciously unfair; but, instinctively, he supported the workers with a fanatic zeal. I never heard him speak in the Cortes, and as I studied his strong face from the gallery, I could not rid myself of the feeling that, in his impatience, he thought parliamentary processes futile. He lived with Spartan simplicity, and, because he was incorruptible, he had become the idol of the working class, which so often had been betrayed by false friends. He became a tremendous power in the socialist union, which ultimately determined the course of the socialist party.

Nothing, I think, did more to foster the notion encouraged by the Fascist and military propagandists preparing an excuse for their rebellion that a Leftist victory would mean extreme measures than the defeat of Besteiro and the overwhelming victory of Caballero, the bogey of the conservatives. True, Besteiro was nominated a few days later, but, psychologically, the damage had been done.

Among the old leaders seeking safe constituencies, none was so pathetic as Lerroux. He had become a liability, and more than one constituency, though pressed by the leaders of the Right, refused to accept him as a candidate. Finally he ran in Barcelona, where he made his one speech of the campaign. It was an amazing speech—from Lerroux. The greater part was devoted to a glorification of the church he had antagonized so excessively during the greater part of his career. He spoke, he said, "with emotion" of the symbols of religion. He always slept with the image of the Virgin at the head of his bed. He who had assailed the church for years, and supported the religious clauses of the Constitution, hotly demanded the elimination from the fundamental law of the very provisions he militantly had supported in accordance with the preachings of his lifetime. It was clear that he was desperately afraid and was throwing himself upon the mercy of Gil Robles.

The Fascists went in under false colors, for José Primo de Rivera was refused admission into the Rightist coalition that would have assured his election. The avowed Fascists were not strong enough in any one constituency to elect him without an alliance, and this he was denied. He had not been forgiven his bad manners when he broke the pious spell thrown over the Cortes as the Rightists virtuously vindicated their leaders on the scandals, by shouting "*Viva Straperlo.*" His friends put him up in a number of districts hoping that he might win in one.

Count Romanones ran as usual in his province of Guadalajara, which he swayed as did the great landowning nobility of England in theirs in the eighteenth century. Azaña and Prieto ran again in Bilbao, where their election was almost certain. Gil Robles stood again in Salamanca, Fernando de los Ríos in Granada, Calvo Sotelo and Portela in Galicia.

5

In the midst of the campaign there were diversions. After the funeral services for George V in the little English church, I drove Salvador de Madariaga and his pleasant English wife to their home. He lived in a house of his planning in a new residential section. It was the home of a scholar and it was there I saw Zuloaga's portrait of Madariaga.

That day Madariaga interested me by his gloomy pessimism over the future of democracy. He doubted if it could survive the increasing monopolization of the agencies of publicity by the special interests. With the electoral campaign in Spain, he had but an academic interest. "I have lived most of my life outside Spain," he said again. He was temperamentally antipathetic to practical politics and was more political philosopher than politician.

That winter even the social scene was poisoned by the venom of the struggle. One felt it when, a month later, Alcalá Zamora gave his usual dinner to the chiefs of missions. The grand stairway was lined as before with the rigid guards, and the rooms were warmer than ever, but there was a chill in the air. There was the same opulence of food, the same wilderness of flowers, and, later, in the throne room, there was a concert with the brilliant orchestra leader, Sr. Arbos, directing; and after that the usual cold supper. But the atmosphere was chilly and tense, and nothing appeared quite normal. Men seemed mannequins that night, or actors in uncongenial roles. Alcalá Zamora played his part well, smiling cordially throughout, though the hustings over the country roared with the threat of Gil Robles to drive him from the palace if he won. It was to be Alcalá Zamora's last dinner in the palace.

6

It was not until the last week that the Rightists and Leftists unlimbered their heavy artillery the same day in Madrid. The speeches in one theater were relayed by radio to many cinemas taken for the overflow. The attempt of some extremists to howl down Azaña was a gift of the gods to the Fascist and military propagandists. Meanwhile, Portela had formed his Center party, but soon he went over to the Rightists for some political reason. And

Gil Robles, after a period of silence, was renewing his attacks on Alcalá Zamora and threatening his impeachment.

Then a real sensation. Word reached Madrid that the headquarters of the labor unions in Granada and Badajoz had been ordered closed, and that a meeting of more than eight people had been prohibited in Badajoz. These stupid orders were speedily rescinded by Portela, who knew they would justify a resort to violence. . . . Meanwhile, Juan March was assuming immense proportions as the dictator of the Rightist coalition, contributing a fortune to the campaign fund and exercising the right of veto over candidacies. . . . And then, less than a week before the election, another scandal broke. Sr. Paya, Sub-Minister of Finance, publicly charged that Juan March had vetoed his candidacy in Murcia because Paya had interfered with March's plan to "rob the Treasury" of eighteen million pesetas. March was seeking a refund of that amount to his Porte Pi Oil Company, and Paya had rejected the claim. Then, charged Paya, March crowded the corridors of the Ministry of Finance with agents, armed with bribe money, and these, along with their master, had been ejected. The vetoing of Paya's candidacy in Murcia was March's revenge. Paya complained to Santiago Alba, who scouted the idea, but in the evening he was reported to have telephoned Paya that he had learned from CEDA leaders that it was true, and that Gil Robles could do nothing about it. Few realized at the time what a commanding position March had among the Rightists, but many were recalling the comment of Jaime Carner, Minister of Finance under Azaña, that "either the Republic will destroy Juan March, or Juan March will destroy the Republic."

But another scandal did not shake the supreme confidence of the Rightists.

7

That confidence I could not understand. A lifetime of study of political psychology and reactions convinced me that the Leftists would win. The dearth of constructive action by the Gil Robles-Lerroux combination in more than two years of power, the savagery of the Moors in the Asturias, the imprisonment of thirty thousand men, the rejection of agrarian reforms, the nonenforcement of the labor laws, the abandonment of the educational program, the scandals—it did not seem a record to make a popular appeal. Calvo Sotelo was denouncing the Republic openly. Gil Robles was complaining that the curse of Spain was too much education. The peasants were getting two and three pesetas a day. I tried to find in the record some possible appeal to the mass of the voters, and without success. But among my colleagues of the corps, I was almost alone, and among my social associates in Madrid, entirely alone in this view of the outcome.

True, the Rightists were holding great meetings in the larger cities to cheering crowds, but these meetings were exclusive, with admission by card, and thus packed with picked partisans, not unlike those in front of Mussolini's balcony or Hitler's tribunal. Even then the extremists of the Right had adopted the Fascist technique. The papers were filled with the speeches and pictures of the cheering throng, and to those superficially impressed, this made the contest seem one-sided. When I expressed surprise that the Leftists were holding so few meetings, my wrong impression was corrected, and I learned that their meetings outnumbered those of their foes. But their meetings were in the villages and small towns, where admission was not by card. They were going out where the greater part of the people lived and were working on the wavering. I could not understand the confidence of the Rightists. True, Portela, now making common cause with the Rightists, could manipulate the electoral machinery. True, the syndicalists had not formerly joined the Popular Front, and Rightist leaders had assured me they could be bought. True, the combination of the Right had the greatest campaign fund in Spanish history, but even so, the drift seemed plain to me.

There was one of the leaders of the extreme Right who was a realist. Returning to Madrid from a speaking tour, Calvo Sotelo publicly deprecated the optimism as vastly overdone. His scouring of the villages had convinced him of an unmistakable leftward drift. He warned that all the women who had voted with the Rightists before would not do so again. But he made as much impression as a feather in a cyclone.

Four days before the election, we drove to the Casa de Campo, and in the poorer section through which we passed I observed the walls plastered with the posters of the Leftists. An unusual number of armed men in uniforms was noticeable. Yet the campaign had been without violence. *The processes of democracy were working out peacefully within the law.*

Never had the Casa de Campo been more beautiful. We got out and walked a bit in the woods. Driving home, we met Cardinal Tedeschini on his stroll. I knocked on the window, and he came laughing to the car in high spirits and quite happy. He invited me to dinner on Wednesday after the election. I was sure the dinner was to be a celebration of the expected Rightist victory.

8

On election day the rain came down in torrents. There were no disorders in the capital, though there was some uneasiness in aristocratic circles. One grandee of my acquaintance went to the polls in a dowdy coat and with a cap, in order not to attract attention. The nobility, offering their cars to convey voters to the polls, had them insured against burning or any other destruction, and their chauffeurs were instructed to abandon the car should it be attacked. But nothing happened. An election in Chicago would have seemed a riot in comparison.

During the day, reports came in of minor disturbances elsewhere. Some voting boxes were smashed in Valencia, Pamplona, and Santiago de Compostela. . . . There was a fight between groups of opposing partisans in a little town near Oviedo, and one man was killed . . . Thirty armed men were found on a roof in Saragossa and dislodged by the police . . . In some pueblos no election boxes were received, and this was the blunder—or the crime—of the government conducting the elections.

At eight at night, an American businessman triumphantly telephoned me that the Rightists had won a sweeping victory and were celebrating at the headquarters of Gil Robles. But three hours later, the same voice brought a different message. The parties lead by Azaña had swept Catalonia, the Asturias, Santander, Madrid, and, indeed the country. Enthusiasm had died down in the headquarters of Gil Robles, and the few remaining were disconsolately filing out into the night. There was no doubt at midnight.

The morning revealed a remarkable reversal of the verdict of
1933—*and this with thirty thousand political prisoners of the Left in
prison and deprived of their vote.*

The casualties among leading politicians were appalling. Lerroux, defeated, had ended his long career under a cloud. Roca, his
friend, was out. Martínez Velasco, leader of the agrarians, was
retired, and his friends were ascribing his defeat to the CEDA.
Count Romanones was returned again from his province of Guadalajara, but Goicoechea, the official leader of the monarchists,
was out. So, too, was José Primo de Rivera.

9

Since unscrupulous propaganda during the Fascist war was to
give the outside world fantastic notions of the significance of the
election, a brief analysis of the vote may be helpful. The socialist
party, more moderate than that of Attlee in England, elected
ninety-nine members of the Cortes; the party of Azaña, eighty-
seven; that of Barrio, thirty-nine; the Esquerra of Catalonia, thirty-
six; and the communists, fifteen. In the combination of the Left,
the combined strength of the straight republican, democratic
parties of Azaña and Barrio outnumbered the socialists by twenty-
seven votes. The combined vote of the socialists and the communists
gave them but a hundred and sixteen out of more than four
hundred and seventy members, and the hostility of these two was
bitter and notorious.

Among the parties of the Right, that of Gil Robles alone elected
a respectable number—eighty-eight. The Bloc Nacional, the monarchists with Fascist leanings, won but thirteen seats, the Carlists
but nine. The once-strong party of Lerroux was practically wiped
out, with but four elected. The Center party of Portela won but
sixteen seats.

And the election machinery had been entirely in the hands of
the defeated.

A few months later, when the propaganda specialists of Hitler
and Mussolini took over in Spain, the world would be told that
the country was divided into two groups only—the communists and
Fascists; but the best the communists and avowed Fascists could do
in the election just before the rebellion was to have a combined

strength of but twenty-nine members out of four hundred and seventy.

However, the Rightists were paralyzed with amazement and fear, and the fear was akin to hysteria. The day after the election, the two country clubs near Madrid were deserted. The garages sheltering the cars of the aristocracy were filled all day, for their owners were afraid to venture out. Social functions were canceled. Cardinal Tedeschini telephoned to me postponing the dinner that never was to be given. Many of the nobility thought instantly of flight, as on the fall of the King. The day after the election, it was impossible to make reservations on trains for several days ahead. Juan March did not stand on the order of his going but turned tail and ran. The Rock Hotel in Gibraltar was packed to overflowing with the Spanish nobility and aristocracy, and the monarchist organ, the *A.B.C.*, bitterly attacked them as lacking in patriotism and courage. That day the Duke of Montellano called upon me, calm and unafraid. A friend had telephoned him asking what he was doing with his children and was told that he was keeping them in that day, but that they would go out the next. In truth, his little daughter was out in the embassy garden that very day.

Why the hysteria?

The election had been peaceable, but with the Leftists' victory, a few hundred young extremists conceived the notion of storming the prisons and releasing the political prisoners at once. Since the Left manifesto promised amnesty, the stupidity of the performance is manifest. The government became alarmed when the police refused to shoot into the crowd, and when some soldiers, sent into the Puerta del Sol, seething with celebrators, fraternized, its fright increased. It declared a "state of alarm"; but when the rumor spread that it planned to declare a "state of war," the conviction grew with many thousands that the victors were to be robbed of their victory by a military *coup d'état*. The labor unions responded with a threat to call a general strike, and the government wisely refrained from going further. But it again clapped on the censorship, which was not wise.

Was the victors' fear of a military *coup d'état* that would leave the thirty thousand political prisoners in jail a mere pretext? *Most emphatically it was not.* The threat had figured with astounding frankness in the daily conversations in the cafés and streets for many months. No one doubted that there had been a manipulation of the army when Gil Robles was the minister and General Franco was the Chief of Staff. And Portela had favored the Rightists in the elections. Under the rules, the new Cortes would not meet for a month, and in the meanwhile, the new government would not take power. This, reasoned the suspicious, would give the Rightists a month in which to perfect their plans and carry them out.

It was not positively known then that immediately after the election result was known, General Franco called on Portela with the suggestion that the government be turned over to him; or that before dawn on the night of the election, Gil Robles had approached the Prime Minister with the proposition that Portela assume dictatorial power. But this was heard in undertones. Later, Franco was to deny it, but Portela confirmed it.

Then, two nights after the election, unquestionably strange things happened in Madrid. Conspirators in the army were known to be meeting in secret at night in the little church of San Luis. In the aviation barracks of Cuatro Vientos there was an actual rising. One of the officers, relieved from duty and told he might go home for the night, went, instead, to his favorite café, frequented by military men. When he replied to inquiries about his absence from his post, his companions exclaimed in a chorus: "Ah, a *coup d'état!*" He hurried back to the barracks and was refused admittance. Returning to Madrid, he gave the alarm. Soldiers were rushed to Cuatro Vientos. They surrounded it, and some officers were arrested.

In the light of the events of the following July, there was ample justification for the uneasiness of the victors at the polls. Martínez Barrio, who was not an alarmist, went to the palace to warn Alcalá Zamora that unless there was a legal transfer of power, a general strike on the morrow would be the acceptance of the challenge.

Six months later, in Fuenterrabia, Count Romanones told me that active plans for the rebellion began the moment the victory of the parties of the Left under Azaña was known. Plans, of course, were made long before.

10

In the midst of the uncertainty and excitement, no one could have been more unhappy than Gil Robles. The day after the election, the *A.B.C.* bitterly attacked him, and thereafter criticism fell upon him in showers. For two and a half years he had been master, and the collaborationists of 1933 resented his failure to make good on the promises of the campaign. The two and a half years had been barren. The King was not back. All the peasants were not off the land. The labor laws, if not enforced, had not been repealed. Even his warmest supporters had been annoyed by the rashness of some of his public utterances. Some could not forgive him for his close alliance with Lerroux, and the friends of Lerroux could not forgive him for his final desertion of their favorite. His policy had proven ruinous to all the parties of the Right but his own. Lerroux was defeated and his party wiped out. Martínez Velasco, agrarian leader, was defeated and his party reduced to minor importance. Goicoechea, monarchist leader, had been defeated and his party had made no gains. And among the more liberal of his own party, he was criticized for his failure to support the land program of Fernández. Many thought he had lost his head in the clouds, unable to see where he was treading, while marching blindly to the intoxicating clamor of his young idolaters shouting, "All power to the Chief" and "The Chief is always right." Heartsick, his nerves shaken, he announced his temporary retirement, and Fernández was proclaimed his temporary successor.

Realizing now that the victors at the polls could not be robbed of their victory without a fight, and that public order would be threatened as long as the Rightists retained their grasp upon the government, Alcalá Zamora, on the highly patriotic advice of Portela, summoned Azaña to the palace, but he refused to go. Portela then called him on the telephone and was informed that Azaña was too busy to talk. It was his determination not to consult or consider the assumption of power until the official declaration of the poll. But when, the same day, Portela resigned, Azaña again was summoned to the palace, and went. There is not the shadow of doubt that for forty-eight hours Spain was on the verge of an eruption.

11

Charged with forming a government at six in the evening, Azaña announced his Ministry three hours later. Instead of taking the War Office himself, he gave it to a general, which might have moderated the fears of the army officers if they had any real fears. Augusto Barcia, the able, clean leader of Azaña's party, was made Minister of State. Santiago Casares Quiroga, the intimate friend of Azaña's, was made Minister of Public Works, and Domingo, Azaña's former Minister of Agriculture, was made Minister of Education. For the Ministry of Finance, Azaña went outside the professional politicians, and selected Gabriel Franco, who had been chairman of the Finance Committee in the Constituent Assembly.

Of course, no communist was ever considered or thought of, but there was not even a socialist in the government since they had asked no place, in accordance with an agreement made before. All the ministers, except the two technicians, were selected from among the followers of Azaña and Barrio, with one republican from the Left party of Catalonia, and one Basque.

Thus—and this is important in view of the propaganda later:

There was not one communist in the government.

There was not even one socialist of the mild type of Besteiro.

There was not one who could be described as an extremist; not one who was not a republican and a democrat in the French and American sense.

This cannot be too strongly stressed, since when the rebellion began, it was to be justified as aimed against a "communist government," and Hitler in Berlin and Mussolini in Rome were to justify their armed intervention with the smug and hypocritical assertion that they "could not tolerate a communist government in western Europe."

3

THE AXIS WAR
ON SPANISH DEMOCRACY

Chapter XIV

The Conspiracy Unfolds

THE next day, Augusto Barcia made his protocol call at the embassy as Minister of Foreign Affairs. He was an able lawyer and a worthy representative of the liberalism and culture of the country, for, like Unamuno, Azaña, and Fernando de los Ríos, he had been president of the Ateneo Club, composed for a full century of the best minds of the nation. A man of medium height, graceful in his bearing, jovial but dignified in manner, he had impressed me by his ability, dignity, and poise. He was moderate in his views and methods and he had not one drop of intolerance in his blood. During his exile in Buenos Aires after the Fascist rebellion, he was to write a brilliant five-volume interpretation of San Martín.

The Spanish of the Right turned out to be shockingly bad sportsmen. Instead of turning momentarily from politics to their business, with some semblance of philosophy, as political losers would have done in the United States and England, they presented a scowling countenance to the world. In social circles in Madrid, it was as though there were a general mourning for the dead after a major battle. Society closed its doors and drew the window shades. Before the election, there had been much gaiety among the young, but thereafter there were no parties. The youngsters reflected the gloomy pessimism of their elders. That this silly mood was encouraged by those creating the atmosphere for a military or Fascist *coup* I have no doubt.

From the moment the election result was known, the irresponsible and unscrupulous tongue of Fascist propaganda began to clatter. One night a member of my staff excitedly telephoned me that churches were "burning down everywhere"; that Companys, the Catalan President, released from prison, was arriving in Madrid that night, and that the Swedish Minister, notoriously reactionary, had said that "we shall be lucky if we get through this night without bloodshed." While unimpressed by this tiresome reiteration of the Fascist cry of "wolf," I telephoned the Associated Press and found that the church burnings were the old ones and that none had been "burned down." Most of these outrages were the work of irresponsible young rowdies, who, in most cases, merely poured kerosene on the stone steps, applied a match, and ran. That night passed in absolute serenity, and so it was all over Spain.

The alarm of the victors fed on the fear that before the new government could take control, a military *coup d'état* would intervene to prevent the release of the thirty thousand political prisoners. To await the meeting of the Cortes thirty days later would invite continuous unrest. Azaña appealed to the Permanent Committee of the Cortes, composed of members of every party, with the Rightists in substantial majority, to authorize the immediate amnesty for the political prisoners, and it responded instantly with unanimity. With the release of the prisoners, the fever subsided, and quiet was restored. The popular festivities of the week of the carnival enlivened every town. Madrid was filled with merrymakers in costumes, both attractive and grotesque, with children in gay colors riding on the tops of taxis. Only the social sets pretended to see danger, but there was perfect order.

But when great throngs gathered in the cities, exuberant with the intoxication of the triumph, to celebrate the liberation of the prisoners, there was a potential danger. At an immense meeting in the bull ring in Madrid, utterances from some extremists were heard on which the tribe of Goebbels thrived. The demand was made that Lerroux should be tried for murder in the Asturias. Some, marching in processions, laughingly demanded "Gil Robles' head," but no normal person took this seriously. But the criticism of Julián Besteiro by extremists as a "mere reformer" implied a revolutionary trend, and Prieto was thundering in the revolutionary strain.

"You, Gil Robles, you Goicoechea, who have slandered us in spit and paste [the posters], you will have to answer to us, face to face."

The electoral upheaval, however, had cast into the Cortes a real revolutionist, Dolores Ibarruri, a communist deputy from the mining region of the Asturias. She was called "the Passion Flower" by her admirers. She had intelligence and a simple eloquence, and leading the tiny flock of communists in the Cortes, she dominated them by her personality. She invariably dressed in black. Her strong face shows in the bust by Jo Davidson. She was the only one of the tiny group of communists who had significance, and the Fascists were to make the most of her.

2

Time would disclose that the numerically insignificant communists, astutely led, perfectly disciplined, would not be the important disturbers of peace. The problem of Azaña was not the socialists or even the communists, but the syndicalists and the anarchists.

For fifty years the anarchists had a large following in Barcelona. Anarchy did not come to Spain with the Republic. It had taken root in the country as early as 1868, and by 1873 it had a membership of three hundred thousand, with two hundred and seventy local centers, the most important in Barcelona. Their terroristic activities had begun in the reign of Alfonso XII, with outrages in Barcelona, with an attempt to assassinate the King, with the murder of Cánovas del Castillo, with a revolutionary strike in 1902, with the attempt to kill Premier Maura in 1904, and with the rioting in Barcelona in 1909.

Nor did the syndicalists come to Spain with the Republic. They had appeared as early as 1892, with a policy of intimidation similar to that of the anarchists, though the latter bitterly resented them, and there were bloody encounters between them.

Then, with the growth of socialism, and the creation of the powerful General Union of Workers, the two decentralizing groups were driven together; and when, in 1910, the syndicalists organized their National Confederation of Labor to combat the more moderate socialist General Union of Workers, the anarchists joined; and through their more intensive intimidation, often dominated it. But at the same time the anarchists maintained their own organization, the Iberian Anarchists' Federation, secret, illegal, pledged to anarchy in the raw.

But neither the syndicalists nor the anarchists were in the *Frente Popular* in the elections. They had contempt for Azaña's ideal of representative democracy, and, after the election, they remained what they had been under the monarchy—enemies of the constituted authority.

After the release of the prisoners, there was general order in Spain, though here and there incidents occurred, involving few participants, and most of these were boys. But it was crystal clear that a high-powered propaganda had been prepared to create the impression that the country was in a state of anarchy—the now familiar technique. Here, in a quarrel over politics, a man was stabbed in a bar; a hundred miles away a dozen young socialists and Fascists engaged in a fight and some were hurt; fifty miles from this unimportant brawl, a score of peasants went on a grandee's land and cut some trees; far away from there a small strike was called, affecting one small town; in Pamplona a church was robbed, by foreigners, ordinary criminals. All such incidents were carefully and systematically assembled day by day and published in the antidemocratic papers under a standing headline: "Social Disorders in Spain." The foreign press made the most of this. It was as though in the United States every fight, every killing, every robbery, every crime, every strike, no matter how insignificant, was noted and published on the front page of *The New York Times* daily under the standing caption, "Social Disorders in the United States."

When nothing could be found, something was manufactured, since I figured in some of the "incidents" and I know. Stories were told of dire dangers on the country roads, of threats, of shaken fists, of ferocious faces peering leeringly into passing cars. The propaganda was directed by Nazi agents as a justification to world opinion for the Fascist rebellion to which at that hour, as we now know, both Hitler and Mussolini were committed.

I determined to see for myself.

3

In early March, 1936, General Fuqua, Biddle Garrison, and I drove toward the much publicized dangers. It was a pure, crisp day, and the air from the snow-capped mountains as we drove eastward toward Valencia was cold. We lunched in a village at a tavern with an unpromising exterior, but the crude dining room was clean and the food excellent. We entered through a court paved with cobblestones that might have been contemporary with Cervantes, and as we left, an old woman at the door bade us "Go with God." We reached Valencia in the evening without having seen one scowl or clenched fist. The villages were serene, the people friendly. The consul in Valencia told me that at the celebration of the electoral victory, the city was packed with exultant marching men—*without any incident*. They had pledged themselves to maintain perfect order—*and they did*. The police, hidden from view on side-streets, were ready for an emergency—*that did not come*. The consul had not seen a drunk man that day.

The next afternoon we resumed our journey, driving south along a magic coast toward Alicante. Nowhere, I think, can there be a drive more beautiful than along this coast road by the Mediterranean. The road was congested with traffic, for this was the harvesting season for the orange crop. Orchards waved their ripe fruit at us as we passed; great trucks loaded with oranges crept by; great piles of oranges by the roadside awaited the loading. Along the highway, too, for miles, were piles of artichokes which singing peasants were loading into wagons. Everyone seemed merry, busy, happy.

At length we reached the unique *parador* of Infante, where we passed the night. A short distance from the highway on the very edge of the sea loomed a huge black rock, a miniature Gibraltar, and there, beside it, stood the *parador*—the most elaborate I had seen. The large, attractively furnished rooms looked directly upon the sea, and one could sit on a stone terrace beside the water for tea or breakfast.

The drive thence to Alicante is enchanting, with charming vistas of the sea, orange groves, and avenues of palms. That day we lunched at a resort called Bascot, beloved by the comparatively few who know it, for its pine woods, its hills and valleys, its distant sea views, and its big fresh-water bathing pool. Long before, the old mansion had been converted into a hostelry.

4

Walking through the garden, aflame with flowers of every hue, we came to the edge of a deep valley, heavily wooded, and among the trees a modern castle was pointed out to us and we were told the story.

Not many years before, a Spanish count, whose ancestral home was the mansion now turned into a hostelry, fell in love with a beautiful gypsy girl of Alicante. For a long time she denied his appeal for marriage because of the bitterness of the tribe against alliances outside the clan. At length she agreed to marriage on one condition, that he would build her a castle wherever she might wish. The marriage was consummated, and the castle built. Within two months after they had taken up residence in the castle, the beautiful gypsy was dead. It was whispered among the superstitious peasants that she had died of the curse put upon her by the gypsies. The count was crushed and could no longer bear the sight of the castle that had become the mausoleum of his romance, and he went away, never to enter its door again. The castle was locked and barred. Soon the peasants were sure that in the night they could see the ghost of the gypsy countess hovering in the air above the castle of her dreams. Even in the bright sunshine, that pile of masonry in the wooded valley seemed a bit eerie.

5

Thence between rows of palm trees we drove into Alicante, where, at night, the streets were thronged with lighthearted groups of the young, who seemed carefree and friendly. But the next morning we saw what a mad mob can do, not only to property but to a good cause. Passing through the old town of Elche, I was reminded of the church of Santa María, where the primitive passion play had been given annually for many years by the natives—more primitive, less professional, less mercenary than that of Oberammergau. No effort has ever been made to commercialize the drama. The church itself could scarcely accommodate more than the parishioners, and though the occasional stranger was welcomed, the play primarily was intended for the villagers only. I wished to see the church where this passion play had been given for generations.

We drove through the narrowest streets I have ever seen to reach it. The doors of the church were closed, and some women were standing solemnly at the entrance. I had not heard of the attack on this church during the three days of disturbances, but peering through an opening in the door, it was plainly to be seen that there had been a fire. The walls and ceiling near the altar were stained by smoke.

And then I heard the story. A mob composed of anarchists and rowdies had broken in, smashed the altar, piled all the images together upon the ruins, and given them to the flames. The eyes of the women at the door were suffused with tears, and their eagerness, in assuming us to be officials from Madrid, come to restore their church, was touching.

In the village of Montaedo, not far away, we lunched that day at a long table stained by time in the basement of The Two Brothers, whose walls were hung with interesting old prints and bull-fight posters. The atmosphere was warmly cordial and the food and service excellent. The street was crowded with loungers so manifestly peaceable and friendly that we did not hesitate to leave the car unattended among them while Pepe had his lunch.

6

Thence onward to Almería.

For many years, Americans were fond of the huge juicy Almerían grapes, and the prosperity of the province rested to a considerable degree on the American market. A decade or more ago, our Agricultural Department banned these grapes because of the appearance of the Mediterranean fly. Years passed. The vineyards of Almería no longer were afflicted with the fly, but the ban continued. Meanwhile, France, which had taken some of the Almerían product, excluded it from her market to "protect" her own grapes from competition, and so Almería fell on evil days. No matter how great the crop, it brought no income, and cruel poverty fell upon the people. Convinced that a formula could be found that would permit the readmission of this delicious grape, I urged Washington that one be sought, and at length one was agreed upon. The gratitude of the people of Almería was sincere, since it meant a more bountiful life for them. I was invited to visit the town and be feted, but I am glad I did not go. The plan we had devised provided for refrigeration, which shriveled the skin and ruined the sale in our market.

7

I had asked a friend in southern Spain why some decent peasants in that region were anarchistic. "I think I can guess," he said. "These people are dreadfully poor and illiterate, but kindly and altruistic. If the larder of one is empty, that of a neighbor is thrown open. They get along together on the most amicable terms. They feel that, left to themselves, they would have no troubles. But the government makes laws interfering with their fishing; the Civil Guards enforce these laws with no show of sympathy; other governments forbid the admission of their products on some pretext or other, and they come to the conclusion, in their elemental thinking, that they would be happy if it were not for government."

When I saw the poverty of this once-happy community, I began to understand. Here surely I would find lawlessness and a hostile attitude, but nothing remotely like it could be seen. Almería haunted me the rest of the journey. Misery brooded over it. Stark poverty stalked its listless streets. The leading hotel was the worst I had seen in Spain, and yet there was pathos in the eagerness of the manager to please. That night the town was like a city of the dead. There was no form of entertainment, for the mass of the people had no pesetas for amusement. We found a large, crude café where the people congregated and gossiped while sipping a sweet spring water which cost them scarcely anything at all.

And in Almería, where poverty was unjustly, unnecessarily imposed, we found nothing but courtesy. Surely this was not the "turbulent Spain" of which the people of London and New York were reading.

8

Most of the next day we were driving over a fascinating road, looking down upon the sea, toward Málaga. The blue sea, the green fields, the purple grapes, the small towns, clean and freshly white-washed, with their red roofs shining in the sun, made an unforgettable picture. Though it was Sunday, we saw a woman busy with her whitewash brush upon her house. It was evening when we reached Torremolines and found lodging at the Santa Clara. At the home of Jay Allen I met a small, slender man with gray hair and a pinched, parchment face who proved to be Sir George Young, for many years in the British Foreign Service, but now retired. I lunched with him the next day in his charming old house, where I found his brother-in-law, Professor H. A. L. Fisher, who was slowly recovering from a breakdown following the completion of his *A History of Europe*. Tall, slender, with a student's stoop and a shy English smile, he looked his role in life. Sir George was to leave Torremolines a few months later to escape the bludgeons of the Fascists.

That night, at a place of entertainment in Málaga, I had my first contact with the incredible Fascist propaganda flooding the world from Spain. There, officers of the Foreign Legion, returning to Africa from the Asturias, were telling a startling tale. Solemnly they assured us that when the Legion disembarked at Cádiz to change boats, a mob attacked them and they were forced to shoot, ten being killed by the volley. Then, they said, the mob ran amuck, burning churches and convents. The story was told with the best barracks-room swagger, and General Fuqua, professionally interested, asked many questions, which were answered glibly. I have no doubt this story reached the foreign press. A day or so later we learned positively that on that occasion there had been no mob, no attack upon the Legion, no shooting, no burning of churches. I was convinced then, as I am now, that such fantastic stories were part of the systematic plan for creating the impression that Spain was in a state of anarchy to justify the Fascist rebellion in the offing and the intervention of Hitler's and Mussolini's troops.

Unable to find lodgings the next night at the Rock Hotel in Gibraltar, crowded with Spanish noblemen and aristocrats in flight from fear, we passed the night at the charming María Cristina in Algeciras in Spain with the English, who were not afraid.

The next morning we were on our way to Seville. Warned that the main route, via Cádiz, could not be used because floods had washed a bridge away, we went inland by way of the medieval town of Medina-Sidonia, and this took us through a region of rich resources and rare beauty. For two hours we drove through thick forests of cork trees, most of the trees skinned from the ground to the branches.

We had just arrived at the Hotel Madrid in Seville when Pepe came running in to say that in Madrid an attempt had been made to murder Jiménez de Asúa, a brilliant young socialist deputy, vice-president of the Cortes and internationally known as an authority on penal law and prison reform. Though the attempt had failed, one policeman had been shot. It seemed ineffably stupid. It would invite, and it was no doubt hoped it would invite, reprisals.

The next morning I breakfasted by the open French door of my room looking out on a delightful patio, fragrant and colorful with trees and white and yellow flowers. Birds were singing rapturously in the trees. In the afternoon we visited the cathedral, and that night we walked the narrow streets, finding the smart shops of the historic Sierpe open as late as one o'clock.

Except for the isolated instance at Elche, we had seen nothing of the lawlessness, so picturesquely ascribed in the foreign press to the region through which we had passed in meticulous search of the anarchy of which we had heard daily, nor had we heard of anything of the sort.

9

The next day we had our "incident."

We had lunched at Córdoba and had hurried on to spend the night in the medieval town of Úbeda in the fine old palace in which Isabella the Catholic had tarried during the conquest of Granada, and where St. Theresa had lingered on her way to the opening of a convent. It had now been converted into a *parador*. We planned to spend the night in this beautiful palace and see the fine Renaissance churches which are the glory of the town. It was a delightful drive through an opulent countryside, with small villages at close intervals, and with villagers promenading on the paved highway. Taking possession of our rooms, we set forth at dusk on an exploration of the town. A narrow street led from the *parador* to the plaza, lined with attractive little shops. We found the Plaza de Toledo thronged with loungers. Nothing could have seemed more peaceful. Satisfying our curiosity, we started back to the *parador*.

We were walking single file along the narrow sidewalk, and General Fuqua had just disappeared around the offset, when I was amazed to see an armed Assault Guard bearing down upon me on the run in a threatening manner and in a frenzy of excitement. Shouting incoherently the while, he was running his hands over me before I realized I was being searched for arms in the street. A number of idlers stood at the opening into the plaza watching the strange exhibition. It was so absurd that for a moment I was more amused than indignant. The guard was in such a state of excitement that he could not listen to my explanation of my identity, and, at length, giving it up, I suggested that he accompany me to his chief. This seemed both to astonish and relieve him, and he smiled.

Just around the corner in the plaza was the police station, and at a little desk sat a man in citizen's clothes, the socialist chief of police. I was in the midst of my protest to this dignitary when I heard a chuckle, and turning, I found General Fuqua grinning gaily in the custody of another guard who had been sent to fetch him. The police chief seemed to find the incident diverting, and certainly not one calling for an expression of regret. He coolly explained that they were searching all strangers, and when I suggested that the rule surely did not apply to an ambassador accredited to Spain, he laughed heartily at my simplicity.

"We know no personalities," he said righteously.

I would not have missed the incident for anything, and at length, when we left, everything was forgiven. But a large crowd had assembled in the plaza facing the station, evidently convinced by the spectacular dash of the guard upon me that we were desperate characters. As we passed out into the street, there were two or three low hisses and a few boos. We ignored this and walked on slowly, but not without a realization of how easy it would have been for a mischief-maker to have aroused the passions of a mob.

By the time we reached the *parador*, I was indignant, and Garrison was sent formally to protest to the mayor. It was Saturday, and on Sunday the peasants of the region were to celebrate the electoral victory at Úbeda, and if we were not wanted there, we could leave that night. Garrison found the socialist mayor, unshaven and with weary, bloodshot eyes, surrounded by his advisers, looking equally worn, but sincere and conscientious. Scarcely had Garrison begun when the Mayor interrupted:

"I have just heard about it," he said. "I am very sorry. Tomorrow the peasants are to celebrate in Úbeda, and we have been warned that mischief-makers are coming to start rioting and to burn our churches. We socialists may not be religious, but these churches are our most priceless possessions, and we do not intend that harm shall come to them. We have been busy for two days and nights preparing to protect them and to preserve order. We asked the government for assistance, and a number of Assault Guards, strangers here, have been sent in, and the officer who made the blunder is one of these. I am sorry. We do not want you to leave. We want you to stay and see the churches. It is unfortunate that, on top of the warning, three strangers should have been seen in the plaza on the eve of the celebration, since we have had repeated warnings that Fascist agents were being sent."

That seemed good enough to me. I was delighted that these socialist officials were determined to protect the churches and preserve order. So I swore Fuqua and Garrison to silence and kept the incident from the press. Scarcely had I reached Madrid when a representative of the government appeared to apologize and to thank me for my attitude.

During the next few months I was to hear much of the occasional outrages, the threat of which had so aroused the fears of Úbeda. It was significant that few were incited by the people of the community in which they occurred. Frequently the ringleaders were strangers who had mysteriously appeared and as mysteriously had disappeared.

Who instigated them? Who bore the expense of travel? One thing is certain—it was not the government; it was not the socialists; it was an enemy and not a friend of the Azaña government. I am sure that many incidents were inspired by Fascist provocateurs. There were so many "tourists" from Germany swarming over Spain at the time!

We had traveled for days, for hundreds of miles, and seen no outrages, received no affronts, and we had found the villages and the countryside as peaceful and law-abiding as those of Westchester in New York. Our only incident grew out of the determination of the friends of government to preserve law and order.

10

We returned to Madrid in time for the opening of the Cortes. A long procession lined the streets, awaiting the opening of the public galleries. I was impressed by the absence of familiar faces on the floor. Lerroux was gone. If Gil Robles was there, he was inconspicuous. Santiago Alba, humiliated and disgusted, leading the four surviving members of Lerroux' party, sat sad and disillusioned.

But it was Largo Caballero who aroused my curiosity and misgivings. He sat in the front row, his bald head gleaming, his hands constantly in motion as he talked with deputies around him. He agreed to the Popular Front on the basis of a definite program, but even now he was manifesting impatience with the processes of a representative democracy and was threatening the Cortes with "the man in the street." It did not so much matter, he said, what the government wanted; the man in the street would tell it what it could do. His rash statements at this time were complete negations of his campaign speeches. Hinting at force, they were eagerly seized upon by the extremists of the Right for their propaganda. He was playing into the hands of the Fascist agents. At this time, too, he was flirting with the syndicalists while threatening the constitutional program to which he had agreed in the campaign. His honesty and sincere devotion to labor I could not doubt, but his judgment in these days was worse than bad.

Meanwhile, Prieto and the more moderate of the socialists were in no mood to follow Caballero's leadership in this direction, and there was an open schism.

In the meantime, the provocateurs were increasingly active. Some young Fascist gunmen fired on the house of Caballero . . . Groups of anarchists and syndicalists were trying to terrorize the workers of the socialist union . . . None of this, however, affected the mass of the people—any more than a shirtwaist workers' strike affects New York, but these petty clashes, exaggerated in the foreign press, conveyed a false impression.

With clashes between extremists, Azaña summoned José

Primo de Rivera, whom he respected for his courage, and asked him voluntarily to leave the country on some pretext until the excitement died down. Had the Puerta del Sol been packed with a raving mob of anarchists, young José would have been content with nothing less than a ride on a white horse into their midst. But José refused to go, and Azaña put him in prison for his own protection. I know that his friends, and I heard that his family, were convinced that Azaña had thereby saved him from almost certain destruction.

In the meantime, high-pressure Fascist propaganda was going beyond all bounds. I heard fantastic tales of Rightists beheaded in sleepy Murcia, where we had just been, with their heads carried on pikes; of Fascists and monarchists elsewhere butchered and their bodies "fed to pigs"; of motorists stopped on the highways and compelled to pay large sums for permission to drive on. One night the United Press telephoned me they had heard that during that afternoon, while driving in the country near Madrid, I had been stopped and forced to pay. I had not been outside the embassy grounds all day. But the next morning a grandee told me he had heard the story, and that I was reported to have made such a furious protest to the Foreign Office that rigid orders had been given for the better protection of the country roads. "Oh, yes," said the Duke, "I have heard you acclaimed a public benefactor on the strength of the tale."

But through March, the real drama was the schism between Caballero and Prieto which had begun as early as the insurrection of October, 1934, and had now broadened.

Chapter XV

The Fascist Provocateurs

Azaña postponed his speech setting forth his program until the Cortes could be organized through the settlement of contested elections by the Electoral Commission. Though composed for the most part of the Leftists under the chairmanship of Prieto, fully as many decisions went to the parties defeated at the polls as to the victors. I am sure the decisions were reached judicially, regardless of political considerations, and the Rightists had no legitimate cause for complaint. Once only did political considerations enter and that was in the contest of Calvo Sotelo in the constituency of Orense. It was less his enmity to democracy than the arrogance of his hostility to the regime that made his name provocative. But even in his case, after the decision had gone against him, the commission reversed itself, and, rumor had it, on the intercession of Azaña. Meticulous respect for the evidence had been the rule, but the opposition was in no appreciative mood.

No one doubted that the election in Granada, where the Rightists had been given the victory, would be annulled; no honest person doubted that it should be, since the election there had been notoriously dishonest, with armed men and intimidation playing the major roles. No one questioned that an honest election in Granada, where the socialists were strong, and the popular Fernando de los Ríos was a candidate, would have given victory to the combination of the Left. But money had been used lavishly and intimidation had been brazen. Protests to Portela, conducting the elections, were without avail. On election day, Fernando de los Ríos, entering the city where he was a candidate, had been met at the outskirts by armed men and turned back. It was an incredible piece of stupidity. He had represented Granada in the Cortes continuously since 1919, except in 1923, when he represented Madrid.

The debate was to be bitter. The resignation of the chairmanship by Prieto on the eve of the submission of the report on Granada was ascribed by *El Debate*, *Ya*, and the *A. B. C.* to his opposition to the report annulling the election, and Prieto's silence was puzzling. Gil Robles and the CEDA were out in force, and when the report on Granada was read, Fernández, acting CEDA leader, rose and announced the retirement of his party from the Chamber. Its members rose, cheered, and began to file out. The deputies of the government coalition laughed and waved handkerchiefs in farewell. Gil Robles, who had watched the childish performance from outside the enclosure, joined in the exodus, and Azaña, who entered at this moment, looked on the demonstration coldly and with a contemptuous smile. Then a spokesman for the tiny monarchist party repeated the performance, and there was more laughter and waving of handkerchiefs. Only the meager Carlist group was permitted to leave in silence.

When order was restored, Martínez Barrio, President of the Cortes, asked that the debate be conducted on a dignified plane, regardless of the desertions, and recognized Sr. Ventosa, the last Finance Minister under the King, a pleasant, able man. He aroused Prieto with the assertion that he had protested against the decision by his resignation. Prieto looked like a huge bull on the charge when he sprang to his feet to declare his warm adherence to the decision and to denounce the CEDA as "too cowardly and dishonest to stay and defend its crimes." Wild cheers greeted the denunciation.

Fernando de los Ríos followed. A polished orator, his manner of delivery, intonations, gestures were all the more effective because of their restraint. In a voice vibrant with emotion, he described the condition of the Andalusian peasantry. "You people of Castile and the north have no conception of the situation in Andalusia, where

the ancient nobility feel it necessary to resort to force and intimidation to maintain the medieval conditions that prevail there," he
said. Seldom have I heard so much feeling expressed in a conversational tone. It was superb eloquence. The greater part of the
Chamber rose and gave him an ovation.

When Prieto rose to speak directly on the issue, he bitterly
attacked Portela for permitting the outrages in Granada. With the
CEDA press indecently attacking Portela every day, Prieto could
not understand how the Prime Minister could have acquiesced
in the commission of crime. Very nervous, his hands twitching,
Portela interjected that he had ordered the governor of Granada to
stop the outrages. "You did," said de los Ríos quietly from his chair,
"but they continued, and I notified you by telegram the day before
the election."

There had been crookedness in the counting, the suppression of
free speech, the expulsion of Don Fernando on election day, the
lavish use of money. It seemed incredible ineptitude to withdraw a
party from the Cortes on the nullification of a notoriously dishonest election. I wondered if this march into the street was a
rehearsal for a military or Fascist rising and was intended as a
gesture of contempt for parliamentary procedure. Soon the pouting
party would return, but the memory of an infantile performance
would abide.

2

One day the Duke of Montellano, whose palace I occupied,
offered to add some art works of his cousin's, the Duke of Fernán-
Núñez, to those in my leased house. The palace of the latter was in
the old quarter that might conceivably figure in street fighting in
the event of trouble. Should a fire spread to his palace, it would be
difficult to save the priceless paintings and old Gothic tapestries. I
agreed to accept them on condition that they be added to the
inventory and made binding in the lease.

The next day, the Dukes of Montellano and Fernán-Núñez,
with a number of carpenters, appeared to supervise the hanging of
the paintings. These included Goya's magnificent portrait of the
Fernán-Núñez who had been Ambassador to England in the days
of Goya, another of the duchess, painted not without the touch of

malice that Goya reserved for ladies of the nobility and court, a
Greuze portrait of a beautiful lady, and two portraits of Du Barry,
once the property of that frail beauty, purchased by the Earl of
Pembroke, and later acquired by Fernán-Núñez. These paintings
were to hang on my walls throughout the rebellion undamaged,
unmolested.

Fernán-Núñez was a handsome man, rather tall and slender,
elegant and patrician. As the workmen hung the pictures, we talked
of the possibility of a military *coup d'état*. *To those outside Spain who
later were to take, hook, line, sinker, the Fascist lie that the rebellion was to
forestall a communist revolution, it may be surprising to learn that in three
and a half years I had never heard such a suggestion from anyone, while all
were talking confidently of a military* coup d'état. In the event of the
latter, the duke thought Madrid would be taken immediately, and
the rest of the country would acquiesce.

But as the time to strike approached, with Fascist agents from
Italy and Nazi agents from Germany on the ground, the most
fantastic stories were set afloat. "Bela Kun has arrived in Cádiz to
launch a communist revolution." No, said others, "he had landed in
Barcelona." Why bother about details? The aristocracy and
nobility were preparing for flight if they had not already gone.
Diplomats who had lived modestly suddenly moved into fine palaces
for a consideration little more than the protection of a foreign flag.
It was clear that the reactionaries knew of plans hidden from the
masses.

More alarming, Largo Caballero was threatening the government coalition with disruption before Azaña could present his
program to the Cortes. The socialists were dividing on Caballero's
action, and a feud was developing.

By the end of March, it was perfectly clear that a military *coup
d'état* was in active preparation. I learned from an authentic source
that this rising was to come in two weeks. The conspirators had
canvassed the barracks within a radius of twenty miles of Madrid
and were assured that all the officers were ready. General Varela
was to be in charge. At five in the morning, eight thousand troops,
with artillery, tanks, and machine guns were to march into the
city and take possession of the Ministries of War, Communications,
and Interior. That, thought the conspirators, would be enough.

My informant, like Fernán-Núñez, was sure that the easy taking of Madrid would be conclusive.

In the meanwhile, the government was not asleep. It had tapped the wires in all the barracks and officers' quarters, and agents were listening in. So ran the rumors in the latter part of March, 1936.

3

On April 4, 1936, Azaña presented himself to the Cortes in a characteristically great speech in which he pledged himself to carry out the program of the government coalition, but he warned that he would not be stampeded into anything beyond. The effect was astonishing. The speech was praised without stint by almost every sector of public opinion as statesmanlike in tone and context, and as distinguished by the purity and beauty of language that no other Spanish orator could approach. Even the Rightists thought he had chosen the psychological moment. He frankly said that he had expected some outbursts from friends of the thirty thousand long imprisoned without trial, but had assumed that these would be sporadic and not general. He could understand the hysteria of these. To have put them down with bloodshed would, he thought, have made matters infinitely worse. This speech had the momentary effect of soothing the jangled nerves of the conservatives.

The next day I had a twenty-minute talk with Azaña at the Presidencia. I found him serene and confident and I had never seen him in a happier mood as he talked freely and cordially of mutual friends and Spanish-American relations.

And then, in a flash, Prieto moved for the impeachment of Alcalá Zamora.

4

The diplomatic gallery was packed to capacity, the public galleries were overflowing, but until five in the afternoon the floor of the house was deserted. Count Romanones was the first to find his seat. The gong sounded in the lobbies, and with a rush and roar, the deputies stampeded into the chamber. Every seat on the floor was occupied. Gil Robles and his party were squeezed into the section directly in front of the Blue Bench; and behind the Blue Bench sat the followers of Azaña and Barrio.

Barrio opened the session with an appeal for dignity and decorum, and recognized Ventosa, who pled quietly for a postponement and a report from a commission. Prieto replied coldly that only the Cortes could determine the issue—the Cortes in open session. On a rising vote, no more than thirteen of the Rightists voted for the Ventosa motion. When the negative vote was taken and the greater part of the deputies sprang to their feet, the fate of the President was sealed.

Prieto presented the case for impeachment, speaking conversationally, with his usual fluency and with occasional flashes of eloquence that stirred the Chamber. He charged the President with constantly interfering with the work of the Cortes and the program of the government, with a disregard of his constitutional limitations, and with lacking sympathy for vital parts of the Constitution. He read from Gil Robles' speeches, ringing with the same charge and promising the President's impeachment in the event of a Rightist victory. He closed to loud republican and socialist applause. The cheering grew in volume, became an ovation. From his seat, Prieto waved his hand in recognition, but this only increased the storm. Finally he had to rise and bow his thanks, and half the Chamber rose with him.

Though Gil Robles' party had decided in caucus not to participate in the speaking or the voting, he was stung by Prieto's taunting into a reply. Speaking with evident emotion, with his usual rapidity of utterance, he sought to explain his change of heart on the impeachment. He had proposed impeachment under Article 81 for the dissolving of the Cortes, but since the election had shown a change in popular sentiment, the dissolution had been justified. For the moment he thus found it convenient to admit the validity of the elections.

Azaña took his place on the Blue Bench to listen to Prieto and Gil Robles. He sat motionless, his face a mask. Then he retired to the lobby.

Then rose Calvo Sotelo to speak for the Fascists and the monarchists. His was a trim figure, slender and elegant, perfectly tailored. His features were clear-cut and his expression crafty. His coal-black hair was brushed back and apparently held in order by oil. He talked directly, not eloquently, like a businessman addressing a board of directors, and he seemed to me deliberately provocative. His manner was arrogant, and, toward his opponents, insultingly contemptuous. He scoffed at the Constitution, ridiculed the constitutional limitations of the President, and declared that he should have more power. He was clearly thinking of the dictatorship he had served. "You want a dictator," shouted an excited young man from among the fifteen communists. It was quite true, but Calvo Sotelo replied with equal truth that there was a dictatorship in Russia.

Portela, the former Premier, who had advised the last dissolution, now rose to assume the responsibility and save the President. Tall, lean, his face pale and pinched, his expression grim and angry, his snow-white hair rumpled, he spoke with force and feeling. But when Miguel Maura, his enemy, interrupted with cynical and sardonic remarks, the old man shook his clenched fist at his tormentor and screamed insults with such vehemence that his face was purple.

But the humiliation of the President was to be overwhelming. Out of the two hundred and forty-three votes cast, but five were in his support, and these entirely from the Portela party. Gil Robles and the monarchist leader led their parties out without voting. In view of all they had said against Alcalá Zamora and their campaign promise to impeach him, they could not vote to save him; and because the motion of impeachment had come from the Leftists, they could not support it.

I was personally sorry for Alcalá Zamora. Temperamentally incapable of keeping within the narrow limitations of his position, he habitually had intrigued against all the governments of his regime, but I was sorry to see him humiliated. He had certain intellectual qualities I admired, but, intentional or not, his manner was supercilious. As often as not he had been right in his controversies, but he passed from power a very lonely man.

5

The observance of the fifth anniversary of the Republic promised an opportunity for provocateurs. A great procession of the soldiers and civilian societies was to march up the Castellana to be reviewed by Barrio, the Acting President, and Azaña. National dignitaries occupied a second tribunal, and the third, which alone was roofless and open to the rain which was falling, was assigned to the diplomatic corps. There we waited impatiently in the dreary drizzle. At length, in a car, accompanied by the brilliantly uniformed Presidential Guard, appeared Barrio with two or three high military officers. There were waves of applause. The cheers fell from the housetops, from which many were watching in the rain. And then the procession was sweeping by to martial music.

Suddenly, quite close to us, and just behind the stand of the President and Azaña, there was a startling boom, like the explosion of a bomb, immediately followed by the rat-a-tat-tat that everyone took for machine-gun fire. The thought flashed on many that this was an attempt to assassinate Barrio and Azaña. Instantly the people panicked to the sidewalk, men and women rushing wildly, aimlessly, in terror. A secret-service agent, bending low, hurried to our stand and motioned the occupants to the floor. The scene that followed was amusing—in retrospect. The beautiful and charming Señora Castana, wife of a Foreign Office official, was crying out frantically about her children, who were safe at home. The attractive young wives of the German Counselor, Hans Voelkers, and the Italian Secretary were sitting on the wet floor facing each other solemnly, while holding umbrellas over their heads. I remained standing, trying to see what was happening. A lady with me stooped low for the doubtful protection of a board railing, and when I assured her that the danger was over and urged her to rise, she did not move. Later, she explained that the Polish Minister was sitting on her knee.

The Presidential Guard had instantly gone into action, riding into the crowd at the seat of the trouble. Meanwhile, the soldiers in review were sweeping by with verve as though nothing had happened. But a little later a detachment of mounted Assault Guards charged, with a great clatter, down a narrow intersecting street which ran by the British Embassy. No one knew the reason. Lopez Largo, Introducer of Ambassadors, told me that some "communists" had run amuck and that the machine-gun sounds came from their pistols. This was utterly false. Thus, early, the Fascist technique was in operation. By now the rain was coming down in torrents, and we left, as most of the corps had done before. We found Pepe with the car, parked a block away. He looked disgusted and indignant. "Boom-boom," he said. "No good."

Later the truth came out, in part. A small group of Fascist youths had exploded a nondestructive bomb and this had ignited a bundle of cannon crackers. The police with difficulty saved the culprits from violence. One of the youths was too drunk to walk alone. Some thought the explosion was intended as a signal. Down the Castellana there was some booing, and a Civil Guard was hurt. After I left, a Captain Herrais, of the Engineer Corps, was seen fighting his way toward the reviewing stand of Azaña and Barrio, waving a pistol. He was intercepted and seized. I was unable to learn the reason for his action.

Was the confusion arranged to cover an assassination of Azaña or to precipitate a riot? And who was responsible? Certainly it was not the government; assuredly it was not the republicans or the socialists. Fascists? They were responsible for the explosion. Extremists of the Left unquestionably had booed the Civil Guards after the explosion when one of them was killed.

6

The next day when I drove some friends to the Escorial, the countryside was perfectly serene and very sweet in its spring dress, but even there I found an indication of tension. I had visited this majestic mountain of stone many times, but this time I found something new—two Assault Guards, with pistols in their belts, unostentatiously accompanied us. My guests supposed it was a special attention to an ambassador, but I am sure all visitors were thus accompanied in those days to prevent a possible act of vandalism. It was to be my last visit to the Escorial.

Always I made the same tour and had the same emotions. Always the court, paved with uneven, time-worn flagstones, depressed, while it fascinated me; always, the broad granite stairs seemed gloomy and bitter cold. How like a grim prison corridor were the narrow halls with their cold granite walls leading to the apartments of the great Philip. Severe and cheerless as a prison cell the rooms of Philip's sister, the Regent of Flanders. An ancient organ with its broken bellows, the worn Córdoba leather upon the floor of the small interior bedroom—these alone remained to suggest the Queen long dead.

But the study of Philip seemed alive with the spirit of the man— small, simple, more like a monastic cell than the working quarters of the mightiest monarch of his age. There stands the tall narrow desk where Philip wrote on and on interminably; and there are his books in leather, the classics of the Greeks and Romans. And there beside his chair the camp stool cut in two on which he rested his ailing leg while working. But from a window in the room we got a touch of beauty. Below, a walled-in garden of boxwood; beyond, the country reaching to the mountains. But Philip's bedroom! How small and dark, with its little altar in the corner. Through a window the monarch could look out on the high altar of the cathedral and participate in the mass. Here Philip passed to his accounting. From Madrid they carried him here to die in a curtained reclining chair, and for seven days stout servants bore him over the rough highway. That chair still stands in the little room opening upon the Hall of the Ambassadors.

This, the most ornate room of Philip's day, is neither long nor wide. On the platform stands a throne; the floor is covered with worn Córdoba leather; and at one end is a beautiful door through which Philip entered to greet and awe the ambassadors of far realms. Beside the throne, a large marble fireplace—the only one in the palace that Philip knew. At one end of the room is the small table where he signed state papers. More than the gallery of the masterpieces, more than the cathedral of exquisite beauty, these rooms of Philip awed me.

Nothing could be more beautiful or magnificent than the crypt where sleep the monarchs. Marble and onyx and gold. At one end, an altar; and around the walls, shelves with red marble caskets, all alike, and selected centuries ago. The silence of eternity broods there—silence but for the comments of the republican guide who tells us that Alfonso brought visitors there and pointed out his waiting casket with a shrug, but that the Queen could not bear the place and always waited in the cathedral. We observe that there are but a few caskets left—these waiting for Alfonso, the Queen, and his mother, and there are no more.

"Will Alfonso be brought here when he dies?" I asked the republican guard.

"Certainly," he said. "He is part of the history of Spain."

It is interesting to know that the Escorial remained in possession of the loyalists to the end of the war, and that it was respected. These "barbarous hordes," more savage, we were told, than the terrorists of the French Revolution who dragged the kings from their tombs at St. Denis and consigned their bones to quicklime, did not disturb the Spanish monarchs in their marble beds.

7

Returning that day from the Escorial, I learned that there had been some trouble in the Castellana and that extra soldiers had been sent to the embassy. These, fully armed, were pacing the Castellana by our garden.

That day, the Civil Guard, killed as a result of the Fascist disturbance on the anniversary of the Republic, was buried, and reactionary politicians planned to convert the funeral procession into a provocative political demonstration. Gil Robles insisted on walking at the head of the procession. The Minister of War, fearing trouble, requested that the line of march be changed from the Castellana to evade the possible trouble-makers, but the constituted authority was ignored. Black-shirt arrogance was becoming commonplace. Hardly had the procession moved when a pistol was drawn. Officers fell upon the young culprit, who narrowly escaped a lynching. Shots were fired from a building in the course of construction, and soldiers rushed into the building and fired on some of the workmen before discovering that none of them were armed and that strangers had gone into the building, fired, and fled. The provocateurs! There was a bitter reaction among the workers.

Meanwhile, the government was sending officers on ahead to search on the curb for arms. At length orders were given the Assault Guards to end the procession; some Civil Guards resisted the order of the government, and, in an exchange of shots, another victim fell.

8

That afternoon I went to the Cortes for the debate on the public order, and to hear Azaña's reply to his critics. I was convinced from the temper of the discussion and the methods of some engaged that there were two extremes in Spain, numerically then unimportant, determined on chaos. Gil Robles frequently interrupted Azaña, who heard him coldly, and bitingly replied. But it was not until Calvo Sotelo, the provocateur of the Cortes, rose that there was pandemonium. His manner was arrogant, as usual, supercilious, intensely and consciously provocative, with the evident desire to arouse a demonstration from the fifteen communists, and they fell into his trap. The meager minority of the two extremes took possession of the Chamber by mere noise, staging a disgraceful scene, while the great majority sat in disgusted silence. The purport of Sotelo's speech was that the government of Azaña, without even a single socialist, was "communistic"—because fifteen out of four hundred and seventy members of the Cortes were communist. Azaña listened to this Fascist demagogy with cold contempt.

I left the Cortes that evening confident that two tiny groups of extremists, numbering no more than thirty out of four hundred and seventy, had deliberately lynched parliamentary government that afternoon. They had roughhoused the Cortes, after the fashion of a barroom brawl.

9

Another day brought another ominous portent. The syndicalists, dominated in their union by extremists, had urged a general strike in protest against the Fascist activities at the funeral. The more conservative union of the socialists was opposed, and it greatly outnumbered the syndicalists in Madrid. When, despite the opposition of the socialists, the syndicalists called the strike, it was assumed that it would fail. It succeeded; and it succeeded because the syndicalists intimidated the workers of the socialist union into joining.

Nothing could have been more advantageous to the Fascist propagandists. Here was evidence that despite their comparatively small number, the extremists could and would impose their will by terrorism. The socialists saw it, too, and were bitter in their resentment.

However, the twenty-four-hour strike passed without incident. Everything was closed. No taxis were in the streets. No trams ran. Though there was perfect quiet, the usual wild stories to disturb the timid were set afloat by the agents preparing the rebellion. We heard that a military *coup d'état* would take place that night, and that "communists" were "fighting in the street." That night I gave a dinner, and some of the guests walked, rather than risk their cars, and one arrived in a dilapidated station wagon belonging to his company.

The strike passed without a single incident, but the intimidating fact that an extreme element had imposed its will on a great majority of the workers, through terrorism, remained. And the Fascist and Nazi agents made the most of it.

10

One afternoon, Oliver Baldwin, son of the British Prime Minister, called upon me and laughed heartily over the drolleries of Spanish politics. The day before, he had seen Azaña and had found him "very clever." He chuckled. "What a country," he continued. "I told Azaña I would like to see José Primo de Rivera, who is in jail, but supposed it was impossible." "Not at all," said Azaña. "I will arrange it"—and he did. Where else in the world, asked Baldwin, would such a thing be possible?

"And Primo—did you see him?" I asked.

"Yes, the court of the prison was crowded with expensive motorcars from which women of quality were emerging to see him, bearing flowers."

The next morning, I went to see Luis Quintanilla working on his frescoes on the life of Pablo Iglesias, founder of the socialist party in Spain. A marble pergola was the memorial, and the frescoes were for its walls. It had a perfect setting, facing the Casa de Campo. Quintanilla was in a boyish mood and explained the process. I was impressed when among the workers at the memorial a number were pointed out to me as guards, in disguise, since threats had come from the Fascists that they would destroy the frescoes. Later, they did, during the military struggle around Madrid. Quintanilla introduced me to a young sculptor who had done the huge bust of the socialist founder, a charming, eager young man, who would soon give his life fighting for democracy in Spain.

11

May Day came. The "reds" were to swarm into the street, overcome the police, and terrorize the city with looting and shooting—so ran the inspired gossip. It was a day of brilliant sunshine. I stood in the garden behind the shrubbery, and through the iron railings of the fence, watched the procession on the Castellana. No police or Assault Guards were in sight. A large part of the procession was composed of children who sang merrily as they swung along. The sole disorder was caused by Lass, my Scottie, who poked her indignant nose between the railings and barked ferociously. The "reds" looked at the dog and laughed. . . .

But two days later, two men were murdered in the street—and not by "reds" . . . In San Sebastián the editor of an Azaña paper had been murdered . . . An attempt had been made to assassinate Jiménez de Asúa and had failed, though a police guard with him had been killed . . . Armed men were sent to guard the apartment of Azaña . . . The home of Largo Caballero had been fired upon . . . And no attempt had been made on the leaders of the Right since Primo de Rivera had been confined . . . *In the midst of these provocative crimes, it was Prieto, not Calvo Sotelo, who thundered in the Cortes* in denunciation of these criminal attempts.

12

Then came the poisoned-candy hoax.

Almost a century ago, when thousands died in a typhoid fever epidemic, the word mysteriously went forth that the Jesuits had poisoned the wells, and an infuriated populace sallied forth with kerosene and torches to burn churches and convents. This was in the days of an absolute monarchy. This remains the classic example of the whispering campaign in Spain.

One morning in early May, 1936, some shooting in the workmen's section of Cuatro Caminos proclaimed trouble. Word came to the embassy that a dangerous mob of men, and more ferocious women, were firing convents and churches and pursuing priests and nuns. This was grossly exaggerated. However, the fury of the mob forced the police to take extreme measures to suppress it.

Then came the explanation. Some fiend had given currency to the lie that on May Day a priest had given poisoned candy to children. Every mother whose child had gorged on a green apple, with resulting pain, thought it the victim of the mythical priest and fared forth in fury to get revenge. The story had spread like wildfire, and in a very short time had penetrated to every section of the city. The dissemination of this story had been organized by experts in such work. It was clear that whisperers had been stationed at strategic points and the precise minute fixed for the spreading of the tale. The counselor of the embassy, Hallet Johnson, had heard it from his servants, the Spanish messenger had heard it in his section far away, and Marcella, my wife's maid, had heard it on her way to church.

The government instantly broadcast a denunciation of the lie. The labor unions flashed the news to the workers that it was a vile canard. The communists charged by radio that the story was circulated by the extremists of the Right. Young socialists rushed to the scene of the trouble personally to remonstrate with the mobsters and were severely beaten. None of these could have been responsible. Who was? It might have been the work of anarchists, but many thought it a device of common criminals to create a riot with the view to looting the churches and convents under cover of the confusion. Still others ascribed the outrage to Fascist and Nazi provocateurs to promote attacks on churches that could be used, in accordance with their familiar technique, for propaganda in other lands. This was my own conviction.

Chapter XVI

Just Before the Rebellion

IN MAY no one could doubt that reactionary forces hostile to a democratic regime were intensively fomenting incidents that could be used in justification to the outside world of the rebellion being prepared. The Fascist technique was to divide all people into two classes—communists and Fascists. And because democrats were not Fascists they were communists! The loss of the elections had convinced the beneficiaries of the feudalistic system of society that the days of their privileges were numbered unless an armed minority could maintain them by force. Axis agents, spies, propagandists, provocateurs from Germany and Italy were actively engaged in Spain, and these were busy creating "incidents" that the press was publishing in other countries as proof of a state of anarchy.

In early May I drove my wife to Torremolines, near Málaga, where she had taken a tiny cottage by the sea, and I welcomed the opportunity again to test by my own eyes the stories of the "outrages" of peasants on the highway. We left Madrid with the intention of noting every incident that might be termed offensive. Between Madrid and Bailén, where we stayed the night, I counted four children, ranging in age from six to twelve, who greeted us as we passed with the tiny clenched fist of the *Frente Popular*, and a friendly grin. From not one single man on the road had we received so much as an unfriendly glance. We reached Bailén about five o'clock, and because the air was sweet and caressing, we went for a long walk along the paved road, lined with trees. It was the hour when the peasants were returning from the fields, and we passed forty or fifty riding home on mules or donkeys. Without one exception, they greeted us with a nod and smile.

The next morning, the country was fresh and fragrant as we started for Granada. Never had I seen such a riot of wild flowers by the roadside and in the fields. Great fields literally were aflame with red poppies as far as one could see, and others glowed with yellow daisies, or with a purple flower I did not know. The villages we passed were very quiet and the people cordial. Reaching Granada in time for lunch, we spent the afternoon meandering among the wonders of the Alhambra. That night I went alone to the caves of the gypsies in a rough part of town to see them dance again, and without the slightest reason for apprehension. The town was quiet. It was as safe as Broadway at midday.

After a morning in the midst of the magic beauties of the summer quarters of the Moorish kings, we drove to Málaga over the old road, less picturesque but less nerve-racking than the new, and arrived at five o'clock. I was looking forward to a few days in this enchanting region when Garrison appeared with a message that changed my plans.

2

Azaña had been elected President.

It seemed to me a blunder to transfer him from the position he held of responsibility and power to the more circumscribed Presidency at this critical moment. Great pressure had been brought to bear upon him, for it was feared that his declination would open the way for an extremist. And so it came to pass that the electors assembled in the Retiro and elected him, and the message from Madrid informed me that I had been designated to represent the United States at his inauguration on Monday afternoon—and it was Saturday evening.

On Sunday morning, we went to Torremolines and took possession of the cosy little stone cottage in a walled-in garden that looked down upon the blue waters of the Mediterranean, and after lunch I began the return journey with Pepe. It was a dreamy afternoon of pensive sunshine as we drove over the mountains and through Granada, without stopping, and reached Bailén for the night.

When, early the next day we were on our way, it seemed nothing could be more lovely than riding up from the Mediterranean to Madrid on a fresh May morning. The countryside was drenched with glistening dew, and the grass and trees were a brilliant green, and odorous. The country was perfectly quiet, the villages sleeping in the sun. We reached Madrid in time for lunch, and having changed into the idiotic American "uniform," full evening dress in the daytime, I drove to the Cortes for the ceremony. An unusual array of soldiers, mounted and on foot, gave the surrounding streets much color by their uniforms, and this was all that made the meeting of the Cortes different.

On the floor of the Chamber, a yard from the rostrum of the President, a platform had been erected on both sides, one for the diplomatic corps, and the other for high functionaries of the army and navy. The long table of the President of the Cortes had been removed, and a small one substituted against the wall where Jiménez de Asúa, president pro tem., sat. The floor of the platform was covered with a large rug, glistening with gold braid, which had been used formerly when the King appeared. The curtains that customarily concealed the door through which the King was wont to reach the tribune were parted in the center and drawn back.

Slowly the deputies trickled in and found their seats. Besteiro, laughing happily, chatted with friends, but Fernando de los Ríos, just behind him, was strangely solemn. Even Largo Caballero was in a lively mood, but Prieto, just behind him, was quiet and serious.

Finally Asúa announced the result of the election, and a committee was named to escort Azaña to the Chamber. There was a wait of twenty minutes, and then the patter of horses' feet on the pavement, the shouts of command, and the buzz of excitement from the street, announced the arrival. The deputies rose to a man. The generals in the opposite tribune rose. We were the last to rise, since the dean, the Argentine Ambassador, was slow to move. It was not until Azaña appeared between the drawn curtains that the diplomats stood up. It was not a friendly delay.

Azaña, pale as usual, beamed with good humor, bowed to the deputies, then to the diplomats, who returned the salute, and then to the generals. Without a word, he turned and faced Asúa, who read the oath to support the Constitution and defend the Republic. In a low conversational tone, Azaña took the oath. He had not uttered more than twenty words. Then, bowing again, he turned to leave. The Chamber burst into applause which intensified into an ovation, increasing in volume until he was compelled to pause and bow again. Cries of "Long live the Republic" were ringing in the Chamber when he disappeared between the drawn curtains.

That night, he moved into the "Prince's house" in the hunting park of the Pardo to await the completion of arrangements for his reception in the palace in Madrid. It is a modest but attractive brick mansion in the center of the hunting park of El Pardo.

3

The ministers resigned, and Azaña summoned the party leaders and invited Prieto to form a government. He patriotically declined, lest the socialist schism be accentuated. The task was then assigned to Azaña's friend, Casares Quiroga, who had shared his imprisonment.

The new minister was a slender man in frail health. His face was thin, his cheeks slightly sunken, but his cynical, mocking eyes that betrayed a satiric strain gave him a Voltairean countenance. He was able and clever. His republicanism was a conviction and his democracy a faith. Nothing could better illustrate his political character than his reply to my congratulations on his first speech as Prime Minister: "Spain wasted the entire nineteenth century making speeches." Women found him an interesting talker, for his conversations were not bromidic. Personally and politically, he was devoted to Azaña. He was a Galician and he had the robust qualities of his race.

Augusto Barcia continued as Minister of State, and all the other members were drawn from the parties of Azaña and Barrio, except one who represented the Left republicans of Catalonia. *There was not one extremist of the Left from top to bottom. There was not even an evolutionary socialist as radical as Ramsay MacDonald. But this was the government actually in power, by will of the people, when the generals, in alliance with Hitler and Mussolini, precipitated the bloody, wasteful war on the pretext of wiping out a "communist" or "red" government. This miserable pretext was to serve its purpose throughout the war with the gullibles and the Fascist-minded in the United States and England.*

4

A few days later, Azaña received the diplomatic corps at the palace. There was more form and smartness than had been seen since the fall of the monarchy, and some of my colleagues, who had been scornful of the ultrasimplicity of Alcalá Zamora, were equally resentful of Azaña's departure from it. Officers in brilliant uniforms lined the stairway. We went through the old guard room into a magnificent apartment, and thence on through the porcelain room where Washington Irving presented his credentials to the child Queen Isabella, in the presence of her nurse, to the room where we were to be received. In an adjoining room a military band played the national anthem, and Azaña appeared, followed by his ministers and the Military Household, headed by General Masquelet. These grouped themselves behind the President. Azaña was pale, as usual. The doyen read an address, Azaña replied, and then passed down the line shaking hands with the heads of missions, smiling graciously. Thus did he approach the Italian Ambassador.

In execrable taste, in contemptuous disregard of the proprieties, and with true Fascist impudence, the Ambassador of Mussolini, at that very hour deep in the conspiracy soon to flare in the military and Fascist rebellion, appeared in a spirit of insult in a black shirt and in boots. And when Azaña approached, ready with an outstretched hand, the Italian Fascist drew back and gave the Fascist salute. It was the sort of insult that had been rebuked at the King's levee at the Court of St. James. Azaña disregarded the deliberate insult and passed on, smiling.

Having reached the end of the line, he turned and, with his ministers and Military Household, moved on to the banquet room, where a long table in the center groaned under the weight of food, and where champagne was being served. Azaña seemed in a happy mood.

That night at a dinner at the Japanese Legation there was much criticism of the boorish conduct of the Italian Ambassador, even among the enemies of the Republic, and the next night at my dinner for the Minister of Foreign Affairs it was still the subject of severe comment.

5

Meanwhile, to all outward appearance, the country was peaceful. One May morning, the venerable Jacob Schurman, former American Ambassador to Germany, and then in his eighty-third year, called upon me. When he announced that, unaccompanied, he was leaving for a journey into Andalusia, it did not occur to anyone to warn him against it. He spoke with appreciation of the exquisite courtesy he had met throughout his Spanish journey. Had he seen any indication of anarchy or lawlessness? He had not.

Even the nobility and aristocracy that had fled from fear some time before were venturing back. The great palace of the Duke of Medinaceli in the Plaza de Colón, repository of paintings, books, and trophies covering centuries of that family's prominence in Spanish life, had been closed with the advent of the Republic, and the family was living near Biarritz in France. Nothing in the palace had been disturbed in the five years of the Republic, and this May the duchess returned for a few days, and it was under her ciceronage that I saw the treasures of that splendid house. Later I wondered if she also knew of the plans of the conspirators and was making sure that some transportable treasure had not been overlooked. She died during the war at her country place near Biarritz.

6

And then, in early June, the incident at Yeste rekindled the apprehension of the timid. From time to time, after the election, there were minor incidents among the peasants. With them, the issue of agrarian reform in the campaign had been very real. Their wages were pitifully small. The vast majority were desperately poor, with neither plow nor hoe. Literally, they were medieval serfs bound to the soil around them forever unless some magic put them in possession of a little patch of land they could call their own. They knew the triumphant coalition at the polls had promised them land, and, with the victory, these illiterates assumed the thing was done. The land was theirs, and theirs the choosing. It was difficult for many of them to understand that this required time and governmental action. And so, here and there, groups of peasants merely moved upon the land they themselves selected.

In some instances, great landowners, with enormous holdings in various parts of the country, resentful of the victory of the Leftist parties and in vengeful mood, decided not to cultivate this farm, or that; and yet peasants living in the vicinity of this uncultivated land were dependent for mere existence on its cultivation. Unless the fields were plowed and seed was sown, they had no means of livelihood, and starved. It was unthinkable to them that they were not summoned to the fields. Each spring, as long as they could remember, they had gone upon the land and plowed in the spring; and so, from habit, they did this year as they had always done. This made them "trespassers," and the reactionaries called them "reds."

Azaña, and every intelligent thinker, including Fernández, of the CEDA, Gil Robles' Minister of Agriculture, knew that a nation with eighty-five per cent of the workers penniless peasants would inevitably invite a dangerous social struggle, and that a small peasant proprietorship would make for law and order, stability, and a reasonable conservatism. Already there had been too much delay, and Azaña was bending to the task of creating a peasant proprietorship as rapidly as possible between March and July, 1936.

The great landlords were furious, though some conservatives among them reasoned that by yielding some of their enormous holdings for a consideration, they could save the rest, and that by yielding nothing they might eventually lose all. I was not astonished that the great landowners felt the way they did, human nature being what it is, but I was astounded by the undercurrent of hostility among some posing as liberals with a humanitarian interest in the peasants.

Such was the atmosphere in which Azaña was trying to save Spain from a bloody social revolution.

The incident at Yeste then must be viewed in the light of the situation. For some time, peasants in the neighborhood of Alicante had been going on the land of great estates and cutting down trees for fuel. The government ordered the authorities to end the practice and sent Civil Guards. Six of the trespassers were arrested. This aroused the fury of the peasants to such a frenzy that the mayor of Yeste requested the Civil Guards to release the prisoners. But, incited by their leaders, the peasants attacked the guards with pitchforks, clubs, and rocks, and one of the officers was killed. When many of them were wounded, the guards opened fire, and eighteen peasants fell.

The extremists of the Left took advantage of the opportunity to assail the government, and the shortsighted, demagogic politicians of the Right joined in, to embarrass the ministers. The next day, one of the fifteen communists in the Cortes proposed to question the government, but agreed to await the report of the judge charged with the investigation. It was commonly understood in the cafés and streets that the few communists and the socialists would demand the immediate disbandment of the Civil Guard, whom the masses had come to look upon as enemies. The incident at Yeste was a club in their hands.

A few days later the government was ready for the interpolation. In the meanwhile, better counsels had prevailed, and the attack on the guards was abandoned. Even so, I expected a lively session of the Cortes and attended. The opening speeches of the young communists and socialists convinced me, by their moderation, that the first frenzy had yielded to a more reasonable spirit. Meanwhile, Casares Quiroga, on the Blue Bench, sat with one hand in his coat listening intently. Dolores Ibarruri, from whom a passionate denunciation might have been expected, sat with her head resting against the back of her seat in silence. Gil Robles was silent but intent.

At length the Minister of Justice, speaking authoritatively but without feeling, said the facts were different from those stated. An investigation was in progress, he said, and at its conclusion such arrests as the facts demanded would be made, regardless of which side was affected. He was cheered by the Left republicans and the Center, but all the Rightists and the fifteen communists sat silent. The debate was over. The government had not yielded to violence.

I was convinced that subversive forces had incited the peasants of Yeste to their acts. Clearly, the extremists, Fascists, and anar-

chists were bent on mischief. Already some Fascists were insinu-
ating themselves into the anarchists' ranks, urging acts of violence
that could be used as an excuse for drawing the sword in a military
coup d'état.

7

In early June I gave my annual presidential dinner for Azaña.
A few days before, a witty countess, who hated the Republic, knowing my daughter Patricia would be the hostess in the absence of her
mother, undertook to advise her how to "please the President."
She was to say, "How charming Spain was ten years ago"—which
was in the days of the Dictator.

That night, Azaña drove in from the Pardo hunting lodge in
high good humor, discussing plans to extend the beautiful gardens
of the lodge and to establish the summer capital in Santander.
Patricia found him an easy table companion and quite as charming
as Spain had been "ten years ago"; and after dinner he was interested in the panels in the Goya room and in Zuloaga's portrait
of the Duchess of Arion. He spent the evening in the ballroom
talking entertainingly. Señora Azaña, a small woman with a very
attractive face, with expressive blue eyes, and a soft, pleasant
voice, was much younger than her husband. Her brother, Rivas
Cherif, the dramatist and writer, had been Azaña's close friend
from their early youth in the monks' school in the Escorial.

There was nothing that night to indicate that in five weeks
Spain would be engaged in a sanguinary war with guests of the
evening on both sides of the barricade.

8

The next day, five weeks before the war began, I started south
with Garrison to bring my wife home. So many circumstantial
stories had been told and published outside Spain of peasants demanding money of motorists on the road that I had provided myself with a number of small bills. But I found this story as false as
the rest. Nothing could have been more serene and pleasant than
the drive to Granada five weeks before the war.

It was to be my last view of Granada before the rebellion. The
next morning when I looked out the window on the historic town,

nothing could have been less suggestive of trouble or a clash of arms. A cosy domestic corner was spread before me. Directly below my windows two roads branched, each lined with houses gleaming white in the sunshine. They were spotlessly white, and the roofs were red. Before the window of each house a small iron balcony was banked with red roses. Now and then a housewife appeared on a balcony to peer idly up and down the road, to hum a song, and disappear. The home scenes of the women, the crowing of the cocks, the pranks of the playing children in the road, the patter of the footsteps of the Civil Guards sauntering along, the barking of dogs, the cackling of hens, imparted a sense of intimacy to the scene. For two hours I sat drenching myself in the sunshine as patient donkeys passed, laden with green boughs for the home fires. In the distance, through the sunshine, the snow glistened on the tops of the Sierra mountains. Two planes swooped low, the engines roaring— a warning of what was to come to this Granada, so happy and peaceful that June morning.

That afternoon, we drove over the mountains to Torremolines, our eyes alert for the "disturbances" of the overpublicized peasants' strike in the province of Málaga. We saw nothing more disturbing than peasants basking in the sun.

9

I lingered a few days on the enchanting hilltop of Torremolines and came to love it—a charming old village with narrow streets, interesting old houses, and little villas facing the sea. I found Sybil and Helen, the companion, in the midst of their court of children on the terrace of the tiny stone cottage with its walled-in garden. The little tots had appeared on the day of their arrival, and regularly now, they appeared for tea and to sing and dance "for the lady." That is Torremolines. Their fathers were workmen, fishermen, Civil Guards, and they were neat and clean. They had been a bit distressed because "the lady" did not go regularly to mass, and one day when she went with them to please them, they were disturbed because of her failure to respond properly to the prayers, until Helen explained that "we say our prayers in English." Nothing could have been sweeter than these scenes in the garden with the blue sky above, and the blue waters of the sea just showing above the garden wall, and the little girls in bright clean dresses laughing, dancing, singing. Soon thousands of such children would be blown to bits by the Fascist bombers of Mussolini and Hitler.

Every morning a goatherd appeared at the door with a great pounding, and when Helen appeared, he summoned one of the goats by name and it stepped forward primly to be milked, while Helen waited with a pitcher. Another robust bang at the door announced the arrival of a fisherman, his produce dripping from the sea, and ridiculously cheap. And then came the vegetable man from the country to give, for a few pesetas, enough to feed a famishing crowd.

I stayed with Hawker, the host at the Santa Clara, having a cosy room in the brick barracks, and learned that the syndicalist extremists had entered the little paradise of even this tiny village. The woman cook, having become impossible, was discharged. Because she was a socialist, Hawker went to the socialist headquarters and explained. He found their union reasonable. They would send him another cook and guarantee satisfaction. The syndicalists then persuaded the cook to join their ranks, with the promise to force Hawker to take her back on pain of death. There had been some threats. The villagers were mostly with Hawker and the socialists.

10

One gorgeous Sunday morning, Jay Allen accompanied us to Majas, a unique mountain town of seven thousand people, twenty kilometers away. Centuries ago, the Phoenicians lived there, and the town wall they built is still partly standing. Along the road we passed a family, husband, wife, children, and a pig, camped beneath a few fig trees, and Allen explained that in this section it was not unusual for the owner of fig trees to rent them for the season. The renter with his family then settled down beneath the tree, bringing his pig along to eat the bad fruit that fell. The happy family was stretched on their backs in the shade of their own fig tree. The pig grunted us a greeting as we passed.

Winding among the hills, we finally found ourselves in a beautiful village of clean, narrow streets. There we found a simple eighteenth-century church, resembling the mission churches in California. Across from the church was the bull ring, and between the church and the ring I was surprised to find some trees had been cut down. It was said that the youth of the town needed a football field, and this was the only available space. Again I was impressed by the enormous popularity of football in Spain, which competed then with the bullfight.

Torremolines and Majas—beautiful, unspoiled, once seen never forgotten. When we left the cottage in the village of Torremolines, the ten children fought for the privilege of carrying our luggage to the car. One, having nothing to lug, burst into tears, and I had her help with a satchel. When, during the Fascist war, this little village was bombed by the Fascists, we thought many times of these children.

11

The next day we were at the María Cristina in Algeciras. The old Moorish town was feverish with the fair, excited over the coming bullfight in which Ortega would appear. Seville was tranquillity itself. The "anarchy" the foreign press was featuring under the inspiration of the Goebbels agents was nowhere to be found. The next day we lunched at Córdoba and drove on to Úbeda, where we had had our "incident" three months before. My failure to publicize the misunderstanding had been appreciated, and when we reached the palace *parador*, we found two Assault Guards waiting to escort us in the town. Through the open French window leading onto the balcony of my room, I had a leisurely view of the façade of the fine old Renaissance church of San Salvador, built in the eighteenth century. The gray, heavy stone is mellowed and stained by time. On the ledges and roof were moss and flowers.

But more interesting to me was the smaller church of Santa María, just across the little plaza. It had been begun in the twelfth century, and, though lacking the exterior charm of San Salvador, it impressed me more. A kindly priest accompanied us. The iron grill before the altar is the best of Spanish workmanship of an age when Spanish artists in iron were incomparable. Our priest took us to see the two-and-a-half-million-peseta present of Louis XIV of France, given because his Queen, a Spanish princess, was a patroness of the church. This took us into a bleak room where some of the necessary keys were kept. One or two of these are always in possession of the priest. We came to a huge door built as though to withstand the battering of an army. Two keys were used in opening it, but another door, just beyond, barred the way, and two more keys were used. Passing through the second door, we found ourselves in a small, drearily barren room, dusty, neglected, and empty but for an iron trunk. Again two keys were used to open the trunk, and the priest called attention to the complicated machinery of the lock, making utterly impossible the opening of the trunk without these keys. Then, reverently, he reached into the trunk and drew forth a large figure in gold of three angels with flowing robes, and then, a huge fan-shaped jewel that fitted on the head of the central angel. This was of rubies of great size. It was a scintillating piece of work—this present of Louis XIV to the little church of Santa María.

The next day we reached Madrid. Again, on every hand, we heard about the outrages of the roads, of cars held up at the point of guns, of riots and perils everywhere, and again I marveled. I had driven hundreds of miles, for many days, almost the full length of the Mediterranean coast, and up from Seville through Córdoba, Málaga, Granada, in February, March, May, and June, 1936, with as much security as though I had motored through Westchester, in New York. But the gossip about a military rising continued to be heard. It was understood that the time was fixed for October. So all arrangements were made to spend the hot months as usual in the summer capital of San Sebastián.

Chapter XVII

The Sword Is Drawn

T OWARD the end of June, in the election of the officials of the socialist party throughout Spain, Prieto won a decisive victory over Largo Caballero and his more impatient policy. The next day I met Virgilio Belrandez, director of *Política* and found him a man of intelligence and sound sense, prone to speak with moderation. He doubted if a *coup d'état* was probable, though he admitted that extreme Right elements were raising huge sums of money for some purpose. He realized that the greater part of the higher officers of the army were enemies of the regime, but thought them handicapped by the sincere loyalty of under officers and men. And he was positive the Civil Guard would remain true to its traditional loyalty to the constituted authority.

But a few days later, when I drove one evening in early July to Toledo to participate in the ceremony of dedicating the newly renovated telephone building, I might have had a head-on collision with the rebellion. I had Garrison and Lester Ziffern, of the United Press, with me, and after crossing into the province of Toledo, we were puzzled by the extraordinary number of Civil and Assault Guards at close intervals. We were wondering about it when a car whizzed by going toward Madrid and then stopped with a grinding of brakes. We drew up and waited. It was Gonzales Lopez, the provincial governor, who had come personally to conduct me into town. Nothing of the sort had ever happened before on my numerous visits to Toledo, and I ascribed the unaccustomed attention to the new governor's exaggerated notion of the courtesies expected. He was a short, heavy man with a large head and features, and I learned that it was he who had ordered the Civil Guards to stop the cutting of trees at Yeste. His car preceded mine into town, and to the telephone building. This was a seventeenth-century structure with much history and beauty plastered over, and the company had restored it to its original state.

After the ceremonies there, we went to a banquet at the home of Gregorio Ledesma, former mayor, whose son I knew. Seldom have I seen a more picturesque spot. The gardens of the house were on three levels, and the tables were spread on the highest, under the stars. It was a night of brilliant moonlight, and we dined on the top level of the garden, men with flaming torches moving about on the lower level as in medieval times.

Of the company about the table, most of whom I knew, some were monarchists and some republicans, some aristocrats and some democrats. The mayor was a working man and the host was an aristocrat. There were some officers of the military school of the Alcázar, including the General Moscardo who was to figure in the much-fictionalized siege of the Alcázar, and then known as an enemy of the democratic republic. Two weeks later, these men about the table would be struggling desperately in the streets. But the night was mellow, and the air fragrant with flowers and foliage, conducive to the spirit of fraternity. It was two o'clock in the morning when we rose. As we were preparing to leave, the governor approached to say that he would accompany me as far as the provincial line. I protested that it was quite unnecessary for him to bother. He shook his head, entered his car with his wife, and we followed. The full moon literally flooded the countryside, and we could see for miles. We did not meet a single car nor a single soul. At the provincial line, the governor drew up, and we alighted to say good night, and then, to my surprise, I noticed a car behind us filled with armed guards. "I leave you here," said Lopez, "but this other car will accompany you to the gates of the embassy." Again I protested that it was not necessary. "No," he said, "they will go with you. I will not take the responsibility." It sounded melodramatic, but I said no more, and, followed by the car of armed men, we sped toward Madrid.

It was later that I learned that these precautions were taken in fear of an armed rising, though few expected trouble before October. I was, therefore, probably the first diplomat in Spain to travel with an armed escort in the Spanish war.

2

The next morning, Sybil and I, Jesse Moore, of Indianapolis, a guest, and Helen and Lass, the Scottie, started for Fuenterrabia, where I had taken a villa near the summer embassy in San Sebastián. We lunched at a charming *parador* near Burgos and stayed the night in that fascinating old town. That night we saw the illuminated cathedral again, and the next morning again we visited the ancient monastery of Huelgas. It was pensive and peaceful in the sunshine of its walled-in grounds. Lunching at Vitoria, soon to be the center of rebellion, we arrived at the villa at Fuenterrabia in time for tea.

The Villa Lore Artean was the home of the Marquise Villasinda, widow of a former Spanish Ambassador in Rome. It was pleasantly set upon a hill along a beach road from the quaint Basque village, and so high above the road that we looked down directly upon the beach and sea, gay with bathers, and colorful with red and green dressing tents. The house was attractive within, but the extensive and valuable library of old books, the marquise had inconsiderately locked up. During our all-too-brief sojourn in this delicious spot we were to spend most of the time on the grounds, having tea at a large round stone table between two giant trees that formed a frame for the beautiful castle near Hendaye. At night we could see the lights of Saint-Jean-de-Luz twinkling in the distance. In the rear were tennis courts, flower gardens, and a small pine grove.

A little farther on, on the beach road, was the villa of Jean Herbette, the French Ambassador, where, in other days, the Pact of San Sebastián had been signed. Nearer the village, and facing the little harbor of the fishermen, was the villa of General Manuel Trevino, the Mexican Ambassador.

Late one night, less than a week after our arrival, Lester Ziffern telephoned me from Madrid to inquire into the truth of "the report" that I had been "held up by the reds" on the way down. The Fascist propagandists had imagined another "outrage." Ziffern was just ringing off when he broke in again:

"Oh, by the way," he said, "Calvo Sotelo was murdered at three o'clock this morning, apparently by Assault Guards."

3

This parenthetical intelligence was startling in the extreme. No one among the open enemies of the regime approached him in ability or audacity. That he was conspiring for the destruction of the regime through a military *coup d'état* was common knowledge. The next day I heard the details. In the funeral procession of the murdered Civil Guard, Lt. Castillo, of the Assault Guards, had shot a young Fascist for reasons never made clear. The Fascist youths openly boasted that they would kill the colonel, and on the previous afternoon they had made good their boast by shooting him at his door, where he stood with his arm around his wife. At four in the morning, a carload of men wearing the uniforms of the Assault Guards appeared at Calvo Sotelo's apartment and told him he was under arrest and must accompany them to the police station. He asked permission to telephone the police and was refused. He then leaned out the window and asked the Assault Guards assigned for his protection if the guards in his apartment were legitimate, and they answered in the affirmative. Thereupon, he dressed and accompanied them from the house. He did not return. Morning came and there was no news. Later it was learned that the assassins had taken the body to the Municipal Cemetery and asked that it be laid on the slab of the morgue. When, in the morning, everyone was discussing the disappearance of the murdered, the custodian thought of the unknown body on the slab and notified the authorities. The body was then identified. It was evident that the Assault Guards had avenged the death of a fellow officer. All this was common knowledge, and Winston Churchill's statement in *The Gathering Storm* that this was a communist murder is utterly without justification and completely false.

Instantly the clever propagandists seized upon the death of Calvo Sotelo as an excuse for the rebellion which had been worked out in detail long before and was known to Hitler and Mussolini. Gil Robles discovered an affection for his rival and denounced the crime in an inflammatory speech sprinkled with Biblical quotations, one of which was erroneously thought to have given the word to strike to the members of his party.

That day the Council of Ministers sat continuously, preparing for drastic action and for the defense of the regime. The Cortes was adjourned for eight days. Because of the vicious propaganda, the socialist deputies went for the week end to their provinces, where they were caught and murdered. But for the incessant clatter of tongues, Madrid remained quiet. There was not a ripple of excitement in San Sebastián or Fuenterrabia, but the next morning when I drove to the embassy in San Sebastián, the news was sensational enough. Special permission had been given the embassy in Madrid to telephone me that the long-expected military *coup d'état* would strike at noon. All telephone and telegraph communications were cut. I had telegraphed Washington. Meanwhile, Pepe had heard in the streets that Madrid, Saragossa, and Seville were in the hands of the rebels—which was not true. That afternoon I drove to Saint-Jean-de-Luz, and in the little cinema in Irún I saw the pictures of the Schmeling-Louis fight. No one seemed excited in Irún; and when the Minister of the Interior radioed that the *coup d'état* had failed, it was generally believed.

The next day Madrid was tranquil, and Civil and Assault Guards were cheered in the streets. There was some shifting of positions in the government, and Barcia, close to Azaña, became Minister of the Interior. Later I learned that Prieto had been unable to form a government because Leftist extremists, outside the Popular Front, had refused their co-operation. The same was true of Barrio. These extremists, the anarchists and syndicalists, were to remain the problem of loyalist governments throughout the war.

Meanwhile, into the village of Fuenterrabia trickled the story that Seville, Cádiz, Pamplona, Burgos, and Barcelona were in possession of the rebels. With Barcelona excepted, this was true, but few credited it at the moment. All means of communication had been cut off. When Walter Schoellkopf, First Secretary of the embassy, called at the villa for a dispatch to Washington and telephoned me on reaching San Sebastián of his experience on the way, the prospects darkened. He had repeatedly been stopped on the road by armed men who appeared to be searching for arms, but on learning his identity, they passed him on politely.

But things were happening. A general strike had been called in San Sebastián as a protest against the military rising. Returning that day from Saint-Jean-de-Luz, I found the frontier closed and guarded by armed men, but I was permitted to pass. It now looked like war in earnest. Rightist politicians were in flight from Madrid. Gil Robles sped across the border to his enclosed garden in Guetharia the night before the rising.

The next morning, Hallet Johnson, Counselor of the embassy, motored to the embassy in San Sebastián and telephoned he had found the road closely guarded by armed men who stopped all cars and made the passengers account for themselves. The men were decent enough, but dangerously careless with their loaded guns. In San Sebastián, Johnson found great excitement, for it was then known that Burgos, Vitoria, and Pamplona had been taken over by the army, and it was thought a march on San Sebastián was imminent. Barricades sprang up in the streets and at intersections, and the streets swarmed with armed workmen. No streetcars or busses were running, no trains to or from Madrid. All stores were closed. The wires between Madrid and San Sebastián were cut. It was a cloudy, gloomy day, in harmony with the outlook.

On the fourth day, the sweet peaceful village of Fuenterrabia turned to Mars. The beach in front of our villa was deserted and lonesome. Armed fishermen and peasants passed up and down the beach road carrying guns or pistols at disturbing angles. Most were young and joyous. To them it seemed a lark. Many had never had a gun in their hands before. Now and then a car, driven at a reckless speed, flashed by with armed men under the flag of the Republic or the red flag of the socialists.

Then came authentic news from Madrid. General Fanjul, with the aid of a part of the garrison of Cuartel de la Montaña, in the old part of the city, near the palace of the Duke of Alba, had undertaken to take the town, but the loyalists had replied with artillery until the rebels ran up the white flag. Fanjul was captured, tried, and shot. Another officer committed suicide. The government ordered all business houses in Madrid to open their doors.

In Barcelona, much reliance had been placed on General Goded, able, ruthless, ambitious soldier, who had betrayed almost every government he had served. But the loyalists made short shrift of the rebellion, and Goded was tried by court-martial and shot.

And then the greatest blow of all fell on the rebels. Pepe came running to the villa from the radio at the little beach bar. "Sanjurjo is killed!" he exclaimed. General Sanjurjo, who was to have led the rebellion for which he had been saved by the mistaken clemency of Azaña, had been killed in a plane crash on his way from Portugal.

Calvo Sotelo—Sanjurjo—Goded—three of the very strongest men among the conspirators—all dead or doomed within four days. And General Franco—where was he?

An airplane roared above the clouds en route to San Sebastián; and from San Sebastián came Garrison carrying messages, with three young workers in the back seat as guards, toying with their unfamiliar guns in an intimidating manner. It had been a perilous journey, with armed groups along the road firing wildly at planes above them, and time and again the occupants of the car were compelled to take refuge behind walls. Garrison complained bitterly that all the way his young guards sat with their guns pointed at his back, while chatting and gesticulating with animation. They were nice friendly young fellows with the best intentions, and I gave them lunch. But Garrison had a sickly smile as he drove out of the grounds on his return trip, with a grinning, waving guard playing with a huge old-fashioned gun pointed at the base of his skull. Soon these happy youths would die in the mud for the Republic.

4

The morning I had arranged to go to San Sebastián all communications were cut, and Herbette, who had gone the day before, had been unable to return. The booming of the bombardment there could be clearly heard. In the quaint, hushed streets of Fuenterrabia, fishermen were gathered in groups, looking grim.

All cars had by now been requisitioned and the garages of the aristocrats of the village were empty. Their cars sped through the street flying the republican or socialist flag. A rich Madrileño was amused at the end of the day when his Rolls Royce was returned with the complaint that it had "no speed." The beach was deserted, since swimming was forbidden, due to the ease with which a swimmer could reach France. A boat flying the republican flag floated lazily near the shore in charge of an armed man.

Then, in the plaza, we heard the beating of a drum—a small boy the drummer. Always I shall remember the spirit of the men who fought for democracy in Spain as symbolized by that small, earnest child, summoning the people to the defense with his drum.

Thus summoned, the villagers were forbidden to leave their houses after nine o'clock at night. That night, a small army was busy filling bags with sand for the barricades being prepared for Irún. Visitors were constantly calling at the villa for information or advice, and with requests. The Countess of Romanones and her daughter were seeking news of their children and grandchildren marooned in San Sebastián. Like all the other occupants of the villas, they described themselves as "rebels," and all were confident it would be over in a week. "They began planning this before the election," Romanones said to me. "Everything has been perfectly arranged and it will be speedily over." "How long?" I asked. "Four days—five at the most." For so it had always been in Spain. A thousand soldiers would march from barracks to the Cortes and turn out the deputies, and, in former times, the citizen, leaning against a building in the sun, would turn, with a yawn, to his companion with the comment that they seemed to have another boss. But that was before Spain had awakened from her long sleep.

Nine-tenths of my colleagues informed their governments that the war would be over in a few days—a month at the most; but I advised Washington that it would be a long, bitter war since it was not a contest between a professional and an untrained army, but one between an army and a people. Ten days after I was told the war would be over in "five days at the most," I asked my informant, Count Romanones, what had happened. "They counted on the navy, and the men were not with them; on the Basques, and they are against them; and they did not count on the rising of the people."

I had based my opinion on the rising of the people.

On the fifth morning I looked out the window on a peaceful village, but when I prepared to go to San Sebastián I found all communications had been cut and that the road was impassable. At the radio of the little beach bar, where, in happier times, the summer colonists were accustomed to get their cocktails, I learned that the revolt of the artillery in San Sebastián had been crushed, and that the soldiers were shut up within their barracks. The Casino, where the rebels had entrenched themselves, had been taken. Some young Fascists who had pushed into the María Cristina Hotel, endangering the lives of women and children, had been firing from the windows into the streets.

And then, the rolling of the little boy's drum in the village street again. Because of the flight of Fascists toward France, all residents were ordered to take no one into their houses without informing the authorities.

In the late afternoon of that day I walked over to the Villa Menda Rea of Count Romanones. Rugged, grimly smiling, he met me at the door. I found him pessimistic about an early ending of the war, because this was something new in Spain since the Napoleonic invasion—a rising of the people in defense of their liberties. I sought to cheer him with the story of an affront by the loyalists to a Leftist lady of the diplomatic corps who was his pet aversion and who had been refused permission to cross the border, and he laughed and wrung his hands in an ecstasy of delight. When, to tease him, I referred to the "Passion Flower" as his colleague, he kissed his fingertips at me, and then quickly said that she was "a clever woman with brains." But when I told him she had ordered the communists not to enter houses or take private property in Madrid, he grinned incredulously and mentioned the requisitioning of automobiles. "That, however, is permissible in war," he said, "but they have been up here for my wine." I reminded him that there were no communists in Fuenterrabia. The venerable statesman, who so many times had served the King, was all serenity when I left him at the door.

The next day the telephone communications were cut even among houses in the village, and we were as completely isolated as though we were on another planet. The fighting continued in San Sebastián. The streets teemed with surging men in savage mood, shooting to kill. The diplomats caught there in the Continental Hotel dared not venture out. Bullets plumped against the wall in the room where Schoellkopf worked. One night two hundred rough men pushed into the hotel, demanding food. Garrison made a mad ride to Sarauz at his peril to rescue an American woman, and guards with him in the car sat in a crouch with guns aimed, and fingers on triggers, as the car swayed around the innumerable hairpin curves.

By the sixth day the situation was maddening. It was clear that Madrid could not be reached. Even San Sebastián was unattainable. The telephone was silent.

In driving in the village I met Mme Herbette and drove her to the City Hall, delighted for an excuse to penetrate the ancient narrow street of the Fuenterrabia of the days of Charles V and Isabella. The day before the rebellion broke, I visited the Calle Mayor, so narrow and old, and saw the old palaces where lived the courtiers of centuries ago. I had visited the somber stone castle built by the great Emperor, if not by Isabella. The thick walls, the dismal prison room, the gruesome dungeon, reached through a round hole in the floor with an immense stone cover to shut out light and life, were relics of a savage age of autocratic power. I had gone to the top of the four-story fortress and viewed the country for miles around in France and Spain. From this position I could look down on the medieval church, black with time. I had entered the church to find a priest pounding wisdom into a small group of little boys on their knees, and the sharpness of his voice and the vigor of his manner implied that he had no easy task. Some of the windows of the church were beautiful, but on the whole the church was somber and depressing. This castle and church brought back the fifteenth century.

On this sixth day of the war, the church and castle were unchanged, but the narrow streets were now crowded with Basque fishermen, determination and indignation written on their rugged faces. Most were armed, but, without exception, they were polite and friendly. I had a permit to drive my car, stamped with the seal of the provincial governor. "It is perfectly correct," explained a functionary of the City Hall, "but not enough." He took the permit and disappeared. When he returned, four stamps had been added—those of the Republican Party, of the Socialist Union, of the Socialist Youth, and the National Party of the Basques. Nothing could have illustrated better the divided authority at the beginning of the war.

On driving Mme Herbette home, I noticed a big French flag on the house and another at the gate of the villa. That gave Sybil and Miss Moore an idea, and they hurried down into the village to buy material for an American flag, since the war had caught us without one. Though almost dark, they went with perfect confidence into the village among these fishermen who were being described by the hysterical or dishonest as "vicious reds."

And that night, the sixth, a few Basques went up the hill to the centuries-old fort of Guadalupe and took it over from an officer and fifteen men. The day before the war began, we had driven there to see the tiny church of the fortress and to view the scenery from this commanding height. The dark little church smelled of age and was as primitive as the old fort. We saw no soldiers. Across the winding dirt road we sat a while above the turmoil of the world, where the absolute silence was broken only by the rustle of the wind-touched trees. Then down the road came a low rumbling sound, and a primitive two-wheeled cart drawn by two huge oxen lumbered slowly by. A few days more and hell would be popping all about this peaceful scene. The fort, with its cannon, commanded the village of Irún, and the unwarlike nature of these villagers was revealed in their failure to take possession for almost a week.

At ten o'clock that night I was startled by the now unaccustomed ringing of the telephone. The speaker at the State Department in Washington seemed strangely startled and relieved to hear my voice. It appeared that the telegrams we had sent had not reached Washington. I had "disappeared," according to the American papers. The press had carried many weird tales. I had "taken refuge in an old fortress in Fuenterrabia"—the old dilapidated castle; with my staff I was hiding from the ferocious "reds" in a hotel basement in San Sebastián. Garrison, my secretary, had made a mad dash through the mountains at the risk of his life to save me. I had "bribed a fisherman" to smuggle a message across the frontier to France. Mme Herbette had informed the d'Orsay that she had seen me in Fuenterrabia! I was amazed and amused. The State Department spokesman kept repeating, as though unwilling to trust his ears: "Are you SURE you are all right?" It was as though he thought me a prisoner talking in the presence of my jailor with a gun at my back. So early had the Berlin and Rome propaganda about the "reds" taken hold in the United States.

I then demanded and secured permission to talk to San Sebastián, and got Johnson on the phone, and his high-pitched voice and rapid utterance were evidence enough of his excitement. He described conditions as "horrible." Desperate men had pushed into the hotel and "everyone was lucky they had not had their throats cut." Learning that all Americans had been evacuated, I told him to join me with the staff at Fuenterrabia until traveling conditions made possible a return to Madrid.

The next morning, I was looking out over the sea from the balcony when I sighted a ship, and, observing it curiously through glasses, was able to see the Stars and Stripes. It was the *Cayuga*. It cast anchor two miles out, and a boat was lowered. I drove into the village to the fishing wharf to meet it. The entire village seemed assembled, and I wondered about the mood of the crowd. The officers in smart uniforms were standing as the boat rose and fell on the waves. I hurried across the sand to meet Lieutenants Cowert and Jones, and I had never felt so proud of the Spanish masses as when these fishermen and peasants, with guns held awkwardly, saluted our officers as smartly as they could.

When we reached the villa, it was filled with women, long shut in their houses, eager to get word to worrying relatives in other lands over the wireless of our ship. The officers agreed to send the messages. The daughter of a marquise was much excited. "If the rebels lose, we are finished," she said, over and over again.

5

It was an eventful day. In the afternoon, the mayor of Irún telephoned me that two young men, claiming to be Americans but without their passports, had been arrested near the loyalist forces, with some damaging papers on their persons. Would I drive to Irún and give my judgment about them? I drove immediately to Irún, which even then seemed a town that had passed through war, or was ready for it. The streets were barricaded at close intervals with enormous sandbags. The plaza in front of the City Hall was filled with fishermen, peasants, and villagers in blue overalls that might have been terrifying to that tenderly nurtured element that imagines men in working clothes to be brigands or "reds." They politely made way for the car and crowded about curiously when I got out. In front of the City Hall, sandbags were piled seven feet high, the full length of the building. Soldiers, with muskets, guarded the door. The mayor was pleasant, friendly, intelligent, unflurried in the midst of the excitement. He told me the two boys had been found in a very suspicious spot without passports and with some notes that had caused concern. On a paper was written: "Two trucks of ammunition, two cannon," etc. I suggested that the boys were keeping a diary and had made some notations for their next entry. "Perhaps," said the mayor, "but we do not know." "May I talk with the boys?" I asked. "Certainly." A moment later, two boys, clearly American, but with sheepish expressions, entered. One turned out to be Clifford Chester, son of an executive of the Telephone Company in Madrid, and the other D'Arcy Wright, both students at Dartmouth College. They said they had been staying at the Eskualduna Hotel in Hendaye, and, being bored, they had decided to take a tramp along the French frontier. They followed a map carefully so as not to cross the border, but the map was defective and they crossed it unaware. "Have you got the map?" I asked Clifford. He drew it from his pocket and showed that the spot where they were taken was in France, according to the map. "Show it to the mayor," I said. He looked at the map and seemed satisfied. "And how about those notations on the paper" I asked. Clifford blushed and said he had thought he might become a journalist and he was "practicing." The mayor smiled. "I don't want to interfere with your defense of Irún," I said, "but if you want my judgment, I would stake my life that the boys have told the exact truth." "That is good enough for me," said the mayor, and, rising, he shook the boys' hands.

In the plaza I found Captain Townsend Griffiss, Assistant Air Attaché of the embassy in Paris, waiting for me. He had been sent down presumably to find me, dead or alive, and he had found me in the midst of a throng of determined-looking fishermen and artisans receiving every courtesy.

Returning to Fuenterrabia, I had my first contact with the pathos of war in front of the Concha Hotel. A car drew up, and robust workingmen helped a few old and middle-aged women out. The women were in tears and embraced in silence. One of the men told me they had come from Rentería, where an attack was expected from the Carlists of Navarre. The men, sons and grandsons of these women, were hurrying back to fight.

6

Sunday, the eighth day, was ushered in by the exploding of bombs in San Sebastián. I went to the City Hall to inform the mayor of the coming of my staff and to ask instructions as to their hours and conduct. He was a young man of agreeable appearance and fine courtesy. He said the village would be honored *and would carry out any instructions I might care to give.* And so no instructions were given or received.

At lunch, Gabino rushed in to announce that Patricia, who had been with the Schoellkopfs in London, had telephoned from Hendaye. I drove to Irún and crossed the border without trouble. Patricia had left London alone over the protest of her hostess, and against the advice of Grouitch, the Yugoslav Minister, and Sir George Graham, but she was not afraid of the Spaniards and she loved Spain.

7

It was at this time that I wrote Cordell Hull setting forth the elements supporting the rebellion.

(1) The monarchists, who wanted the King back with the old regime.

(2) The great landowners, who wished to preserve the feudalistic system by ending agrarian reform.

(3) The industrialists and financiers, who wished to put, and keep, the workers "in their place."

(4) The hierarchy of the church, hostile to the separation of church and state.

(5) The military clique that had in mind a military dictatorship.

(6) The Fascist element, which was bent on the creation of a totalitarian state.

A little before, the Fascist party was numerically unimportant, but with the defeat of the reactionaries in the election, great numbers of the young of the monarchist and CEDA parties, despairing of defeating the democrats at the polls, and disgusted with Gil Robles' failure, were turning from ballots to bludgeons and joining the Fascist group.

At that moment, while convinced by the arrogant conduct of Pedrazzi, the swaggering black-shirt Italian Ambassador, that material aid was to be given by the totalitarian States, I had no positive evidence of their participation. This was to come immediately afterward and, as we shall see, to be the determining factor, along with the appeasement policy of the Western democracies, in the destruction of democracy in Spain.

8

On the ninth morning, the *Cayuga* returned with some lugubrious passengers who solemnly filed into the villa. Among them were Lieutenant Cowert of the *Cayuga*, Captain Griffiss of the embassy in Paris, Counselor Hallet Johnson, First Secretary Schoellkopf, Biddle Garrison, and Eddie Flynn, the political leader in New York, who was my personal friend, and had been brought along for that reason. They sat down in the library in sober silence. Then Johnson, acting as spokesman, said that all were agreed that I was staying in Spain at my deadly peril, and that I should cross the border without delay. I resented, and opposed the idea, since I saw no immediate danger and felt strongly that there could be no justification for leaving. Cordell Hull had urged that I should not endanger my family by staying, and later I heard that he had telephoned Johnson to persuade me to leave. Then Captain Griffiss made his contribution. He had flown over the region and he reported that the rebels were in the mountains on one side, and the loyalists on the other. A battle was certain soon, and the defeated, retreating to the coast, would pour into Fuenterrabia and "probably attack, murder, and pillage." In case of an emergency, he said, I could not reach a ship without going into the center of the village and riding in a small motorboat for two miles, within shooting distance of the shore.

Meanwhile, all the others sat in silence staring at the floor. I repeated that there was no immediate danger. After a gloomy luncheon, the discussion was renewed, and finally, in exasperation, I asked Flynn when he had become hysterical. He blushed, and ascribed his panic to the statement of Captain Griffiss. "If anything should happen, and they had to send marines in to get you out, and some were killed, you would never forgive yourself," he said. I was astounded, but a bit shaken in my determination to remain against all advice. Hull, Ambassador Straus, the Army, Navy, and State Departments were all agreed that I should cross the border. Though sick at heart, I called Flynn upstairs with the family, to whom, thus far, I had not mentioned the reason for the visit. Sybil was indignant. Patricia was amused at the idea of danger. The argument began at ten, and it was almost five when finally I agreed to go. But never had I felt so mean as when I faced the necessity of telling the servants that I was leaving them in a trap—for if it were a trap for me, it was more of a trap for them. Patricia assumed the painful task of breaking the news and reassuring them. They were surprised and a little worried, but courageously they set about packing such belongings as we had to take. With the banks all closed, I borrowed all the pesetas in possession of my visitors and gave them to Gabino for the servants' food. The latter asked if I could help in getting his wife and child to the villa from a town beyond San Sebastián, and I drove to the City Hall again. The friendly mayor, with a consideration I shall always remember, agreed to send a car with guards to fetch Gabino's family—and he did.

So panicky were some of my advisers that it was feared I might not be permitted to cross the frontier, and it was arranged that the others should not enter the motorboat until I had crossed and signaled from the other side. In twenty minutes we reached the Golf Hotel in Saint-Jean-de-Luz, where we were greeted by Edna Ferber, the novelist, and a group of reporters.

9

The story of my opposition to leaving Spain was published in the American press. On July 27, the Associated Press carried the story that "four American diplomatic officials sailed today for Fuenterrabia to induce the American Ambassador to cross the border, since Bowers previously had refused to leave." But very soon, papers motivated by malice were criticizing me for my "flight," and the State Department was strangely silent, with full knowledge of the circumstances under which I left. I was ignorant of these libelous attacks, too busy with the crisis affecting Americans, until many friends sent me clippings and expressed indignation. At length I made a formal and blunt protest to the department and sent a copy to President Roosevelt with the observation that when a London paper had a similar criticism of the British Ambassador, the Prime Minister in the House of Commons instantly announced that the ambassador had crossed the border on the orders of the government "for good and sufficient reasons"; and that while I thought it more dignified and decent for the facts to be given by the department, I was quite capable of defending myself on the record, and would not hesitate to do so.

The President replied at once:

The White House
January 15, 1937

Dear Claude:

We are kindred spirits! The unfair attacks of that part of the press which had no interest in reporting either the truth or the facts are enough to make any of us boiling mad. Some day we may have a chance to sit down together and plan our own form of revenge. . . .

I don't think it necessary for me to tell you, but I hope you will pay absolutely no attention to these irresponsible people. They have just acquired the habit, which is impossible for them to break, and I think the American people gave them a sufficient answer as to how public opinion rates them in the November election. . . .

We are all following your scene, and, as you know, I am very much aware of the great difficulties which are yours. The job has been an outstanding one and as a historian you should get some comfort from the knowledge that history . . . will record it so. . . .

I have a memo from the State Department that your letter has been formally answered by Acting Secretary Moore. You probably will have received it by this time. [Included in *F. D. R.: His Personal Letters*, Vol. I, pages 651–2.]

The statement by Judge Moore, in the absence of Secretary Hull, said that I had gone to Saint-Jean-de-Luz under circumstances I have outlined, and explained the silence of the department on the ground that the attacks were so clearly malicious and political it had not thought it worth while to deny them.

I had scarcely reached the Golf Hotel in Saint-Jean-de-Luz when Wilbur Carr, Assistant Secretary of State, telephoned from Washington asking if I would go aboard the *Cayuga* and visit all the ports of the northern coast to evacuate our people, and personally contact our consuls in Bilbao and Vigo. Preliminary to leaving on this mission, I returned the next day to Fuenterrabia, where I found a serene determination among the people, the servants at the villa with the American flag displayed, happy and unafraid, and the Basque fishermen, with guns held awkwardly, as courteous and likable as ever.

Chapter XVIII

The Floating Embassy

IT WAS raining dismally, and there was a heavy sea when, with Schoellkopf and Garrison I went on board the *Cayuga*, a two-thousand-ton ship, to scour the entire northern coast in the evacuation of Americans. Along this full length of the picturesque coast of the Biscay waters, from the French frontier to near the Portuguese border, we had consulates at Bilbao and Vigo only. In no other port was there a consul on whom Americans could lean so for help or advice. Consequently, there was no one in these parts to assemble Americans for embarkation, and, in all but two, it would be necessary for us to land and personally search for our people in the town and surrounding country. Because of the breakdown of all communications in Spain, we had no idea what we should find, or what difficulties encounter. Our primary purpose was to get the Americans out of danger; and the other purpose was to confer with the consuls in Bilbao and Vigo who had been unable to communicate with us by telegraph or telephone concerning conditions in their territory. I was to be the only ambassador or minister personally to participate in the evacuation work.

The moment we drew out of the harbor in Saint-Jean-de-Luz, the ship began to pitch and roll. That day Schoellkopf and I were seated at a table in the center of the captain's office going over telegrams, when we were startled to find ourselves at the far end of the room with chairs and table in precisely the same relative position as when in the center. After that, the chairs and table were securely tied. We established an office for the "floating embassy" in the large, pleasant quarters of the captain.

And now, for the first time since the war began, we commenced to lose the feeling of being completely isolated from Spain. It was utterly impossible in any spot in Spain to get the most remote notion of what was transpiring in any other spot beyond the neighborhood, because all means of communication had been cut. But the moment we reached the *Cayuga*, with its wireless facilities, messages began to pour in from consuls theretofore shut off. One message intercepted, origin unknown, interested us greatly: "Keep clear of the *Cervera*"—a rebel ship the government had declared a pirate and which was said to be in the waters of Gijón.

It was five in the afternoon when we reached Bilbao, whose harbor, with five warships, had a martial air; and the moment we arrived the captain of the crack German battleship, the *Deutschland*, then in the harbor, wirelessed greetings. We had last seen this premier of the German fleet at San Sebastián, when its captain, illadvised, undertook to land armed men for the evacuation work. The Spaniards instantly bristled, and, but for the intervention of diplomats of other nations, who persuaded the captain that such bellicose gestures would endanger the lives of all our nationals and make evacuation work impossible, the wharf would have been stained with blood. Soon we were to have a similar contact with this inexplicable Teutonic psychology.

The captain of the British ship, making his ceremonial call, brought the information that Germany was sending bombing planes to the rebels. I am not personally positive that this was true at the time. However, on July 27, 1936, nine days after the rebellion broke, William Shirer, of the Columbia Broadcasting station in Berlin, wrote in his diary:

"The Nazis are against the Spanish government, and party circles are beginning to talk of help to the rebels." On August 25 he wrote: "Press now quite open in its attacks on the Spanish government. And I learn from dependable sources that the first German airplanes have already been dispatched to the rebels." And on November 12 he wrote: "Dodd [American Ambassador] tells me our consulate in Hamburg reported this week the departure from there of three German ships loaded with arms for Spain.'

It is positively known that about the middle of November, Hitler sent one combat group (3 squadrons of Junkers-52), a fighting group (3 squadrons of Heinkel-51), a company of radio operators, a company of telegraphists, a company of "listeners" and meteorologists. Soon the Nazi Condor Legion would be doing yeoman service against the Spanish democracy, commanded at different times by Generals Sperrle, Volkmann, and Von Richthofen. So proud was Hitler of the part he played in the destruction of the Spanish Republic that on February 4, 1939, Shirer reported in his diary: "A big German film company completed last summer, at the cost of several million marks, a movie based on the exploits of the German Condor Legion. . . . Hitler, Goering, Himmler saw it and praised it."

Whatever doubt there may be of the exact time the armed forces of Nazi Germany appeared in Spain, an embarrassing incident leaves us in no doubt as to the very early arrival of the Italian Fascists. Six hydroplanes, sent by Mussolini to the rebels, in compliance with prewar arrangements, were forced down in North Africa in French territory within a few days after the beginning of the war. The French sent General Denain, Inspector-General of the French air force, to investigate, and he reported that the planes had taken off from Sardinia, destined for Melilla and Ceuta, then in possession of the rebels.

Less than a month after the war began, a German tri-motor Junker 52 was forced to land in the airport in Madrid for gasoline, and it was taken over by the Spanish government. It was a military plane. On orders from Hitler, Hans Voelkers, the German Chargé in Madrid, well known to me, called on Augusto Barcia, the Foreign Minister, to demand the immediate release of the plane. I knew Voelkers well, and I can well understand his embarrassment. Within an hour after he left, the French Chargé called on Barcia with instructions from the flabby Delbos, the French Foreign Minister, to ask that Hitler's demand be immediately respected. He made a second call within an hour to say that Delbos begged that satisfaction be given Hitler. That same day Delbos, in Paris, summoned the Spanish Ambassador with an urgent appeal, and Voelkers called again in Madrid to say that Hitler "demanded" immediate action. He was told that the plane was a warplane and that the Council of Ministers would determine its disposition. The council unanimously agreed not to release the plane, and the crew was turned over to the German Embassy, the plane was sealed, and Voelkers was notified.

After all this, no one with any pretense to elemental honesty, in office or out, could pretend to doubt that Italy and Germany, the Axis, were engaged in a war of aggression. Within two months, everyone knew that Fascist Italy and Nazi Germany were waging a war on the Spanish democracy by prearrangement.

2

Soon we adjusted ourselves to life on board the *Cayuga*. Consul Chapman, who had joined us on board for dinner at Bilbao, painted no pleasing picture of conditions there. The government of the Basques was reasonable and self-respecting, the Basques were friendly and accommodating, but some syndicalists, with their anarchistic fringe, were sometimes defiant of the constituted authority.

Meanwhile, news was pouring in over the wireless. Saragossa had been taken by the rebels in a surprise attack of the army, and government troops were marching on the town . . . Americans from Madrid were going by train to Alicante to be picked up by the *Quincy* . . . Gil Robles had taken up residence in Portugal.

That night Captain Hall, of the battleship *Oklahoma*, came on board for the night. He was in command of our vessels in northern waters, and, at the moment, three of our warships were in the harbor. After dinner, we went to the engine room and saw the picture *The Kid from Spain*. Directly in front of the curtain, three rows of the seamen sprawled, lying almost flat, their heads raised a little on the pillow, so as not to obstruct the view. We sat with the officers on chairs in the front row, and when the ship lurched, the chairs were apt to slide. Behind us were all the other sailors, and soon these would be joined by men, women, and children taken on board for evacuation.

It rained all night, and in the morning we looked out on a heavy sea. The air was damp and chill, the skies were gray and gloomy. Chapman came on board early with the disturbing news that the Basque government proposed to take over the American Firestone plant and might displace the executives and demand the secret formulas. Should such a demand be made, it would be refused, and it was feared permission to leave the country would be denied the executives. It sounded ugly, and it was in keeping with the stories assiduously spread about the "communist" nature of the Azaña government, through the unscrupulous propaganda radio stations of Germany, Italy, and Portugal. This story was too good to have been improvised. It had clearly been inspired by the Axis allies of the rebels. I arranged to have the executives of the plant accompany me when I called on the governor for the facts.

With Schoellkopf, Garrison, and Lieutenant Jones, I went ashore. Unpleasant possibilities loomed in the sensational stories afloat. There was, no doubt, some curiosity, uneasiness, and resentment over the presence of so many American warships. The previous day, the British had been refused permission to embark their refugees from the nearest and most convenient pier. And we had heard blood-curdling tales of armed desperadoes in the streets.

Landing a mile from town, we telephoned the governor, and, in a few minutes, two armored cars arrived, with a clean-cut, snappy captain of Assault Guards in charge who might have stepped out of a ceremonial occasion at West Point. Reluctantly, I took along the correspondent of a press association, but with the distinct understanding that he could not be present at the interview with the governor. But he was.

The drive to the city was uneventful. It was over the road leading from the city to the pretentious villas and mansions of the rich. In that of the Marquis Ibarri I had dined three years before. But that morning there was nothing to foreshadow violence. The all-but-deserted highway was perfectly tranquil. Down the road, a group of citizen-soldiers would move toward the center of the road as we approached, but a wave of the hand of the captain with us, and they stepped back. The city streets were peaceful, and but few armed men could be seen. But for the absence of automobiles and the queer silence, the city seemed entirely normal.

We went to the governor's office prepared for controversy, to be greeted by Governor Novas with a warm, disarming cordiality. He was a republican of Azaña's party, surprisingly young, and most personable, with a pleasant face, and friendly eyes bubbling with good humor. He shrugged his shoulders and smilingly apologized for not having had time to shave, and for the stiff way he held his neck, because of a cold.

I mentioned the rumor about the taking over of the Firestone plant and the reported demand for the secret formulas. Novas smiled incredulously. Because of the exigencies of war, he said, the government, like any other, anywhere, was forced to requisition the use of industrial plants for the manufacture of war material, but nothing was wanted from the Firestone plant but tires for army cars and trucks. "We do not want the executives to leave," he said, "since we know nothing about operation; and we certainly have no desire for the secret formulas, since we are not going into business." The executives of the company readily agreed to produce tires to the capacity of the plant, and thus an amicable arrangement was made within five minutes. When I asked if we could count on the extension of all facilities later, should any of the executives desire to leave, Novas gave assurance.

Very informally, even parenthetically, I explained the presence of our warships in the harbor; and expressed regret that the British had been forced that day to use the most inconvenient pier for the embarkation of their refugees. Novas raised his eyebrows in honest astonishment and summoned the harbor master, a competent and gentlemanly Basque. He, too, was amazed. And then it came out that turns were taken in the guarding of the piers, and that some syndicalist extremists had evidently been on guard when the British arrived with their refugees. It was admitted that the government occasionally had brushes with these extremists, syndicalists and anarchists. "What time will you embark your people?" asked the harbor master. We told him. "Very well," he said, in a determined voice, "I shall be there to see them into the boat."

I left Novas with the feeling that I had met a gentleman. After some shopping, we returned to the ship. When the correspondent joined me in the car, he said:

"God! What sinister eyes that man had."

"What man?" I asked, astonished.

"That governor."

And then the explanation flashed upon me. The correspondent represented an association that was supporting the Fascists on the theory that the loyalists were communists bent on pillage and murder, and when I read his story—for he had slipped into the governor's office during my interview—I was not surprised. I read with amazement that we had passed groups of murderous-looking men as we rode in the "armored cars" in command of a villainous-looking captain of Assault Guards. We had been stopped repeatedly, and once when we were ignoring the order to halt, we heard the cocking of the guns and hastily backed up. But, in the end, it seemed that I had handled the governor with the "sinister eyes" properly enough. I had told him bluntly that when Americans wished to leave I expected him to see that they had no trouble. And then, pausing dramatically as in a melodrama, I had looked into the "sinister eyes" and said: "That is the reason the *Oklahoma* is here."

Thus Novas was repaid for his kindly consideration for the Americans. Soon I was to get accustomed to this type of propaganda when a part of our press would refer to the loyalists in Spain as "hordes from Russia." Goebbels was trying it out in Spain and finding it easy.

3

That afternoon, while the refugees were being embarked, I remained on board for the ceremonial calls. The British commander of the *Comet*, a young, ruddy, hearty Britisher, came with another story of German ineptitude. He had just visited the German destroyer, the *Albatross*, and had found the captain and his men on deck, armed, and preparing to land. "But you can't do that," stormed the red-faced British. "You will make it impossible for all of us." The German had seemed startled on hearing that Bilbao was not swimming in the blood of the slaughtered.

Scarcely had the Britisher left, when a messenger from the *Albatross* came to inquire if I would see its commander. I had a vision of a bluff, blustery, stone-faced Prussian, and I had no doubt I would dislike him. Then, in dress uniform, the commander appeared, and I almost gasped. My prejudices vanished the moment I saw him. A tall, manly young officer, with pink cheeks and a charming, frank face that beamed with friendliness, saluted. I could not bring myself to mention his plan to land armed men.

Instead, I told him of my visit to the town and of the absence there of armed men or trouble. That he understood my meaning was evident in his explanation that when, in response to orders from Berlin, to go full-speed ahead from the Baltic to Bilbao, and he found five warships in the harbor on his arrival, he had assumed there was serious trouble.

A little later, the commander of the French destroyer, sword, braid, and all, came on board, and then the harbor master appeared to ask if the embarkation of our people had been satisfactory. Such were my experiences in Bilbao in the last days of July, 1936.

After dinner, we were on deck when we steamed out, enjoying the beauty of the shore line, with the great green hills and cultivated fields. As we passed the *Deutschland*, all hands were lined up at attention; and as we passed the *Oklahoma*, the band was playing the "Star-Spangled Banner."

4

We awoke the next morning in the harbor of Gijón. The pilot, accompanied by a keen-looking young man in workman's jeans, came on board, reporting that the day before, the *Cervera* had shelled the town, but that the damage had been confined to the killing of two men and the wounding of five Germans in a hotel where they were awaiting evacuation. We were just about to go ashore, when a ship appeared on the horizon. The officers of the *Cayuga* inspected it through glasses. "It's the *Cervera*, probably returning to shell the town again," they reported. It was approaching at considerable speed. Since, in the absence of a consul in Gijón to assemble our nationals, we would have to search the town with deliberation, it was manifest that nothing could be thoroughly done under the guns of the rebel ship. Besides, with the *Cayuga* in the line of fire, we might easily be involved in an incident, or our appearance at the moment of the reappearance of the *Cervera* might be misunderstood. We decided to go on to Vigo and stop at Gijón on the way back.

5

We reached Vigo in the early afternoon. I had long planned to visit the city, but now that I was there, I could not land. The town

was in possession of the rebels and to go ashore would entail a call
of ceremony on the military commander. Seen from the deck of
the ship, the city looked attractive, with its fort-crowned mountain
in the background. It, too, was a city of silence.

When Consul Cochran came on board, I got my first description of the Fascist methods in taking possession of a town. On the
day the rebellion broke, the army in Vigo marched out of the
barracks to the roll of drums. In the public square, a startled population stared curiously at the soldiers. An officer stepped forward
and began reading the proclamation of martial law, and announcing that the People's Republic had been put aside by the armed
forces. An irate republican tried to snatch the paper from the
officer's hand. That was all—but it was enough. Without more
ado, the order was given to fire into the crowd of unarmed men.
The citizens fell back and ran. When the smoke lifted, some were
stretched upon the pavement, dead. This was but the beginning of
the "New Order" in Spain. There were very few extremists in
Vigo, but there were liberals, democrats, and republicans, and in a
hectic rush they were caught in the dragnet, arrested, thrown into
prison. The jail designed for eighty was soon packed with almost
three hundred prisoners. Thereafter, "all was quiet."

But all was not serene with Consul Cochran. In the political
capitalization of the death of Calvo Sotelo, "funeral services" were
celebrated in all churches of all towns in rebel territory, purely for
propaganda purposes. Quite properly, Cochran declined the invitation to join in an antigovernment demonstration. But when the
British and Portuguese consuls appeared, officially, tongues began
to wag the story that the American consul was a "red." When,
soon afterward, the British consul conceived the idea of a ball
game, with members of the crew of a warship of a democratic
nation participating, and with the announced intention of turning
the proceeds over to one of the rebel organizations, Cochran quite
properly stayed away. These two offenses against Fascism made
him a marked man. And when, after being insulted in the street
by rebel soldiers, he forced a public apology over the radio, the
fury of the armed masters of the city knew no bounds.

I listened to Cochran's story with incredulity, but when the
British consul called upon me with his interpretation of the war,
I was quite ready to accept the Cochran story. I listened with

astonishment as he poured forth the philosophy and propaganda of Fascism. Observing my evident surprise, the consul frequently paused, solemnly to assure me of his devotion to democracy. When, at length, I accepted his assurance with the comment that naturally he was a democrat, representing the people that he did, he had the grace to blush. Clearly it was his opinion that any liberal, democrat or republican was a "red." That absurdity was soon to take deep root in conservative and fashionable circles in both the United States and England.

Notified of our coming, Cochran had assembled Americans wishing evacuation, including three Bryn Mawr girls who were unable to understand the gravity of the situation. In a little Ford, they had been rattling for days in the midst of the perils without suspecting danger until, on reaching the outskirts of Vigo, they were startled by heavy firing in the city. They telephoned the police station to learn the reason. "Where are you?" demanded a voice. They told him. "Well, stay there until we send for you," barked the voice. They still were giggling, persuaded that the rebellion was a lark out of comic opera. While waiting for the *Cayuga*, they had made friends with some young Fascist soldiers, who had taught them the Fascist salute and songs. These youths rowed to the *Cayuga*, giving the salute, singing the songs, and the American girls, bending over the rail, were joining with a will, until it was suggested that in view of our neutrality, of the fact that the ship was a governmental vessel, and the American Ambassador on board, it would be desirable to dispense with antigovernment, antidemocratic demonstrations.

6

That night we went on to Coruña through a heavy fog that kept the captain on the bridge all night. The fog dissipated before the morning sun, and Coruña was spread out before us. Again, for diplomatic reasons, I was tied to the ship. Seen from the sea, the town is in the shape of a crescent, stretching a long distance along the shore. At one end, and a little beyond the town, loomed the "Pillar of Hercules," a famous old lighthouse known to song and story. The town was very still. Its silence was broken only by the target practice at the barracks.

And again I heard how Fascism took possession of these towns. The army had marched into the city that had no premonition. The civil governor and some Assault Guards died speedily without ceremony before a firing squad. It had been an easy conquest. In towns like Vigo and Coruña, the armed forces were hostile to the Republic, since Gil Robles and Franco, when in the War Office, had seen to that. And the population was unarmed. In that year's election, thirteen of the sixteen deputies from Galicia were of the Left or real republican parties, and but three were enemies of the democratic regime. But those who voted for the thirteen were unarmed; and those who voted for the three had the army. It was that simple. A small armed force had imposed its will on an unarmed population.

In the afternoon we went on to Ferrol, a navy base and a ship-building center to offer evacuation to the American wives of Spanish naval officers, and I sat on deck enjoying the entrancing sea view and the green hills while some of the party went to the town.

We reached Gijón at nine in the morning and immediately went ashore. We were greeted in friendly fashion and furnished a car to take us into town. Despite the recent shelling by the *Cervera*, the city was calm and orderly. But the City Hall presented a scene of intense activity. The reception room was filled with unshaven men. The mayor was coldly calm, unhurried, lightning quick in his decisions. Learning our mission, he volunteered to broadcast for us. While that was being done, we went to the Cuban Consulate to inquire about Cubans and Argentinians who might wish to leave. The office was crowded with men, women, and children. As we were leaving, the Spanish guide who had accompanied us remarked that the consul did not know that the loyalists knew that the consulate was filled with enemies of the regime in hiding. It was my first contact with the system for the protection of fifth columnists by democratic nations in the diplomatic corps that was to shock me later on.

This guide, an educated man, who had attended Cornell University, introduced himself as familiar with two of my books. As we rode through the streets, he pointed out the effect of the shelling by the *Cervera*—the wreckage near the pier of the inner town, the great hole in the pavement in front of a hospital where a shell had burst. All this he pointed out with the nonchalance of a guide piloting tourists through the ruins of ancient Rome. He told us that Civil Guards, distrusted by the masses, were imprisoned but not harmed. Explaining why the miners in Oviedo did not use dynamite to blast out the rebels in that town, he said they did not want to hurt women and children. "We want the respect of the outside world," he said.

When we returned to the pier with our refugees, we found the *Cervera* dangerously near, its boats lowered out of range of the guns that were turned toward the town. There was nothing to do but risk it. We embarked our refugees in a motorboat without an incident. As we passed the *Cervera* on our way out, it signaled in the customary manner. And there were queer happenings on the sea that night. The officers on the bridge of the *Cayuga* had seen a mysteriously darkened ship prowling on the waters and had thought it an Italian ship carrying provisions or ammunition to the rebels. This was when it was still thought bad taste to mention above a whisper Italy's notorious participation in the war.

7

The next morning we were at Santander. It was here that we took on board the most winsome of the refugees, Gloria Sileo, a nine-year-old girl from Brooklyn, spending her vacation with her Spanish aunt. The child, both pretty and bright, was keen to return to Brooklyn before school opened. The aunt was large and jolly and eager to go herself. To evacuate the child alone would have been a problem, and the rule was rigid against taking Spaniards without a permit from the authorities. My appeal to the mayor was successful.

There was little in the streets of Santander that day to suggest a war. The city was beautiful in the hot sunshine, and the business buildings and private houses suggested comfortable living conditions. Men and women jostled one another on the sidewalks, merry and apparently carefree, and the stores and banks were open. We were graciously received by the governor, whose rooms and corridors were crowded with a constant stream of callers going in and out. The captain of the port, tall, distinguished, and handsome, was charming, and this "red" talked regretfully with Garrison of the lost pleasures of the city's fine golf course.

While we were waiting by the open window, we were startled by children's voices raised in song. They were packed into a trolley car going by, and in the midst of so much tragedy, it was a strange and welcome interlude.

My last view of this pleasant town, which Azaña hoped to make the summer capital, was through the porthole of my cabin just as we sailed. There loomed the King's favorite palace like a picture in a frame.

8

The next morning we were in San Sebastián. We had seen it last when men were fighting in the streets and diplomatic privileges meant nothing to men playing with death. Now the government was in control. The loyalist guards who met us as we landed were rough enough in appearance, but they were fighting men in fighting days. They met us in a friendly spirit. We walked to the old quarters of the summer embassy in the Continental Hotel and marveled, as we went, at the gross exaggeration of the "destruction" wrought on the María Cristina Hotel and the Casino. It is remarkable that most truthful people will misrepresent and exaggerate in war days to give a thrill. This was impressed upon me in the beginning when an American woman, evacuated from San Sebastián, told staring reporters in Hendaye, on disembarking from the *Cayuga*, of seeing the entire coast line lighted by the fires of burning churches and convents *when not a single church or convent had been touched*. The devout Basques did not harm their churches or convents; that was a speciality of the Nazi aviators, as we shall see.

That day the people were moving about the streets in normal fashion. There was little traffic, and the sidewalk cafés along the Alameda were deserted and lonesome. Near the post office, groups were gathered about the front page of a newspaper pasted on the wall. We joined the group in reading a denunciation of Gil Robles as a "traitor," a "perjurer," a "liar," responsible for the blood welter in which Spain was plunged. The crowd read in moody silence.

We drove at noon to Hendaye to the Eskualduna Hotel, where most of the diplomatic corps had taken quarters.

That ten-day journey along the northern coast of Spain in the first days of the Second World War gave me much to think about. The sheer beauty of the rugged coast, the green wooded mountains, the cultivated fields, are unforgettable. The towns were enveloped in tragedy, silent, grim, and mostly sad. They suggested the stage setting for a tragic drama. The people were ready to die, if need be, but it seemed so hopeless. This corner was completely shut off from any possibility of assistance from the loyalist government in Madrid, since the territory held by the rebels stretched for miles between. Should the rebels attack, they could constantly be reinforced from rebel territory, but no loyalist who died could be replaced. The Basques, the Galicians, the Asturians, the people of Santander, were surrounded and isolated. For a while they would be able to get material and food by sea, but troops could not be moved in by water. Even so, the morale of these people was remarkable. They seemed to realize that they faced overwhelming odds, but they faced them gamely with a smile.

The journey back to Saint-Jean-de-Luz had been interesting, for the refugees were gay, sunning themselves on the deck by day and at night crowding into the engine room for the pictures. It was a paradise for the children—movies every evening, and a boat for a playhouse every day. The sailors fed them chocolate bars, and they romped about with smeared faces.

9

I established the embassy in two large cheerful rooms with French doors opening onto a balcony in the Eskualduna Hotel at Hendaye, and the next day I drove across the border to Fuenterrabia, where I found the servants at the villa contented, though the war was drawing near, and we could hear the rumble of loyalist artillery in the mountains . . . Cochran telegraphed from Vigo that the military authorities were ignoring his intercession for an American in prison, and that he was receiving threatening letters on the stationery of the military headquarters. I advised his transfer after Fascist youths debated one night outside his door whether to kill him regardless of the effect on international relations . . . An amusing story drifted in from Madrid, where the pretty and charming young Countess Villada and her husband had "lost" themselves by going to a hospital to escape notice. She worked as a nurse and he as an orderly . . . In San Sebastián, officers taken in rebellion were being court-martialed in batches of eight, granted all the customary privileges of defense, and condemned. They were, on their request, permitted to die in uniform.

This tragic phase came close to me. One afternoon I was informed by the daughter of Sr. Padilla, former Spanish Ambassador to Washington, that her brother, an officer, was to face a court-martial that night in San Sebastián. It usually meant execution at dawn. The association of the father with Washington seemed to justify a deviation from the usually rigid rule to keep entirely out of the savage struggle. There was no time to cable Washington, but I joined the British Ambassador in a telegraphed appeal for clemency. That night seven, not eight, were condemned, and young Padilla was saved, but he died within a year fighting those who had granted clemency.

The Eskualduna Hotel, one of the largest in Europe, delightfully situated facing the sea and a beautiful beach, was swarming with diplomats, war correspondents, and the Spanish aristocracy seeking to save relatives caught in the vortex of the furious struggle. For days we were deluged with telegrams, and the telephone rang literally day and night. There was no entertainment in Hendaye outside the lobby of the hotel, but in free moments we found the house of Pierre Loti, rambled over the extensive grounds of the castle built for the Empress Eugénie by the sea, or went to Cambo to walk in the elaborate gardens of Rostand.

Meanwhile, rumors flew fast about the march of the rebels on Irún, about the increasing number of Moors on the fighting front, about the Carlists' marching from Pamplona, and then bombs fell on Irún. The battle was not remote.

Chapter XIX

The Decisive Battle of Irún

IN SEPTEMBER, 1936, it was evident to any intelligent observer that the war in Spain was not a civil war; nor had it begun as a civil war in the usual meaning of the words. Arrangements had been made long before for the military participation of Hitler and Mussolini, and they were now pouring their forces into Spain.

It was to be a war against democracy, and in this war the Moors were to play an important role. It was not for nothing that General Sanjurjo and José Primo de Rivera had gone to Germany in February, 1936, even before the elections, where they had been established at the Kaiserhof Hotel in Berlin, reserved exclusively for guests of the government. It was at this time that the bargain was made with Hitler; that with Mussolini had been made two years before.

Spain then was to be the testing ground. Here would be staged the dress rehearsal for the totalitarian war on liberty and democracy in Europe; here public reaction to outrageous methods would be tried out; here the new method of warring on civilian populations would be ventured; here the term "fifth column" would be coined, and its use tried.

Meanwhile, General Franco had reached Spain from the Canary Islands. In London a plane had been engaged by C. W. H. Bebb to convey him, and, to give the excursion an innocent ap-

pearance, some "tourists" were to accompany the plane as pas-
sengers. These were Major Hugh B. C. Pollard, his daughter,
Diana, and her friend, Dorothy Watson. In appreciation of this
coverage for Fascism, Bebb was to be given the Imperial Order of
Red Arrows by Franco, and Major Pollard was to be made a
General of the Order, and the girls were to get medals. Thus Franco
reached Spain and assumed command of the Spanish-German-
Italian-Moorish military forces.

2

Irún, the frontier station on the Spanish side, is utterly without
charm, barren of artistic treasures, either those of canvas or stone.
But it guards the entrance to Spain.

A mile away, off the main road from San Sebastián, lies the
more charming and historic village of Fuenterrabia.

As the struggle for Irún approached, great lorries of arms and
ammunition, purchased by the Spanish government in accordance
with its legal right, poured in a stream across the bridge at Hendaye
to the defending forces. Thus Irún became a strategic point of the
first importance.

It was inevitable that a determined effort must be made by the
rebels and their allies to capture the town and thus end the inflow
of war material to all the loyal northern provinces, cut off completely from the major part of loyalist territory. In the last days of
July there was a momentary expectation of an attack from the
Carlists, said to be creeping through the mountains from Pamplona.
From the windows of the Eskualduna one could look down on
Irún and on the sweet little Basque village I had been forced to
abandon. The two heights of Guadalupe and San Marciál, whence
Irún could easily be shelled, were in possession of the government,
and their cannon, booming at intervals, effectively held the enemy
in check.

In San Sebastián, the rebel ship *Cervera* was shelling the town,
doing some damage to property and taking its toll of human lives.

The next day the gun of Guadalupe continued to roar, but more
impressive now was the new note, the rat-a-tat-tat of machine-
gun fire not far away. That night there was a thrilling electric
storm, with the skies aflame, and everyone in the hotel sprang to

the windows, convinced that Irún was being heavily bombed from the air. But the next day all was quiet on the Irún front.

The road from Biarritz to the frontier was congested with motor-cars carrying the curious, who availed themselves of every elevation along the road to peer through field glasses across the border. All they saw was the quiet of Irún, the sweet serenity of Fuenterrabia, the sea and sky. Great numbers drove along the very narrow, winding road beside the Bidassoa River, marking the frontier, toward the mountains of Navarre, in the hope of seeing the Carlists or the Moors—quaint partnership—slinking among the trees. This picturesque road had become dangerously congested, for once in the creeping line, there was no possibility of turning back. The cars crept at a snail's pace. Hundreds of pedestrians tramped by the roadside, glasses or cameras hanging around their necks. The harassed gendarmes bristled with annoyance, and, at a point where the road widened, we were forced to turn back. That day we were closer to danger than we thought, for on the morrow we were awakened by the thunder of the guns.

Then it was that bombs fell from the air on Irún. Far out on the water, the *Cervera* was firing at intervals at three-hundred-year-old Guadalupe, and a tremor ran through the hotel with each explosion. We watched, fascinated. A flash of fire on the distant ship, and then, after a surprising interval, the explosion of the shell as it fell somewhere near, but never on the old fort. The ancient cannon there returned the fire, but the ship was out of range. We could see the splash on the water as the shell landed many yards from its objective. From comfortable chairs on the balcony we watched the futile battle all day long.

3

That night a letter, written on the stationery of the mayor of Fuenterrabia, was handed me. It was dated from the fort of Guadalupe and was in the handwriting of a member of a distinguished family in Madrid. It brought the horrors of war close.

This afternoon [it said] the committee of the *Frente Popular* of Irún and Fuenterrabia communicated to us, a committee of five of the prisoners, the decision adopted yesterday because of the victims of the aerial bombardment of Irún and San Sebastián to shoot five of the prisoners for each innocent victim of Irún. To prevent this taking place, we have decided to write to persons of our acquaintance in Navarre in order that they may inform the general in command of the forces of Navarre. As I do not know anyone in Navarre, I dare to address myself to you, given the great friendship which unites you and my family, in order that you may communicate this to the general who commands the forces of Navarre, and that he may be able to attend to our wishes.

Begging you to forgive the haste with which I write this letter, I remain your affectionate friend, etc.

At the bottom of the sheet, Count ——, well known to me, and at whose country house I had been a guest, had added:

My dear friend: I being also one of the prisoners join in the request of our friend, begging that you intercede with all good interest in the favorable solution of this situation, for which your good friend will remain deeply grateful.

Another bombing of Irún, another mangled child or woman, and these two men might face a firing squad. That day I spent hours trying to contact some of the men who constantly went back and forth from France to the rebel forces until I learned from the mother of the Duke of Algeciras that her son-in-law, the Marquis del Mérito, was crossing in the early morning and would stop at the hotel. He read the letter gravely the next morning, shaking his head and muttering, "It is terrible." He promised to deliver the letter.

That day, the *Cervera* fired a few shots at Guadalupe without effect and soon was lost behind the horizon. And that day a letter was brought me from across the border from the Countess de la Maza, who was confined by the loyalist authorities to the Concha Hotel in Fuenterrabia. Should the lawless element get control, she asked the refuge of my villa there. This lady, sister of the Duke of Fernán-Núñez, a tall, handsome woman, fond of horses and country life, was a friend and I readily gave consent. Her experience, as I heard it, illustrates a phase of Spanish character. On receiving my note she had the temerity to summon the military commander to her hotel to show him my letter, with the bland announcement that should conditions justify, she would insist that he send an escort with her to my house. Momentarily stunned, he burst into laughter and gave his promise. The Spaniards admire courage and audacity, especially in a charming woman, and they have an appreciation of humor. It was about this time that Muñoz Seca, the dramatist whose drawing-room comedies long were popular in Madrid, was arrested by the anarchists during the period of the terror and put on "trial." He won his enemies with a comedy.

"You may take my life," he said in tremulous tones, "you can take away my reputation, you may take my property"—and here his voice came strong and defiant—"but there is one thing you never can take away from me, and that is the horrible fear I have of you just now."

The crowd at the "trial" was delighted, and the dramatist's life was spared for a while.

4

One night San Sebastián was cruelly bombed from the air, and we heard there would be reprisals on rebel prisoners. It had been a savage attack. The entire upper story of a maternity hospital was demolished. The governor invited the press correspondents on the border to visit the city and see the ruins. Jean Herbette, the French Ambassador, who had not yet deserted his loyalist friends, publicly denounced the bombing as barbarous and personally conducted French correspondents to the scene.

Worried now about the servants in Fuenterrabia, I drove across the border. Irún and Fuenterrabia were grimly silent. All the aristocratic summer residents in the villas, all enemies of the Republic, were confined to their houses, with armed guards patrolling up and down in front. Only soldiers paced the streets, and they walked with the silence of shadows. In the quaint little plaza of the main street, old women with wrinkled faces sat on benches under the trees knitting and gossiping in undertones. On the veranda of the Concha Hotel, the Countess de la Maza was calmly sewing. But at the villa I found consternation among the women. The constant bursting of shells on the hill just beyond the house made the building tremble, and the noise was nerve torturing. The women were on the verge of hysteria, but my Italian chef was terror stricken. Even that early everyone knew that Italy was actively in the war, and he was in mortal terror lest a mob tear him limb from limb because of his nationality. His condition was so pitiful I promised to take him across the border with me, but, noting the abject terror in his face, I roughly told him to rid himself of that expression of guilt and fear or he would be suspected at the frontier. With a supreme effort he calmed himself, and when we paused at the frontier, he had a wan, silly smile on his face, but his hands, held low and out of sight, were twitching violently. The "red" guard, a large friendly Basque, who rode in front with Pepe, knew the chef's nationality and sensed his fear with astonishment, and when he left the car at the International Bridge, he turned with a smile and shook the Italian's hand, as he winked at me.

I arranged then to take all the servants into France as soon as possible. Three times committees had appeared at the villa to take possession of the house for military purposes, and once to get books for the hospital, but the mere announcement that the villa was the home of the American Ambassador sufficed. They apologized and left.

5

While we were at Fuenterrabia that afternoon, a battle was being fought not far away, and the rebels were repulsed. The next day it was mysteriously quiet but for a few shots at Guadalupe from the *Cervera*, with the usual results. Then, for two days, silence. At night we listened to the radio from Madrid—to military orders, too often to speeches of extremists who had seized the station in the first days of chaos and were doing irreparable harm beyond the frontiers. But mostly we heard gay music, which, under the circumstances, tempted tears. Frequently, parts of operas, some *flamenco* singing, and once we were stirred by the pulse-moving strains of Sousa's *El Capitán*. Always at the end the "Hymn of Riego," the national anthem of the Republic, came over the air defiantly. In the midst of a rebellion, supported by the arms of two nations and the Moors, with irresponsible terrorists in the streets at night, it was remarkable that there was no lapse in the entertainment of the people. But it was a time of striking contrasts everywhere. While the *Cervera* was shelling the fort and town, a great number of Basque fishing boats from Fuenterrabia were basking peacefully in the sun upon the sea, the fishermen unmoved, indifferent to the rebel ship, plying their trade as though death were nothing.

The battle of Irún was developing slowly. For a day or so there was little fighting, but a correspondent coming from General Mola's army told me that at Burgos he had seen Moorish troops. Though it was common knowledge that the Moors were being brought over by the thousands, an effort was being made in these early days of the war to conceal or camouflage their presence. There was still some feeling about the Moors in Spain. The censor with Mola's army instructed the correspondents to refer to the Moors as "the army from Morocco," *if they had to mention them at all*. But soon the presence of the Moors would be proclaimed from Burgos, and Moorish cavalry would act as the guard of honor when the Hitler Ambassador would present his credentials to General Franco.

Meanwhile, Mola was bringing up reinforcements from Africa, mostly of the Foreign Legion, and bigger guns. The citizen army was proving rather tough for the professionals.

6

Then the major struggle for Irún began. The air throbbed with the roar of artillery, the droning of planes, the explosion of bombs falling on Irún. That day the Foreign Legion, leading the attack against the improvised army of the loyalists, threw itself into the fight with all it had, with the aid of tanks and armored cars. The untrained loyalists met the onslaught without blanching and fought with the spirit and courage of veterans. At one time they blew up a road, and while the rebel tanks plowed through, the armored cars were stuck. With their vast superiority of equipment, training, military leadership, the rebels gained but two hundred yards, and without taking a single strategic point. That night the young commander of the loyalists laughed with boyish glee and said that since the army had put forth its utmost and failed, Irún would not be taken.

On the second day the battle was not resumed until ten o'clock, and the fighting was intermittent. For a time, the rattle of machine-gun fire, the cracking of rifle shots, the boom of cannon, the crash of exploding shells—and then, long intervals of silence. That afternoon the recruits fighting for the democratic regime had the temerity to countercharge, and they regained some ground they had lost the day before. That evening Captain O'Reilly, Assistant Military Attaché of the embassy in Paris, who saw the fighting, told me he doubted if the rebels would take the town.

7

That afternoon we drove to the old castle of the Empress Eugénie and walked for two hours in the beautiful grounds as far as the sea, where the rocky coast is most picturesque. The meadow was aflame with fragrant clover. Here and there, patches of woods made a frame for the castle in the distance. At land's end there was a precipitate fall to the sea. Some distance away, across the water, we noticed a young man and woman in scant bathing costumes climbing over the mountainous rocks and taking perilous chances until they found what seemed to them a secluded spot. There they sat, loverlike, while shivering reverberations shook the air, and shells sped with a weird whistling sound over our heads from the *Cervera*, some distance out at sea. It was an unforgettable scene— the blue skies, the bluer sea, the meadows red with clover, the hum of bees, the chirp of birds, the hellish sound of battle, and the lovers on the distant rock shut in from all behind them by a granite wall, and with only the sea before them, utterly oblivious to the whistling shells. Life went on in the midst of death. Here was love and hate. Not far from the clover field, young boys were dying in the mud.

That day the offensive failed again—and failed so signally that on the morrow all was silent throughout the day but for the occasional booming of the superannuated cannon of Guadalupe.

8

At midnight we were awakened by a terrible din, and we knew a fierce night fight was on—the first of the war in this section. In the mountains a bitter battle was in progress for the capture of San Marciál. An almost full moon cast a dramatic radiance on the country, though nothing was clearly visible but the flashes when the guns roared from the hilltops.

Later in the afternoon, the rebels had made a desperate effort to take the fort, but wave after wave ascending the mountain side, led by the Foreign Legion, was literally mowed down by machine-gun fire. The night attack was intended as a surprise. Under the cover of darkness, the Foreign Legion had moved up a ravine in the rear and fallen upon the first of the loyalist trenches. There men had grappled, man to man, and fought with hand grenades. But San Marciál remained in possession of the loyalists, and numbers of the Legionnaires who had marched up the hill never marched down again.

Infuriated by his failure to take San Marciál, General Mola called off further attacks for three days, threatening in the meanwhile he would send a flock of planes from Pamplona to pepper Irún with incendiary bombs. That day a number of the Foreign Legion escaped across the river into France, complaining that they had been forced to bear the brunt of the battle. For several days there was no action, and press correspondents, returning from the front, told me that Mola was waiting for reinforcements.

Two or three days later, when the struggle was renewed, Irún was subjected to a ruthless bombing, but despite the ferocity of the attack, the rebels made but little progress, and more Legionnaires waded across the Bidassoa to France under cover of the night.

The rebel command was becoming desperate. If a little unfortified town, defended by fishermen and mountaineers untrained in war, could not speedily be taken with trained troops, the rebels clearly were finished. Mola took command in person. With a professional army, though many were mercenaries, and with vastly superior equipment, a desperate attack was made on San Marciál, and the outlying trenches successfully were stormed.

And just at this critical juncture, the French government and that of Chamberlain and Baldwin moved effectively to the side of Mola to break the resistance of the defenders of European democracy.

9

History is still curious about the genesis of the plan through which the European democracies aligned themselves stubbornly, if ignorantly, on the side of the Fascists against the Spanish democracy. In his brilliant and illuminating book, *The Gravediggers of France*, Pertinax, the ablest and most dependable of French journalists, tells an interesting story, which I quote:

Toward the end of July, 1936, this diplomat, Señor de Cárdenas, the Spanish Ambassador [in France], although an ardent royalist, still represented the republican government of Madrid. Before resigning, he apparently wanted to be sure that the rebellion would not peter out. He had, therefore, to comply with instructions received from Madrid and ask Léon Blum for warplanes. The Premier at once received him at the Hotel Matignon and, without a shadow of hesitation, granted his demand. "Good, I'll give orders right away." The ambassador's vexation and anxiety can easily be imagined. Were the Spanish generals, then, despite the Fascist air forces that had rushed to their help, to suffer defeat at the hands of the French Popular Front, and, what was worse, on his own entreaty? Cárdenas frantically looked for a monkey wrench to throw in the wheels, a monkey wrench which would still not belie him in his role of loyal agent. A telephone call came to his rescue. "Would you mind waiting a few minutes in the garden?" asked the Prime Minister. "This is urgent business and I cannot put it off." Señor de Cárdenas did not wait to hear the request the second time, but scurried off to the garden. Shortly afterward he returned with this bright suggestion: "On behalf of my government, allow me to thank you for your willingness to lend assistance. But would it not be wiser to consult Madrid as to the types of planes best fitted to the task?" "How right you are. Let me hear at once what you find out." The ambassador dashed to the British Embassy, where he had friends. They agreed immediately to unleash the Rightist press. Its howls rose to heaven. Sir George Clerk, Phipps' predecessor, did not mince his words, and some of his staff terrified drawing rooms and editorial offices. Léon Blum and Yvon Delbos, his Minister of Foreign Affairs, fearful of losing the British alliance, were cast headlong into the so-called nonintervention agreement. Thus they backed down before what was to be an Italo-German monopoly of waging war in Spain. [Pertinax, *The Gravediggers of France*, p. 433.]

It is now fairly established that this plan was hatched in London and that Blum was practically blackmailed into acceptance. Otherwise, England would withdraw her guarantee to maintain the frontier of France and support France in a possible war with

Germany; and would consider herself released from her obligations under the Locarno Pact, unless France abandoned her right, under international law, to sell arms and ammunition to the democratic republic that both England and France recognized as the legitimate, legal government. This amounted to an ultimatum, and the Blum government yielded to the threat. Mr. Churchill would have us believe that the plan was Blum's and that he acted on his own initiative. When two nations thus seek to shift responsibility, there is something of which to be ashamed.

It was not a complete surrender, since the proposed pact, presumably to localize the war, applied to all nations, including Germany and Italy. It was proposed to ask Italy, Germany, Portugal, and Russia to agree to set international law aside and deny the constitutional government of Spain its right to buy arms and ammunition to defend itself against a foreign invasion or a Fascist insurrection. It also stipulated that no arms should be sent to either side.

Honestly intended, and honestly carried out, this would have kept all other nations out of the Spanish war. Meanwhile, the United States declared itself neutral as between the contending forces, and it put on an embargo against the sale of arms to Spain. Thus we, too, denied Spain her right under international law.

But this was only the beginning of the betrayal of democracy. In common fairness and decency, none of these nations of the Nonintervention Committee should have put the proposed agreement into practice until all of them had affixed their signatures. *The battle of Irún was at a critical stage; the defense of Irún was essential to the defense of the northern provinces; but instantly, without awaiting action on the part of Germany, Italy, and Portugal, the democracies signed, and stopped all sales to the Spanish government. At the critical stage of a decisive battle, the defenders of Irún were deprived of means of defense.*

The result was this: When the defenders of Irún fled across the border to Hendaye, because of the exhaustion of ammunition, they found six freight cars loaded with ammunition from Catalonia sent across the southern border of France. This munition had been stopped by "nonintervention" at the critical hour.

But Germany and Italy were not so precipitate. Since the democracies had tied the hands of the democracy of Spain—why hasten to tie their own? And so, for days, while withholding their signatures, they were sending more arms to the rebels and their Nazi and Fascist allies—planes, tanks, artillery. This was to continue on a huge scale for two years.

The position of Blum was pitiful. On September 6, 1936, at Luna Park in Paris, he told of his emotions in refusing the plea of a delegation of Spaniards to lift the embargo. "When I read the story of the taking of Irún and the agony of the last militiamen, do you believe that my heart was not with them?" he asked. But his explanation that had he not refused, Hitler and Mussolini would have released material to Burgos was utterly absurd, since they were releasing it on a large scale even then.

Thus did the Nonintervention Pact operate dishonestly from the first day. Never for two and a half years was the pact to be regarded by the Axis powers; and during this time, the legal and constitutional government of Spain, recognized as such, was hampered in every way in buying the supplies it needed and for which it was prepared to pay in gold.

At this time it was positively known that Italy was sending Savoias, Capronis, and Fiats to Franco, and that Hitler's pocket battleships were protecting rebel ports from bombardment by the Spanish navy. Soon Hitler's battleship, *Deutschland*, would be steaming slowly up and down the harbor of Ceuta, making it impossible for the loyalist *Jaime* to fire.

10

So at a critical stage of the battle of Irún the lorries with arms and ammunition for the defenders ceased rumbling across the international bridge, and the loyalists were left naked to their enemies. What Mola had not accomplished had been done for him by the Nonintervention Pact, conceived by the governments of democratic peoples. They struck a deadly blow, perfectly timed, at the loyalists at the crucial moment, and thus made impossible a successful loyalist defense of the whole of northern Spain.

That day I saw pitiful scenes. Hundreds, thousands, of women and children and old men poured across the border from their ruined homes that no longer could be defended. Penniless, friendless, they staggered into an alien land, bringing as much of their pathetically meager belongings with them as they could carry on their backs. Many of the old women, with fear and misery stamped on their faces, carried chickens under their arms—their sole reliance against starvation. Many bore bedding on their heads as they stumbled along. Some carried a few kitchen utensils. And all their faces were marked by tragedy and horror. Sons, fathers, husbands in some instances escorted their families into exile, and with stoic calmness bade them farewell, kissing the mother or the wife, who wept bitterly. The eyes of the men were dry. So, too, the eyes of the older women. The men lifted toddling babies in their arms for a last kiss, and then with a wave of the hand they returned to the fighting, wherever they could find it. A small boy with a harassed, desperate expression sat on a coping, his arms around a loved dog. "Is that your dog?" asked Fred Kelly, the writer, who was with me. The child had come to look on all strangers as enemies, and, assuming that the dog was now in danger, he clutched it tightly in his arms and nodded affirmatively, turning a defiant look on his interrogator. Touched by the child's fears, Kelly gave him fifty francs—a fortune! The mother rushed to the donor with tears streaming down her face and covered his hand with kisses.

From the beach we could see men filling bags of sand at Fuenterrabia, preparing for battle in the streets of Irún.

11

The next day Irún fell because of the lack of ammunition. Some of the defenders, with a few rounds of shot left, stood at their posts and died in their tracks. Others, more realistic, escaped in boats and made their way to Bilbao to continue the struggle. And some, in fury, set fire to buildings that might serve the enemy. This was shocking to some who later were to applaud the "scorched earth" policy of the Russians.

Just before leaving, the loyalists, pictured as savages a little later, went to the imprisoned rebel families in the villas of Fuenterrabia and told them it would be best for them to leave. They hurried to the beach and, in the boats of the "red" fishermen, crossed the narrow strip of water to Hendaye. Such was the tolerance and chivalry of the loyalist Basques. But the next day when the loyalist noncombatants were fleeing across the border, they were fired upon as they ran. It was the Fascist technique— forerunner of the practice that was to shock the civilized world a little later. Old men who had crossed hobbled along the road painfully with burdens on their backs; women carried children in their arms and bundles. And across the border, Irún was burning. Great clouds of black smoke obscured the view, but now and then red flames shot through.

12

The effect of the fall of Irún on the rebels and their ardent supporters among my colleagues was incredible to me. These agreed that the war was practically over. They were sure that the rebels would take Bilbao at once and then hurry on to the immediate capture of Madrid. I reiterated to Washington my conviction that the war would be prolonged because the struggle involved not merely armies, but a people.

At this time, after Irún fell, in talking with Jean Herbette, the French Ambassador, I thought I had a touch of the sun or had lost my hearing. This socialist, whose reputed sympathy with the government had given him partial treatment, sat across the table from me, serene, apparently happy, renouncing the constitutional regime with no semblance of regret and assuring me that the "generals would now get together and end the war." Overnight he had become a partisan of the rebels.

One effect of the fall of Irún was a change in the government in Madrid. Deprived by the betrayal of the army of the instrumentalities of force to maintain order, Azaña's most pressing problem was the restoration of order and the unification of all forces opposed to Fascism. In his government of conservative republicans and democrats, described by the Fascist propagandists as "communistic," there was not one who could have influence with the extremists. Dr. Giral, the Prime Minister, was of Azaña's party and with no influence with the extremists who were a threat to solidarity in the face of the foe. With the inevitable losses in the early stages of the war, before some semblance of order could be brought out of confusion, there was grave danger that, in desperation, irresponsible extremists might play on the fears of the people and seize power. The immediate problem was to control and discipline these elements and persuade them to march in step. There was one man of political prominence they might follow—Largo Caballero, who had spent months before the war cultivating these tumultuous forces. He was a favorite with the working class and of the powerful Socialist Union. Thus, when Giral resigned, he was succeeded by Largo Caballero.

The first reaction outside Spain was that the extremists had seized power, and that "communism" was in the saddle. I did not share this pessimistic view. If anyone in the crisis could align the undisciplined element behind the constituted authority, Largo Caballero could. His appointment impressed me as an intelligent attempt to bring all the anti-Fascist forces under the discipline of the constitutional government. I knew he was honest and that he was not a communist.

I had some slight personal relations with Álvarez del Vayo, the new Minister of Foreign Affairs. He was a very clever man who had distinguished himself in the work of the League of Nations in the Chaco mediation. Azaña, in the beginning, had designated him for the embassy in Germany, but, to his credit, the government of Hitler declared him *persona non grata*. He was then sent as ambassador to Mexico, where he had been a friend of Josephus Daniels and his wife. His father, General Álvarez, had been trained at the Escorial and at the Infantry Academy of Toledo. After studying at the University of Salamanca and in Germany, he had been associated with Sidney Webb and Mrs. Webb in the School of Economic and Political Science in London. Before the fall of the monarchy, he had been Spain's most brilliant foreign correspondent, representing *La Nación*, of Buenos Aires, in Berlin. Having studied for two years at the University of Leipzig, he knew Germany. He spoke English clearly but with a pronounced German accent. His protruding chin, his clear, penetrating eyes, the vigor with which he spoke, chopping off each word as with a meat cleaver as it came from his lips, all conveyed an impression of force. He was to demonstrate his ability in his forceful Notes to the League of Nations and in his moving and prophetic speeches before the Assembly of the League in the last days of September, 1937.

I also knew Dr. Juan Negrín slightly before the war. I remember a delightful luncheon with Negrín, Luis Araquistáin, Jay Allen of the Chicago *Tribune,* and Prince Bibesco, the Rumanian Minister to Spain. Negrín was a distinguished scientist, long associated with the University of Madrid. He had been educated largely in Germany. His was an interesting personality. His culture was wide and deep and he possessed much ability—but we shall return to him later. He entered the government at this time as Minister of Finance with great reluctance, and when first instructed by the socialist party, of which he was a member, to accept, he "refused vehemently." He gravely questioned the wisdom of creating a government with a representation of the left wing of the socialists. He foresaw a long war with an international angle that might be decisive, and he feared that the reaction to such a government in other lands would be detrimental. Finally yielding to party discipline, he accepted, and in the field of finance and economics he was to perform miracles for almost three years. (Letter from Negrín to Prieto, June 23, 1939.) He was a progressive or liberal, and an individualist.

13

After the taking of Irún, the fall of San Sebastián was inevitable, and after its fall there was a lull. The rebels and their German and Italian allies did not march immediately on Bilbao and Madrid, as most of my colleagues had predicted. Meanwhile, General Franco had assumed supreme command of the rebel forces and their German, Italian, and Moorish allies. There was a kind of drawing-room glamour about Franco. He was a bit theatrical in his manner and he had a taste for elegant uniforms. Twice he had been described to me before the war as "a good man to lecture on strategy at West Point." A small man, with an intelligent, but not a forceful, face, he was immaculate in dress and he bore himself with an air that pleased his admirers in social circles. But in political judgment he was deficient, and his vanity was colossal.

The line-up for the struggle was now complete.

Chapter XX

The Diplomatic Front

THE diplomatic corps was established in Saint-Jean-de-Luz, twenty minutes from the frontier, in September. The British had taken an old house facing the railway station in Hendaye, where the ambassador had an amusing cubbyhole of an office. Here in Hendaye and Saint-Jean-de-Luz were Sir Henry Chilton, the British Ambassador; Jean Herbette, the French; Daniel Garcia-Mansilla, the Argentinian; Robert Everts, the Belgian; Orazio Pedrazzi, the Italian; and the ministers of Norway, Sweden, Holland, Uruguay, Peru, China, Turkey, Poland, Japan, Egypt, Czechoslovakia, Ireland, Colombia, Rumania, Venezuela, and Finland. According to custom, the embassies and legations had been established in the summer capital of San Sebastián when the war broke, and the missions in Madrid were represented by a single secretary or, in some cases, a mere caretaker.

Saint-Jean-de-Luz, a charming, picturesque Basque village by the sea, is saturated with history. Relics remain to remind the lovers of the past of the far-off days when the brilliant court of Louis XIV, and the more ceremonious court of Philip IV, appeared in the village with pomp and color for the marriage of the French monarch to the daughter of the Spanish. The granddaughter of Henry IV, following the court of Louis XIV on the occasion of the marriage, records in her *Mémoires de La Grande Mademoiselle* that "we arrived in Saint-Jean-de-Luz, which was a most agreeable little town. The houses were very clean, and that of the Queen, at one end of the village, had a view overlooking the river and the bridge that crossed over to Sibours—the village on the other bank where the cardinal and most of the people of the Court were lodged." This was in June, 1660. Never again for almost three hundred years was Saint-Jean-de-Luz to be literally filled with diplomatic and political people; never, certainly, such a mingling of the Spanish and the French. Facing the wharf of the fishermen, still stands the old palace where the bride had lodging, and close by the equally interesting palace where Louis XIV awaited the hour of the ceremony in the church still standing and in use through the years as a place of worship. In the old Place Louis XIV, where now, on summer evenings, Basque lads and lasses dance, flirt, and wage confetti battles, stood the guillotine in the days of the Terror.

Along the narrow, winding lanelike roads are comfortable and pretentious villas. It was pleasant in the morning to stroll along the narrow, crooked Rue Gambetta and peer into the shop windows of neat little stores. Under the trees by the Bar Basque, men and women sat with their cocktails, both noon and night, gossiping with the salty malice of seaside resorts. On the hills about, looking out over a charming rural landscape, loom red-roofed villas, and a mile away is the famous Chantaco golf course, and in its neighborhood are many of the choicest houses, surrounded by ample grounds.

It was here we settled in a downpour of rain in the Villa Eche Soua, designed to reveal entrancing vistas. It stands on a hill on the edge of the golf course. The very lofty ceilings, with huge Basque beams, are typical. Huge windows of one solid glass offer in three directions, from one position, the rolling countryside, with green pastures dotted with flocks of sheep, with cultivated fields and peasants at the plow, with patches of wood and cattle grazing in the shade. On the near horizon loom the Pyrenees. Even on the darkest, rainiest day, the view is pleasing, with the wind blowing the rain in misty waves across the fields.

2

The months passed here brought some painful disillusionments. I had assumed that the nations recognizing the Spanish government would at least refrain from active, militant, open propaganda in favor of its enemies. But from the first day of the war, a very large proportion of the diplomatic corps was aggressively aligned with the enemies of Spanish democracy. Germany, Italy, Portugal would naturally be expected to denounce the constitutional regime and to sneer at its democratic character. I could even understand how democratic nations, looking upon the struggle as a "civil war," could adopt a policy of neutrality and stand aloof. But when, almost at once, the complicity of the Axis powers became notorious, I could not understand how diplomats, presumably representing democratic nations, could earnestly compete with their Fascist colleagues in bitter hostility to the government to which they were accredited and in extravagant glorification of the invading Axis armies.

Convinced from the beginning that the alliance of Hitler, Mussolini, and Franco marked the initiation of an audacious attempt to wipe out democracy in Europe, I was surprised by the complacency of some of my colleagues and shocked by the bitter pro-Fascist partialities of others.

With the issue world-wide and clearly made between totalitarianism and democracy, I observed that while the diplomatic representatives of totalitarian states were aggressively Fascist, an appalling proportion of the diplomats of democratic nations were either cynically indifferent to democracy or actually antidemocratic in spirit, as revealed in their conversation. That, I was to conclude, was a primary reason for the long, dismal procession of diplomatic victories for Fascism, making a new world war inevitable; and I concluded that the preservation of democracy and a free society demands that no one be tolerated in the diplomatic service of a democratic state who is not a convinced and militant democrat.

That there were real democrats among the heads of missions accredited to Spain, I have no doubt; but, intimidated by the violence of the abuse of the constituted authority, and finding themselves in a minority, most of these took refuge in silence. It is ironical that the diplomatic representative of every nation soon to be trodden neath the iron heel of Hitler was openly smiling on the totalitarian crusade against democracy in Spain. One minister who had been a particular friend of mine all but ceased to speak to me early in the war because of my attitude, and his country would soon be dragged at the chariot wheels of his idol who was "saving the world from communism." As I have said, Jean Herbette, misrepresenting France, had gone over bag and baggage to Franco and the generals within three weeks. My British colleague, Sir Henry Chilton, was violently against the loyalists from the first day, and he habitually called them "reds." On his retirement, Geoffrey Thompson, a brilliant diplomat, succeeded as chargé, and he saw the significance of what was going on and reported what he saw, I have no doubt, to Whitehall. But he was soon recalled. It was rather lonely for democrats in the bizarre capital of Saint-Jean-de-Luz.

3

From the first days of the war it was manifest that an effort was being made to use the diplomatic corps as a sounding board for Fascist propaganda. The *doyen* of the corps, the Argentine Ambassador, was an intense partisan of the rebels. He had grown old gracefully—a small man with snow-white hair and beard. His eyes were blue and beaming, and he spoke in a voice low and caressing, rubbing his hands the while. I am sure he accepted the propaganda of the Nazis and Fascists as gospel truth, and that his mind was hermetically sealed against any information favorable to the government to which he was accredited, or unfavorable to its enemies.

Even in diplomatic circles the most incredible tales were told. I am sure a colleague believed it when he assured me that Madrid was being defended by "fifty thousand Russians." An ambassador with whom I was talking in a tailor shop in Bayonne about the scandalous conduct of a portion of the corps in Madrid puzzled me with his explanation of the German in Bilbao, a spy in the First World War, and serving as consul there for Austria. He had been caught with a satchel at the harbor containing minute plans of the harbor and the defense works that he was to pass on to the military authorities in Salamanca. He was arrested, properly tried, convicted, and shot. "Oh, yes," said my colleague, lowering his voice to a confidential tone. "I have just heard the true story of the incident from *a German* in Paris. It seems that this good gentleman, the consul, during his many years in Bilbao, had had an obsession about the harbor, and he was always amusing himself and exercising his ingenuity by drawing plans for an attack on or a defense of the town. You see . . ."—and his voice was deep with sympathetic understanding—"you see, it was just his hobby. But unfortunately for this good gentleman, some of these plans with which he had amused his idle moments were found, and he was taken out by the reds and shot."

I knew the consul had been caught red-handed at the wharf with the satchel in which were the drawings of his "idle moments" to be smuggled to the rebels in Salamanca. Momentarily I was persuaded that his excellency was pulling my leg, for, if serious, he would have had too much finesse to have given a German as his authority when an Englishman would have served the purpose better. I looked hopefully for a twinkle in his eye. Alas, there was none. He seemed very sad. And I wondered if the foreign offices of the world were being served with such tripe as this.

4

The *doyen* lived in Cibourne on a hill, reached by a dangerously winding road and it was here that a series of meetings of the diplomatic corps was held. During the three years in Madrid before the war there had been no formal meetings, but now for a time they were to come in quick succession, and each was clearly designed to discredit the legal government. The first, called less than a month after the war began, was for the professed purpose of offering mediation. The effect of such an offer at that time would have been publicly to proclaim by the representatives of all nations that the rebels and the government were on a common level of legality. It was certainly a deliberate affront to the government, intended to discredit it at the earliest possible moment. I could not reconcile my attendance with any semblance of neutrality and I refused to attend. Meanwhile, so many others questioned the propriety of such a gesture that the meeting resolved itself into a talk-fest, and the plan was abandoned. I know the British Ambassador was instructed from London to take no part.

At this time I learned from Eric Wendlin, Third Secretary of my embassy in Madrid, that a similar attempt to use the corps as a medium of propaganda against the government was being made there. The German and Italian chargés were agitating among their colleagues for the immediate departure, *en masse*, of such members as were there, and for the closing of the embassies and legations with a loud slamming of doors. The plain purpose was to create the impression that the fight of the legal government had been lost before it had begun. It originated with the two countries that notoriously were allies of the rebels and were seeking a pretext to recognize Franco at the earliest possible moment. The Cuban chargé denounced the scheme for what it was, and, it, too, was abandoned.

Meanwhile, at Saint-Jean-de-Luz the activities of many of the corps continued hectic and transparent. The announced purpose of the second meeting was to offer the corps as an intermediary in the exchange of political prisoners. This was puzzling. The prisons of Madrid were filled with undoubted enemies of the constitutional regime who were potential spies and informers if left at large. No government on earth would have tolerated their moving about at will under similar circumstances. General Mola had boasted that these were Franco's "fifth column," who would act from within when Madrid was attacked from without. But if Franco had prisoners, no one could name a single one of the slightest political importance. Correspondents with the rebel army had told me that no republican, democrat, labor leader, or socialist of the least importance in the regions conquered were left alive "to incite to trouble afterward." The socialist deputies in the Cortes caught among their constituents had been "liquidated." It was impossible at this juncture to have thought a successful issue possible. But the plan did offer an opportunity for propaganda.

Thus it was proposed publicly to announce that the corps would make an offer "in the interest of humanity." Then, with that impressed on the public mind, the government would be approached first; and only in the event of an acceptance there would the subject be so much as broached to the rebels. Since the government undoubtedly would refuse the one-sided proposal, Franco would not be embarrassed by an approach. Would the corps then announce that its humane plan had been thwarted by the refusal of the constituted authorities? It was clear enough that by meddling without an invitation, the corps would invite a deserved rebuff. I neither attended the meeting nor signed the note.

When, in due time, the expected rebuff came, with the pointed suggestion that were the corps interested in humanity, it might give some thought to the rebel generals who had plunged a peaceful country into a welter of blood, I was not surprised to note that the the initiators of the plan were plainly pleased. Curiosity impelled me to attend the meeting called to determine what should be given to the press. The announcement I had foreseen was ready for approval. Refusing to sign, I suggested a bare statement that the corps' efforts thus far had been unavailing, but that it would hold itself in readiness to render any humanitarian service *when invited by both sides.*

But just then the Italian black-shirt ambassador appeared.

Orazio Pedrazzi had been a conspicuous black shirt before Mussolini marched on Rome in a Pullman coach. He carried himself with a swagger. He walked into the room of the villa in Cibourne with the nonchalance of an acknowledged master among his disciples, and sat down and began to talk in a high-pitched voice. Many of my colleagues listened in what seemed to be a reverential silence. It was as though a much-loved governess were telling bedtime stories to her little charges. This was the beginning of the period when all Europe was eager to kowtow to Mussolini. Pedrazzi instructed—it seemed an instruction—that the corps merely announce that the government in Madrid had refused the humanitarian offer.

"Well, that settles it," said the Colombian Minister beside me.

"Settles what?" I asked.

"What we are to give the press," he said.

"But who settled that?" I asked.

"Why, didn't you hear the Italian Ambassador?" he asked in amazement.

I had, but I had heard no one acquiesce or utter a word, nor had I understood that Mussolini's envoy had been made the official mind and voice of the corps. I refused to sign the propaganda notice and left the meeting. For some reason, in the end, nothing was given the press.

Pedrazzi undoubtedly was entitled to Mussolini's highest dec-
oration. In the first weeks he seemed to dominate an astonishing
number of the corps, and not least among them the diplomats of
nations presumably democratic. He was to have a Roman triumph
in the little town of Saint-Jean-de-Luz. When, despairing of taking
Madrid, which was to have been the signal for the recognition of
Franco, Hitler and Mussolini accorded recognition without rhyme
or reason, Pedrazzi became literally a lion. Garcia-Mansilla, the
Argentine Ambassador, conceived the brilliant thought, as *doyen*
of the corps, accredited to the Spanish government, to send him
away with a resounding cheer, omitting, of course, the cry of,
"Duce! Duce!" At the Bar Basque, the most conspicuous place in
the village, frequented by the war correspondents, he arranged a
farewell dinner which might well be interpreted as a celebration by
the corps of Italy's recognition of the rebel government. The greater
part of my colleagues attended there in public to honor the envoy
who had insulted the President to whom they were accredited,
who had conspired against the constitutional government they
recognized, and whose government had just taken its stand openly
with the rebels. In my six years in Spain no such special honor had
ever been accorded any other departing colleague, and Pedrazzi
was a new man in the corps and not noticeably popular. I did not
attend the fiesta.

Such was the tone in diplomatic circles in Saint-Jean-de-Luz.

5

At the beginning of the war, Gil Robles, engaging in political
propaganda from his walled-in garden in Guéthary, ten minutes
from Saint-Jean-de-Luz, was ordered to move north by the French
government and he went to Portugal. It was assumed that France
would not permit her frontier to be used as a base of operations
against the constituted authority she recognized in Spain.

Just when, or why, this policy was changed I do not know, but
changed it was. The rebel authorities opened headquarters in the
Villa Nache Enea in Saint-Jean-de-Luz, where an entire staff was
stationed. Many wondered at the effrontery. The narrow road in
front was often congested with military cars, and couriers came and
went between the villa and the rebel headquarters in Burgos and

Salamanca. One day a Paris paper protested, and a spectacular "raid" was staged, but "nothing was found" to indicate that the house was not "just a private residence." There was much giggling at the cocktail bars over this quaint announcement from the French government. The next day the villa hummed with its usual activity. Months then intervened, and another "raid" was widely publicized and the announcement made that this rebel base was closed; but the next morning the entire staff was at their desks as usual.

A few kilometers away, at Biarritz, the Count de las Andes discharged the functions of Franco's agent without the slightest molestation. It was not until more than a year after the war began that complaints bore fruit in a much-publicized order from Paris sending him on his travels—but he traveled not one inch. The public could be fooled by a press announcement.

The climax of this bizarre story of the complacency of the French fifth column, which was to bring France under the contemptuous heel of Hitler and the infamous Laval, came with the queer exploit of Major Troncoso, the Franco Military Commandant in Irún, with whom the socialist French Ambassador was on intimate terms. In the harbor of Brest, a Spanish government destroyer was resting, after having undergone repairs, and this figure from a Dumas novel made his plans to steal it from under the nose of the French police. The plot failed, and some of the conspirators were arrested.

The next day, Troncoso swaggered into police headquarters in Hendaye to boast that he had conceived and directed the bold attempt! In other words, he confessed to the French authorities to a serious crime against the laws and the dignity of France. The astounded French police listened in respectful silence and permitted him to swagger out and across the border without so much as a reprimand.

When this incident became public, there was some consternation in high official circles in Paris, and some muttering about a possible dismissal of the too-complacent officers. And just then Troncoso again crossed the border to demand the immediate release of his "chauffeur," really a Marquis, who had been caught red-handed in the attempt at Brest. This time Troncoso was arrested.

In these days it seemed that the French fifth column was dominating the French government. The Troncoso incident, however, was a bit too much. Driving to the office one morning, I noticed a large poster with the name "Herbette" in large letters, and I got out to read it. It was a denunciation of the French Ambassador as a "traitor to France," and a demand by the majority political parties of the region that he be deprived of his post, with the threat that otherwise "direct action" would be taken on the following Saturday. On Friday, Paris announced his recall. He retired to Switzerland.

6

There was nothing remotely like neutrality in social circles on the Basque coast. These were composed of what is popularly known as the fashionable international set, and it was aggressively pro-Franco, incredibly bitter against Roosevelt, and most agreeable toward Mussolini. It was not rare to hear high praise of Hitler, whose officers in German military uniforms roared across the border from Spain to dine at the Café de Paris, crowding other people's cars to the curb. This atmosphere was not surprising. The villas and hotels were crowded with refugees of the Spanish nobility and aristocracy, and a stranger strolling on the waterfront in Saint-Jean-de-Luz would have assumed he was in a Spanish town, since many of the pedestrians he passed would be speaking Spanish. These crowded the Bar Basque in Saint-Jean-de-Luz and Sonny's Bar in Biarritz at the cocktail hours to exchange news and views. Most of them had crossed the frontier at the beginning of the rebellion, and many had made their way from loyalist territory by devious means to Biarritz to roost for the duration. These formed the social nucleus of the Francoist claque on the Basque coast.

But the incessant beating of the tom-toms in glorification of the Fascist cause was by no means confined to these. In truth, the Spaniards were more restrained than their supporters from democratic nations. Few of the latter had any real knowledge of Spain or with the problems and personalities of Spanish politics. I am sure that, in their ignorance, they accepted the propaganda that everyone in Spain not with the rebels was a "communist"; that the contest was between property and "anarchy"; between the socially pure and the unwashed multitude; between the infidel and the Christian. I found the ideology of democracy most unfashionable. One night at a party I was approached by a bubbling lady with the question:

"You are a Fascist, aren't you?"

"No."

"Then are you a communist?" she screeched, with a look of horror.

"Have you, by any chance, ever heard of a democrat?" I asked.

With a supercilious lifting of the eyebrows she turned away, no doubt to whisper that the American Ambassador was a "red."

I finally began to wonder if patriotism now referred less to country than to class. Puzzled by the hysteria of an ambassador of a democratic nation, and his extravagant support of the rebel cause in the very first days of the rebellion, I asked him why he was so intensely bitter. "We must stand by our own class," he spluttered. I was not conscious that property rights were so sacrosanct in Berlin and Rome.

So extravagant was this partisanship of the fashionables with the Fascists that for months one heard that Italy had become the great power in Europe that speedily would smash the British Empire— and all this with an air of satisfaction. When a British vessel was bombed by an Italian plane, I often heard expressions of satisfaction; when a British merchant ship was forced at the point of guns into a rebel port, I often heard facetious comments at the cocktail bars. The abuse in the Axis press of such British statesmen as Robert Cecil, Winston Churchill, and Lloyd George, and of democracy, met with many approving smiles. It was the golden age along the French Basque coast for the most dangerous enemies of France. But a little later, when the hordes of Hitler swept in, it was amusing to observe the precipitancy with which the erstwhile champions of the Axis' cause folded their tents and fled. They left their beautiful villas, and Nazi officers moved in as nonpaying guests.

With Saint-Jean-de-Luz the center of the international phase, this section was overrun with spies, and no one could be quite sure that his companion was not a carrier pigeon. They swarmed at the cocktail bars, and it came to be a favorite game to mention the war and note the instant silence that fell on the adjoining tables.

Even so, I know of no lovelier place, summer or winter, than the Basque coast of France. The local French officials extended every courtesy to the diplomats. Even the Nache Enea was often helpful in facilitating the crossing into Spain of those entitled to go over under our regulations. Luis de la Yrupo, the Marquis of Arcos, a personal friend, later my colleague for a while in Chile, invariably was graciously accommodating in Saint-Jean-de-Luz; and the Viscount Momblas, whom I had known and liked as the head of the cultural section of the Foreign Office, was quite as much so in Biarritz.

7

Meanwhile, incredible tales trickled out of Madrid about the novel activities of some embassies and legations there. With their houses packed with Mola's fifth column, enemies of the regime, not a few, leased other houses, unfurled their country's flag as a protection, and filled them also. When one of the embassies was choked with "guests," the members of the staff were ordered to pack their apartments. These "guests" soon mounted up into the thousands.

Then, floating out of Madrid, came whispers that the inmates in some of the embassies and legations were paying "guests." All this had been discussed with wonder in Saint-Jean-de-Luz—discussed in undertones—when one of the "guests," who had paid admittance, amused himself by tossing a handmade bomb among some soldiers in the street. When the astonished militiamen ran toward the house to investigate, they were fired upon from one of the windows. They thereupon stormed the house and arrested the inmates. In the case of some embassies and legations having "guests," an admission fee, measured by the financial capacity of the "guest" was charged. He paid to enter; he usually paid to stay, since, at intervals, donations were demanded "to ▮▮▮▮ten the militia"—as they were falsely told. When the militia took action in the case mentioned, a pro-Fascist ambassador from a democratic country undertook in behalf of the corps to take the government to task. The action of the police was described as an "outrage." Del Vayo replied by sending a copy of the government's telegram to the Foreign Minister of Finland, whose legation was involved:

On December first, a bomb was thrown from the house used as an annex to the Legation of Finland. No one was injured. On the third another was thrown from the same house, inflicting injuries to a passing child. These acts were repeated, exhausting the patience of the authorities. They planned a scrupulous search of the building, but when they arrived they were greeted by heavy rifle fire, which resulted in wounding one of the group. Gaining entrance finally, they found 525 Spanish subjects, many affiliated with the Spanish Falangists. . . . The authorities confiscated rifles, pistols, machine guns, and bombs.

These acts are evidence that a part of the fifth column was hiding in certain buildings, under the immunity of foreign flags, in vague invocation of a humanitarian principle permitted by the government. This constitutes a scandalous abuse of the diplomatic prerogatives. Consequently we request the dismissal and immediate departure of Mr. Cachero from Madrid.

The reply of the pro-Nazi spokesman of the corps in Madrid was pitifully weak: "I am sure you will appreciate the danger of permitting the press to continue publishing items which can affect the security of other diplomatic missions"—to which, properly, might have been added, "that are engaging in the same flagrant abuse of diplomatic privileges."

Another incident, resulting in an indignant protest, was the search of the Peruvian consulate, where was found a radio station, some messages from Burgos, and hostile commentaries on the regime. The Peruvian Minister made a virtue of his claim that the fifth columnists "wanted to listen to the official news from the Salamanca station," and he had refused permission.

At length, the situation became intolerable, and on October 13, 1936, Del Vayo reminded the diplomats that "the right of asylum constitutes a form of shelter whereby the refugee is enabled to find with a foreign representation a temporary shelter"—and temporary only. This interpretation is that of the United States and England. A man in swe. ent peril of his life, pursued by a mob, could take refuge in an embassy or legation, which would turn him over to the constituted authorities. But the diplomats engaged wholesale in the protection of fifth columnists were not even following the rules laid down at Havana, which prescribed that the heads of missions accepting refugees should immediately notify the government of their identity. "Except for one," wrote the minister, "none of the diplomatic representations accredited to Madrid has forwarded to the government the names of the persons to whom they are extending refuge." In truth, most of them made a virtue of concealing the identity of their "guests." Del Vayo then set forth the government's interpretation of the right of refuge:

1. Asylum may be granted only in urgent cases, and only for such time as is necessary for the refugee to find security elsewhere.

2. The diplomatic agent . . . shall notify immediately the Minister of Foreign Affairs of the persons to whom he has extended asylum.

3. The government . . . may demand that the refugees be removed from the country within the shortest time possible; and the diplomatic agent of the country which granted the asylum may demand the necessary guarantees of protection for the safe conduct of the refugee.

4. The refugee may not be disembarked at any point within the national boundaries.

5. During their term of asylum the refugees shall not be permitted to engage in any activities detrimental to public order.

Del Vayo concluded brusquely: "The granting of asylum has given rise to the practice of many notorious abuses, which, in themselves, violate the terms of the Havana Treaty. The government wishes to notify the members of the diplomatic corps . . . that it will no longer tolerate these abuses and will not hesitate to see that they are punished."

This note, correct in every detail, was nevertheless a bombshell thrown into the corps, but it had little effect, and fifth columnists remained under the protection of foreign flags throughout the war.

In his memoirs, Del Vayo says that "two embassies, those of the United States and Great Britain . . . refused to take in refugees" and that "in every respect the conduct the United States Embassy was exemplary." He describes my purpose and conduct as "very different from those of a majority of my] colleagues" and adds that my "opinion that the peace of Europe depended largely on a republican victory is by now an open secret." (*Freedom's Battle*, page 240.)

The moron who threw the bomb from the Finnish Legation gave the game away, and everyone made merry over the new commercial business. As many of the paying guests emerged and reached Biarritz with the false passports they had purchased, many a company rocked with laughter over the droll tales of the "racket."

One day two Spaniards called upon me in Saint-Jean-de-Luz and told of their experience with an embassy which had done a lucrative business in the "racket." They had paid a round sum for admission, and every few days their "host" appeared, suavely, to announce that since the militia was showing a disturbing interest, it would be necessary to take up a collection to "sweeten" them. The money was collected and went into the capacious pocket of the humane diplomat. At length, arrangements were made with the government for their evacuation. On the way to the coast, a member of the staff accompanied them for their "protection," and approached them twice with demands for money to "sweeten" some officers, who "acted queerly." The climax came when, near the coast, the attaché approached again. "Now," he said unctuously, "we must collect the money for your passage." They knew that arrangements had been made for their passage on a British ship which had been sent for the purpose, but rather than create a scene, with escape so near, they submitted again to the "diplomatic racket."

A few years later when I was ambassador in Chile during the Second World War, the story was circulated that I had stood on the balcony of the embassy in Madrid smoking a cigarette and watching the butchery of men pleading for entrance at the gates. Aside from the fact that there was no balcony, that I did not smoke cigarettes, that I was not in Madrid during the war, and that no one was butchered at the gates, it was a good story. I ignored this Fascist lie, but Henry Halfant, of the Rumanian Legation in Madrid at the time, who was then in Santiago, denounced the absurd lie in a letter to the press and included it later in a book.

8

When the honorary consul of Austria in Bilbao was caught trying to get the defense plans of the city to Salamanca, the Basque government placed certain restrictions on the movements of some of the consuls there, none too soon. A Spanish lawyer, acting as the consul of a country under a dictator, appeared in Saint-Jean-de-Luz to persuade the diplomatic corps to join in a protest. In his conversation with me he showed himself to be an ardent Fascist. I refused to join in a protest, and none was made.

That evening at dinner in the village, attended by this consul, I witnessed a scene from an Oppenheim novel. The consul of a totalitarian state, in San Sebastián, entered the dining room and drew the consul from Bilbao into a corner of the room and engaged him in a long conversation in low tones. The meeting clearly was prearranged, and at the close of the whispered conversation the consul from San Sebastián immediately departed. This was when plans were being made for the attack on Bilbao. I could not but wonder how the consul from Bilbao had escaped the firing squad as I reflected on how easily he could transmit military information to the rebel authorities in Salamanca through the Fascist consul in San Sebastián, and the conviction was forced upon me that diplomatic immunity in the Spanish war covered a multitude of political crimes. And I was forced to the conclusion that in the bizarre story of Mola's fifth column, a portion of the diplomatic corps accredited to the Spanish Republic, should insist, as a richly earned right, to at least—dishonorable mention.

Chapter XXI

The Terror: the Epic of Madrid

During the first months of the war, Spain had its Reign of Terror. Deprived, by the desertion of most of the army and of the Civil Guards, of the armed forces necessary to any government, anywhere, for the preservation of law and order in the midst of panic and passions, the legal authorities of Madrid and Barcelona were unable to prevent the crimes of the extremists and the criminal element inseparable from any great center of population. The capital was teeming with enemies of the government as the rebel army, with every military advantage, was approaching. Under the pretext of defending the regime, these most dangerous enemies of the regime took matters in their own hands. When, in the first days, the anarchistic element in possession of the radio station had broadcast through Europe and the United States wild speeches, irreparable harm was done to the loyalist cause. It was in these days that criminal groups, posing as emissaries of the police, pounded on doors in the darkness of the night, pillaging the houses and often dragging the owners to death in the street. It was the golden harvest time for private revenge. The jilted girl informed on her disloyal lover who paid the penalty of his inconstancy with his life.

In time, certain anarchistic groups established their private prisons, unknown to the government, to which their victims were dragged, subjected to the mockery of a revolutionary trial, and sometimes condemned to death. The daughter of Vice-Admiral

Salas, one of the victims, told me of her own experience. Arrested, imprisoned, she was twice tried. She found herself in a little room facing three disreputable looking "judges" seated behind a rough pine table. She was questioned for hours, insulted with foul innuendos, and then sent back to sleep on the stone floor of her cell. Her life was saved through the intervention of three members of the Socialist Union and Prieto, who had heard of her plight. The place of her incarceration was found and the government demanded that she be turned over to a legal tribunal, which fined her two thousand pesetas, and released her.

It was during these early months that the atheistic anarchists set fire to churches and killed some priests, though the number was grossly exaggerated in the foreign press. Until the creation of a real national army, the authorities were unable to cope with the situation. A friend of mine who saw Azaña at this time found him in an impotent fury. Dr. Juan Negrín, then Minister of Finance, rushed to a neighboring village and snatched a number of intended victims from their fate just in time. When the mob element, taking its cue from the most disgraceful event of the French Revolution, began to attack the prisons to murder the inmates, Negrín and another minister slept for some days in the prisons to protect the prisoners if possible. This was after the mob had broken into one of the prisons and murdered a number of prisoners. In view of the fact that at this juncture the loyalist government was helpless, this cannot be charged against it. But there was another incident in which the responsibility rests upon the government. A youngish man, son of a socialist of repute, had been made chief of police in Madrid and he turned out to be a communist. When the government moved from Madrid to Valencia, this young communist gave orders for the transfer of many prisoners from the prisons in the capital to others outside the city. This order was given on his own. En route to the new prisons, the prisoners were set upon by a mob and slaughtered to a man. It is difficult to believe that the communist police chief was not in on the conspiracy of assassination. I personally have no doubt of it. The responsible chiefs of the government were many miles away and knew nothing of the transfer order until after the massacre. This massacre was the worst crime of the war that can be charged against the loyalists.

Later, when order was restored, both Azaña and Negrín frankly admitted these outrages and placed the responsibility on the disloyal army, which, by its desertion, had left the government without the instrumentalities of force with which to deal with such situations. Toward the end of August (1936), citizens were instructed to admit no one to their houses, and to telephone the police on the appearance of a gang, but for some weeks these murders and robberies continued, until at length a national army was created in the midst of chaos, and the government could assert itself effectively. After that there were no such murders by roving mobs.

2

The scenes of horror in Madrid were accentuated in Barcelona, the stronghold of the atheistic anarchists for generations. There, more than elsewhere, the fury of the mob turned against the clergy, and churches were attacked and pillaged, and some priests were killed. Worse still, the tombs of priests were desecrated. Two elements committed these crimes involving religion—the anarchists, who are atheists, and the criminal element, who attacked the churches for purposes of pillage.

On the advent of the Republic, some Spanish bishops had denounced the Republic and democracy. (*The New York Times*, August 17, 1931.) Cardinal Gomá had ordered the Catholics to vote against the republican forces led by Azaña in the electoral campaign of 1936. Basque priests refused, and great numbers were exiled. Two high-ranking Spanish prelates, Vidal y Barraquer of Tarragona, the Archbishop, and the Bishop of Vitoria, who refused to sign the election manifesto, were driven from the country later by Franco, and the former died in exile in France. These incidents explain in part the resentment of the loyalists, engaged in a war of defense. The extent of this resentment differed radically in different parts of the country. I have before me a confidential report of the agent of a great humanitarian organization which rendered yeoman service in saving children from starvation. He was stationed at Murcia. "It is true," he says, "that I never saw a priest in civilian garb, but within an hour after the news of the collapse of the government, there were many priests in the streets of Murcia. These had obviously been there all the time, and surely the government knew of their presence. We lived on the third floor of a Murcia house. Across the street lived an old man. We saw him often on the roof, reading. When the change of government came, he just put on his priest's clothing and went out into the streets. Those who did not engage in spying or espionage were left alone." This agent read press reports of loyalist funerals, even those of army officers, "conducted according to Catholic rites." I personally know that in Barcelona numerous priests were saved by the Catalan government. I have this on the authority of a Catalan priest who told me his story in Saint-Jean-de-Luz. He owed his life to Luis Companys, the head of the Catalan government, who found ways to conceal him from the mob and to spirit him across the French border. The only priests, so far as I have been able to learn, who were killed in cold blood *by authority and not by mobs* were the fifteen Basque priests who fell before Fascist firing squads.

The story of the murder of nuns was pure propaganda without substance. To prevent such a monstrous crime as the murder of nuns, the government took over an estate near Valencia, where many nuns were living throughout the war, unmolested in their worship. They sewed and knitted for the poor. The American Friends Service Committee in Murcia had nuns working for it in their regular uniforms. In Totana, the loyalist mayor, in charge of the canteen under the supervision of the Friends Committee, asked permission to assign the nuns to the actual feeding, which he says was done "to the satisfaction of all."

That there was looting in the churches in the early stages of the war is certainly true. Every effort was made to prevent it. Again, I refer to the absolute knowledge of a member of the Friends Committee. "I was given the opportunity to visit the Murcia cathedral during the loyalist period," he says. "We had to get a pass, but this was a reasonable request, for the huge building was filled with religious treasures *brought in from the countryside for safekeeping*. There had been trouble in the earlier days of the war because of irresponsible persons who took advantage of the war to do looting. There were many sealed boxes filled with priestly vestments and other church materials, many wooden images and statues of Christ, the Madonna, and the saints. These were stored where the cathedral walls were thickest so they would be safer in case of bombardment. I have reason to know that several individuals who had looted churches were caught and punished by the republican officials."

There were crimes enough on both sides during the Reign of Terror, but those committed in loyalist territory by anarchists and criminals certainly did not have the sanction of the constituted authority.

3

Those committed in rebel territory were less exploited by the foreign press, for woe to the press correspondent who dared mention them. But the horrible slaughter at Badajoz is classic. When large numbers escaped to Portugal, they were driven back to their death, and Moors stained the steps, and even the altar, of the cathedral with Christian blood. A representative of a news radio service appealed to me for assistance in searching for a military photographer of its staff, thought in peril of his life. Some minor officer had given him permission to take pictures in Badajoz after the slaughter, when it was scarcely possible in some narrow streets to walk without stepping on a corpse. The pictures taken were revolting, and, when shown in Paris, spies reported to Burgos, and the photographer was arrested and held "somewhere in rebel territory."

Since this wholesale slaughter is audaciously denied, it is proper to introduce the evidence of press correspondents who visited the stricken city. A special correspondent of the Havas press agency wrote on August 10:

On the Square in particular are lying numerous partisans of the government who were lined up and executed against the wall of the cathedral. Blood had poured in streams from the pavement. Everywhere you find clotted pools.

Reynolds Packard, United Press correspondent, published his account in the New York *Herald Tribune* of August 15, 1936:

As fast as they were captured, the defending loyalists were executed in mass killings, and the militia, realizing that certain death awaited it if captured, continued to fight, despite the capture of the city last night.

A special correspondent of the Paris *Temps*, sent from the adjacent town of Elvas in Portugal, printed his account in the famous journal, August 15, 1936:

Militiamen and suspects arrested by the insurgents were immediately executed. At the present moment about twelve hundred have been shot on the charge of armed resistance or of grave crimes. I saw the pavement in front of the military commandant covered with blood of those executed, and still strewn with their caps or personal objects. The cathedral in which numerous families had taken refuge is in disorder but has not been damaged. The militiamen captured in the choir were executed facing the high altar, before which they were lying in their blood. Arrests and executions *en masse* on the Plaza de Toros continue.

In this connection, this correspondent added the significant statement that when the town was captured, "three hundred and eighty political prisoners [Fascists] were released, safe and sound." But no loyalist prisoners were taken; they were mowed down in mass without a trial.

On August 17, 1936, the Havas special correspondent wrote again from Elvas in Portugal:

Executions continue in mass in Badajoz. It is estimated that the number of persons executed now exceeds fifteen hundred. Civilians have been shot by dozens.

So much for Badajoz.

In the Burgos I knew so well for its serenity and religious atmosphere the massacres and murders in the first days of the war did not figure at all in the foreign press. Franco's first appointment there was that of General Martínez Anido to maintain public order. No one could doubt the significance of this appointment, since Anido served ruthlessly and cruelly in the same role under Primo, the Dictator. Salvador de Madariaga says that "he had nothing to learn from the Gestapo." It was in Burgos that, the day after the war began, labor-union leaders were arrested and promptly dispatched. Ruis Villaplana, president of the College of Commissioners of Justice in the region of Burgos, was summoned by the provisional rebel government there and he remained in the discharge of his duties for months. He has told his story in his book, *Doy Fe* (called, in the English edition, *Burgos' Justice*). When dead bodies were found, as they were with each rising of the sun, it was his duty to examine the body and make reports. The bodies were found mostly in fields on the outskirts. Prisoners were taken out in lorries from the jail at night and shot without trial. Time and again he found on the bodies of the dead the telltale spoon of the prison. He himself had to honor the documents for the "release" of prisoners who passed from their cells to their graves. He once saw sixty prisoners taken from the jail in batches of twenty. Even the beautiful Carthusian monastery of Milaflores, which I knew, was gracelessly dragged into the bloody business over the pleading protests of the monks when a wood behind the monastery was converted into an execution ground.

The massacre of loyalists in the Balearic Islands has been indelibly painted by the brilliant French Catholic writer, Georges Bernanos, who, with pro-Fascist sympathies in the beginning, became so sickened by the horrors he witnessed that he left the country and wrote his vivid book, *A Diary of My Times*.

The story of the slaughter of loyalists in Seville has been told by Sr. Bahamonde, officially attached for a year to General Queipo de Llano, as publicity director. Like Villaplana in Burgos, and Bernanos in the Balearics, he was so horrified that when sent to Germany on a mission, he left the boat in Holland and wrote his book: *One Year with Queipo*.

Neither the laws of humanity nor civilized warfare was regarded in the first days of the struggle. A correspondent told me of seeing fifteen loyalist soldiers in a lorry who had lost their way and had driven into a rebel camp. Seeing their blunder, they threw up their hands as a token of surrender as military prisoners. A few minutes later, a volley from a firing squad rang out. The correspondent raised his eyebrows in interrogation.

"Finished," said the officer, shrugging his shoulders.

Perhaps the most disgusting murder in the early days of the war was that of Federico Lorca, poet, dramatist, one of the geniuses of Spain, liquidated by Fascist elements. When, a few years later, in Santiago, Chile, I saw Margarita Xirgu, the distinguished Spanish actress, present a number of Lorca's plays, the thought of his senseless assassination was sickening.

Even more horrible was the execution of the wife of Ramón

Sender, a great Spanish writer. She was a devout Catholic, member of a conservative family, but her husband was fighting with the loyalists and that was enough. Arrested in the office of the civil governor, she had been imprisoned a month when a priest was sent to confess her and she was taken to the cemetery and shot.

4

But the crimes of the loyalists were not by real supporters of the government. The anarchists and extreme left-wing syndicalists were elements hostile to Fascism and foreign invasion, but they stood aloof from the democratic regime of the Republic, as they had from the monarchy. Neither had any regard for either the monarchy or the Republic; neither had any sympathy with real democracy; and both hated Azaña and the socialists. In the first days of the war, this anarchistic fringe rendered an incalculable service to the rebels with their wild harangues, their mobbing and murdering, their firing of churches and attacks on priests, their sowing of dissensions behind the firing line. In time, their unwitting co-operation with the rebels became the subject of jests in a comedian's monologue in a Madrid theater. An unhappy fellow, determined to kill himself, slashed his wrist, but was hurried to a first-aid station and saved. He then decided on poison, but the druggist was low in stock and gave him a harmless powder. It then occurred to him to go to the headquarters of the anarchists in the palace of Fernán-Núñez and shout for Franco. That, he thought, would mean short shrift. Slipping by the guard at the door, he rushed up the stairs to where a group of anarchists were chatting in a room. "Viva Franco!" he shouted. The anarchists sat in dead silence for a moment. Then one of them put his finger warningly to his lip and whispered: "Not so loud, comrade, the guard downstairs is a republican and might hear."

Certain it is that not a few Fascists and enemies of the regime insinuated themselves into the anarchists' ranks to encourage excesses that could be used to the detriment of the democratic cause.

5

With the desertion of the army in the beginning, the government's problem of how to create an army of defense seemed hopeless. The one possible temporary solution was to utilize all the anti-Fascist political parties and groups as a nucleus for the fighting force. Each party, union, or segment whipped its members into a fighting unit. These included, along with the democratic and republican parties, the communists and anarchists. But this did not create an army—it was a conglomeration of military units without a supreme head or co-ordination. Each group had its commander, recognizing no superior. Each had its flag, and all the flags were not those of the Republic. No one division was strong enough to undertake offensive action, and, in the absence of a supreme head, it was impossible to bring them all together in a crisis. Each group dug in where it was and performed miracles of valor in holding on; but if one was hard pressed and in need of reinforcements, the others did not move, and there was no supreme commander to make them move. The army itself was chaos.

Azaña, Barrio, Prieto, Negrín, knew what was needed and sought the unification of all groups into one, but for months the stubbornness of some made this impossible. How such an "army" as then existed was able for months to withstand the onslaught of the trained rebel troops, the Foreign Legion, the Italian Fascists and the German Nazis is one of the miracles of history.

6

In the midst of the resulting chaos in Madrid, Franco began his march on the capital. The defenses there had been utterly neglected. In Toledo, in the beginning, some sharp fighting in the streets had driven the enemies of the government to the shelter of the granite mountain of the Alcázar. There were the monarchists, Fascists, army officers, and reactionaries of importance. A fantastic tale was soon told which gave a false impression of the siege of the Alcázar. The outside world was fed on the attractive story that the granite mountain was defended by young cadets, since the building was used as a military school. The truth is that the school was on holiday and there were not more than twenty or thirty cadets among the eleven hundred fighting men. These fighting men, not mere cadets, were under the command of General Moscardo, a ranking army officer, personally known to me.

Rebel planes attacked the city, wiping out the priceless old

Cervantes tavern and leveling much of one side of the historic plaza. The government begged that the women and children be permitted to leave the Alcázar, but it pled in vain. Quarter was offered if the others surrendered. Monsignor Enrique Vasquez Camara, a brilliant pulpit orator, was sent from Madrid to negotiate for the release of the women and children, but without success; and, having celebrated mass and heard confessions and baptized some newborn babies, he returned to the capital. The eloquent priest, like hundreds of other priests, was later driven into exile, and he died ten years later in a French monastery. At length, with Talavera taken, and with the rebels advancing with rapid strides, the mine beneath the Alcázar was fired, the old town shook on its hill, and a large part of the palace was a mass of ruins. But the inmates had retired to a section that was not destroyed.

And so it came to pass that the Moors and the Legionnaires swarmed into the narrow streets of the ancient city. For the second time in history, the Moors entered Toledo on the invitation of Spaniards, and the resulting scenes were scarcely Christian. A few militiamen who stood their ground were mowed down by executioners—not taken prisoner. Webb Miller, the great American journalist, who was in Toledo, told me of seeing numerous headless bodies in the streets—the civilizing influence of the Moors "saving Christianity." He was offered jewelry for a song and when he asked where the Moors had got it, they pointed to the private houses they had pillaged. He was shocked to find many Moors wearing the badge of the Sacred Heart of Jesus—which they had stolen.

It was then, to the sound of warning sirens, that Franco appeared to dramatize the victory and to waste time with press photographers much better spent in hastening to Madrid, which was then wholly open to him and entirely unprepared.

7

In Saint-Jean-de-Luz we waited for the speedy fall of Madrid, where the defending forces were unorganized, untrained, miserably equipped. But weeks were wasted, and in the meanwhile miracles were performed by the Madrileños. Francisco Herrera, publisher of *El Debate*, told me in Saint-Jean-de-Luz that Madrid would not be taken until October. By then, he thought, the resistance of the city would collapse. Another member of the staff of *El Debate* told me that Franco was holding off to permit the people to escape by way of Alicante. But he said the town could easily be taken by storm if necessary. Did not Franco have up-to-the-minute German and Italian planes and tanks? In due time he would make an aerial demonstration over the city as a warning of future horrors if the people remained stubborn. He said the city would probably be taken on October 12, 1936, since that was the day of the festival of the race and the anniversary of St. Pilar, the patron saint of Spain.

But on that anniversary the rebels were no nearer the city than before, and the defenders were infinitely better prepared to meet the attack. More order had been imposed, along with a sterner military discipline, and the people retained their racial gaiety and clung to their amusements until Del Vayo attacked the holiday spirit on the verge of battle.

For the Franco army, with planes and tanks from Germany and Italy, was moving steadily toward the town. The outer defenses fell, since human flesh could not stand up before every modern device for slaughter.

On October 20, 1936, I saw Herbette, the French Ambassador, who said no war material for the government had been sent from France since the "nonintervention pact" was signed, and that certainly no war material bought in Russia had entered through his country. Meanwhile, war material and soldiers were pouring in for Franco from Italy and Germany.

8

Thousands were now digging trenches outside the city, and more were feverishly at work to save the masterpieces of the Prado, threatened by enemy aviation. Under the supervision of the director of the museum, an army regiment was busy packing, boxing, and moving the works of art. Money was spent for that purpose without stint. Some of the less priceless treasures were buried in the basement under layer after layer of bags of sand; some were transferred to Valencia; some were placed in vaults in the Bank of Spain until it was found too damp, when they were taken elsewhere. All over the world, lovers of art were horrified to read in Fascist propaganda that the treasures of the Prado were "being sent to Russia."

9

The rebels were advancing, led by the Moors. Illescas, midway between Toledo and Madrid, where I had often gone to see the El Greco pictures, was taken. The loyalists were fighting desperately to hold them back. And then, a sudden change, an astonishing lifting of the morale of the defenders, as they took the offensive, captured a town of strategic value near Aranjuez, reopened the railroad line between Valencia and Madrid. There were several reasons.

The Nonintervention Pact had pledged all signers on their honor against selling arms and ammunition to either side in Spain, and the American embargo served the same purpose. This had been rigidly enforced against the government, which, under international law, had a right to buy; but there was no pretense of enforcing it against the enemies of the government, and Germany and Italy were pouring tanks, artillery, ammunition, and soldiers into Franco's camp, to the positive knowledge of the Nonintervention Committee, which did not even protest. The Spanish government made charges, with proof, before the Assembly of the League of Nations on October 9, 1936, which, ironically enough, was referred to the Nonintervention Committee.

When the pact had become a loathsome farce, Maxim Litvinov, the Russian on the committee, openly gave notice that unless the one-sided intervention ceased on a stipulated date, Russia would not consider herself bound "to any greater extent than any other signatory of the pact." Nothing was done, and Russia began selling tanks and planes to the loyalists—but it *sold* them, did not give them.

Up until that time I invariably asked war correspondents from the front about foreign war material, and, without exception, they all said they had seen many Italian and German planes, tanks, guns, and soldiers, but they had not seen any Russian material. The amount of material bought in Russia has been grossly exaggerated. None appeared until four months after the planes, tanks, and even soldiers sent by Hitler and Mussolini were notoriously in Spain. The Axis submarines immediately became active, and after the the Russian freighter, *Komsomol*, was sunk by an Italian submarine, it was all but impossible to get war material to Spain from Russia except through France, and this was very difficult.

More important to the loyalists, they got some trained soldiers. From the beginning of the war, young men of many nations poured into Spain to fight with the loyalists. Some were mere soldiers of fortune; some were adventurers ready to fight for meager pay; some unquestionably were communists from other European countries; but the greater number were just anti-Fascists, eager to fight the forces of Hitler and Mussolini. There were numerous British, Germans, Italians, French, and not a few Americans. Among these was the son of Ring Lardner, who went to Spain as a journalist and, seeing the significance of the struggle, gave his services and his life. I recall a young man from Louisville who had distinguished himself at Swarthmore College, and had left the classroom for the battlefield because he felt that in Spain would be determined the fate of European democracy. He fought and died in battle. He was no more a communist that the Cardinal of Toledo.

Among all these there were very few Russian privates in the loyalist army. There were a few Russian aviators and technicians, and I heard of one Russian officer who trained the recruits. There was never at any time more than five hundred Russians in Spain. When the commission of the League of Nations supervised the withdrawal of all foreigners in loyalist Spain, on the request of the loyalist government, they found but one hundred and fifty Russians. This, I know; the members of the commission, impressed by the Goebbels propaganda, entered Spain expecting trickery, and left convinced of the honesty of the loyalist leaders.

These volunteers from many nations, and they WERE volunteers, constituted the famous International Brigade. Taking their place in the front line, they pushed the enemy back. For a time the International Brigade saved Madrid, but the fact that a communist officer from Germany commanded for a time, and many of the privates were non-Russian communists from Germany, Italy, and France, was to be used in propaganda to create the impression in other countries that all the loyalists were communists. Later, when he began to assume too much authority, the commander of the brigade was removed.

10

Let me put down my impression of the part the communists played. I never thought communism could take root in Spain because of the intense individualism of the people. Soon after my arrival in Spain, when the government was on the point of establishing diplomatic relations with Russia, I asked Fernando de los Ríos, the Foreign Minister, the reason the recognition had been so long delayed. He replied that on the fall of the monarchy, Moscow had the impression that because of the sodden poverty of the peasants and workers, Spain offered a fertile field for communism, and, accordingly, sent men and money; but after a year she realized that communism was alien to the Spanish character and she lost interest. The minister said that so long as Moscow actively propagandized against the regime, her recognition was impossible, but with the abandonment of the campaign, her recognition was reasonable and inevitable for reasons of trade.

At the beginning of the war, Russia sent Marcel Rosenberg, who had represented her in the League of Nations, to Madrid as ambassador. I have no doubt Moscow felt that in the chaos of war it might be possible to make headway impossible in normal times. He reached Madrid when the loyalist regime was being openly attacked by the Axis nations and when "Nonintervention" and the American embargo left the loyalists naked to their enemies. He arrived at a dark and dramatic hour, promising to sell arms and ammunition, as part of the policy of opposing Hitler. Naturally, the people in the street, in a high state of excitement, greeted him cordially and gratefully, but this natural reception was used effectively in the foreign press as proof that the loyalists were communists. Later, when England and America warmly welcomed Russia as an ally against the same Axis powers, no one suggested that they were communistic. The Goebbels-type propaganda that the loyalists and democrats of Spain were all communists was referred to by Azaña in his great speech in Barcelona, July 18, 1938, when he said:

It is fitting to point out certain of the errors at the basis of the armed attack against the Republic. There was, in the first place, an error in information, enlarged and exploited by propagandists: the error of believing that our country was on the eve of undergoing a communist insurrection. We all know the origin of that tale. It is an article exported from Germany and Italy in order to cover more serious undertakings. A communist insurrection in 1936. The communist party was the most recently formed and the least numerous of all the proletarian parties in Spain. In the February elections, the communists had obtained less than four per cent of all the votes cast on that occasion. Who was going to make the revolution? Who was going to maintain it? Even supposing that anyone had thought of such a thing, with what forces was it to be carried out? In view of a menace of this nature, or of a similar one against the Spanish state, which was not communist or at all in the way of becoming so, logic would have prescribed that all these political and social forces, frightened at this supposed menace, would have rallied around the state in order to defend it and would have formed a body around it, because, after all, the state was completely middle class.

It is true that the time came when the communists were given representation in the Ministry because of the necessity of unifying all anti-Fascist forces in a grave crisis, just as communists were taken into the government in Italy and France after the World War. The only communist in the government of Caballero and Negrín whose name I had ever heard was Jesús Hernández. He was a Spanish communist and had been from his fourteenth year and he had been trained in Moscow. The little I had heard of him had not been impressive. That he received orders from Moscow he himself has since admitted. Moscow ordered an attack on Prieto, but Hernández tells us in his book that no one favored the attack except La Pasionaria. Toward the close, when the loyalists were fighting desperately against overwhelming odds in guns, planes, and ammunition, Moscow resorted to blackmail to force some concessions and among the commissars stationed with the army were too many communists, but at the side of each of these was a non-communist army officer to check on his actions. This was a grave contribution to the Fascists' propaganda. "Make concessions or face the fact that Russia will discontinue selling arms" is about what they said. But even Hernández says in his book that this help given was utterly insignificant. "If, during the first weeks of the war, Stalin had sent us arms instead of advisers and technicians, we would have beaten the enemy once and for all," he wrote. More significant is Hernández' statement that "Moscow wanted to wind up the Spanish war in order to get on with negotiations with Hitler," which soon resulted in the pact of alliance between Germany and Russia. If the world has learned one thing more than any other since 1945 it is that the inclusion of communists in political combinations for election purposes in Popular Fronts is fatal.

At the close of the Spanish war, when the real leaders of the Republic, Azaña, Barrio, Caballero, Negrín, José Aguirre, Fernando de los Ríos, Prieto, found refuge in democratic countries, England, France, the United States, and Mexico, and leaders of the constitutional opposition, Lerroux and Gil Robles, exiled themselves in Portugal, the only men supporting the loyalist cause who went to Russia were a few Spanish communists, and these, with the exception of La Pasionaria, were speedily disillusioned. Hernández soon left and was expelled by Moscow from the party, and he has told the story of his disillusionment in his book.

The Spanish temperament is not compatible with communism.

11

We were assured in Saint-Jean-de-Luz that Franco would take Madrid on October 5, 1936, since that day was announced in Salamanca. A few days before, he had been at the gates of the city. In the house of the Countess Nostitz I was present when the aide of General Mola appeared, and, after a brief conversation with the hostess, left. He had told her that they could have taken Madrid two days before, but for "political reasons" they had postponed their triumph. I was unable to learn the "reasons."

Certainly the enemy was drawing closer. The Moors and the Foreign Legion were on the outskirts. The loyalists were preparing to defend the city, house by house. But the people were quite calm. On the night of November 5, Colonel Behn entertained American friends in the fortresslike telephone building in Madrid, and the company sent me a telegram of congratulations on the re-election of Roosevelt. While they were dining, correspondents with the Franco army were reporting buildings burning and the palace destroyed.

In truth, the Moors, who led the advance, were five miles from town.

On November 7, 1936, General Franco announced that he would "hear mass" in the city the next day. Because of this announcement, rebel radio stations, particularly that of Lisbon, gave graphic descriptions of the scenes in the city when he rode at the head of his soldiers into the conquered town, receiving an ovation from the "liberated people." Knickerbocker, famous American correspondent, published a vivid description, missing no detail, not omitting the dog that followed the procession barking rapturously. But that night I listened to the radio in Madrid and heard a calm reading of military orders for the morrow. And on that day when Franco was to "hear mass," the loyalist aviation had the mastery of the air, and three hundred and fifty Moors were taken prisoner in the Casa de Campo. The rebels were now in the old royal park, trying vainly to cross the Manzanares. The advance of Franco on the capital was stopped.

Infuriated by the failure, the rebels observed Armistice Day by an indiscriminate bombing of the city for the first time. Naturally, noncombatants were killed or wounded, including women and children. As the days dragged on, and the loyalists took the offensive, another ruthless bombing of the town was ordered, and three hospitals were hit, and an incendiary bomb set fire to another. Because the people took the bombing stoically, it was intensified on the morrow, and bombs fell in the Puerta del Sol and on the historic palace of the Duke of Alba, which was destroyed by an incendiary bomb.

12

Nothing in the cynical propaganda of the war surpassed the fantastic misrepresentation of the destruction of the Alba palace. It was not destroyed by loyalists but by a misdirected incendiary bomb of the enemy, mostly of Mussolini's aviation. Into the flames the loyalist militia rushed at the peril of their lives to save as many of the artistic and historical treasures as possible. But soon the destruction of the palace was being cited as an illustration of the savagery and the criminality of the defenders of Spanish democracy. Even the Duke of Alba wrote Zuloaga from London that his beautiful portraits of the duchess and himself had gone up in flames. Much later, these portraits were on exhibition in Valencia, and I had the pleasure of showing Zuloaga the photographs of them taken by a museum director from London who had gone to Spain to ascertain the truth. These two portraits were among the treasures rescued by the valor of the loyalist militia.

13

But Madrid held, almost gaily, and Hitler and Mussolini were embarrassed. They had planned, on the capture of the capital, to accord recognition to Franco, with much beating of drums. That was to have been the first of October; then the twelfth; and then the fifth of November; and then the seventh, and the ceremonial entrance of the "army of liberation" seemed as remote as ever. The morale of the enemy was in need of strengthening, and so, with Madrid untaken, Hitler and Mussolini accorded recognition to the Franco regime. The only effect was to prove beyond all doubt that Fascist Italy and Nazi Germany were waging a war of aggression in Spain, without a declaration of war—the new Fascist technique.

The event was celebrated in Madrid with the most savage bombing of civilians the war thus far had seen. Bombs crashed on the Gran Vía, in the crowded Puerta del Sol, in the section of the workers, where they took a heavy toll. They fell on the royal church of San Jerónimo where Alfonso had been married, and crashed on the Trinitarian Convent; they fell in the garden of the British Embassy and they wrecked the Rumanian Legation. So barbarous and senseless was the bombing that the British protested with a warning of the inevitable reaction of mankind.

But Madrid remained unmoved. The loyalist army kept the offensive, taking a heavy toll of the enemy. The German officers fumed and fussed because of Franco's "weakness" and "sentimentality." The way to take Madrid, they said, was to wipe it from the map with shells and bombs, as, later, they would take Warsaw; but Franco had scruples as a Spaniard. However, bombing from the air continued, and one day the beautiful historic palace of the Mendozas in Guadalajara was hit. It was a stupid crime, since it was a school, in charge of the nuns, for the orphans of army officers.

Meanwhile, German and Italian officers were becoming more

arrogant, and the best hotels were reserved for the Nazi officers on their demand. I heard at the time that Jewish employees in these hotels were instantly dismissed on orders. In Seville, they monopolized the best hotels; in Salamanca when a Spanish nobleman with a press correspondent as guest sought lunch at a hotel, they waited almost an hour for service. Angered and embarrassed, the nobleman, observing that strangers who had entered much later were given preference, summoned the headwaiter. That worthy shrugged his shoulders and spread his fingers. "But what can I do?" he asked. "The Germans insist on being waited on first." The Spanish nobleman waited. The master had precedence over the nobleman.

14

The rebel aviation, mostly foreign, rained death and destruction on the city, and women and children died on Christ's birthday. But the most sadistic bombing was reserved for New Year's Eve. For years, on this occasion, thousands of the young gathered in the Puerta del Sol to celebrate with singing and dancing in the street. The old clock in the Ministry of the Interior, facing the plaza, was almost as well known for its striking as Big Ben in London. According to an old tradition, one making a wish, and eating a grape with each of the twelve strokes, had his or her wish granted. On New Year's Eve, the picturesque and historic old plaza was teeming with laughing youth. And then, a sudden roaring in the sky, and the explosion of a bursting bomb.

15

Just after Christmas, 1936, an American industrialist in Spain assured me "confidentially" that "Madrid will be taken on January 10." A few days before, the rebels, strongly supported by the Germans, Italians, and Moors, began a desperate offensive on a large scale, aimed at cutting off the Escorial and the Prado. The fighting was fierce and bloody, utterly reckless of human life, and, with heavy losses, some progress was made. The business section of Madrid and a large part of the working-class quarter were showered with shells and bombs. Again the British Embassy was hit, this time by an incendiary bomb, and an English officer and a woman were injured by a bursting shell. The British government again protested.

At this time, heavy Italian reinforcements were landing in Cádiz and being hurried to Seville, en route to the fighting. That same day, Rome and Berlin issued another denial that any of their soldiers were in Spain, and the Scripps-Howard papers published Franco's incredibly false interview denying that there was a single foreigner in his fighting forces!

Two days after the Italian reinforcements reached Cádiz, the Western democracies took extreme measures to prevent any of their people from crossing the border to fight against the Fascists. Appeasement was in full flower.

Thus, within four days, four nations had taken decisive action that served the Fascist and Nazi cause—and two were nations whose people were democratic. But in Madrid, the people, serene and strangely confident, held on. They had a battle cry: "Make Madrid the mausoleum of Fascism."

Chapter XXII

Pranks of "Nonintervention"

M EANWHILE, through the autumn, winter, and spring of 1936–1937, the defenders of Madrid were strengthening their position. The hoped-for panic was nowhere seen. Instead of panic on the approach of the Moors, who led the van of the approaching enemy, the people sobered, grew gravely calm and grimly determined. The forces of disorder, and the criminal element, were now put down by the iron hand of military authority. General Miaja made short shrift of them.

If Miaja was not a great military genius, he was a trained and seasoned officer with an abundance of common sense, a stubborn will, and with excellent defensive tactics. He was a staunch defender of the Republic who believed it the primary duty of the soldier to support the constituted authority. Some years later, when, with Martínez Barrio, he called on me in Chile, he impressed me as a Spanish version of General U. S. Grant—stubborn, tenacious, if not brilliant. The people's faith in his loyalty and integrity stiffened their morale.

Bombs fell on the beautiful city from German and Italian planes, the people were reduced to rations and forced to forego heat in winter, but gladly they went about their appointed tasks. Their love of Madrid was such that, though freezing, they spared the trees that are the glory of the streets. They gathered in the familiar cafés for gossip, crowded the cinemas, and laughed at the comedians on the stage.

2

Meanwhile, the Nonintervention Pact was proving itself a dishonest farce. The Fascist powers fought openly, defiantly, with arms; most of the democracies fought just as effectively, if unconsciously, as collaborationists of the Fascists under the mocking cloak of "nonintervention." When men of good minds assumed that Italy, Germany, and even Portugal were observing the pact, the dishonesty of the pretense stood out like a sore thumb. This pact had become a mockery by October, 1936. It denied the Spanish government the arms and ammunition while turning a blind eye to the glaring violations by Germany and Italy. Arms and ammunition poured into the Portuguese ports consigned to Franco, and, without inspection at the customs were hurried through to Franco's forces. It was common knowledge. Later, deliveries were made openly through Cádiz, Vigo, Passejas, and Málaga. On September 16, 1935, John Whittaker, Knickerbocker, and Floyd Gibbons, war correspondents, informed me that rebel aviation consisted largely of German bombers and Italian pursuit planes, and that in Seville they had seen German officers in the cafés. Another correspondent, distinguished in his profession, told me of his astonishment on landing in Seville because of the number of Italian planes, and on being greeted by Italian officers he had known in Abyssinia. All this was in the shoddy days when British ministers were assuring the House of Commons, on their responsibility as ministers of the Crown, that they had "no information" that any Italians were in Spain. I knew that the British Embassy in Hendaye was informing London to the contrary.

In late October, Minifie of the New York *Herald Tribune*, Gorrell of the United Press, and Weaver of the *News-Chronicle* of London were arrested by the Franco forces near Aranjuez, detained at Talavera, transferred to Salamanca, and expelled through Irún. I met them at the border, and Gorrell wrote his story on the typewriter in my house. The three had driven from Madrid in taxis with a man from the War Office to see for themselves what was happening near Aranjuez. They were startled on the way by the appearance of a large number of the Moorish cavalry thundering toward them on the road. They stopped the cars and sprang out.

One chauffeur turned his car and escaped, but the other was caught, and, with his hands above his head as token of surrender, he was shot down. The Moors, noticing the buttons on the coat of the War Office guide, tore them off, and as he stood with hands held high as token of surrender, he too was shot down. After he fell, the Moors riddled his body with bullets. So was Ring Lardner's son to be murdered by the Moors.

The correspondents now noticed behind the Moorish cavalry a number of Italian whippet tanks bearing down upon them as if to run them down, firing as they approached. Gorrel sprang into a ditch to escape a tank which lost balance and fell into the ditch, upside down. Humane instinct triumphing over caution, Gorrel reached into the tank and helped the driver out, only to find himself looking into a pistol level with his eyes. The operator could not speak Spanish; neither could any of the operators of these tanks. They were of Mussolini's Fascist army.

The correspondents wrote their stories. The Nonintervention Committee was annoyed, not because of the proof of the violation of the pact but because of the publication of the proof. Nothing was said about it.

Then, early in December, 1936, when German soldiers, technicians, engineers, and aviators landed in Cádiz, the British government "deplored it"—and hastened the passage of a law making it a crime to sell arms or ammunition to the loyalist government! The delectable Ribbentrop, later to be hung at Nuremberg for his crimes, thereupon informed the Nonintervention Committee of the pleasure of Hitler that steps had been taken to prevent "intervention." Thus the collaboration with the Axis powers in the war of extermination against democracy in Spain was complete.

3

The Germans sent no infantry to Spain, but their intervention was far more effective than that of the Italians, who did. The rebel artillery was operated and directed by the German Condor Legion, as Hitler was to boast. In his conference with Ciano he said that "Italy and Germany had done very much for Spain in 1936." (Notes of Minister Schmidt, September 28, 1940, State Dept. Bulletin, Vol. XIV, page 300, March 26, 1948.) The *Forza Armata*, organ of the Italian army and navy, in its issue of June 3, 1937, said that from December 26 to April 27, Mussolini had sent one hundred thousand Italian soldiers, forty thousand tons of war material, conveyed in fifty-two ships in one hundred and thirty-two voyages. Certain it is that the antiaircraft defenses were in charge of the German Nazis, since this is admitted by that ardent Francoist, Georges Oudard, who says that Spanish rebel and Italian officers were not permitted to examine them at close range. The airdromes were built by German engineers, and when the attack on the Basques began, it was made by German aviators in command of German officers. At the air bases, the commanders and instructors were German, and the fine engineering work was done by German engineers. Hitler was not exaggerating when he boasted of his decisive part in the Spanish war.

4

In November, 1936, the Foreign Minister of the Spanish Republic demanded a meeting of the Assembly of the League of Nations to take action under Article II of the covenant, but it was not until December that it met and adopted resolutions admitting the aggression against Spain, but the Nonintervention Committee required time to "study" the facts with which it was entirely familiar.

When in January, 1937, Mussolini and Chamberlain announced their agreement on Mediterranean matters, from four to six thousand more Italian soldiers landed at Cádiz; Mussolini denied that Italians were in Spain; and the British Minister solemnly quoted Mussolini in the Commons. A few days later I had authentic information that more Germans had landed and been sent to Seville for distribution to the different fronts. In February, 1937, heavy Italian reinforcements were sent to Málaga, and when the French press published circumstantial stories of the inflow of Italian Fascist soldiers, Del Vayo made a radio appeal for common honesty. Nothing happened except the arrival of more Italian soldiers at Cádiz, brought in the Italian ship *Lombardi* in several trips. Again the British Minister in the Commons seriously replied to an interrogation that he had the assurance of Mussolini that neither men nor material had been sent to Spain since "Nonintervention" went into effect five months before!

At this time, the common topic of gossip in Saint-Jean-de-Luz was the notorious lack of camaraderie between the Italian and German forces across the border. I heard it frequently from war correspondents and from Franco supporters going back and forth to San Sebastián.

5

Meanwhile, the staggering faith of some British ministers in the integrity of Mussolini's assurances was causing some concern in France, which now demanded some system of control to enforce the bedraggled "Nonintervention" farce. The demand was accepted "in principle," but there was the usual delay until the French Ambassador in London made a belated gesture of indignation and demanded action. But two or three weeks were required by the committee to shake off the fumes of Morpheus. At length, it was arranged. Agents of several nations were to guard the French frontier to prevent supplies going to the Spanish government; French and British were to patrol the northern coast and the south up to Málaga; and the entire coast from Málaga north was to be guarded by the ships of Germany and Italy, whose governments were waging open war against the legal government. Some realists doubted the wisdom of assigning German and Italian ships alone to hover over the coast of loyalist territory; and some, lacking a childlike faith in Mussolini, feared that under cover of darkness these hostile ships might shell the cities while pretending it was done by Franco. Naturally, the Spanish government protested, but nothing could have been less impressive to the now notorious committee on "Nonintervention."

The patrol system was a farce from the beginning, and Italian and German ships continued to pour men, arms, and ammunition into Spain.

6

It was not until Franco ordered all ships out of the waters of Barcelona by announcing a mere paper blockade that France and England became uneasy. How, they asked, could he enforce the blockade? He certainly had very few submarines, and if, magically,

they appeared, no one could doubt their origin. He had few ships—
pitifully inadequate for a blockade. He warned shipping away by
saying the waters were mined, though at the beginning of the war
he had but two mine layers. And so, stouthearted British sea cap-
tains kept going all the while without an incident, bearing food.
That the Axis warships were giving ample assistance to Franco's
meager navy was certain. They could at least wireless Franco's
ships the movements and positions of merchant ships and government vessels.

Unhappily the honeymoon of the Axis powers and the Nonintervention Committee was cruelly interrupted. The long series of
outrages had begun—the taking of British, French, and Norwegian
ships into rebel ports with the confiscation of their cargoes. The
torpedoing of neutral vessels soon became too commonplace to
figure in the press. So successful was this Fascist game of piracy
that soon the Italian submarines would undertake to terrorize all
shipping from the Mediterranean.

7

When enough Italian soldiers had arrived, the attack on
Málaga began. On January 13, 1937, rebel ships shelled the city
and the next day the rebel army, with thousands of Italians, under
command of Queipo de Llano, fought a bloody battle with heavy
losses on both sides, at Estepona, about forty miles from the
city. German bombers were active. The war vessels shelled the
road. Inside Málaga there was confusion, dissension, lack of co-
ordination, and the extremist elements who had fought each other
in the streets continued to quarrel among themselves. Early in
February the city fell, followed by the usual executions. Chambers
Mitchell, former secretary of the London Zoological Society, an
old man of seventy-two, living in Málaga, and neutral in the war,
and Arthur Koestler, correspondent of a London paper, were
arrested and narrowly escaped execution. Mitchell was saved by a
British warship, and Koestler by the protest of the world press.
They both survived to write their illuminating stories.

The Nonintervention Committee slept through it all.

But the fall of Málaga was a blessing for the Spanish government. For months the leaders had urged the merging of all party

and labor military units into a national army with a common command responsible to the government. The easy Fascist triumph in Málaga brought a sobering realization that without such a reorganization the fight was lost. With public sentiment now aggressively with it, the government acted with decision. The factional military units ceased to exist and in a surprisingly short time the effect was seen.

8

Elated by the success at Málaga, the rebels pushed their preparations for an offensive against Madrid. A great army, with the most modern equipment from the Axis powers, with three divisions of Italian troops, was assembled for a march on Guadalajara. Italian generals were in command, the Italian troops were given precedence on the insistence of Mussolini, who sent a flamboyant message expressing supreme confidence in their triumph. With heavy artillery, tanks, and planes, the legions moved. For a few days the offensive prospered, and then the loyalist army, now reorganized, with plans drawn by General Rojo, a brilliant officer, launched a counteroffensive, retook Brunete in a fierce assault which threw the Italians into a panic. They retreated, lost formation, and it became a rout. Loyalist planes swooped low, peppering the fleeing with machine-gun fire.

At the cocktail bars in Biarritz and Saint-Jean-de-Luz, where Francoists met for cocktails and gossip, there was open mirth among the Spaniards over the discomfiture of the Legionnaires of Caesar, and there was frank jollity among the Spanish officers. Slapping each other on the shoulder, they greeted each other with smiles and laughter. They had resented the insolence of the Italian Fascist officers before the battle; it was to be their battle; very well, then, it was their rout. A colleague of mine in Salamanca at the time described to me the scarcely concealed satisfaction of the Spanish officers.

But the telegram of Mussolini to his army in Spain was embarrassing to the Nonintervention Committee, and Del Vayo made it the subject of a vigorous protest to the League of Nations, but this meant less than nothing, and actually was resented. One of my colleagues assured me that it was in "bad taste"! The League had ceased to command respect or to deserve it. When I asked Herbette, the French Ambassador, what he thought the League would do, he laughed heartily.

"Is this a serious conversation?" he asked.

So low had been reduced the prestige of the League.

But another attempt to take Madrid had failed.

9

The six months of fall and winter in Saint-Jean-de-Luz were not exciting. We had moved to the villa of Eche Soua in a torrential rain, and scarcely had we arrived when a visitor was announced. It was Zuloaga, the famous Spanish painter. He seemed remarkably youthful for his age. He had the carriage of an athlete. His face was a little lined, and such hair as remained was white. His blue-gray eyes were keen and quick to kindle with amusement. He talked with animation.

When the war broke, he was living at Zumaya, near San Sebastián, in an old convent he had converted into a home, studio, and museum. He had never interested himself with politics, though his intimate friends in the intellectual and artistic circles were the academic republicans who had made republicanism fashionable in the last days of the monarchy. The preface to the English edition of Pérez de Ayala's *Tiger Juan* paints a charming picture of a scene on the lawn of Zuloaga's house, with Unamuno, Zuloaga, Pérez de Ayala, a poet or two, and Belmonte, the matador, in conversation. They were all republicans. During the loyalist occupation of the region, the painter was unmolested, for he, too, was a Basque. But Fascist propaganda had thought it wise to kill him as proof of the savagery of the loyalists. That afternoon, with the rain lashing at the windows, and with the fire crackling, he told me with a chuckle of the manner in which he had learned of his demise.

Shut off from the world, and unwilling to mingle with it under the circumstances, a friend had given him a radio—his first. The family grouped itself about it and turned it on. The first words that emerged left them gasping: "I am sorry to announce that Zuloaga, the world-famous painter, has been savagely murdered by the reds."

It was after his first visit that the "reds" murdered him again.

"He had been arrested by the Basques, tried, condemned, and executed" by his own people. He had not been in Bilbao, the scene of the "outrage," but Americans read the story with indignation. In reply to a cable from Fernando de los Ríos from Washington, the Basque President Aguirre indignantly denounced the story as a lie.

Zuloaga came to see me that day in a state of excitement over the possible fate of a small El Greco portrait of the head of St. Lawrence, which he thought the real masterpiece of the immortal artist. He had it in a safety-deposit box in a bank in San Sebastián, and when the loyalists left for Bilbao, the boxes were transferred to banks in that city. Zuloaga had been unable to sleep in fear that the canvas might be destroyed by someone ignorant of its value. I promised, unofficially, to call it to the attention of President Aguirre, and he was childishly delighted. "Get my El Greco," he said, "and I will build a monument to you that will fill Central Park." But early the next morning his hostess came to tell me that he had not slept a wink that night. He was afraid that the acceptance of any favor from the Basques would put him under suspicion, and it was then but a few steps from suspicion to the Fascist firing squad. He would rather I did nothing. In time, the canvas was found undamaged and returned to him.

I was to see him several times and to delight in his visits. At the time of his first visit, he was neutral, but, before long, living in Fascist territory, and not so sensitive to German Nazis as Unamuno, he had become a strong partisan of the Fascists. An exhibit of his paintings was arranged in Rome, and at Zumaya he continued to paint—mostly portraits of the German and Italian officers.

10

That winter San Sebastián was fairly gay. The Spanish in Biarritz and Saint-Jean-de-Luz went back and forth across the border to hear the gossip of the cafés and bars, and some returned permanently to Spain because their funds were tied up there. The old Bar Basque in San Sebastián, the meeting place of the monarchists before the war, was packed. Chicote, whose cocktail bar in Madrid was internationally famous, opened a bar in San Sebastián, and soon the city was aristocratic Madrid in miniature. Young boys in the army, on leave, found it lively and amusing. In bars and cafés Mussolini's officers in their smart Fascist uniforms surveyed the Spanish scene with a supercilious condescension.

But behind the gay exterior there was tragedy. Executions at night were not unusual. Because gossip ran riot, the billboards flamed with orders to the people to hold their tongues, warning that Franco's spies were everywhere. The liberties of the people were reduced to the Fascist standard. Young women gave up the beach when the new moral standard prescribed something like Mother Hubbards as bathing dresses.

But even in the rebel army all was not serene. The monarchists, Fascists, and Carlists were irreconcilable, and often there were incidents in the streets. In front of the Italian consulate, where Spaniards occasionally staged affectionate demonstrations, hung a huge picture of Mussolini, and woe to the unhappy wight who failed to give it the salute of Rome. Soon, as much reverence was exacted for the picture of Franco. Garrison, of my staff, who had narrowly escaped attack because he did not think to uncover before the picture of Mussolini, was roughly ordered to remove his hat in respect to the picture of Franco in the commandant's office in Irún.

It required tact to get along in San Sebastián. A young attaché of my staff, there to serve an American in trouble, was asked by an old woman in the street if he were a Fascist or a Carlist. He replied that he was neither. "Which do you like best?" she demanded. "I like them both," he said coyly. "I don't," she snapped. "I am a Carlist, as my people were before me. I like the Carlists best."

11

That winter Alcalá Zamora's son returned to Spain to fight for the Republic that so signally had honored his father, and the old man wept over his son's "ingratitude" and "wiped his eyes on the public." Later, the former President complained that his safety-deposit box in Madrid had been opened and his money and diary taken. At the same time, the box of Lerroux was opened, and here came a revelation in character. It contained no money—nothing but a few sentimental relics—a youthful picture of himself with a young girl, a few old letters, a blue ribbon. It was very human, reflecting the mellow side of the old political leader.

Meanwhile, General Wilhelm Faupel, once on Hindenburg's staff, and a noted strategist, arrived in Burgos to present his credentials as German Ambassador. He was received colorfully and escorted to Franco by Moorish cavalry in Moorish uniforms. He knew nothing about politics or diplomacy. His business was war—and that was his business in Spain.

A little later, when the Italian Ambassador presented his credentials, Franco, with tongue in cheek, said in his speech that some parts of the country were still under the rule of "foreigners." Addressed in the presence of the Moors and to an ambassador whose army of foreigners was on Spanish soil, numbering many thousands, this was in the best Fascist manner.

It was about this time that Azaña went to Valencia and made a notable speech setting forth as the program of the government the redemption of the campaign promises of 1936 and the maintenance of the democratic Republic. He bluntly accused some, meaning anarchists and some syndicalists, with failure to co-operate in a unified defense of the regime. Like all his speeches, this one was memorable and meaty, and it was received with great enthusiasm. It would have been helpful in the United States and England in counteracting the effect of the wild harangues over the radio of extremists in the first days of the war, and I was amazed that it had not been given in advance to the foreign press.

12

For the radio was playing an important part in determining world opinion on the struggle in Spain. Listening to the weird, incredible propaganda of the radio, I was impressed with the illimitable possibilities of this medium in confusing the public mind as to events, with fantastic falsehoods and innumerable contradictions. Night after night, the radio stations in Italy, Germany, and Portugal poured into millions of ears the Fascist propaganda, giving but one side, and this colored by the imagination of Dr. Goebbels. The French and English stations gave both sides as news. Thus all the radio advantage was with the totalitarians who did not scruple to manufacture "news," to distort it, or suppress it. The broadcaster of Lisbon was the most fertile and shameless in his inventions; and after he announced, in bored tones, that when the "reds" left San Sebastián, they carried off twenty or thirty girls of the best families as victims of their lust, I listened no more to Lisbon.

Our favorite entertainer was General Queipo de Llano, commander of the rebel army in the south, who talked nightly from the station in Seville. These talks were as disjointed as they were picturesque, as unreliable as they were amusing. If not an Andalusian by birth, he was one by temperament. His hostility to dictatorial regimes had driven him into exile in the days of Primo de Rivera. He had served for a time as the head of the military household of Alcalá Zamora, and I suspect he was a republican by instinct, and, compared with Franco and Mola, a liberal. As a showman he was superb. In the early days of the war when the rebels were worried over the failure to take Madrid, his broadcasts of gasconading optimism on imaginary victories were as helpful as a victory in the field.

For more than eighteen months he was to comment nightly on the "news" with a soldier's rough wit, to abuse the loyalists in the picturesque phraseology of the fish market, and to ridicule the "Passion Flower" with the ribald humor of the barracks. He talked so much like a man half overseas that the loyalists dubbed him "the drunkard of Seville" and they put on a clever radio skit under this title, punctuating the general's wildest statements with cries of "*Viva Vinos.*" But in time he was to become a thorn in the side of the more pretentious gentlemen of the army in Salamanca, and he was silenced. Whether he actually made the speech at La Linea, with huge amplifiers to carry the words into Gibraltar, announcing that in due time Spain would take the Rock back, I do not personally know. It was naturally denied by Franco, and the Chamberlain government accepted the denial, though Englishmen in Gibraltar who heard the speech were less surprised by the denial than by its ready public acceptance. Whatever the facts, immediately after the incident it was made the subject of a sharp interrogation in the House of Commons and soon thereafter Queipo's retirement from the radio was announced. This deprived the war of some humor. Queipo's place in history as the greatest radio warrior of all time is assured.

1 3

At this time my dispatches to the State Department covered every phase of the struggle, as Cordell Hull reported at a press conference. The substance of them was that the struggle was now a war of Fascism against democracy, and the beginning of a World War by the Axis powers to exterminate democracy throughout Europe. I read daily the Franco papers of Burgos, Salamanca, and San Sebastián, all teeming with contemptuous attacks on democracy and on the United States and England. At this time appeared a book of "history" prepared for the schools by the Franco authorities, in which England appeared as a moribund nation of "shop-keepers" without courage, and the United States as a land of plutocratic bond holders in the last stage of putrefaction.

At this time there was great suffering and semi-starvation among the children in all parts of Spain, and I was shocked that the American people were doing nothing for their alleviation. Thinking it possible that the policy of neutrality we had imposed might have given the impression that donations would be frowned upon by the American government, I wrote Cordell Hull, who immediately issued a statement that neutrality was not involved, in that food and clothing would go to the needy children and mothers on both sides. I was asked by Mrs. Roosevelt to take the honorary chairmanship of the American committee organized to collect food and money, and one evening I made a transatlantic radio address from Saint-Jean-de-Luz, appealing for help. Later, when I went to Paris to record another appeal on a gramophone, I narrowly escaped death in the wildest ride I ever had, since Ernest Hemingway drove me to the studio from a cocktail party, the car swerving dangerously and narrowly escaping collisions with trucks and pedestrians by its zigzag course, as the novelist talked with boyish enthusiasm of the loyalists' resistance.

1 4

It was at this time that the Quakers entered Spain to investigate and supervise the distribution of American donations. Even in this humanitarian work we were to encounter the hostility of the Fascists to the United States. With food and clothing being sent into their territory, I learned from American newspapermen that the Franco officials stoutly, and even resentfully, denied that we had sent anything at all. I learned that the labels showing the origin of the sacks were removed before the distribution. I know that the Franco press never in a single line acknowledged the service or expressed appreciation, but, on the contrary, it denounced us as "reds" for sending food to the starving children in the industrial centers of loyalist territory.

Not wishing to send our ships into the fighting zone, it was arranged to send them to Bordeaux and to notify the loyalists in Barcelona and the Francoists in Burgos. The loyalists gratefully accepted and had the goods sent by train across France to loyalist territory, but the Francoists complained because we did not unload at San Sebastián. Later, an agent of the Quakers told me of a strange occurrence in Vigo. A ship with flour arrived there and it was almost a month before the military governor permitted it to be unloaded. When, finally, he gave the order, it was with instructions that a meager part of the cargo be given to a bakery, and the greater part to the rebel army. The Quaker agent protested and threatened to send the ship away. Then only did the flour reach the homes of the children for whom it was intended. Such were our experiences in trying to be impartial in our charity.

Too much credit cannot be given this efficient and fair Quaker organization for the magnificent work it did in Spain.

Chapter XXIII

Martyrdom of the Basques

IN THE spring of 1937 the rebels were ready to undertake the subjugation of the provinces of the northern coast, which were isolated from other loyalist territory and effectively shut off from assistance. Powerfully supported by Italian and Moorish troops, with heavy German artillery and German planes and aviators, Franco's army was prepared to strike first at the Basques.

There is no finer, nobler race in Spain than these. Their origin is lost in mists of history, but they have stoutly lived from time immemorial in the shadow of the Pyrenees, and scholars have called them "the oldest race in Europe." Robust, courageous, fiercely independent, passionately devoted to their liberties, intensely individualistic, and deeply religious, they have changed but little in character through the centuries.

The Moors conquering most of Spain to maintain their conquest for seven centuries swept northward as far as Tours, but the Basque provinces and the Asturians never lowered the Cross to the Crescent. Because of their heroism, the people of Vizcaya were granted autonomous rights, which were not lost until the second Carlist war, and all the inhabitants were ennobled by the state.

The Basques are the most energetic and progressive, and have the most initiative of the Spaniards. Nature has blessed them with great deposits of iron and coal, and has given them a coast line from Bilbao to Fuenterrabia rich in natural harbors. With the coming of the industrial age, Bilbao became the Pittsburgh of

Spain, the fourth city in population. The Basques harnessed the mountain torrents and made them turn the wheels of industry. Paper mills sprang up beside the mountain streams. Thousands of miners produced iron ore and coal to feed the furnaces of factories. The harbor of Bilbao teemed with shipping from every quarter of the globe.

Fishermen, seamen, artisans, peasants, manufacturers, merchants, bankers—all the Basques prospered. High-minded, clean-living, deeply religious, it is commonly agreed that in no other region is Catholicity more sensitive or profound. The people profited by better teaching. The Basque priests, usually of healthy peasant stock themselves, have a sympathetic understanding of their people, entering intimately into their lives as counselors and friends, sharing their instincts and fidelities, entering enthusiastically into their pleasures, competing with them on the pelota court.

When the rebellion broke, the Basques instantly lined up with the loyalists. Their churches continued to function as before; priests and nuns walked the streets in safety; mass was heard as through the centuries; and priests blessed the armed forces of the Basques. Soon a German paper was denouncing the Catholics because Basque priests were fighting in the trenches beside their people, though I believe this was an exaggeration. Even so, this loyalty of the Basque Catholics to democracy embarrassed the propagandists who insisted that the Nazis and Moors were fighting to save the Christian religion from "communism." When Basque priests went forth to tell the members of their faith that the best Catholics in Spain were with the loyalists, the fury of the rebels blazed. One spoke to a great crowd in New York City; a delegation of them went to Ireland to confront and confound the false propaganda there. It was clearly necessary to get the Basques off the front page of the newspapers.

And there was another reason—the iron ore of the Basque provinces. Franco needed this ore to trade for arms and ammunition; *and Nazi Germany needed it to prepare for its war against European democracy.* The Basques were sending the greater part to England, and the pledge of the rebels to divert it to Germany had been given. Hitler had frankly announced in a public speech that his soldiers were in Spain because Germany needed the iron ore.

Thus Franco did not push toward Bilbao to save the church—the church was in no danger; nor to save the priests, for they had the reverence of the people and performed their functions in perfect peace; nor to put down communism, for the Basques were not communists.

2

My wholehearted sympathy was with the Basques. I knew them as a race of sterling worth, honest, clean, kindly. Their fishermen turned soldiers, saluting a bit awkwardly at Fuenterrabia, had won my heart, and when I visited Bilbao to evacuate our people, I was impressed by the poise, fairness, and intelligence of their leaders.

In December, before the offensive started, Arthur O. Minnich, representing a great financial institution in New York, asked my aid in advancing his mission to Bilbao, where his people had securities of great value and four hundred thousand pesetas in the bank. He wished to get the securities and send them home, and to draw the pesetas to buy iron ore. I gave him letters to President Aguirre and his Minister of Finance. He was cordially received. Permission was given for the transfer of the securities, and soldiers were assigned to safeguard them to the ship. He was allowed to withdraw the pesetas. With these he bought iron ore and shipped it to Liverpool, where it was converted into money.

"These people 'reds'?" he snorted on emerging. "Why, they are decent people with respect for law and property."

Generous enough to ascribe his success in part to me, he called to tell me of his experience. He was a large, forceful man with the poise of common sense, and I could readily understand his appeal to the Basques. At a dinner given him by the ministers he gave an amusing account of his wife's fears because of the atrocity stories she had heard, and of her insistence that he, who never had carried a pistol, take one with him. He laughingly added that he had "parked" the pistol in Saint-Jean-de-Luz. "Ah," said Eliodoro de la Torre, the Minister of Finance, "it is not right to deceive your wife, and since you promised, you should have a pistol." And putting his hand in his pocket, he drew out a beautiful ornate pistol and passed it to the American businessman. I am afraid the proffer was made in the Spanish sense of courtesy, which expects a polite declination, but Minnich knew nothing of the Spanish custom and gratefully accepted in good faith. Months later, the minister called on me in Saint-Jean-de-Luz and smilingly verified my theory. The directors of the bank adopted a resolution thanking me for my co-operation.

In December I sent the destroyer, the *Erie*, to Bilbao to continue the evacuations, and we found conditions there fairly normal. Streetcars were running, street cleaners were at work, traffic police were at their posts, shops were open and busy, religious services continued in all churches, and the people in the streets were calm and unafraid. Because more than one hundred thousand refugees had crowded into the city, food was rationed, but it was easy to find a satisfying meal in both quantity and quality at restaurants at reasonable prices.

3

The operations against Bilbao were under the command of General Mola, supported by a large force of Italian and Moorish soldiers and aided by powerful Nazi bombing planes and aviators. But very strong defenses had been built around the city, and the mountains threatened a desperate resistance. It was the hope of Mola to starve the people into submission. It was announced from Salamanca that the harbor was blockaded, but it was a paper blockade. Then the warning was broadcast that the harbor was mined, and the Basques truthfully announced that mine sweepers were busy day and night. The British government, however, tried to discourage its merchantmen from entering the harbor, but the hearty British seadogs called Salamanca's bluff and sailed in and out without the slightest incident. When the warning failed to end the delivery of food, the enemy launched a war of piracy on the high seas. The bombing of ships of neutral nations became common-place. Many were forced to rebel ports, where their cargoes were unloaded. The protests of the British Ambassador were answered, after a long silence, with insulting phrasing.

When this bombing or detention of British ships became a favorite outdoor sport without disturbing the complacency of the Chamberlain government, the Labor and Liberal parties in the Commons drove the Ministry into a corner in a five-day debate and they forced the promise from the government to protect British commerce on the high seas. Franco countered with the threat to fire on British destroyers escorting food ships, even outside territorial waters, and British merchant ships were instructed from London to stay in the harbor of Saint-Jean-de-Luz or Bayonne to await further instructions. The great battleship, the *Hood*, was ordered from Gibraltar to Saint-Jean-de-Luz, and the little harbor was crowded with destroyers and merchantmen.

At length, the Chamberlain government announced its decision. It would not tolerate any interference with British shipping by Franco, to whom belligerent rights had not been granted. *Therefore*, it strongly urged British ships to bow to Franco and not go to Bilbao. This was interpreted to mean that British ships would protect British shipping on the high seas, but would not challenge Franco's right to sink them in the harbor. But the old seadogs of England asked nothing more, and, gaily enough, they steamed into the harbor of Bilbao.

But almost immediately came a clarification of the policy of Chamberlain. He admitted the right of British ships to deliver their cargo in Bilbao; that they had this right under the Nonintervention Pact; that Franco had no right to interfere, since he had not been given belligerent rights. *This being true*, food ships for Bilbao should not attempt to deliver their cargoes—because the waters there were mined! Thus was darkness made visible.

It was now clear that the dominant wing of the Chamberlain government was willing to make its contribution to the starving of the women and children of Bilbao, but the British food ships continued to pour into the harbor, and the people were not starved.

4

The overwhelming advantage was with the rebels. Cut off from the possibility of reinforcements, every man lost in battle was irreplaceable to the Basques, while Mola could draw on reinforcements from the immediate surrounding territory. The Basques had no planes, no antiaircraft guns, no way of getting them from the loyalist government. Planes from Barcelona could not cross over Franco territory without a perilous landing for refueling in the enemy zone. But Franco had a perfect fleet of German and Italian planes sent by Hitler and Mussolini. This terrible advantage was to determine the fate of the Basques.

But, even so, the offensive progressed slowly. The Basques fought gallantly and died heroically, but the bombers beyond their reach roared above them and planes machine-gunned them on the ground, and they had no planes with which to meet their enemy. Often the Basques lost a position by day because of the planes and retook it at night when it was man to man.

And then came the martyrdom of the little old town of Durango "in the most terrible bombardment of a white civil population in the history of the world up to March 31, 1937." It was a peaceful and religious town, and many people were at mass in the three churches. The Nazi bombers, circling above the town, could be heard by the worshipers in the ancient church of Santa María, in the Church of the Jesuit Fathers, and in the chapel of Santa Susana the nuns could hear the sinister roar of the planes flying very low. The Nazi aviators dropped tons of heavy bombs.

One crashed through the roof of Santa Susana's chapel, and nuns were literally blown to bits, mingled with pieces of the holy images.

Another heavy bomb smashed through the roof of the Church of the Jesuit Fathers, and Father Rafael Billalabeitia, who was officiating at the mass when the roof crashed in, died under its wreckage, along with others.

Still another heavy bomb shot through the roof of the old church of Santa María just at the moment when Don Carlos Morilla was elevating the Host, and he lay dead, with numerous worshipers about him. Of the many killed and mangled, beyond recognition, many were children, but only pieces of them were left to be laid on a slab and numbered 1, 2, 3, etc.

5

And then came the atrocity of Guernica.

General Mola had threatened that unless the Basques surrendered he would not leave one stone standing on another in the whole province—and quickly followed the crime of Guernica.

This was the "Holy City of the Basques," sacred in the history of the race. As the ancient capital, it had stood for centuries for race, religion, liberty, and independence, and under its famous tree the Assembly of the Basques had met to make the laws, and in its shade some of the noblest figures of the race had taken the oath of office as rulers. Here José Aguirre, a splendid character and a devout Catholic, had sworn as President to preserve the independence and liberty of the people.

It was a small town of no military value, and the massacre fell on a market day when the peasants were there with their livestock and produce. The market was at its fullest at about four-thirty in the afternoon, when, suddenly, the sky was blackened by a great fleet of Hitler's bombing planes, resembling a swarm of locusts; and, with cold-blooded deliberation, taking their time, since there were no defending planes—and "Nonintervention" had seen to that—the little town was peppered with explosive and incendiary bombs until it was a mass of ruins. Before the planes returned with the incendiary bombs, Father Aronategul, the parish priest, was seen making his way through the debris with the sacrament for the dying, walking through the deserted streets with the holy oil. He knew how, and by whom Guernica was destroyed, and he said so to me.

When the Condor Legion was welcomed home by Goering, he said one reason the Nazis were in Spain was that "our air fleet burned to show what it could do." It showed it at Durango and at Guernica.

When the revolting news reached Saint-Jean-de-Luz, I was horrified, most of all by the heartless complacency with which the bestial crime was accepted by many. The atrocity was so stupid I could not ascribe it to a Spaniard, who would have had some sentimental regard for the historic town. The reaction of the outside world came quickly. Humanity recoiled with horror and disgust before the barbarous pagan act. When Lord Robert Cecil publicly denounced it as the "most savage act in history," the jubilation in Fascist circles became less audible and more discreet, and General Franco hastened to deny foreknowledge of the crime. But Mola's threat had not been forgotten.

Thus a town sacred to a civilized people, with a population of but seven thousand, unfortified, unarmed, was nearly wiped out. With the thunder of denunciation rolling in upon them, the victors

took refuge in denials, and then, on second thought, they planned
to convince the world that the "reds" had wrought the ruin. How?
By planes? They had none. Then with fire, they said. It was too
silly. The Basques did not destroy their Holy City nor mangle their
women and children. I like to think no Spaniard would or could.

Then Father Alberto Onaindia, an eyewitness, told his story:

I arrived at Guernica on April 26, at four-forty P.M. I had hardly left
the car when the bombardments began. The people were terrified. They
fled, abandoning their livestock in the market place. The bombardment
lasted until seven-forty-five. During that time, five minutes did not elapse
without the sky's being black with German planes. The method of attack
was always the same. First there was machine-gun fire, then ordinary
bombs, and finally incendiary. The planes descended very low, the
machine-gun fire tearing up the woods and roads, in whose gutters,
huddled together, lay old men, women, and children. Before long it
was impossible to see as far as five hundred yards, owing to the heavy
smoke. Fire enveloped the whole city. Screams of lamentation were heard
everywhere, and the people, filled with terror, knelt, lifting their hands to
heaven as if to implore divine protection. . . . As a Catholic priest, I
state that no worse outrage could be inflicted on religion than the *Te
Deum* to be sung to the glory of Franco in the church at Guernica which
was miraculously saved by the heroism of firemen from Bilbao.

They who had seemed elated when the news of destruction
reached Biarritz began to hang their heads a bit. But overnight,
Father Onaindia, whom I met later and found a man of charm and
culture, became a "vicious character." Louder and louder, with
the impudence rising to a scream, grew the protestations that the
"reds" had "burned the town."

I knew this to be a lie. Correspondents, with no motive for
misrepresentation, who visited the ruins, came to see me, and these
threw light on the audacious propaganda. David Darrah visited
the ruins in the company of a Fascist officer. Though he understood
Spanish, he pretended ignorance and spoke in French. They came
upon an old man digging in the wreckage. "How did it happen?"
asked the correspondent. The Fascist officer translated into Spanish.
The old man replied that the planes came in enormous numbers
and kept on dropping bombs until everything was ruined. The
officer translated: "He says that just before the Army of Liberation

entered the town, the anarchists set fire to everything." Darrah thanked the officer—in French.

A little later, Virginia Cowles, an American correspondent, told me her story, on emerging from an inspection tour of the ruined town. She was accompanied by a young man from the bureau of propaganda at Burgos, who clearly accepted the fiction of the "reds' " responsibility. They, too, found an old man among the ruins, and she asked how it happened. He replied that "the planes came and bombed the town until nothing was left but wreckage." The young man flushed. "But the town was set fire by the reds of course," he prompted. The old man shook his head. "Incendiary bombs," he said. The young man hurried the correspondent away, muttering angrily that "he must be a red." Soon they came upon an old woman searching among the ruins, and the question was put to her. Waving her arms, she said: "The planes came and the sky was black with them and they bombed and bombed and bombed." The young man hurried the correspondent from the town.

When, later, Miss Cowles told some Fascist officers of her experience, they laughed heartily. "Why of course we bombed the town," they said, "and bombed it good. Why not?"

6

But the Basques did not succumb to terror. Desperately they contested every foot of ground, a gallant people, backed into a corner, shut off from reinforcements, denied the right to buy war material for their defense, and fighting Moors, Germans, Italians, and not least of all, the Nonintervention Committee. With the horror of Guernica before it, the loyalist government made desperate efforts to get planes to the Basques. The distance prohibited a straight flight from Barcelona to Bilbao, since this would necessitate refueling in rebel territory. It was therefore planned that the planes should land at Toulouse in France, under the pretense of having been driven from their course by winds. It was hoped they would be ordered back to Spain at the nearest point, which would have permitted the completion of the flight to Bilbao. This was not without the connivance of at least one member of the French Ministry. But at Toulouse, the Scandinavian control officer ordered the planes back to Barcelona and sent one of his men along to see that they went. Thus, meticulously did they enforce "nonintervention" against the loyalists while turning a blind eye on the open flaunting of the Axis powers. A few days after the planes were sent back to Barcelona, machine guns, parachutes, and rapid-fire German cannons were landed in rebel territory and hurried over the public roads to the rebel army.

Meanwhile, deprived of the means to defend themselves in the air, the Basques were being bombed by Nazi and Fascist planes, and to save the children, the Basque government arranged for their evacuation. Great Britain notified Franco that her warships would escort the vessels bearing the children from Bilbao. Franco replied with a challenge of Britain's right to perform this purely humanitarian service. To remove children from the reach of bombs was described as "intervention" by two indignant ambassadors of democratic nations, with whom I talked in Saint-Jean-de-Luz. But the British here stood firm, and day by day ships laden with children steamed out of the harbor.

7

Meanwhile, with no grounds for hope, the Basques did not falter in the field. The enemy was advancing slowly, with a large Italian army playing a major role, and Nazi planes making their contribution. A press correspondent who flew to Bilbao from Saint-Jean-de-Luz told me that the bomb shelters were flimsy retreats in the basements of flimsy buildings that could not stand the impact of a bomb. The correspondent had found the Basques hoping and praying for planes via France; but these planes, landing for refueling at Pau, were seized by the French authorities.

I was not surprised when the bitterness of the Basques was directed against the Western democracies that had betrayed them into the hands of the Axis powers. In the First World War, scores of Basque ships were sunk by German submarines while carrying food to England, but the only British statesman who seemed to remember was Lloyd George. Aguirre did not forget, and this is what he said:

We have done our duty. I wish I could say I thought Britain and the Western democracies had done theirs. Britain and France will have to answer to history for their abandonment of the Basques.

In the last hours, the civilization and humanity of the Basques glowed like a flame against the darkness of the barbarous paganism and hypocrisy all about them. It was at this juncture that Jesús Marie de Leizaola, the Basque Minister of Justice, assumed command, to prevent last-minute excesses from marring the Basque record of humanity and legality.

It was after the surrender that he came to see me in Saint-Jean-de-Luz. He was a tall man, with a strong face, his full lips firm, his dark eyes sad and brooding. He had made a reputation at the Bar and for years had been a staunch supporter of Basque autonomy. In the Constituent Assembly he had opposed all measures of a religious nature, for he was a devout Catholic. As Minister of Justice, conducting the treason trials, he had insisted that the accused should have every right guaranteed in normal times for their defense. He was not moved by personal hate in these prosecutions. The German spy, serving as consul for Austria, caught trying to sneak the defenses of Bilbao to Salamanca, he had known and liked. He prosecuted and convicted him, and the night before the execution he had gone to the condemned man's cell to comfort him. Such was Leizaola.

The army of the Italians, Moors, and rebels, sweeping toward the city, was on the outskirts, and with full knowledge that if caught he would immediately face a firing squad, he turned a deaf ear to the pleas of his friends to flee. He and his compatriots had fought a good fight and kept the faith, and now that they were overwhelmed by foreign troops and Nazi planes, he determined that Bilbao should be surrendered in a civilized way without reprisals on prisoners, or the arson and pillage that so often precedes the moment of surrender. With every moment precious, and the enemy sweeping on, he ordered all but the Basque battalions from the city. He then ordered the blowing up of the bridges as a military measure. He refused the suggestion to blow up the university and the old church of San Nicolás as potential machine-gun nests, to save the library of the university and the church because of its beauty. He then ordered all prisoners released; and, lest they be molested, he remained on at night, personally to protect them against the possible fury of the crowd. As these prisoners emerged and started down the road, a crowd collected, and Leizaola ap-

peared upon the scene, placing himself between the prisoners and
the crowd, and announced that he had ordered their liberation.
They were untouched. And then, his work done, the city preserved
from wanton damage, the tired minister drove out of the city toward Santander in the nick of time.

8

And then came the infamy of Santoña.

The surrender at Santoña was made to the Italian army on
written and signed terms of capitulation, after two members of each
of the political parties and the labor unions had been sent as hostages.

Weeks later, Leizaola and Sr. Monzon, the Basque Minister of
the Interior, came to me, unannounced, with a letter from President
Aguirre, setting forth in detail the treatment of the terms of capitulation as a scrap of paper. These ministers were trying, in this
allegedly advanced stage of civilization, to find some avenue of
approach to Mussolini to appeal for the observance of the agreement his officers had signed. Because of the flagrant violation of the
plain terms of the capitulation, and since this outrageous act was
carefully concealed from the outside world, I set them forth in full,
as they were left with me.

Owing to the progress of the enemy at Torrelavega, twenty-fourth of
August, the armed Basque forces found it impossible to continue the
struggle, because of their isolation from the Asturian region. Two of their
representatives consulted with the command of Franco's Italian Legion,
and, under its guarantees, a capitulation, with the following essential
clauses, was agreed to:

ON BEHALF OF THE BASQUE FORCES

(A) To lay down arms in order and to deliver the material over to the
Italian legionary forces who would occupy without struggle the region of
Santoña.

(B) To preserve public order in the zone they occupied.

(C) To guarantee the life and liberty of political hostages in the prisons of Laredo and Santoña.

ON BEHALF OF THE ITALIAN FORCES

(A) Guarantee of life to all the Basque combatants.

(B) Guarantee of life and authorization to leave the country of all the Basque leaders and functionaries in the territories of Santoña and Santander.

(C) To consider the Basque combatants, subject to the capitulation, free of all obligations to take part in the civil war.

(D) To guarantee that the Basque population, loyal to the provisional government of Euzkadi, is not persecuted.

This capitulation was made known publicly to Colonel Faeina, Commandant of the legionary column which occupied Laredo, to the Basque combatants. And, in the presence of many foreign ships in the bay, and the civil population of Santoña, the capitulation in so far as what the Basque forces should fulfill was executed in full.

As to the obligations contracted by the command of the Italian Legion, the fulfillment began to be verified by the provisions of Clause B, the combatants going on board the merchant ships, under the English flag, *Seven Seas*, *Spray*, and *Bobbie*, in the Port of Sontaño, more than two thousand persons with whom relations were established with the acceptance, signature, and seal of the Italian legionnaires the twenty-seventh of August, from eight to twelve.

But, without explanation, the order to go on shore was given by two officers of Franco's, the ships mentioned then leaving empty the twenty-ninth of August.

Since then, all manifestation of the fulfillment of the capitulation is wanting on the part of the auxiliary Italian Legion which guaranteed.

(Signed) José Aguirre

It was an amazing story of treachery and military dishonor. The Basque ministers informed me that the Spaniards who had appeared upon the scene to forbid the honoring of the terms of the capitulation after the Basques had discharged their pledge, were Falangists; and that they claimed to be acting on the personal orders of General Franco. From other sources I have heard that the Italian officers were indignant because of the order to disregard the terms to which their signatures were attached.

When I expressed amazement that nothing of this had appeared in the press, the ministers explained that they feared publicity lest the scandal arouse the anger of the enemy and lead to bloody reprisals on their prisoners.

A few weeks later one of the ministers called again on me and left a written statement that the hostages demanded by the Italians on a condition precedent to the discussion of a capitulation *had been executed by a firing squad*. And again I marveled at the silence of the press outside Spain.

9

Still later, I learned from the same source that scores of prisoners had been executed, including fifteen Basque priests, who fell before a firing squad. Their names are known. This is the roll call of the executed priests:

Martín de Lecuona, assistant priest of the parish of Renteria (Guipuscoa)–shot on October 8, 1936; Gervasio de Albizu, assistant priest of the parish of Renteria (Guipuscoa)–shot on October 8, 1936; José de Sagarna, assistant priest of the parish of Berriatua (Biscay); Alejandro de Mendicute, Chaplain at San Sebastián (Guipuscoa)–shot on the night of October 23–4, 1936; José de Ariztimuño, writer, poet, priest–shot with a group of eighteen other people at the cemetery of Hernani (Guipuscoa); Joaquin de Arin, rector and archpriest of Mondragon (Guipuscoa)–shot on the night of October 24–5, 1936; José de Marquiegui, assistant priest of the parish of Mondragon (Guipuscoa)–shot on the night of October 24–5, 1936; Leonardo de Guridi, assistant priest of the parish of Mondragon (Guipuscoa)–shot on the night of October 24–5, 1936; José de Peñagaricano, assistant priest of the parish of Marquina-Echebarria (Biscay)–shot on October 27, 1936; Celestino de Onaindia, assistant priest of the parish of Elgoibar (Guipusaco)–shot on October 23, 1936; Joaquín de Iturri-Castillo, priest of the parish of Marin (Guipuscoa)–shot on November 6, 1936; José de Adarraga, shot together with Father Ariztimuño; Father Otaño, of the Order of the Immaculate Heart of Mary, organist at Tolosa (Guipuscoa); Father Roman, of the Order of Carmelites, Superior of the College of Amorebieta (Biscay); a military chaplain of the Spanish Army, born in Pitillas (Navarre), name unknown. It seems certain that on November 19, 1936, the corpses found in the cemetery of Vera (Navarre) were four priests.

In addition to the executions, five hundred Basque priests were driven into exile. These priests were not communists, nor anarchists, nor syndicalists, nor politicians, nor labor leaders, nor criminals. They were priests.

That Basque priests were executed was admitted by Cardinal Gomá in the significant exchange of historic letters in January, 1937, between his Eminence and President José Antonio Aguirre, than whom no Catholic more devout can be found in all Christendom. In his speech of December 22, 1936, Aguirre had expressed his astonishment and sorrow that the Spanish hierarchy had made no protest against the execution of priests by the rebel authorities. In an open letter in reply, January 10, 1937, his Eminence had admitted the executions but had said that "*the hierarchy was not silent on this matter*," but that the protest had not been made public since publication would have been "less effective." There is a touch of irony in the words "less effective," since the secret protest, if made, had not been effective at all. If any protest, secret or otherwise, ever was made against the exiling of five hundred priests and the execution, I have been unable to find it.

There are few nobler documents than the answer of Aguirre, who, as a devout Catholic, like all his people fighting for democracy, never deviated one hairbreadth from the profound respect due from one of his faith to a prince of the church. "This letter," concluded Aguirre, "is the expression of sentiment, possibly blunt, but believe me, Eminence, sincere, and expressed with the clarity and affection, on which you may rely, of your faithful servant and friend who kisses your pastoral ring." The status of Aguirre as a Catholic is established in the reply of the cardinal, who, in referring to Aguirre's speech protesting against the silence and the seeming acquiescence of the hierarchy in the shooting of the priests, said that "it has left on my soul the impression that I was listening to the voice of a convinced Catholic"; and in his personal letter to Aguirre he had written: "I know you to be good. . . . I bless you with all my affection."

The proof that the Basque priests were shot by the Franco or nationalist government is overwhelming. Among the documents in the German foreign office found after the World War ended is the telegram from the Nazi Embassy in Madrid, signed "Schwendemann," reporting that "Franco has complained strongly to the Italian chargé d'affaires about the Pope's attitude toward the nationalist government" and that the Pope had complained sharply about "the execution of Basque Catholic priests by white troops." (State Dept. Documents on German Foreign Policy, Series 10, Vol. 3, Document 168, telegram 620, December 27, 1936.)

Thus it is clear that Basque priests were shot in cold blood, not by irresponsible mobs as in Madrid, but on the orders of the rebel government.

10

Toward the end of May, 1937, the German warship *Leipzig*, one of the guardians of the droll Nonintervention Committee's control of the waters washing government territory, was bombed by loyalist aviation. It was a blunder, but not a crime. The aviator had jubilantly wirelessed the government that he had damaged one of the Spanish rebel ships. Manifestly he would not have boasted of his act had he not been convinced that the ship was Franco's, as, in effect, it was. I was surprised that the world was shocked when the victim was a Nazi ship, and I wondered if the democracies were afraid to register indignation when their own ships were hit.

And then, as a result, the crime that was deliberate.

Acting on their own, without warning, the Nazi warships shelled the coast of Almería. This savage act was an act of war— the British and the French admitted it; though surely no more an act of war than the sending of troops, planes, tanks, and artillery for almost a full year. But now there was a refreshing reaction against the shelling of Almería and there was much buzzing in the chanceries, and Hitler was dissuaded from repeating the offense. The democracies had the courage to decline the proposal of Hitler for a joint naval demonstration against the loyalist government; and, with a show of injured innocence, Italy and Germany announced their withdrawal from the system of "control" which had been a mockery from the beginning. For a time it was feared that Franco's foreign allies planned to use their ships to make his paper blockade good. The "nonintervention" democracies were alarmed. The farce of "nonintervention" had been so convenient for stabbing a constitutional democratic government in the back under the cloak of impartiality; and so, to save this handy instrument of hypocrisy and deceit, it was proposed that British ships, with

German and Italian officers on board, should guard the eastern coast. The Axis powers refused.

Thus, mid-July, 1937, found the "nonintervention" scheme feeble and trembling before the laughter of the vulgar, and another proposal was made for its preservation. This promised Franco belligerent rights, provided all foreign troops were withdrawn. This had the merit of being a return to the original pretext, but no one really believed that Hitler and Mussolini would seriously consider the withdrawal of their officers and troops, along with their artillery, planes, and tanks. But the plan provided an indefinite delay, and in the meanwhile, "nonintervention" could continue to deny the constitutional government its legal right to buy arms and ammunition. At intervals, and between yawns, this was to be discussed without action for a full year.

11

It was now clear, after a year of horrors, that the rebellion was not a rising of the people against the democratic regime. Had this been true, the army, the Moors, the Italian and German troops would have triumphed within a month. It was just as clear that it was no "civil war" in the usual meaning of the term, but a war of aggression openly waged by Hitler and Mussolini.

And it was clear that it was not a war for the church, supported by hordes of Mohammedans from Morocco, and the persecutors of the church from Germany, since the Basques, the most devout Catholics in Spain, had written their denial with their heartblood while fighting like tigers for democracy.

Chapter XXIV

Politics and Piracy

MEANWHILE, the Fascists with Franco were annoying the monarchists and great landowners, and ruffling the sensibilities of the Requetés with an indifferent attitude toward the church. In truth, they were becoming a bit supercilious toward Franco himself. Assuming the swagger of Mussolini's Black Shirts, their audacity was increasing in their demonstrations, resulting in conflicts with the Carlists in the streets. Soon they forced Franco to accept the full Fascist program of José Primo de Rivera, with a reservation as to interpretation.

This program was as pointed rocks beneath the surface of the waters the rebel ships would have to navigate to reach the harbor sought. José, in a notable speech, had dismissed the monarchy as a "superannuated" institution and had promised the breaking up of the great estates—thus taking his cue from the Republic. The industrialists writhed without grace over the pledge to nationalize the key industries, and the smile of the financiers, backing the rebellion, over the threatened nationalization of banks was pale and wan. The hierarchy of the church, in the manifesto of the bishops, confessed to grave fears over the drift, and the Carlists were so horrified by José's program that they habitually referred to their Fascist comrades as "our reds."

To end the confusion, Franco sprang another *coup d'état* toward the end of April, 1937. He ordered the dissolution of all existing organizations, and the inclusion of all in one, under his autocratic control. When the unification of the Carlist and Fascist militia was ordered, Manuel Hedilla, the then Fascist chief, who took himself seriously, demanded that he be made commander of the joint militias. This was a challenge to Franco's domination. When Hedilla appeared at Franco's headquarters demanding an interview, he was permitted to cool his heels and temper in the waiting room, and then arrested, with permission to leave the country.

Whatever may have been Franco's original thought, he had found the Fascist element, cheered on by the Italian Fascists and German Nazis, too strong to fight, and so he joined them, and made himself their head. I found the Fascist papers that crossed the border had the blank spaces of the censor at the time.

2

The dissentient elements in Franco's territory were more than matched by those in loyalist territory, where the anarchists were the worst offenders against solidarity and discipline. In early May, the loyalist government moved against them with cold steel. A crisis had been provoked by the anarchists and the P.O.U.M. (United Workers Marxist Party), which was composed of Trotsky communists. It was generally believed that many of these were Franco agents. In factories, they were urging the seizure of private property and strikes to slow down production in the midst of war. In Aragon, not a few anarchists in the army who had been fraternizing with the Fascists deserted and hurried to Barcelona to joint the rising against the government.

That day, Consul-General Claude Dawson in Barcelona telephoned me that open war against the anarchists had begun, with barricades in the streets, and with firing from the roofs of buildings. That night, I got in touch with Del Vayo, then in Paris, who reported that the rising of the anarchists had been crushed. But the outlook in Barcelona did not please the leaders of the government. For weeks the enemy had confidently predicted the surrender of Barcelona without the firing of a shot. Luis Companys was afraid to act decisively, and the crisis came with his confession that without help he could not maintain law and order. This cleared the

way for action by the national government, which sent troops into
Catalonia in command of General Ponzas.

3

Meanwhile, I was confidentially informed that Largo Caballero
was nearing an eclipse. One of his real admirers told me he was
suffering from high blood pressure, that he had days of near in-
accessibility, and that he no longer was possible as a leader. The
feud with Prieto had not abated, and the old fighter still clung to
the delusion that it was possible to harness the anarchists to the
chariot of a democratic state. I was told confidentially how Caballero was to be forced out. With the resignation of the two communist ministers, a crisis was produced, and, in the reorganization,
when Caballero demanded the posts of Prime Minister and Minister of War, with the merging of the War, Navy, and Air Offices
under his direction as Minister of Defense, he was put aside. Whatever may have been his physical condition there is no doubt that
his loss of power was due to the insistence of the communists. He
was a proud Spaniard and prone to look on all foreigners with
suspicion, and any attempt of a foreign power to influence his
actions was intolerable to him. The communists, taking advantage
of the Republic's dependence on war material purchasable from
Russia, pressured the government, I am sure. He had served a vital
purpose at a critical juncture, but his hour had passed. He had
seemed to me to have the zealot's impatience with democratic
processes, and to favor a dictatorship of the proletariat, but Luis
Araquistáin, who knew him intimately, denies it plausibly (*New
Leader*, December 10, 1951). When the Nazis entered France,
Caballero was sent to a concentration camp, from which he
emerged at the end of the war a physical wreck. He died in Paris in
March, 1946, following the amputation of his leg. No one ever
questioned his utter devotion to the workers, his love of Spain, or
his rigid honesty.

4

Dr. Juan Negrín, who now became Prime Minister, was a man
of broad and deep culture, a scientist and physician trained in the

laboratories of Germany, where he had gone for his education when young and remained until he was twenty-five. He had been a favorite pupil of the great biologist, Ramón y Cajal, who had received the Nobel Prize.

He was of the faculty of the University of Madrid when I met him and he had much to do with the creation of University City. He was motivated solely by his intellect, which was of fine fiber. He stood for law and order. He was the calm type, not moved against his reason by his emotions. When I met him at a small luncheon soon after I reached Madrid, I was impressed by his intellectual superiority and his lack of pose. He listened more than he talked that day, but everything he said was worth hearing. He had the mind of a scientist rather than of a politician or orator, and I never heard him speak in the Cortes, where he was a deputy. His integrity and courage were both physical and moral. Robustly built, of medium height, with a round face, keen, gray, spectacled eyes, a dark mustache, he would pass readily as an American or English businessman. Soon he was to astonish the press correspondents in Geneva by answering questions in five languages. I had admired him as a man of real distinction long before he became Prime Minister. One of his political opponents gave me his impression of Negrín: "Though of enormous talent, he is very impulsive, indifferent to restrictions, and always wants to follow his own line. He is an intense individualist, a man of strong initiative and powerful in action. As Premier, he decided momentous questions without advice or consultation. He is enormously courageous —afraid of nothing."

He had a gargantuan appetite and irregular habits, eating at all hours, and sitting up with friends until early morning, but never permitting this to interfere with his duties. In the most tense days of the war, he almost always received the executive of an American utility at his home at seven o'clock in the morning. This American industrialist shared my estimate of the man. He was as remote from communism as it is possible to be.

The appointment of Prieto as Minister of Defense was quite as significant. Clever, resourceful, dynamic, audacious, he seemed at the time a Spanish Lloyd George of the First World War.

Del Vayo continued as Minister of Foreign Affairs.

5

By this time the international phase of the war loomed larger when great German siege guns were permanently emplaced commanding the Strait of Gibraltar, causing a mild stir in the House of Commons. French troops took up quarters in an abandoned hotel between Hendaye and Saint-Jean-de-Luz, where I frequently saw French officers tinkering with an antiaircraft gun. France was becoming uneasy. Meanwhile, Franco's forces were moving toward Santander at a snail's pace.

Taking advantage of the lull, I sent the destroyer *Erie* to Santander to evacuate Americans at last willing to leave, and two days later we rescued seventy, whose repatriation was provided by the American Red Cross. The Santander our people saw in July, 1937, had deteriorated sadly since my visit of almost a year before. The streets were dirty, the walls plastered with propaganda posters, and yet some gaiety remained, and in the hour of the *paseo* the streets were thronged as in happier days. But among the promenaders now were men who limped or carried their arms in slings. The stores were depleted, for the people, in reckless mood, were indulging in an orgy of spending. The officials were courteous and efficient.

But it was different in Gijón. We had hoped, with the aid of the radio, to draw Americans from Asturias to the boat at Santander, but Governor Tomás refused them permission to leave. When we reached him by phone at two in the morning, he angrily refused. "Too many Spaniards have suddenly become foreigners," he barked. I understood; we were forced to suffer for the sins of others. "No," he shouted, "not without explicit instructions from the government in Valencia." It was impossible to wait that long.

Receiving assurances later from Valencia, we sent the *Kane* back, and it was already in the waters of Gijón when the warning came from General Queipo de Llano that in firing upon food ships in the harbor, no responsibility would be assumed for any accident to the *Kane*. This message arrived late at night when both Garrison and Codener, the vice-consul at Bilbao, were on shore on duty and beyond reach. I telephoned Admiral Fairfield, of the *Raleigh*, at Villafranca, and we decided to risk a loading in the morning. The work of the admiral during the first and second years of the war was admirable, and his co-operation with the embassy perfect. I heard nothing but praise of his judgment, poise, and courtesy.

But at Gijón we again ran afoul of Governor Tomás, who had gone to Valencia, leaving instructions that no one should be permitted to leave without his personal inspection. I asked Valencia for an explanation. Much embarrassed, it sent imperative orders to Gijón, and the *Kane* went back.

Meanwhile, General Fuqua, military attaché, who had not visited the loyalist army on this front, asked me to assign him for the trip. He left Barcelona one morning and, driving his own car and without pausing for lunch, he reached Biarritz in time to dine with me that evening.

Scarcely had the *Kane* reached Gijón when the rebels began to bomb the ships in the harbor, and Secretary Hull telegraphed me of his anxiety. Again I consulted Admiral Fairfield by telephone. He had been in touch with the commander of the *Kane* and had learned that the ship was anchored outside the harbor and out of danger. We decided to risk another day.

The staff landed and called upon the governor and the general. The latter, who knew Fuqua, greeted him, Spanish fashion, with a hug. He had no illusions, and, knowing defeat inevitable, he said the Asturians would keep on fighting to the end. Fuqua was given every facility to visit the front. It was on Fuqua's return from this front that a bit of comedy, characteristically Spanish, relieved the drab feature of the excursion. The general had shown Fuqua a remarkable book, setting forth in detail, with drawings and maps, the defenses around Bilbao. Fuqua's eyes sparkled.

"Marvelous," he exclaimed.

"Do you like it?" asked the Spaniard.

"Wonderful!" said Fuqua.

"Then it is yours," said the Spaniard.

"No, no," protested Fuqua, having in mind the custom of offering anything admired by another, with the expectation that it would be declined with thanks.

"No, no, many thanks, but I would not think of it."

"But I want you to have it," said the Spaniard.

"No, no," said Fuqua, laughing.

"But I insist," said the Spaniard.

"Oh, well, if you insist," said Fuqua.

A little later, the Spanish general, noticing Fuqua's shirt, of a type then much favored in Barcelona, commented on its beauty.

"Do you like it?" asked Fuqua.

"Very much," said the Spaniard.

Instantly, off came the coat of Fuqua, and over his head the shirt, and with the Spaniard protesting vehemently, the American passed the shirt to the Spanish officer.

"It's yours," he said.

"No, no," protested the Spaniard.

"But I insist," said the American.

And so the Spanish general literally got the shirt off Fuqua's back. It was the latter's intention to get another shirt at the hotel, but he found his suitcase had been taken to the boat, and he was forced to finish his inspection in Gijón in his undershirt, to the mingled amusement and disgust of the "reds" in the streets.

That time Governor Tomás, a stern, cold, ruthless man of iron will, gave permission for the Americans to leave, and our evacuations of the northern coast were finished.

6

All this time, the rebels with the Italian army were making slow progress toward Santander. The trained Moorish troops accompanied Italian soldiers dragging the heavy German artillery, while German and Italian planes roared above them. The overwhelming odds were impossible for the defenders, and toward the last of August the Italian army led the triumphant march into the conquered city.

This habitual granting to the Italian army the place of honor was no more distressing to the Spanish officers than to the Nonintervention Committee, playing possum. At that precise moment it was pleading with Mussolini to resume his part in the farce of "nonintervention" control, when, with cynical frankness, Mussolini sent a telegram of congratulations to Franco:

While the brave Legionnaires (Italian) enter Santander in intimate collaboration with the nationalist (Francoist) troops, obtaining in the name of Western civilization one of the most brilliant [sic] *victories of the war against Asiatic barbarity* [sic], *I am gratified to be able to testify to your Excellency my pride at having these troops under my command and my sincere admiration of their fearlessness and capacity in realizing such a rapid* [sic] *victory.*

If even this could not shake the faith of the world that "nonintervention" was prospering, the reply of Franco might have aroused a mild suspicion:

I am particularly proud that Italian Legionnaires have during the ten days' fighting contributed mightily to the splendid victory of Santander, and that their contribution received coveted recognition in your telegram. This brotherhood of arms guarantees the final victory, which will liberate Spain from any menace to our common civilization.

In addition to emphasizing the predominance of the part of Fascist Italy in the victory, Mussolini announced the names of the ten Italian Generals who had led the army on Santander.

7

In spite of all this, the Nonintervention Committee, in a desperate effort to continue the game of make-believe, literally begged Mussolini and Hitler to carry on the mockery. A new plan to revive the dead and putrid corpse was then prepared, *and it was submitted first to the author of the telegram and the commander of the ten generals for his approval.*

Quite soon, England and France learned what Franco meant by the liberation of the Mediterranean, since our "common civilization" was now menaced by piracy on the sea, with mysterious submarines attacking merchant ships all the way from Turkey to Barcelona. They were not Franco submarines. That they were German and Italian was perfectly understood. They proposed to starve loyalist Spain. But the Chamberlain government dared not be unmindful of British trade and the sinking of British ships. And there was something else involved—the mastery of the famous sea.

Hastily, a conference of all the Mediterranean powers was called, and while Italy would not attend without Germany, which was not invited because not a Mediterranean country, the other nations sat down at Nyon and agreed to drastic action. War vessels were to patrol the sea and sink any submarine attacking any ship not Spanish, or any that refused to show its colors. This served for a while. But the bombing of ships continued until a British ship was sent to the bottom with its crew.

8

But on the international front, Mussolini continued his triumphant march. A new lease on life was given the odorous Nonintervention Committee to make sure no arms or ammunition reached the loyalists. In a great speech at Valencia, Azaña quite properly denounced it as "the most brazen invention in the interest of the rebels since the war began," and as having been conceived, *as it was*, to tie the hands of the League of Nations.

This, from Azaña:

So the London Nonintervention Committee, substitute for the League of Nations, is really not substituting or replacing it, but it is drugging and suppressing it. And though the Nonintervention Committee was set up so that no one could intervene in the Spanish conflict, the only nonintervention this committee has secured has been the nonintervention of the League of Nations.

And now the League was about to meet, and something was required to paralyze its arms. Dr. Juan Negrín, by the rule of rotation, presided over the opening meeting, when his speech, in perfect taste, and without a reference to the war in Spain, made a deep impression. The next day he presented the case for Spain before the Assembly, setting forth a procession of damning facts no one dared deny. And if the facts were facts, it was obligatory on the League to act. But Negrín was heard in an embarrassed silence. More vehemently than Negrín, Del Vayo followed, making the most of the exchange of telegrams between Mussolini and Franco and ending by saying that "the word 'aggression' will be written in indelible letters on the four walls of this Assembly."

There was no possible escape now from the admission of an aggression of outside forces against Spain. The duty of the Assembly was unmistakable. That night the statesmen of the world of make-believe were in a huddle, seeking some way to say it without disturbing the complacency of the aggressor nations. Carefully refraining from mentioning Germany or Italy, a compromise proclaimed the presence of "battalions" of "foreign troops" in Spain. But the resolution did admit that "nonintervention" had been a failure and did declare it would have to be abandoned unless foreign troops were withdrawn.

To head off further action by the League, another committee hastily was formed to deal with the withdrawal of foreign troops. Britain, France, and Italy would attend to that. Italy had not as yet accepted membership. And powerful forces were begging the League to take no action that might "embarrass" the nonactive committee on paper. "Don't rock the boat," they cooed. But even these bloodless, teethless resolutions, calling for a unanimous vote, were vetoed *by Albania and Portugal.*

Thus, with infinite relief, the conspirators, conniving knowingly with the Fascist powers, stripped the League of Nations of the last vestige of respectability. The League adjourned. And then, with tongue in cheek, Italy demanded that the withdrawal plan be referred back to the cherished Nonintervention Committee which the Assembly of the League had just declared a failure.

Thus, with Franco's great offensive being prepared, Spain had to face its fight for life against the Fascist powers still deprived of the right to buy arms and ammunition.

9

In October, 1937, I was told, long in advance, of the decision to move the government to Barcelona. With the rebel offensive advertised for the Aragon front, the psychological effect of the move seemed doubtful to me. I had observed that Catalonia had been very much self-contained and had not co-operated to the extent of its capacity in the defense of the regime elsewhere. Conscious of the slacking of the industrial segment of the population, I now heard of its sabotaging of war activities. The factories that could, under pressure, produce war material were turning out very little. With Spaniards hungry or starving, foodstuff was being sold in France, and the money banked there so it could be of no use to the regime fighting for democracy. I was told that the government was going to Barcelona to direct war activities on the spot, to make factories forge the instruments of war, and to stop the sale of foodstuff across the border. Thus, Thanksgiving Day found the road to Barcelona congested with motorcars and trucks moving the offices and officials to the new temporary capital. A year before, to the day, the move had been made from Madrid to Valencia.

The effect at first was as I had foreseen. The rebel and Fascist press fairly screamed that the war was over and the "flight" of the loyalist government prepared. But this soon dwindled to a murmur, and then to silence.

10

Slowly the rebels and their alien allies were pushing toward Gijón, meeting the desperate resistance of the fierce Asturian mountaineers. It was a hopeless struggle, since the world had organized to deny the democracy of Spain the right to buy arms to defend itself against Fascism. With all hope gone, there was a frenzied effort to escape by sea. The harbor, another Dunkirk, was crowded with boats of every description, packed with soldiers, civilians, women, children. Hundreds were in wretched trawlers. Rebel planes circled above them, sinking some boats with their human cargo. Even when they reached the open sea they were pursued by air, and bombed. They who escaped the bombs drifted into one of the wildest storms that ever lashed the angry waters of Biscay. Observing a French ship sinking in the storm, one of the refugee boats from Gijón heroically went back to rescue the crew.

The taking of Gijón was wildly celebrated in Franco territory, but the troops, rebels, Italians, and Moors, marched into a dead city. A few spectators looked on grimly and in silence. The Moors swaggered in the streets. Out in the mountains a few Asturian miners prepared to continue the fighting.

It was at this time that Lloyd George, with undiminished fire, thundered in the House of Commons:

Bilbao, Santander, the Asturias were all defended by as brave men as ever went into battle—traditionally so, historically so, and racially so. But they had no munitions; they had no guns. Who is responsible for that? Nonintervention. Who is responsible for keeping nonintervention alive? His Majesty's Government. If democracy is defeated in this battle [that of the Aragon front], if Fascism is triumphant, His Majesty's Government can claim the victory for themselves.

Meanwhile, with Neville Chamberlain wooing Mussolini with unmaidenly ardor, Italian planes were bombing neutral shipping, and then, twelve miles from Barcelona, Italian planes sank the British ship *Jean Weems*. At that very hour the Chamberlain government was about to accord recognition to the Fascist government through "an exchange of consular and diplomatic agents." Fearful of the effect on public opinion, Chamberlain had an announcement carefully prepared for home consumption, to the effect that no form of recognition was implied. The identical announcement was to be released at the same moment by the Franco government. The British gave their statement to the press, and then Mr. Chamberlain learned something about the Fascist technique, for Salamanca in its release added that "this is better than the recognition of belligerent rights, since it is a recognition of sovereignty"—as indeed it was intended to be. Soon the Duke of Alba would be going in and out of the Foreign Office in London on official business and receiving more courtesy and consideration than that accorded to the accredited ambassador of the Spanish Republic. When pressed in the Commons whether Alba had the usual diplomatic immunity and privileges, ministers of the Crown persisted in a blunt denial, but soon the cat was out of the bag when a functionary of the Foreign Office (T. H. Glasse) asked the L. C. C. Motor License Department to excuse the secretary of the Duke of Alba from taking the examination for a driver's license, with the explanation that "the Duke of Alba and his staff are regarded *officially* as diplomats in all but name, and His Majesty's Government have agreed to their receiving privileges and facilities on the same scale as members of the conventional diplomatic missions in London" (London *News-Chronicle*, March 30, 1938).

His Majesty's Government clearly had been pulling the leg of His Majesty's parliamentarians in the House of Commons.

11

I followed the British negotiations with Dr. Sangroniz, chief of Franco's diplomatic cabinet, with interest, convinced that an effort would be made to force the United States into a similar recognition. The verification came speedily when, after the fight was over in Bilbao, I proposed sending Consul Chapman back, and asked a *salvoconducto* from the military authorities. After many days of silence I was informed that the reopening of the consulate in Bilbao depended on our agreeing to "an exchange of diplomatic and consular agents." I reported to Washington that I was unalterably opposed to a camouflaged recognition of the Fascist regime. Soon a nice young man, known to me in Madrid, and now with Franco's diplomatic office, came to my house to complain that we were "interfering with the work of Franco's consul in New York," and to demand that Franco's agent in the United States, whom he called "ambassador," should have the same official access to the Secretary of State as that accorded to the ambassador of the Spanish Republic. More, this agent must be permitted to pass on the cargo of ships for Spain. My caller reached his climax with the threat of expelling all our consuls from Spain. I told him I should be sorry to see all our consuls expelled, and let it go at that.

Despairing of action from Sangroniz, we approached General Queipo de Llano through our consul in Seville for permission to reopen our consulate in Bilbao. He readily gave consent and sent telegraphic instructions to the military governor in the Bilbao district and the military commandant in Irún. Nothing happened. The officer in Irún admitted he had received the instructions of the general, but that the order had been received to admit no one without the consent of the diplomatic cabinet. At length, Chapman was summoned to the Nache Enea and informed that a *salvoconducto* was at his disposal to go to—*San Sebastián and back*. This, it was explained, was to permit a discussion with Sangroniz on a purely political matter which did not concern the consul, and I instructed Chapman not to cross the border. Thus matters stood, when, despairing of favorable action, Chapman sailed for America on home leave, never to see Bilbao again. The Bilbao consulate remained closed during the remainder of the war.

12

In November, 1937, seventeen months after the war began, an attempt was made to stampede the loyalists with noisy demonstrations of triumph from the Fascists. They were saying that the end of the fighting in the northern provinces released fifty thousand soldiers who could now move on Barcelona and Valencia; that the loyalist government was verging on collapse and was feverishly angling for peace terms; that the civilian population in loyalist territory was eager to surrender to the Germans, Italians, and Moors. Had I not heard, they asked me, that white sheets had been displayed from the windows in Madrid? I had heard nothing of the sort and I could guess the fate of the people who would display them.

Nothing happened except the appearance of a statement from the loyalist government that neither an armistice nor mediation would be tolerable so long as a single alien soldier was on Spanish soil.

It was at this time that Japan, having made her pro-Fascist alliance with Hitler and Mussolini, accorded recognition to Franco and moved to the position she was to assume soon afterward in the Second World War in the Axis' fight to exterminate democracy in Europe. When the announcement appeared in the press, the Japanese Minister came to see me the same day. At the beginning of the war he had astonished me by saying that since both the United States and Japan were remote from the struggle, he had been instructed to go along with me in decisions of the corps. I had no confidence in the integrity of the "instruction." However, as long as the corps had meetings, the Japanese Minister, who was a decent, likable chap, did go along with me. One day he came to say he would like to spend a week in France, since he had not been in Europe for years, but that he was afraid something might happen in his absence which would be embarrassing to him. Would I permit his secretary to contact me in his absence, and if I foresaw some development of importance, would I tell the secretary so he could send a warning? I agreed. So on the day of the announcement of the recognition of Franco, the little minister was greatly embarrassed when he called. He said on his "word of honor" that he had not received the slightest indication that any such action was in contemplation. He hoped I would accept his word on that since I had been decent to him. But he added that since the news was sent from Tokyo he was sure it was true. The Foreign Office in Tokyo did not always have the confidence of the military crowd. I was convinced of the minister's sincerity and of his embarrassment. That was my last meeting with him.

Chapter XXV

The Axis Massacre in Barcelona

WITH everyone on tiptoe for Franco's two-months' overdue offensive, strange things were happening in France, where stores of secreted arms were being discovered by the police. It was suspected that these arms, of German and Italian origin, were for the use of the Fascist fifth column in France, which ultimately was to toss that country onto the bayonets of their Nazi allies. My contact with this hunt for arms and traitors was slight, but interesting. I was driving Peggy Grippenberg, English wife of the Finnish Minister in London, to the gardens of Rostand, the poet and dramatist, in Cambo. As we drove through the beautiful countryside I was amazed by the unusual number of gendarmes along the highway, and when we reached the outskirts of a village, we were stopped. Pepe identified us, and we were waved on; but in another village, when we turned a corner, we found heavy benches stretched as a barricade across the road. Officers appeared and explanations were made. With her infectious laugh, Peggy asked who was being sought. "That," said the young officer with a smile, "is a secret." In another village police cars formed a barricade, and in one village we saw gendarmes carefully inspecting the interior of a huge lorry.

Rostand's garden was most beautiful in the autumn light, and as we were curiously surveying the house, the custodian, attracted by Peggy's smile, invited us to inspect the interior. When finally she introduced me as the American Ambassador, the old man kindled. "The Germans and Italians are getting their noses up," he said. "The great Republic must jerk their noses down"—and he illustrated by giving his own nose a vigorous jerk. And then, to my amusement, because of my English companion, he added sourly: "And the English are almost as bad"—for Chamberlain was not an idol of the French masses.

So that was the feeling of the common folk in France, as I had surmised.

2

In mid-November, 1937, Eddie Neal, the brilliant correspondent of the Associated Press, just back from the Aragon front, sat in my house and told me why Franco would win within six months. Five armies had been concentrated on that front, with an unprecedented store of ammunition and with an enormous accession of the newest and deadliest bombing planes from Germany and Italy, along with new German guns. "It is not merely that these planes are the very latest," he said, "for the Germans and Italians are sending in the very cream of their aviators, mostly officers. Many of the Italians I had seen and known in Abyssinia."

But days passed and Franco did not stir. The psychological effect of this mysterious pause was disastrous on both sides. His own followers were openly critical, but the prolonged inactivity was more disastrous to the loyalists; since, not knowing where Franco planned to strike, they did not know where to brace themselves. It was therefore determined to take the offensive, to force the fighting, and to choose the ground. Thus they would compel Franco to use up great stores of the ammunition he had assembled and disorganize his plans for the "great offensive."

The loyalists struck at Teruel, held by Franco from the beginning of the war. Since the defenders had had a full year to prepare their defense, the loyalists had little expectation of taking the town, which had but little military value. The real purpose was to cut the road between the army at Teruel and Saragossa. The battle began in a heavy snowstorm in the latter part of December in zero weather, and the new loyalist army fought like tigers in the snowdrifts, with a flaming, awe-inspiring enthusiasm that reached the heights of heroism. The roads were three feet deep in snow, and hundreds of the men wore moccasins as they pressed on, dragging their artillery with them. With an almost superhuman valor they cut their way through the rebel lines, stormed the heights about, and surrounded the town. Ernest Hemingway, the novelist, followed close behind, throwing himself on his stomach at intervals to escape sharpshooters, and he lived to write a graphic description of one of the most audacious offensives of the war. With the fall of the town inevitable, ten prisoners were sent into the city to announce that all civilians who wished could leave in safety the next morning between seven and nine. They were to march out in groups of twenty-five, with each detachment bearing a white flag.

Meanwhile, the startled Franco was hurrying reinforcements from Saragossa under command of the best of his generals, but it was of no avail. The loyalists fought their way into the city, where some of the rebel army and civil leaders had taken refuge in a seminary, in a bank, and in the palace.

With the arrival of the Moors, the Legionnaires, and the Requetés, the rebels were making some progress, which was so absurdly exaggerated that on New Year's Eve the rebel radios announced the recapture of the town, and the rebel supporters in Seville and San Sebastián wildly celebrated. But Teruel was not to be retaken until weeks after the bloodiest fighting of the war.

While these premature celebrations were in progress, the loyalist troops, using hand grenades and dynamite, were storming the buildings in which the enemy had taken refuge, and one by one they fell. From the basement of the palace emerged women and children, emaciated, half starved, leaving behind babies starved to death. The living were fed and attended.

A week after the premature celebrations, the fight was at its fiercest. When the rebels attempted a surprise attack among the snowdrifts, the loyalists, with their machine-guns painted white, lay in wait until the enemy could be mowed down like wheat before the reaper. Franco, making little progress, was losing heavily in men, material, and prestige. Despairing of relief from him, unable longer to bear the agony of the starving, Colonel Rey, of the rebel army, negotiated a surrender. In this savage war, Prieto flashed the message to feed the hungry and to give surgical attention to the wounded. Soon Queipo de Llano was denouncing Colonel Rey as a "swine."

The primary object of the offensive had been served. The plans of Franco were momentarily postponed. Enormous stores of ammunition, long assembled, had been lost. The sacrifice of Franco's men had been appalling, and for weeks I was to hear from day to day of young men and boys I knew who had died at Teruel in Franco's army.

Meanwhile, as his men fought without success, ammunition, artillery, and tanks were being rushed to him from Germany and Italy, and Franco took a mean revenge on noncombatants by peppering Barcelona and Valencia with thousand-kilo bombs—a horrible slaughter of the innocent that was to be a mild prelude to the then unprecedented crime that was to follow.

At length, with the arrival of the new supplies of munitions, planes, tanks, and artillery, Teruel was finally retaken. Hundreds of planes rained high explosives on the defenders and machine-gunned them on the ground. More German and Italian planes were in action than at any one time in the First World War, and the loyalist army could not compete with this.

3

It was after the struggle at Teruel that Ernest Hemingway made me a hurried visit at Saint-Jean-de-Luz and verified the stories I had heard of his hectic life in Madrid. There, he was living dangerously but joyously, in the Florida Hotel, which was frequently being shelled, and he refused to move. He meandered about the city he loved as though nothing unusual was happening, visiting his old haunts, mingling familiarly with the soldiers, who admired him, visiting the front line from time to time. He had rooms in the sheltered quarter of the hotel where he was not directly exposed. Now and then a shell would demolish one room of the hotel, and with boyish glee, he would get a portion of the shell and scratch upon it: "Portion of the shell that destroyed room 36." And soon another shell would wreck another room, and then another, and soon his room was filled with fragments of shells. "Shell that destroyed room 47." "Portion of shell that destroyed room 37." He made a dud shell into a lamp shade for the room he called his "study." Into this strange room, with its sinister relics, crowded young writers, painters, journalists, soldiers on leave, and the room with its portions of shells rocked more frequently with laughter than with explosives.

4

We had been free from incidents involving the United States, but late in January, 1938, the *Nantucket Chief*, an American ship, under the American flag, was found forty miles out at sea and forced by Franco's destroyers to the Balearic Islands, a captive. Under instructions, I made a demand on General Franco for its immediate release in a letter addressed to him not as chief of state, and not signed by me as ambassador, since we had not accorded him recognition. I was positive, therefore, that it would be returned or ignored, and so warned Washington. Immediately after the letter went forth, through the courtesy of the Nache Enea, I learned that the captain had been removed from his ship and sent to prison to await trial on some charge not indicated. I followed at once, without instructions, with another letter demanding his immediate release.

Meanwhile, Franco's new government had begun to function, and Sr. Sangroniz, erstwhile chief of the diplomatic cabinet, was succeeded by General Jordana as Minister of State. As a former governor of Spanish Morocco, he had some experience in diplomacy. Within five days, a courier arrived with a courteously phrased note from Jordana announcing that orders had gone forth for the release of the ship and the captain, who "should by this time be on his way to rejoin his ship." Thus our first incident passed swiftly. I formed a very high opinion of Jordana.

But the British were not so fortunate. Scarcely had they agreed to the semi-recognition implied in the exchange of diplomatic and consular agents, when Italian bombing planes deliberately, and after repeated efforts, sank the British ship *Endymion* and killed several English seamen and a woman. There was no satisfactory answer to the British note demanding satisfaction, and within a few days another British ship was wrecked, and on the heels of that came the torpedoing of another British ship by a submarine, undoubtedly Italian.

These inconsiderate actions annoyed the Chamberlain government, and Mr. Eden told Franco that the end of British patience
had been reached, though this turned out to be hyperbole. Even
so, Mr. Eden's indignation was frowned upon and his refusal to
accept any more of Mussolini's promissory notes, after all the others
had been dishonored with a contemptuous shrug, caused some
distress among his pro-Franco colleagues. It was evident that Mr.
Eden's distaste for Mussolini's methods and political morals was
not relished by his chief. He had become an obstacle to the program
of "appeasement" which Chamberlain was offering to the Duce.
Italian Fascist papers were spewing forth vituperations on Eden's
head, and the word had gone forth from Rome to force him from
the government. Never in history, certainly never in English history,
had a more brazen demand been made by one country on another
for the dismissal of a foreign minister.

And Eden went!

5

I was prepared to see the arrogance of the rebels increase with
the accession of Chamberlain as Prime Minister, when he took over
the functions, if not the title, of Foreign Minister. At the time of his
elevation, an attaché of Franco's diplomatic cabinet said to me:
"Now that Chamberlain is in, we shall have it easier." And about
the same time a press correspondent, notoriously *persona grata* at
Franco's headquarters, said to me: "Now that Chamberlain is in
complete power, it will be easier for Franco." Certain it is that in
rebel territory the elevation of Chamberlain was looked upon as
equivalent to a major military victory, and soon the Nazi and
Fascist press, rejoicing over the withdrawal of Eden, was competing
in paying compliments to Chamberlain. It was when he proposed
to bear sweet gifts to Rome without exacting the withdrawal of
Italian troops from Spain, that Mr. Eden refused to play the
game of make-believe. The English democracy was shocked that
an Italian dictator had been able to bully the British government
into what amounted to the dismissal of the most popular of the
ministers. The Liberal, Labor, and independent press rumbled and
roared, and in the Commons, Lloyd George thundered, Churchill
chided, Attlee and Sinclair protested, but the sodden supporters of

Chamberlain held fast. Scores of protest meetings roared their disgust, but Chamberlain, happy with his romance with the dictators, pledged openly to the extermination of democracy, was unmoved.

And then came Hitler's brutal rape of Austria.

And in Spain, Germany and Italy poured into rebel territory unprecedently large supplies of German artillery, antiaircraft guns, bombers of the latest type, and Italian planes, artillery, and tanks; and high officers of the general staffs of Hitler and Mussolini assumed their roles in the direction of Franco's great offensive in Aragon—without attracting the attention of the Nonintervention Committee, which had never been more free of curiosity.

6

And then, in early March, 1938, a miracle. The rebel fleet, the *Baleares*, the *Canarías*, and the *Cervantes*, was sighted by the fleet of the loyalist navy, and in the engagement that followed, Franco's flagship, the *Baleares*, was sunk. Two weeks later, in Barcelona, Franco took his revenge in the most bestial bombing of a white noncombatant population in the history of the world up until then. It was a Nazi rehearsal for the Second World War.

The horror began on the night of March 16, 1938, and without warning. The bombers, German and Italian aviators, in German and Italian planes of the deadliest variety, could besplatter the pavements of the city of almost two million people with the blood of their victims within fifteen minutes after leaving their base at Palma de Mallorca. They flew at an enormous height, unseen, unannounced, until the death-dealing explosives struck the city.

It was ten o'clock at night. Six Hydro-Heinkel planes flew over the city at a speed of eighty miles an hour, at a height of four hundred meters, dropping bombs; and at one-seventeen A.M. six more came and repeated the bloody performance. And then, at seven-forty A.M. six Savoie-Marchelliti bombers, sent by Mussolini, unloaded bombs of great size; and the Italian planes appeared again at ten-twenty-five with nine-thousand-kilogram bombs.

The second night, at ten-seventeen the Heinkels returned for another indiscriminate slaughter; and at one-fourteen A.M. they came again. At six-fifty-nine A.M. Mussolini's planes had their turn at experimentation, and again at eight-thirty A.M. Then, at one-fifteen, the Junker planes from Hitler appeared for their tryout and they repeated the performance at three P.M.

This detailed information came to me from General Fuqua, my military attaché, who was on the spot.

That a city of nearly two million people was being used as a laboratory for testing new and deadly weapons of destruction was evident. A new type of explosive was being tried. It was described to me by Fuqua as insignificant in size, weighing no more than from fifty to a hundred kilos. It had little power of penetration, but its explosive and expansive force was tremendous. The effect was uncanny. General Fuqua was in the consulate in the Plaza de Cataluña, talking at a telephone on the wall close by a window looking out on the plaza when the planes appeared. Continuing his conversation, he stepped in front of the window to observe the people running in the street, when suddenly, with a thunderous explosion, the window literally crumbled, covering him with powdered glass, and without so much as scratching him, but he found himself in the middle of the room upon the floor.

Nothing on such an appalling scale involving the white race had ever been known before. The bombs were not aimed at military objectives. They were dropped designedly in the center, the most populous section, of the city, where people were dining, walking, sleeping in their beds. When these raids ended, nine hundred men, women, and children were mangled corpses, blown in many cases to bits, disemboweled. Forty-eight buildings were wrecked and seventy-five were partially destroyed.

After each bombing, the hospital corps, assisted by volunteers, rushed into the streets carrying baskets into which they could cast chunks of dismembered bodies, fragments of human flesh, parts of arms, legs, heads. General Fuqua passed a sidewalk café where many had been blown to bits and the waiters were sweeping up small pieces of bodies into containers. He walked gingerly lest he step on a baby's hand. He saw a shoe with the ankle of a woman protruding. The correspondent of the London *Express* passed another outdoor restaurant where the sidewalk was covered with sticky human blood. Many saw a bus, filled with noncombatants, mostly women and children, stop, in horror, as a bomb fell some distance in front of it, and a moment later another bomb made a clean hit on the bus, and the women and children were mere fragments of human flesh smeared on the pavement.

On the sidewalks, bodies, not entirely dismembered, were laid out, one after another, for a long distance—women and children of eight and nine, their eyes still open, staring with an expression of horror. Men feverishly were digging in the ruins of wrecked buildings for the dead and wounded. A few incendiary bombs were dropped, and here and there fires were blazing.

The monstrosity of this bestial crime momentarily stunned the civilized world, and Chamberlain, whose policy had so righteously denied the government the right to buy antiaircraft guns for the protection of the people, expressed himself as "horrified and disgusted." I had no doubt at the time that the Axis was in training for London and Warsaw—*as we now know it was.*

The chief sponsors of the "nonintervention" sham now protested in the name of humanity, and Franco was forced to take cognizance. Barcelona, thereafter, for a while, would be given a respite, but the bombers transferred their sadistic activities to Tarragona and small towns and villages along the coast, where noncombatants could be mangled in the absence of press correspondents.

A few weeks later, speaking in Free Trade Hall in Manchester, Winston Churchill said:

The agony of the civil war continues. If it had been only a Spanish dispute sustained by Spaniards, we could have been able to look away from the horrors. But the shameless interference of the totalitarian powers, with organized troops and mountainous armaments under the mask of nonintervention, has given its battles greater bitterness and a significance which expands beyond the Spanish peninsula.

7

From early November, Franco had been piling up the greatest hoard of war material ever seen in Spain, and German and Italian ships were steaming into rebel harbors unloading more. Troops were being concentrated—Italian divisions, Moorish cavalry, legionnaires. High officers of the German and Italian staffs had arrived and were busy with the strategy for the "great offensive," for they were to have direction to a large degree. In Rome, Mussolini and Ciano were following the preparations avidly. The loyalist offensive in Teruel had postponed Franco's plans, but only for a little while, since material was arriving while the fighting was in progress around that city. At length, Franco was ready.

He began by breaking through the loyalist lines near Huesca; and then began the march to the sea over a hundred-and-fifty-mile front from the Pyrenees to the northern corner of the maritime province of Castellón. The loyalist army was not prepared or concentrated. The ground was mostly level, and, as the Fascists advanced, announcing their approach with an intensive bombardment of heavy artillery, and with their droves of bombing planes, the broken segments of the loyalist army in the little towns were hopelessly outmatched, and inevitably gave way. There were few battles. On March 27, 1938, the rebels, with their alien allies, crossed the Catalan frontier, with Lérida, the second city in the province, as their objective. Here the loyalists, short of guns, made a heroic stand, and for a while they held the enemy with their bodies, but ultimately gave way.

It was now believed that the Catalans would surrender. The press, the foreign press, which monotonously had announced the end of the war after every loyalist reverse, began to treat the struggle as at an end. In Rome and Milan, the Italian press was beating the tom-toms loudly, boasting of the prowess of the Italian army on Spanish soil. The Nonintervention Committee, dead or drugged, was silent. During the three previous months, when arms, ammunition, and men were being poured in from Italy and Germany, it had considerately not functioned. No meeting had been held—and, without a meeting, no embarrassing questions could be asked. Even the subcommittee did not meet after February 3. There was to be no sentimental interference with the preparations for the great offensive which Mr. Chamberlain unquestionably hoped would give the victory to the totalitarians. He was at this time exchanging cordial amenities with Mussolini. It was given out in the press that the ideas of the English democracy and the Italian Fascists were in such complete accord that the Anglo-Italian pact would be ready for signing by Easter, and Franco was announcing that he would celebrate the sacred day in Barcelona. Of course, the press said the pact would not go into effect until Mussolini withdrew his army from Spain; but if, by Easter, Franco would be in Barcelona, the war would be won for Fascism, and, with no further need for the Italian troops, they could be sent home without hurting the Fascist prospects or Mussolini's pride. It was a time of high hopes for the Axis.

But Easter came, and while the pact was ready, the war went on. In the pact Chamberlain agreed to the Italian conquest of Abyssinia when the Italian troops had been withdrawn from Spain —*after the Fascist victory*. The mass mind was a bit confused over the paeans of triumph, since it had assumed that the Nonintervention Committee was insisting on the immediate honoring by Hitler and Mussolini of their pledged word not to intervene in Spain *during the war*. But the mass mind was sadly lacking in the finesse of international diplomacy in those shoddy times.

8

The war went on. Reinforcements were rushed from Barcelona to the battle front, and, with the stiffening of resistance, the holiday march was over for a time. But loyalist Spain was cut in two.

The government remained in Barcelona. Having anticipated the march to the sea, it announced that General Miaja, defender of Madrid, would be in absolute command in all the territory of loyalist Spain south of Catalonia, and that the struggle would go on, with no surrender. The morale of the loyalist troops did not lower, despite inspired reports to the contrary. I frequently saw friends from among Franco's followers across the border, and all expressed amazement that the morale of the loyalists had not noticeably suffered.

Two things had stiffened Catalan resistance. After the bestial slaughter in Barcelona, thousands, previously lethargic, became active. Franco's announcement on crossing the provincial border that he would deprive the Catalans of their autonomous rights and outlaw their language was a major victory for the loyalists. It was the kind of blunder impossible from anyone with political mind and judgment.

9

At this juncture a reorganization of the government was effected through the retirement of Prieto from the Ministry of Defense and the assumption of the post by Juan Negrín. I had great admiration for Prieto and his achievements, but military men with whom I talked in Saint-Jean-de-Luz took it for granted that the success of the enemy in reaching the sea had made Prieto's replacement inevitable. "In the position of War Minister there must be victories," they said. To the general public at the time the reaction of Prieto was unknown, and I shared the ignorance. When at this time I saw Del Vayo in Paris I inquired about the status of Prieto. The minister spoke in terms of admiration of Prieto and explained his replacement on the ground that he had been overworked and living on his nerves, and that the march to the sea had shaken his morale. Del Vayo had seen him that day in Paris and had his assurance that he would return to Barcelona—as he did. A similar explanation was given me by Negrín in New York after the war was over. He said that Prieto's pessimism was having a bad effect on the morale of the fighting forces. I did not know until much later, when I had the opportunity to read the correspondence between Prieto and Negrín when they were both in Mexico, that a deep wound had been inflicted and a schism created. During the remainder of the war these two outstanding socialists were to meet but four times. In the month of his retirement, when Prieto was living at Esplugas, Negrín visited him, and their last meeting was at Comprondon, where Negrín was staying, when Prieto informed him that he had accepted the designation by Azaña to represent Spain at the inauguration of Aguirre Cerda as President of Chile. He said he went with the thought of interesting the Spanish-American republics in a plan of mediation. We have in the correspondence, Prieto's version of what happened: "You offered some objections to the idea, but they were not enough to make me abandon it." Negrín's version was somewhat different: "I raised no objections to your idea that the South American countries might make an effort toward mediation. I merely expressed the little faith I had in the success of such an effort, a sentiment you shared with me. The only condition I imposed was that if anything slipped

out I would disavow it, and that your proposal must assume the
nature of a personal suggestion."

This was the last meeting between these two leaders four months
before the end of the war. The farewell is described by Prieto in a
letter to Negrín. As Prieto was starting to his car "in the presence
of your guests, the carabineros, the chauffeur, and the men who
formed the escort, you asked me to embrace you, and I did not refuse. On the contrary, I embraced you with great emotion, for I
was embracing a man who, as I left Spain with my heart heavy
with dark forebodings, remained there under the weight of a
crushing responsibility—a man who, free from all restrictions, held
the destiny of the country in his hands."

On all of this, history will pass judgment. It should do justice to
both, for both deserve it. Their disagreement was due in part to
temperamental differences, and to the fact that while one had
abandoned hope of victory, the other had not.

10

In truth, when the Western democracies abandoned the Spanish
democracy and concentrated on efforts to prevent the government
they recognized as the legal constitutional regime from getting
any means of defense, Azaña, Prieto, and others could see no possibility of victory.

Even this late, it was evident that the Nonintervention Committee had to tighten its hold on the arms of the Spanish government if the Fascist powers were to prevail soon, according to the
program of "appeasement."

Thus, in her darkest hour, the government reiterated its program and purpose. Thus the Spanish democracy entered upon a
new phase in its Homeric struggle for the preservation of democratic institutions—*the only fight being made for democracy any place in
Europe, and it was to fight alone, worse than deserted by those who should
have been its friends.*

Chapter XXVI

The Spirit of Munich over Spain

W HEN Castellón was taken after a gallant defense, the confidence of the rebels and their alien allies rose as they moved
toward Sagunto with the promise to take it by July 18, 1938, and
to sweep thence down the straight road and take Valencia by
September. It was important to be there by that time since the rice
crop would be ready. My own faith in the ability of the loyalists to
withstand the overwhelming advantage of the enemy in German
and Italian artillery and planes had almost vanished. But the resistance stiffened, the loyalists fought back with cold, calculating
fury, and their morale miraculously rose. I was told by Del Vayo
that the tactics were to hold every inch of ground as long as
humanly possible and then to fall back a very short distance on new
lines, previously prepared, and take a stand and fight like tigers.
The rebels were advancing at this moment at a crawl and with
terrible losses.

In late May, 1938, I saw Álvarez del Vayo, Minister of Foreign
Affairs, in Paris at a little hotel on the Left Bank. He radiated
energy, confidence, enthusiasm. Sitting on the edge of his chair and
leaning forward, his pugnacious protruding chin thrust out, his
eyes kindling, he spoke vigorously in English with his peculiar
German accent. As usual he was in fighting mood. Knowing him
personally before he was minister, I plied him with impertinent

questions without fear of his resentment, and I am sure he replied with candor. True, he admitted, the time had been when stout Catalan resistance could not have been counted upon. But a great change had come over the mood of the Catalans. The barbarous massacre of women and children had aroused a fighting spirit. The foolish declaration of Franco that he proposed to deprive the Catalans of their autonomous rights and outlaw their language had converted secret enemies into supporters of the loyalists. The sense-less execution of Garrasco Formiura, famous Catalan writer on Catholic subjects, revered by his coreligionists, had changed the situation. Catalonia would fight, thought Del Vayo.

"But the division of your territory—" I began.

"That division was foreseen," he broke in, "and provisions have been made. The government can fight on for a year, and Madrid can eat that long."

With that, he handed me a document of great length, a list of all the food ships that had reached Barcelona, Tarragona, Valencia, Alicante, Murcia, Almería, and Cartagena from the first of De-cember to the first of May. "That, for Franco's paper blockade," he said grimly.

It was hard to resist the enthusiasm of Del Vayo. Then, too, at this moment, incidents behind Franco's lines were throwing a vivid light on dissensions in his camp. General Yagüe, commander of the Moors, and an ace officer in the field, had just scored the propaganda of Burgos and Salamanca. He ridiculed the reports from Salamanca that the loyalist soldiers were "cowardly" and "leaderless" as "a lie"; declared them "extraordinarily valorous"; and asked why, if they were cowardly and leaderless "we have been unable to win a decisive victory in almost two years." He was quoted as criticizing the imprisonment of thousands because mem-bers of a political party, not communists, or because they held union cards, and suggested their release. He created consternation among the great landowners by saying that on the termination of the war, the soldiers "fighting with us and for the Spain in which they have no stake to the extent of a peseta or an inch of ground" would ex-pect land from the great estates. Yagüe was said to have been summoned to the presence of Franco and sternly rebuked.

2

Meanwhile, day by day, the Italian planes were dropping bombs on neutral shipping in loyalist harbors, and the British suffered most. The fact that the planes flew low and machine-gunned the decks made the attacks deliberate. Mr. Chamberlain remained complacent until a British captain, in a sizzling protest to London, hotly declared that "the British flag now ranks lower than the Panama ensign." When Chamberlain told the Commons that the attacks could not have been deliberate, the masters of four British ships described his action, in a telegram to Lloyd George, as "a despicable attempt to shield illegal attacks by Italian aircraft." Soon British feeling was running high, and Chamberlain's party was growing restive. And so protests were made to Franco by Sir Robert Hodgson in Burgos, but these were being utterly ignored. Crowded into a corner by indignant members of the Commons, Chamberlain finally admitted that the attacks had been deliberate, but, with nothing done about it, they continued and increased. By July, 1938, many British ships had been deliberately attacked and British seamen had been killed. While these outrages were at their worst, Chamberlain retired to Hampshire for the fishing, and Halifax, with the title of Foreign Minister, took refuge from the press in his Yorkshire country house. But after the parliamentary recess, Chamberlain admitted in the Commons the deliberate bombing, the sinking of ships, the killing of seamen, with the astounding conclusion that nothing would, or could, be done about it. His statement did not reflect the slightest feeling against the alien bombers, but he contemptuously dismissed the British seamen as "profiteers." Would he permit the Spanish government to buy antiaircraft guns to protect British seamen, if not Spanish lives? he was asked. When he replied that that would be "intervention," there were cries of "shame." Then, in a full-dress debate, a few days later, he reiterated what he had said before and was attacked with a violence seldom aimed at a Prime Minister. He sat in silence under the attacks. No one of his own party raised a voice to defend him.

But the Fascist press of Berlin and Rome glowed with tributes. I wondered if my judgment of Chamberlain was one of prejudice until Lord Robert Cecil, whose prestige as statesman and man of moral worth was universal, turned back the whip of the Premier's party in the House of Lords, on the ground that, as an Englishman, he no longer could simulate any sympathy with Chamberlain's policy. The letter was all the more scathing, coming from one noted for a nice moderation of language. It took sharp issue with Chamberlain on the bombing of ships. That policy, he wrote, was "indefensible." The ships were acting "lawfully," having on board goods they were entitled to carry "under orders given them by the British government." They were attacked "deliberately," and the British seamen killed were "murdered." The sending of mild notes was futility itself.

"I do not recall," wrote Cecil, "an incident in British history at all comparable. I do not believe that any other British minister has ever made a speech like that of Mr. Chamberlain's. It seems to me inconsistent with British honor and international morality."

Thus wrote the descendant of the Prime Minister of Elizabeth who laid the foundation for the greatness and glory of the British Empire.

For a moment, these barbs of contempt seemed to have penetrated. Sir Robert Hodgson was instructed to demand from Burgos an immediate reply to the protests and personally to deliver it in London. When the wholly contemptuous reply was received at Whitehall, Sir Robert was held in London so long that Burgos had reason to wonder if she had gone too far. But she was not permitted to suffer long. Sir Robert went back to Burgos as though nothing had happened, and Burgos smiled behind her fan. No further fears need be felt about the bombing of British ships.

Besides, parliament had recessed for three months.

3

Thus encouraged, the Italian bombers intensified their ruthless bombing of civilians, specializing on small villages with no military significance along the coast. Members of the American consulate in Valencia, living in a near-by village, one day stood on the roof, and, with field glasses, watched the bombing of neighboring tiny towns where they knew not even a cartridge could be found. They saw the planes fly low, machine-gunning the peasants as they ran.

At length they were seen by one of the pilots who turned in their direction, and they hastily retreated to the basement.

It was at this time that the crime against the small town of Granollers, near Barcelona, was committed. The alien planes, driven from the great city and forced to drop their bombs before landing, dropped them on this peaceful town rather than waste them in the open fields. Besides, it was excellent practice. Forty houses were demolished and many people, mostly women and children, were killed or wounded. Sir John H. Leche, the British Chargé in Barcelona, hurried to the scene and reported to London that there had been no military objective. I knew Leche in Madrid and later, when he was ambassador in Chile, as an able and an honest man. And so, day after day, village after village suffered, with Christian civilization mute and acquiescent. Now and then, a mildly uttered protest, without mentioning Spain, lest it "irritate Mr. Hitler," was as effective as whistling against the wind.

4

Then came the second anniversary of the Fascist rebellion.

Franco decorated Field Marshal Goering, whose government was persecuting German Catholics and who, later, was to be condemned to the rope at Nuremberg; and the order of Isabella the Catholic was given to Count Ciano, whose planes were slaughtering Spanish women and children.

But the day was not without its shadows for Franco. The boast that Sagunto would be taken on the day announced had not been redeemed. Azaña made a powerful speech, but the democratic press outside published but brief extracts. Sir Archibald Sinclair, leader of the Liberal party in the House of Commons, telegraphed Barcelona that the war had become "a struggle between ill-armed, ill-equipped, and ill-fed masses of the Spanish people against the German and Italian invaders, who spread destruction on their cities from the air and seek to terrorize them by the cruelty and ferocity of their methods of warfare."

It was at this time I again saw Del Vayo in Paris. He had lost none of his buoyancy and confidence. When I was with him, a telegram was delivered to him from the Spanish Embassy announcing that during the day six desperate attacks by the enemy had been repulsed on the Sagunto front. He read it aloud and smiled. Then resumed the conversation.

5

Meanwhile, Mussolini was demanding that the unconditional withdrawal of the Italian troops be waived, and the Anglo-Italian pact be put into immediate operation. The prestige of Chamberlain's agreement was sadly tarnished. And so the Nonintervention Committee, wrapped in its Rip Van Winkle sleep, aroused itself and yawningly resumed its consideration of the withdrawal plan and finally evolved a scheme that was highly dishonorable. Under this plan, the Moors, furnished by a foreign potentate, became "Spaniards"—for was not Isabella long dead? The German and Italian planes, tanks, artillery, could remain in the service of Franco. Every loyalist port would be rigidly guarded, but the rebel ports would not be spied upon by the Nonintervention Committee. With some ironic comments, Del Vayo actually accepted this offensively pro-Fascist plan.

Even so, Franco distressed his friends and supporters of the committee by taking no notice for weeks, despite Sir Robert Hodgson's pleas for that much consideration. Franco could well afford to stand still. In the midst of the desperate struggle for Sagunto, had not Chamberlain brought pressure on Daladier and Bonnet in London rigidly to close the French frontier to the Spanish government while Franco waited? With the loyalists thus cut off, the Italian liner *Firenzo* was carrying Italian reinforcements and material to Franco and the Axis troops.

6

Meanwhile, in Franco territory—

Gil Robles, long an exile in Portugal, ventured back to his house in Salamanca to be greeted with a deadly fusillade from the Fascist press and to be told that he was "separated from Spain by history, which recalls to us his deceptions, his falsifications, his lack of political dignity." The charge was made that he had been seen driving into the country in a magnificent car to meet conspirators against the Fascist group who favored the restoration of the monarchy. He hurried back to Portugal. In this alleged fight for the church, the head of the church party was not wanted. He wrote bitterly to General Jordana that these attacks could have been made only at the instigation of the Franco government. He was a monarchist, not a Fascist, and that put him beyond the pale.

In Lisbon, Lerroux, living in a villa now, was seen driving about with a flower in his lapel and a big cigar in his mouth, enjoying the fruits of virtue.

In Barcelona, José Juan Roca, former Minister of State, and chief lieutenant of Lerroux, was permitted by the loyalists to die peacefully in his bed.

And amidst the shifting scenes, the most thoughtful were observing that the war designed as a quick military rebellion was developing into a Nazi revolution, leaving disturbing doubts as to the security of property, and even the fortunes of the church.

7

The fight for Sagunto was being stubbornly contested. Despite their mechanical advantage, the rebels moved slowly, and for days they did not move at all.

On the morning of July 24, 1938, Dr. Negrin called a war council, with four ministers and the highest military officers. He told them the situation on the Levant was critical, and, without some act of desperate daring, both Sagunto and Valencia were lost. The only hope, he said, was in an attack on the enemy at some given point that would force the withdrawal of a part of the Fascist army from the Levant to give the army of General Menéndez, which had been fighting continuously for three months, time to recuperate. Also to bring stronger defenses around Valencia. The plan he submitted contemplated an attempt to cross the Ebro River. The difficulties were grave, but there was no other way. He then stepped aside to permit General Rojo to give a full explanation of the plan from a map on the table. The general made it clear that the plan was one of desperation.

And so, on that very night, the plan was carried out. Under the cover of darkness, the loyalist army crossed the Ebro in rowboats and over pontoon bridges, many in their enthusiasm swimming the river. They broke through the rebel lines at many points and on a wide front, and swept speedily on to within the shadow of Gandesa, advancing over a territory of two hundred square miles. Their performance was the epic of the war.

Thus threatened in the rear, Franco had to abandon his attempt on Sagunto to transfer his planes, tanks, and artillery to meet the new danger. He still was hurrying reinforcements to the Ebro front when the loyalists launched a new offensive against Teruel, and then a third on the Segre, where they crossed the river under heavy fire and took war material and prisoners.

The prestige of Franco began to dim. It was at this critical juncture in his affairs that Franco finally replied to the Nonintervention Committee, with stipulations so absurd as to amount to a curt rejection. That the reply first was submitted to Hitler and Mussolini for approval there can be no doubt. He asked belligerent rights before withdrawal; the immediate withdrawal of ten thousand foreigners from each side, without regard to the proportionate number, which would have left the rebels with an enormous advantage; the rigid guarding of the French frontier, and no interference in rebel ports—such the modest proposal.

The Nonintervention Committee put its wrath in a refrigerator, and weeks passed without a whisper or a move from it, until Del Vayo indignantly demanded that the committee meet and consider the replies. Until then, there was no outward evidence that Franco's reply had been received. More Italian reinforcements were entering Spain, and ships were unloading war material in Algeciras, which the committee had not proposed to guard. But a meeting of the committee would have been embarrassing. Prying questions, to which there could be no answer that honest men could understand, were all too likely. So nothing was done at all.

And just then, at a meeting of the League of Nations, Dr. Negrin tossed a bomb which utterly demolished the whole superstructure of propaganda so carefully erected to fool the public. Voluntarily, he announced that, regardless of what Franco did, the Spanish government immediately would evacuate every foreigner in its fighting forces. *He asked the League to send a commission to supervise the withdrawal and to certify the fact to the world.*

Portugal was indignant. What was the Nonintervention Committee for? Lord Plymouth, the chairman, with dignified reticence, restrained any possible impulse to praise the government for its decision. In the end, the Council of the League sent a commission to Barcelona. The less noise, the better; too much publicity would call attention to the relative dependence of the two sides on foreign aid.

8

In the late autumn of 1938 Lady Austen Chamberlain, notoriously partial to Mussolini, made a triumphant tour through rebel territory, hailed as a political figure, with her strangely timed visit interpreted as further proof of the adherence of the Chamberlain government to the Fascist cause in Spain. Certainly the Fascist press in Spain, which I followed daily, was warm in praise of her as "one of us." This might have been dismissed as the irresponsible vaporings of an imaginary reporter, but when in Bilbao she was given a public reception and banquet and the Fascist press reported that she was presented with gifts wrapped in the rebel and Fascist colors, I observed considerable embarrassment at the British Embassy in Saint-Jean-de-Luz. She was given an official welcome, as though she really were the official representative of the Empire, in Burgos. Press correspondents making inquiry at the British Embassy were assured that nothing was known of her presence in Spain, though the London *Times* carried daily reports of her triumphant progress. When she emerged at Hendaye, a correspondent, having been told that she had gone to Spain "to get the truth," asked if she was planning also to visit loyalist territory. She snapped furiously: "Why should I?"

9

The number of foreigners appearing in rebel Spain under the ciceronage of the Fascists was becoming impressive. One afternoon a friend of mine, distinguished as former editor of a leading magazine, who had been traveling in rebel territory with a former governor general of the Philippines, called at the villa. I had observed in the press that they had been enthusiastically acclaimed by the Fascist papers. My friend explained that since there was "so much confusion in America as to the war," he had made the journey to get "the exact truth." He volunteered that all arrangements for the tour had been made "by the ambassador." A bit surprised, I asked if he meant Ambassador de los Ríos. This I asked in all seriousness. He looked at me reproachfully. "Oh, no, by Ambassador Cárdenas," he said, referring to Franco's agent. "Are you going directly from here to Barcelona?" I asked. He seemed as surprised and shocked as Lady Chamberlain. "Since you are seeking the exact truth," I added, "I thought it possible you would want to hear both sides." My friend returned home to publish a series of articles in leading papers that the "ambassador" who arranged the trip would have thought worth while. They stated as "an exact truth" that Franco had paid his way as he went and was under no financial obligations to Hitler or Mussolini. I was to remember this "exact truth" after the war in Spain when Sr. Cambó, representing Franco on the commission seeking loans from the despised democracies, frankly admitted that Franco owed Hitler a king's ransom in marks, and Mussolini a staggering amount in liras. And I remembered again when Franco told the United States and Britain that he could not discontinue sending war material to Germany in the World War because of his debt to Hitler. When the documents of the German Foreign Office were found by the American army, they included a report by Minister Schmidt on a conference between Hitler and Ciano on Spain, September 28, 1940, published in the Bulletin of the State Department (Volume XIV, No. 350, March 17, 1946) quoting Hitler as saying that "economically Germany has given out hundreds of millions for Spain."

And I was reminded of the question of the wise man—"What is truth?"

10

Scarcely had Lady Chamberlain completed her good-will tour through Fascist territory when the storm broke in Czechoslovakia. As early as September, 1936, I predicted to Washington that the Czechs would be the next victims, basing the prediction on the bitter attacks against them by Fascists from Spain. Under pressure, the Czechs had yielded to the persuasion of Lord Runciman and agreed to all the eight demands of Hitler. When Hitler increased his demands, Chamberlain flew to Germany to plead with him, and to loud acclaim. I could not join in the demonstration since I had no faith in Chamberlain as a mediator between Fascism and democracy, and I trembled for the Czechs. Making Hitler's demand for the dismemberment of the most gallant democracy in central Europe, his own, Chamberlain flew back to London, calling his surrender a victory and announcing he had "brought back peace in our time." It was then that the British and French ambassadors demanded that the Czechs accept and threatened, otherwise, to abandon them despite treaty obligations of honor. Yielding to what they described as "cruel" and "indescribable pressure," the Czechs again surrendered. But when Chamberlain flew back to Hitler with the good tidings of great joy, he found the dictator had changed his mind and would insist on infinitely more. His new terms were monstrous—so monstrous that Chamberlain could agree to act only as a transmitter to Prague. The Czechs indignantly rejected the terms. It looked like war—unless Hitler were bluffing.

At that hour, France was mobilizing, the British fleet was mobilized, Roosevelt in blunt language had made his protest, and we now know from Ciano's diary that at that time Mussolini was unable to drag Italy into a war in support of Hitler. The protests in Italy were open—there was trouble in Milan—there were demonstrations in Sicily in cafés—Italy wanted no war. France was bound by treaty to support Czechoslovakia, and Russia was ready to support her ally, France. Two chiefs of staff had warned Hitler that Germany was not prepared for a long war.

These cards were in the hands of Chamberlain and Daladier but were not played in the shameful conference at Munich. There the surrender was abject. The democracies, defeated, did not march out with the honors of war.

I was painfully disillusioned by the momentary jubilation in London and Paris over the most disgraceful bargain in generations. That night I attended a party near Biarritz, and everyone seemed ecstatic over "Mr. Chamberlain's great triumph." To me the Munich bargain seemed the greatest British tragedy since Austerlitz. That night I wrote my interpretation in my diary. The pact of Munich had reduced France to a second-class power, wiped out all its defense alliances, nullified the League of Nations, ended the policy of collective security, made Nazi Germany the dominant power in Europe, reversed the British foreign policy of two hundred years, and had given democracy a brutal, if not deadly, blow.

It seemed significant to me that Mr. Chamberlain immediately let it be known that there would speedily be a "settlement" in Spain—in the spirit of the settlement of Munich.

11

Soon thereafter I met at the International Bridge in Hendaye the young Americans who had fought with the Lincoln Brigade. They had been prisoners near Burgos until I effected their exchange for an equal number of Italian prisoners—the first exchange of military prisoners since the war began.

Two months before, the Marquis de Rialp, chairman of Franco's commission for the exchange of prisoners, had asked me to act as intermediary and had submitted a list of twenty-nine Franco aviators, *all Italian except two Spaniards and one Portuguese*, to be exchanged for fifteen loyalist aviators, *all Spanish except one Frenchman and one Russian*. To balance the list numerically, he proposed to add fourteen American privates. Del Vayo agreed to the exchange of soldiers of the same rank. The outcome was the exchange first of the American and Italian privates. No one had expected the negotiations to succeed. Dr. Giral, acting for the loyalist government, was both helpful and reasonable, and the marquis, though a man of good will, was difficult because of his indecision and vacillation, which I ascribed to his fear to assume responsibility. I came to like him and I got along with him. But Field Marshal Chetwode, distinguished British soldier, found the marquis maddening. One afternoon he came to my villa, apparently on the verge of a stroke, purple in the face. "I have just come from that damn Rialp," he exclaimed. "I could kill him." Sent by his government to both sides, his prejudice against the loyalists, formed in London drawing rooms, persuaded him he should visit the rebel government first, but the embassy intervened. In Barcelona he had been accorded every courtesy and distinction. Invited to a dinner, he assumed from what he had heard in London that the "reds" would appear without coats and in jeans, and he dressed accordingly. He was horribly embarrassed to find the guests, mostly of the government, in evening dress, and

the scene quite like one in London. Because he had gone to Barcelona first, he was kept waiting for some days in Hendaye before he
was permitted to cross, and then he had to hire a taxi to take him to
Burgos. "I found the *gentlemen* in Barcelona," he told me.

The International Red Cross took charge of the evacuation of
the American prisoners for whom I had arranged an exchange, and
I went to the French side of the bridge to meet them. When, as I
approached them, they shouted in a chorus, "Who won the World
Series?" they sounded like normal Americans to me. They were
rough in appearance but not in manner, and they did not whine
about their treatment as prisoners. That they had not lost their
sense of humor was evident in a story they told me.

One day in the prison camp they had been given clean suits in
anticipation of a visit of some English people, including a lady of
title, and a British military attaché with Franco's army. The
Englishman inspected them curiously through a monocle, and the
lady through her lorgnette. They were drawn up in line facing a
Franco officer. "*Viva España! Viva Franco!*" he shouted, giving the
Fascist salute; and they were expected to shout "*Viva*" and salute
similarly. But no *vivas* came from the Americans, and their arms
hung loosely at their sides. The officer turned crimson. The British
attaché snickered.

Turning away with disgust, the lady announced that she would
like to see the British prisoners. Through her lorgnette she surveyed
them with distaste. "Never," she exclaimed, "have I seen such
criminal faces in England." Among them were some boys of fine
families and of education, and the irreverent Americans thought the
lady irresistibly funny.

Soon the boys, after a bath and shave and a change of clothing,
were on board the *Queen Mary* on their way home.

The impression created by the propagandists is that the Lincoln
Brigade was composed of communists from the United States. It
is true that there were communists in the Brigade, but along with
many who were democratic liberals and socialists. Toward the
close, the communists through their aggressiveness and arrogance
imposed themselves on the others and this made it easy to denounce
the mixed Brigade as exclusively communistic.

12

The Francoists were enthusiastic over the "peace of Munich." They assumed that the new Holy Alliance of the Four Powers would now impose a "peace" on Spain by putting their combined forces behind the Fascist cause. Instantly, Lord Perth, British Ambassador in Rome, went into a series of conferences with Count Ciano. It was imperative that everything possible be done to force the "Spanish settlement" so the Anglo-Italian agreement could go into effect with its recognition of the conquest of Abyssinia.

But in the midst of the love feast, Hitler spoke again, and not on Chamberlain's favorite theme of "peace in our time." He told England to "mind her own business" and to "stop thinking she was God Almighty"; and that Englishmen like Churchill, Eden, Cecil, and Duff Cooper, who had resigned from the Ministry as a protest against the Munich betrayal, should have "their mouths stuffed." He warned that it would go hard with England if she dared displace Chamberlain with any of these. It was the new language of the New Order in Europe which began when Rome ordered Eden out of the British Cabinet.

Months had intervened and the Anglo-Italian pact was not in operation. It had been stipulated that it should not go into effect until the Italian army had been withdrawn from Spain; then, later, not until a substantial number had been withdrawn—and none had been sent home. At length Franco *announced that ten thousand Italians who had fought in Spain a year and a half would be sent back to Italy.* This was at the time the League of Nations Commission was *supervising the withdrawal of all foreigners from the loyalist army, at the request of the loyalist government.*

And then, one Sunday, the serenity of Saint-Jean-de-Luz was ruffled by the arrival of an all-English commission, consisting of a rear admiral, a captain, a major, an archivist, stenographers, and messengers, under the chairmanship of Mr. Hemming, Secretary of the Nonintervention Committee. A subcommittee, under the chairmanship of the chief archivist, with two secretaries, stenographers, and a messenger, was established in the Angleterre Hotel in Saint-Jean-de-Luz. It was announced that the purpose of the Hemming commission was to explain to Franco the withdrawal

plan of the Nonintervention Committee which the Spanish government had accepted and Franco had rejected. Correspondents were a
bit confused, because it was denied that the secretary of the defunct
committee was acting for that discredited group, and the impression was given that these men represented the Four Powers of
Munich.

The commission crossed the border, and a deep silence enveloped it. After a while, Hemming emerged and went to London;
and returned. Almost at once he flew back to London. It was understood that Franco had refused even to consider the withdrawal of
Italian troops—the Germans, even more important, were not considered—until after belligerent rights had been granted him. All
the commission did was to witness the departure of ten thousand
weary Italians, an insignificant portion—and these worn out by
eighteen months of fighting. Thereupon Hemming extravagantly
praised Franco's generous concession, and the British consul witnessed the landing in Italy with much beating of the drums. And
on the strength of this, Mr. Chamberlain announced the "Spanish
settlement" and put the Anglo-Italian agreement into operation.

While he was making this statement, British citizens standing on
the sea shore were watching an Axis ship attacking a loyalist vessel
within twelve miles of the English shore, and Fascist ships, armed
in Bremen, were prowling possessively in the waters of the North
Sea.

The spirit of Munich was settling like a low-lying cloud upon the
world.

13

On November 3, 1938, Lord Halifax, successor of Eden, made a
sensational statement in the House of Lords:

*Signor Mussolini has always made it plain from the time of the first conversa-
tions of His Majesty's government and the Italian government that for reasons
known to us, whether we approve of them or not, he is not prepared to see Franco
defeated.*

This meant that the Chamberlain government was entirely
reconciled to giving Mussolini a free hand in his invasion of Spain

and his war on democracy. Some old-fashioned Englishmen were shocked, and the *Manchester Guardian* asked editorially:

> *Can anyone imagine Lord Salisbury or Sir Edward Grey telling Parliament that the English government, far from protesting against such flagrant outrage on public law, was entering in a cordial agreement with Italy—an agreement which implies mutual trust and some common purpose—doing what it could to increase the prestige of that power and to strengthen its influence in the politics of Europe?*

When, immediately afterward, Mr. Chamberlain and Halifax, amidst the blowing of trumpets, announced their visit to Paris for a conference with Daladier and the pro-Nazi Bonnet, it was feared that the purpose was to get an agreement on belligerent rights for Franco. But the friends of democracy stiffened, the English protests were vehement, and the foreign-relations committee in the French House of Deputies unanimously went on record as unqualifiedly opposed to granting belligerent rights. And Daladier's narrow escape from overthrow two days before spoiled everything. The British statesmen made an ugly crossing on a raging channel to be received in the streets of Paris with boos and cries of "Munich." Numerous arrests were made. And so belligerent rights were not granted.

14

Listening to conversations in social circles at this time brought more disillusionments. For twenty years I had neither heard nor read anything but praise of Masaryk and Beneš as statesmen and champions of democracy. But Hitler's indecent attack on Beneš now seemed accepted in strange quarters. I heard the outrageous speech of Hitler smugly parroted. A lady of the diplomatic corps from a democratic country criticized Beneš because he "had irritated Hitler." Soon Hitler would take over Czechoslovakia as a feeding field in arms and food to be used against the nations that had surrendered at Munich, and the puppet government set up would order the pictures and busts of Masaryk removed from public places, and history would be blotted out by decree.

My admiration for the Spaniards grew. Fighting some years before the crisis reached the other countries, they were fighting still.

Chapter XXVII

The Last Phase

ANOTHER winter with rolling black clouds that seemed to perch on the top of the Pyrenees frowned on Saint-Jean-de-Luz. Few Spaniards lingered now along the French coast. Two former Spanish ambassadors to the Court of Saint James lived in Biarritz, though they did not move in the same circle. Neither was aligned with the loyalists, but one was the Marquis Merry del Val, long ambassador under the King, and the other his immediate successor, Pérez de Ayala, first ambassador under the Republic. I saw Ayala occasionally in his cosy flat where he had settled indefinitely to write, and he appeared cheerful and philosophic. I did not see Merry del Val, since he was not friendly to anyone who had sympathy for the loyalists.

Meanwhile, having failed in six offensives to drive the loyalists back across the Ebro after their spectacular advance, Franco was assembling planes, artillery, and tanks from Germany and Italy for another attempt. In the fighting that followed, he was able to put into action more planes than the First World War had seen in any single engagement. He was able to use ninety-five tanks on a four-mile front. Confronted by such overwhelming odds, the loyalists were ordered to retreat across the Ebro, and they moved back in perfect order and without the loss of a single gun. The Ebro fight of the loyalists had been sensational, and the London *Times*

(November 30, 1938), though supporting the Chamberlain policy, in commenting on the significance of the fight, said:

Besides the tactical victory, the chief value of the battle on the government side consisted in proof that the army of the people in bravery and discipline, constitutes a force equal to the best the nationalists can put into the field. Only the latter's great superiority in air force and artillery, estimated by one competent foreign observer as three to one in artillery, and two to one in the air, enabled the insurgents, after prolonged effort, to evict the republicans from the Ebro salient.

This was an admission that the refusal of the non-Fascist nations to sell planes and artillery to the legal government gave to the Fascists the victory they could not have won otherwise. At that time, General Fuqua told me that man for man the loyalist infantry was superior to that of their foe.

Thereafter, for a month, all was quiet on the various fronts. Then, in January, 1939, the League of Nations met again, and Shirer, in his *Diary*, wrote: "Bonnet and Halifax here to see that there is no nonsense to delay Franco's victory," and "Del Vayo made a dignified speech before the Council," and Halifax, "to show his colors, got up in the midst of it and ostentatiously strode out."

2

In the meanwhile, the neutral commission of the League completed its arrangements for the evacuation from the loyalist fighting forces of all foreigners, and these crossed the frontier into France. They bade farewell to the land in which they had left so many comrades underground, in an impressive review in Barcelona. Many carried flowers, and some, little children, as they swung along. Less than ten thousand were found in all, and the major part of these were Frenchmen, Americans, British, with anti-Nazi Germans and anti-Fascist Italians. The "Russian hordes" on which the gullible had been fed dwindled under the actual count of the neutral commission of the League of Nations to less than one hundred and fifty. I was told by an authority I trusted that at no time were more than five hundred Russians in Spain during the entire war.

Thus, with all foreign aid voluntarily renounced by the loyalists, the war entered a new phase. It was now notoriously a war of open aggression against Spain by Hitler and Mussolini, unwittingly, I hope, supported by some leaders of the great democracies.

"Nonintervention" had now become such a cynical mockery that some nations withdrew in disgust, as shiploads of arms and ammunition poured constantly into rebel ports from Germany and Italy. When reference was made in the House of Commons to the great number of German ships in Franco waters, Mr. Hudson, speaking for the Chamberlain government, triumphantly explained that these were not engaged in trade, but in carrying war material to Franco for his forthcoming offensive! No one made any comment.

At this time there was an intensification of the bombing of small towns and villages by Italian planes, and women and children were mangled in the streets and in their homes. The British commission, investigating on the ground, reported that no military objectives had existed. The purpose was to terrorize and demoralize the civilian population behind the lines and to drive them into Barcelona and Valencia to swell the enormous number of refugees, dependent on a hard-pressed government for food. When the alien aviators descended low to machine-gun civilians on a passenger train, the Chamberlain government refused to comment when comment was invited by the Spanish Ambassador in London.

At this time, Franco was demanding belligerent rights, though the Anglo-Italian pact specifically had made the granting of these rights conditional on the withdrawal of the Italian army. Brushing aside international law, Franco assumed the rights denied him, and vessels at his command scoured the high seas, remote from Spain, capturing vessels bearing food and confiscating their cargoes. British ships, as usual, suffered most, but no protest was publicized until a Greek ship bearing Rumanian grain to England was captured. This ruffled the complacency of 10 Downing Street. The admission of the Undersecretary of Foreign Affairs that "certainly this would be interpreted as an assumption of belligerent rights" was not more conclusive than the action of Lloyd's in increasing insurance rates because of these acts of piracy.

With Mussolini now demanding from France "Corsica, Tunis,

and Nice," and Italian planes bombing British ships, Mr. Chamberlain, seemingly undisturbed and unresentful, set forth on his journey to Mussolini—his second pilgrimage to Canossa. It was thought by some that the rebels would smash through speedily to Tarragona, and on to Barcelona before Chamberlain and Mussolini could meet; and then, with the Spanish government in collapse, Chamberlain could grant belligerent rights on the ground that the struggle was over and it no longer mattered. France pointedly announced its opposition to the granting of these rights and implied some distrust of the Chamberlain brand of mediation. When, at this juncture, President Roosevelt issued his stirring warning to the totalitarian states, England responded so enthusiastically that Chamberlain was forced to issue a statement in approval. But as the train bearing Chamberlain and Halifax rumbled on, the Italian press was boasting of Italy's ability to "spit in the face of France," their ally. Chamberlain contented himself with a new promise of Mussolini's to withdraw the Italian army *after the Spanish democracy had been crushed.* The scene in Rome was something new and strange in British history with the Prime Minister warmly shaking hands with the Duce whose bombs were destroying peaceful villages, hitting British ships, and killing British seamen. When the Prime Minister returned to London announcing greater faith than ever in the word of Mussolini, Lloyd George snorted: "The faith of a simpleton!" In *The Gathering Storm,* Churchill, citing Ciano's and Mussolini's contemptuous references to the Prime Minister of Britain, confesses a sense of shame.

Mr. Chamberlain returned to find the march on Tarragona prospering, with four Italian divisions on the march, fantastically outnumbering the loyalists in guns and planes. It was now perfectly clear that unless the great democracies lifted the arbitrary ban on arms to the loyalists, the fate of Barcelona was sealed. For a moment, France seemed awakening, and the party of Daladier almost unanimously demanded the opening of the frontier, but at that very moment the sinister Bonnet was in a huddle with Halifax in Geneva.

When at this time, Del Vayo announced that the neutral commission had completed its task of removing all foreigners from the loyalist army, Lord Halifax's expression of appreciation was most restrained, but Bonnet, with shameless hypocrisy, piously expressed the hope that now Italy and Germany would withdraw under the prodding of the Nonintervention Committee which he knew was disappearing in a stink.

To the surprise of the Francoists, all men and women from seventeen to fifty-five were called to the colors in Catalonia, and fresh but untrained troops, inadequately armed, were hurrying down the roads to Lérida to meet the Italians and the Moors. Young Catalonian women paraded the streets of Barcelona summoning their sex to the factories that the men might fight, and invading the cinemas, urging slackers to the front.

Meanwhile, for six weeks, beginning the first of November, Franco was calling on Hitler and Mussolini for more planes, tanks, artillery. In all the rebel ports there was intense activity. More than thirty thousand tons of war material entered the port of Vigo in December alone. The S.S. *Calabria*, from Spezia, in another port, landed three hundred and ten cases, and a few hundred trained foreign gunners. Into the port of Cádiz poured Italian officers and soldiers—to make up for the ten thousand worn-out men who had been sent home to make the "Spanish settlement." From Genoa, the S.S. *Brescia* carried a thousand men and twenty officers. These facts were matters of record in the British Foreign Office to which they had been given by the Spanish Ambassador, Pablo de Azcárate, whom I knew.

With the crisis approaching, the loyalists had but thirty-seven thousand rifles with which to arm the entire army of Catalonia. So low were they in machine guns that soon an entire battalion of well-organized and trained machine gunners had to retire because they had no guns.

But Hitler and Mussolini had not skimped their ally. Soon the Fascists would be able to have a cannon at every twenty yards on portions of the front. They would have ten, and later, twenty, planes to one; in light and medium artillery they would have twenty or thirty to one; in light infantry arms, including automatics, they would have ten to one; and in heavy artillery they would have an abundance against next to nothing.

The loyalists still pinned their hopes on the lifting of the embargo by the United States. The brazen one-sidedness of "non-intervention" was well known in Washington. At length, I wrote personally to President Roosevelt that, without intending it, our embargo was making us an invaluable collaborator of the Axis powers in their war on the Spanish democracy; and a little later, Roosevelt thrilled the world again in his historic call to arms of the democracies with his blunt assertion that *our neutrality act was operating in the interest of the aggressor*. But the twilight of loyalist hopes was deepening into darkness.

3

The major role of Mussolini's black-shirt army in the taking of Barcelona is established beyond all doubt through the publication of Count Ciano's diary. Almost daily, through January, 1939, reference is made to the Italian army's campaign in Spain. Here we read that the Corpo Truppe Volontarie "has assumed the offensive" (January 3, 1939); that in Spain "we are going ahead full speed" (January 4); that General Gambara's role "has been magnificent" (January 7); that Mussolini was pleased with a report from Franco conveyed by personal messenger, describing it to Ciano as "the report of a subordinate" (January 8); and on January 15, that "Gambara has luckily assumed the role of leader of all the Spanish forces" (January 15). After the Fascist army of Mussolini had reached the environs of Barcelona, Ciano wrote that "we ask that our legionnaires be among the first units to enter" because "they deserve it" (January 24). Even then Mussolini was nervous, sending constantly to Ciano for news, since he feared "a repetition of what took place in Madrid" (January 25). He was also uneasy because of Franco's proposed "political pact with Germany" which Hitler had communicated to Mussolini. Of course, Ciano adds, this political pact "happens to be secret like ours," but if made public, the Italian pact would have precedence since "otherwise people will say that Italy makes war in Spain, and Germany profits by it" (January 27). And when Barcelona fell, Ciano proudly wrote in his diary that "victory in Spain bears only one name, and that is the name of Mussolini." More important, perhaps, it also bore the name of Hitler.

4

With their advantage in metal, the Italian legionnaires, the Moors, and Requetés were approaching the outskirts of Barcelona. Del Vayo made a last desperate appeal to Bonnet for the privilege to buy arms. It was as though a hungry man were appealing to a bank façade for bread. He was coldly refused. Bonnet was more for Germany than for France, but the French were now becoming alarmed over what "nonintervention" had done to them. I had this personally from one of the greatest of French statesmen who had understood the significance of the Spanish struggle from the beginning.

Ciano was a bit uncomfortable because he had heard of the "*rapprochement* between Burgos and Paris," and, in that event, he wrote, "we shall then make known that we have had an agreement with Spain since November, 1936." In truth, though not reduced to a pact, there had been an agreement with Mussolini as early as the spring of 1934. Rumors were rife that France might intervene, and in that event—and here we have a queer light on Fascist reasoning —Italy would "intervene"! But with the governments of the democracies standing as firm as Hitler or Mussolini would have wished against the slightest interference with the Fascist plans, the leaders, out of power, were protesting now with vigor, the liberals, the laborites in England making their position plain.

Mr. Stimson, former Secretary of State in the United States, sternly rebuked our embargo policy as an indefensible denial of international law and regretted he had not done so earlier (Stimson's memoirs, *On Active Service*. Eden, speaking at Coventry, was saying:

> *Franco is conquering Catalonia by reason of air and military power more formidable than this war has yet seen. Whence has this great power of armament come? Everyone knows who provides this armament and who continues to provide it in open violation of agreements and pacts. Meanwhile, Franco's foreign airmen are bombing, foreign artillery is shelling, and foreign infantry is marching across the Spanish soil.*

5

The collapse of the defenses around Barcelona was unexpected among those unfamiliar with the situation. Lister's magnificent brigade retired before the foe only when utterly exhausted from four days and nights of ceaseless fighting without rest. Thus Barcelona fell without a battle in the city. About four hundred thousand men, women, and children poured northward to escape the "army of liberation." For a moment, disorganization and panic fell upon the people and the army, with the road to the frontier so congested with humanity that traffic could scarcely move. But Negrín remained cool, and, within a day, order and discipline were restored, and the army covered the retreat in perfect order and with brilliance.

The government took up its quarters in the old eighteenth-century fort of Figueras, where Philip II and María Luisa had lived, whose cellars offered protection from bombs, and there the Council of Ministers sat in almost continuous session. Hidden there were many, if not most, of the treasures of the Prado, which had been "sent to Russia," as millions of Americans had been led to believe. Azaña was in the near-by village of Oerdillina. He lived toward the close in a very simple house in the village of Abajol.

I drove across southern France to Perpignan, where we had opened headquarters. This uninspiring provincial town was packed to overflowing, and Garrison and I stayed in Carcassonne, making the drive back and forth. The day of my arrival the press correspondents had gone to Figueras to attend the meeting of the Cortes. It met in the wine cellar of the fort, with Martínez Barrio presiding. That evening, Harry Buckley, the English correspondent, described the scene to me. Dr. Negrín calmly outlined the situation. He said the loyalists had been overwhelmed with planes, tanks, artillery, from Germany and Italy. Battling brilliantly against tremendous odds for many days, the loyalist army had reached the breaking point, but it had recovered and could fight on. It had become a fight for liberty and independence and for the future of democracy everywhere. Peace would come only through an agreement on three outstanding points:

(1) The absolute independence of Spain of all foreign influence.

(2) The determination by the Spanish people of the kind of government they wished.

(3) And a pledge against reprisals after the war.

He urged the continuance of resistance and sat down. One by one, the leaders of all the parties rose and unqualifiedly gave approval.

That little band, meeting in solemn session in the wine cellar of the old fort that night, presented the most inspiring spectacle to be seen in any democratic country in the world.

I listened at Perpignan to the stories of men from Spain, of the pitiful plight of the refugees, of the machine-gunning of the roads crowded with women, children, and goats. The next day I drove with Colonel Cheadle, my new military attaché, to the village of La Perthus on the frontier. The black Senegalese troops of France were everywhere. It was a cold day and the roads were slimy, but I noticed many of the black soldiers carrying their shoes and treading the wet, cold road with bare feet. We passed groups of men of military age, refugees from Spain, carrying bundles.

Near the village by the roadside hundreds of women and children stood huddled together in the rain, awaiting transportation to a camp for refugees—old women with wrinkled faces, young women with nursing babes, some expectant mothers, trembling in the rain. I had seen such pitiful scenes two years before at Hendaye when "nonintervention" won its first victory for the Axis.

A year and eight months later, at the *fundo* near Santiago, Chile, of Margarita Xirgu, the Spanish actress, a Spanish serving woman brought in an eighteen-months-old child. The mother, with the then unborn baby, had been among the women I had seen trembling in the rain. The child had been born in a refugee camp in France.

6

I was to see Del Vayo at the Spanish Consulate in Perpignan at five o'clock that evening, but the Council of Ministers had delayed him, and it was after six when he rushed in with apologies. One who had seen him the day before had found him unshaven, red-eyed, and depressed, but now his face was ruddy from the mountain air, his eyes were bright, and his pugnacious jaw was set. "I had some sleep last night—the first in four days," he said, while removing his overcoat. "We held them when the proportion against us in planes, tanks, and artillery from Germany and Italy was four to one, but when the odds were fantastically increased it was impossible. We have re-formed our lines and will probably make a stand"—though I could see he had little hope of holding in that region. "We shall do the best we can, but if we fail, we shall go to Valencia or Madrid and carry on." He admitted the impossibility of transferring the troops to the central zone, but he said the government and army officers would go by planes. "Miaja," he continued, "has an army of five hundred thousand men, fine soldiers, in the central zone; we are now getting in some guns, machine guns and muskets, but we are forced to depend on contraband material."

That morning, February 2, 1939, the French Ambassador, Henry, who was Bonnet's hand-picked man, had gone to Figueras to urge the loyalists to surrender. When I asked if the tale were true, Del Vayo hesitated and then nodded affirmatively. "And the answer?" I asked. "An emphatic no," he said. There flashed before my eyes the picture of a similar scene at Prague when a similar demand had been made on Beneš.

My chief reason for seeing Del Vayo was to inquire as to the fate of the masterpieces from the Prado and the Escorial that had been stored between Barcelona and the French frontier in what had become a fighting zone. "The paintings have caused us great uneasiness," he said, "but just this morning I signed the papers turning them over to the International Committee for the Protection of Works of Art, for immediate conveyance to Geneva. We have arranged for the conveyance." Soon one thousand paintings were on their way. These were the masterpieces the gullible had been told had been "given to Russia."

Suddenly Del Vayo, on edge, sprang up and hurried across the room to the telephone. "I want news of the military operations," he explained, taking up the receiver. "Hello, hello, hello." Then, to me: "It is terrible—there is but one line in Figueras." At length he got through, but the officer he sought was out.

"I have just one request," he said. "I wish you would transmit to your government an appeal to the United States, possibly in conjunction with others, to do what is possible to prevent reprisals in Barcelona, where we fear a massacre."

A few days later, Ciano would write in his diary that in Barcelona Franco had engaged in "painstaking and drastic housecleaning." Among the prisoners were Italian anti-Fascists, and Mussolini was so informed. He ordered them all shot, with the comment that "dead men tell no tales" (*Ciano's Diary*, February 22).

Del Vayo, bareheaded, went with me to the door. That was my last view of Del Vayo during the war.

7

At first, the French frontier was closed against the escape of civilians and soldiers, but through the negotiations of Negrín, it was opened, and thousands crossed the border, as the loyalists, retreating toward the frontier, with their wounded, brilliantly fought rear-guard actions. By the last house, close to the frontier, Negrín stood watching the last parade of the gallant army as it marched into France and into concentration camps. Azaña, in the meanwhile, driving and sometimes walking with his family over a two-thousand-foot pass, crossed into France and went to the villa of Rivas Cherif, hoping, with the aid of England and France, to make terms in the interest of humanity.

But, under the prodding of Bonnet, France, with almost comic haste, was planning to recognize Franco, while the Spanish government existed and functioned, in possession of the capital and a quarter of the country and with five hundred thousand soldiers in the field. The delay was holding up Hitler's march on France and Europe.

8

Thousands of old men, women, and children, with loyalist soldiers, were confined in camps in France unfit for human habitation. The camps of St. Cyprien and Argelte, great stretches of sand, enclosed by barbed wire, had no shelter of any kind. Confronted by an emergency, this cannot be held against the French, but the unforgivable sin of the French government was in giving permission to Franco agents to enter the camps and harangue the soldiers in an attempt to persuade them to join the Fascist army.

Soon Franco was making his triumphant entrance into Barcelona. Eighty thousand troops marched, headed by the Italian army under General Gambara, with German and Italian guns, artillery, and tanks and with two hundred and fifty Italian planes roaring above the marching men. Behind the Italian army, Franco rode in a car, preceded by his colorful Moorish bodyguard, their trappings glistening in the sun. Behind the Italians and the Moors marched the Spaniards. And in the rear, more Italians, the Bersaglieri and the black-shirted Arditti with daggers upraised in the Fascist salute. When the Italian Littoric division swept down the street, it was greeted with cries of "*Duce! Duce!*" A London paper described the scene with joyous gusto under the caption "Barcelona *en Fête*," creating the impression of a city wild with joy. But more impartial witnesses have assured me that the general population showed no enthusiasm but looked on in curious silence.

9

In the midst of these events in Barcelona, the British and French agents who went to Burgos were being bluntly told that in return for recognition there would be no pledge of amnesty; and that no information would be given regarding the foreign policy Franco would adopt. But the "spirit of Munich" was still strong, and "appeasement," though panting a bit, was pressing on. With the German and Italian press making merry over the subserviency of the democracies, crawling on all fours with indecent haste; with the Franco press screaming that France and England would never be allowed to separate the Spaniards from their German and Italian "comrades"; with the announcement from Mussolini that the Italians would stay in Spain as long as their services were required, the Chamberlain government and the French prepared to surrender unconditionally.

One day, Daladier announced to the French deputies that his government had decided on recognition, and that the Chamberlain government was pressing him for immediate action. Three days later, Chamberlain announced that he had accorded recognition without conditions. Thus Fascism had triumphed over democracy in Spain, and with the "Spanish settlement" came "peace in our time"—for six months.

10

The French government, dominated in its foreign policy by the slimy Bonnet, sent Marshal Pétain as ambassador to Franco. He was known to be temperamentally and ideologically in sympathy with the kind of government favored by Franco, and always to have hated the ideals of the French Revolution. He had never been favorable to a republican regime. And, in addition, he had been a teacher of Franco in the military school and was presumed to have influence with him. Stationed in Spain, he frequently crossed the border to Saint-Jean-de-Luz to lunch at the Miramar Hotel, where I had my embassy, and I saw him several times. Tall, erect as a flagpole, seemingly in the best of health, he did not look his age by twenty years; and, later, when he became a collaborator of Hitler's and his apologists sought to excuse his treason by pleading his age and feebleness, I was not impressed. But when he first called on the Dictator at Burgos and was kept cooling his heels in the reception room for a long time while Franco dallied with the diplomat of one of the least significant of nations, and when, at length he was received with such marked coldness that even Pétain noticed, the degradation of France was apparent.

In the meantime, Negrín had flown back to central Spain to resume the struggle. He was trying to raise the morale, to readjust the various services to the changed conditions, and to rally the loyalists for a renewed resistance. He felt sure the resistance could be continued for six months. With the international situation growing more threatening every day, he envisioned the possibility of a European war. He was a "last ditcher."

Chapter XXVIII

I Report to Washington

THE first of March, 1939, I was summoned to Washington "for consultation" with the State Department. During the two and a half years of the war I had not received a summons home for consultation, which may seem rather remarkable. This has been the subject of some comment in the American press. It may not have seemed worth while to the department, since it knew precisely my interpretation of the significance of the Spanish war. Throughout the two and a half years, I personally wrote regularly and sent voluminous reports on every phase of the struggle, copies now in my possession, precisely as Secretary Hull told a press conference at one stage. These dispatches would make a very large volume. There was nothing I could have said by word of mouth that was not clearly said in these dispatches, and my position was perfectly clear, as Mr. Hull makes plain in his memoirs. My opinions were as follows:

(1) That after the first days of considerable confusion, it was plainly shown to be a war of the Fascists and the Axis powers against the democratic institutions of Spain.

(2) That the Spanish war was the beginning of a perfectly thought-out plan for the extermination of democracy in Europe, and the beginning of a Second World War with that as the intent.

(3) That the Nonintervention Committee was a shameless sham, cynically dishonest, in that Germany and Italy were con-

stantly sending soldiers, planes, tanks, artillery, and ammunition
into Spain without an interference or real protest from the signa-
tories of the pact.

(4) That Germany and Italy were using Spanish towns and
people for experimental purposes in trying out their new methods
of destruction and their new technique of terrorism.

(5) That the Axis, in preparation for the continental struggle,
was using Spain to see how far it could go with the silent acquiescence of the great democracies and to test their spirit, courage, and
will to fight in defense of their ideals.

(6) That the Axis powers believed that with the conversion of
Spain into a Fascist state, it could, and would, be used as an entering wedge in South and Central America. I informed Washington
of the open boasting of the Franco press of the determination to
"liberate" South America from "Yankee bondage and atheism."

(7) That the purpose was manifest in a book prepared for use
in the schools bitterly attacking democracy in general and that of
the United States and Britain in particular.

(8) That the attacks, ridicule, and insults aimed at the United
States and England by the Franco press left no possible doubt as to
its position.

(9) That while the Axis powers poured in armies, planes, tanks,
artillery, technicians, and engineers for Franco, the Nonintervention Committee of the European democracies and our own embargo
were making a powerful contribution to the triumph of the Axis
over democracy in Spain; that whereas the war on China was being
waged by the Japs alone, on Czechoslovakia by Nazi Germany
alone, on Abyssinia by Fascist Italy alone, the first country to be
attacked *by the Axis—Germany and Italy together—was Spain.*

(10) That it was my opinion, long before Munich, that the next
attack would be on Czechoslovakia, because of the bitter abuse of
her, without apparent reason, by Germans and Italians who crossed
the Spanish border for food in Saint-Jean-de-Luz and Biarritz.

(11) I had informed Washington that our interests, ideologically, commercially, and industrially, were bound up with those of
democracy in Spain, whose government we recognized as the legal
constitutional government, and that the victory of Franco would be
a danger to the United States, especially in South America.

With these views constantly sent to the State Department for more than two years, I never received any comment from the department. Now we know that there was a cleavage there even in the higher strata.

2

When summoned home so late "for consultation," I had no doubt of the purpose. I did not then know that the summons was on the initiative of Secretary Hull and Mr. Dunn, his adviser politically on western Europe. It is now of record that Mr. Hull wirelessed President Roosevelt, then at sea, that since Britain, the Chamberlain government, had decided to recognize the Franco Fascist regime, "I suggest that Ambassador Bowers, our representative to the loyalist government, be ordered home for consultation in order to free our hands for establishing relations with the Franco government" (Hull's *Memoirs*, Vol. I, page 616).

I sailed on the *Queen Mary* on March fourth, and in mid-Atlantic the wireless brought the intelligence that General Casado had overthrown the republican government in a *coup d'état* in Madrid on the issue of unconditional surrender. Franco, with his Moors, his Italian Fascist army, his German aviators, engineers, technicians, troops and officers, and all the material furnished by the Axis, had been unable for two and a half years to take Madrid; it fell only when the defending forces were divided through the intrigues of one of the great democracies of Europe.

On the fall of Madrid, Ciano wrote in his diary that it was "the most formidable victory for Fascism, perhaps the greatest one so far" (March 28, 1939)—which is precisely what I had been reporting that it would be. *That day, with Mussolini "overjoyed," Ciano described the scene when the Duce, pointing to the atlas open on the map of Spain, said: "It has been open in this way for almost three years and that is enough." And then he added: "But I know already that I must open it on another page"—which is precisely what I had foretold.*

3

The news of Casado's action reached Negrín in a little village near Alicante where he was in council with some of his ministers. At three in the afternoon, he and Del Vayo took to the air in planes held in readiness and turned toward Toulouse, and, flying by daylight over enemy territory, miraculously reached France.

The marvelous fight to save democracy in Spain was over.

I was not surprised to find at home a powerful public sentiment favorable to the Spanish loyalists. It was the instinctive American sentiment, going back to the days when Daniel Webster, Secretary of State, sent a sizzling reply to the protest of the Austro-Hungarian government because of the ovations being given Kossuth in the United States. But it was then too late to realize that our embargo had been a factor in giving victory to the Fascists. I was entirely satisfied with my position throughout. I found there was a sharp division in the State Department on our policy in Spain, though the pro-Franco element was more numerous, and strategically placed. Mr. Messersmith, then an Assistant Secretary, was sympathetic toward my point of view, and he assured me that the same was true of Sumner Welles, the Undersecretary. This, I assume, was true, since in a book written since by Mr. Welles he has ascribed some of the misfortunes of the world to our appeasement policy in Spain.

On the night of my arrival in Washington I spoke with President Roosevelt on the telephone and proposed that I see him and report that night, but he thought it best for me to see Mr. Hull first.

I had known Cordell Hull as a friend, personal and political, for seventeen years. In his *Memoirs* he refers to our first meeting when together we spoke at a state-wide Democratic meeting in Indianapolis, where he thought I had made a "red-hot and eloquent speech which attracted wide attention" (Hull's *Memoirs*, Vol. I, page 485). Two years later, when Hull was National Chairman, he asked me to go down from New York to Washington and spend the day with Senator Pat Harrison going over his keynote speech for the convention of 1924 with him. Pat had made so many revisions of the manuscript that it had grown stale on him and he was depressed, but it was a brilliant discourse and required no change. After that, I saw Mr. Hull frequently and on terms of warm friendship. In a pre-convention conference with Roosevelt at Albany in 1932, he, with Senators Walsh and Wheeler of Montana and Dan Roper, selected me to place Roosevelt in nomination—an honor I could not accept for reasons not necessary to state here. In the preparation of my keynote speech at Houston in 1928 the only people with whom I conferred were Hull and Senator Walsh of Montana. I had a profound admiration for Hull's statesmanship. His speeches in the House before he entered the Senate were literally treatises, especially in the fields of economics and international trade. A man unquestionably of presidential caliber, I had editorially suggested his nomination as early as 1924. Throughout his tenure as Secretary of State, and since, our personal relations remained unchanged. All this, to make clear that our differences on our Spanish policy were political and not personal.

But some observations of his in his *Memoirs* touching on the Axis war in Spain and my mission there call for some comment. He says:

Bowers, himself a liberal, promptly took sides in the Civil War. He felt that the United States should make its policies conform with the vital interests of the liberal forces prosecuting one side of the war.

I did not actually "take sides" until the arrival of Italian planes and German engineers and technicians made it crystal clear that the Axis was warring on Spanish democracy, but that was clear in less than a month after the war began; and while a "liberal," I did not take sides as such, but as a democrat, since I could see but one side a democrat could take. On the issue of Democracy vs. Totalitarianism, so blatantly and offensively proclaimed by the Franco press and by the Fascist radios of Italy, Germany, and Portugal, I was certainly not neutral. No diplomat of the totalitarian states would have dared be neutral, and it was because we had too many "neutral," if not worse, diplomats representing democratic states making a virtue of "neutrality" on that issue that we lost all the diplomatic battles from 1934 until the World War began.

Again Mr. Hull says:

He buttressed this view by frequent references to the assistance rendered by Germany and Italy to Franco. At the State Department, while recognizing that what Bowers had to say about Germany and Italy was true, we had to pursue a broader course, which recognized the grave danger that the civil war in Spain might erupt into a European war.

This goes to the very heart of the difference in opinion between me and members of the Department. They went upon the theory

that this was a "civil war"—so like the "civil wars" in Norway and
Poland—and that the policy of appeasement, sponsored by Chamberlain, would prevent a World War; I upon the theory that the
Fascist states would inevitably accept this policy of acquiescence or
appeasement as evidence of weakness or cowardice and conclude
that the hour had struck for an all-out effort to exterminate democracy throughout Europe, and that this would make a World War
inevitable. I did not have the advantage—if it was an advantage—
of the views of Chamberlain's ambassador in Washington, or of
Mr. Bonnet's, but I heard the Fascists and Nazis and their fellow
travelers from across the border making their boasts, and I daily
read the Franco papers. Within six months after the troops of
Mussolini and Hitler marched with a dash before Franco's reviewing stand in Barcelona in celebration of the Fascist triumph in
Spain, the World War came.

Conceding this, of course, Mr. Hull says, "But Spain was not
the cause of the European war." It is true that the cruel sacrifices of
the democracies of Spain and Czechoslovakia did not incline the
great democracies to draw the sword, but their weak acquiescence
in these wanton outrages was the "go" signal for the Axis powers.
That, I have no doubt, will be the verdict of history when the
tumult and the shouting of the partisans and propagandists have
died out. History will declare that the six months intervening between the Fascist victory in Spain and the invasion of Poland were a
mere armistice in one war—the Second World War. It certainly
requires no argument to sustain the fact that the policy of appeasement and acquiescence did not prevent the World War; I contend
that it made it almost certain. What it did, and all it did, was to
sacrifice the two gallant democracies of Spain and Czechoslovakia
as a peace offering to Fascism, which did not, and in the nature of
things could not, work.

Again, defending the embargo which was a godsend to the
Axis in the war in Spain, Mr. Hull says that "merely authorizing
the export of arms to Spain was not enough, since we would have to
see to it that the arms got to Spain" (Hull's *Memoirs*, Vol. I, page
483). That is not my understanding. I was assured by the Spanish
government, as recognized, that it was prepared to pay for material
bought, and *to take the responsibility of its delivery on itself*. It was not

expected that it would be sent in American ships. Producers in the United States were willing to sell; we exerted ourselves to prevent the sale. The delivery was another matter in which we would not have been involved. But the sad thing is that we set aside international law to prevent the sale. As we shall see, this shocked Henry L. Stimson, a distinguished former Secretary of State and a great international lawyer.

4

My opinion was, and is, that our policy and the policy of Chamberlain was the narrow and not the "broader course," for this policy was predicated on the theory that seemed absurd to me, that through the appeasement of Hitler and Mussolini and the sacrifice of the democracy of Spain, it would maintain peace elsewhere. But for this evidence of fear and weakness, it may be doubted whether Hitler would have felt safe in attacking Czechoslovakia, or in launching his war on Poland. I could not satisfy my conscience that it was the broader course to set aside international law in the appeasement of international Fascism, by refusing to sell the constitutional government of Spain the material for its defense. At any rate, this course, broad or narrow, was vigorously opposed by Henry L. Stimson, who, too late, as he admits, made his protest. In his charming and fascinating memoirs, written by Mr. Stimson in collaboration with Mr. Bundy, I find these words:

His first statement [against Fascism] was made on the war in Spain. It was a closely reasoned legal document for the enforcement of the well-established rule of international law that we "should furnish arms to the government that had been recognized as legal, and to no other." In the case of Spain this was the loyalist government. This is a statement Mr. Stimson was sorry he had not made sooner. He had made no secret of his sympathy with the loyalist side [thus taking sides] but he had held back from direct opposition to the policy of the Administration. In January, 1939, it was too late for any statement to be of any use, for the republican government was at last being overcome by the superior force of Fascist intervention. Stimson was not a left-winger, but he believed, and repeatedly argued, that "the Fascists were incomparably more dangerous to us; more active in their proselytizing; and more dangerous and intolerant of international law and methods." And, of course, in the case of Spain, it remained a clear and simple fact that the republican was the legal and elected government, recognized as such by the United States. [Stimson's *On Active Service*, pages 313–317.]

These were precisely my views, but we took the "broader course," refusing to recognize Spain's right under international law to buy antiaircraft guns to protect women and children against the Axis aviation, to buy heavy artillery and planes to meet the armed forces of the Axis, boasting of its determination to exterminate democracy in Europe. I had hoped that with the revelation of the significance of the struggle proclaimed by the harangues and congratulatory telegrams of Hitler, and by his actions, we would lift the embargo. Finally I wrote personally to Roosevelt that however good our intentions may have been at first, it had become quite clear that actually our embargo was operating powerfully for the benefit of the Axis. Very soon thereafter, Roosevelt said as much in a public speech.

5

When I saw Mr. Hull he received me with his usual cordiality, but he seemed disinclined to discuss the Spanish situation, the solution of which had been determined upon when I was summoned home for "consultation" in order "to free our hands in establishing relations with the Franco government."

I found President Roosevelt seated at his desk in the White House residence, more serious and graver than I had ever seen him before. I got the impression that he was not happy over the course we had followed. Before I could sit down or utter a word, he said:

"We have made a mistake; you have been right all along."

He said more, in explanation, that I do not feel free to quote from my diary. He did say, however, that he had been deluged with contradictory information from many quarters other than from the ambassador to Spain. I knew, of course, that the ambassadors of Chamberlain and Bonnet had given information in contradiction of mine; that our embassy in London reflected the views of Chamberlain; and that other American ambassadors, depending on the propaganda of Franco agents, had joined. I asked him if our minister in Iraq had sent him information "right out of the horse's mouth," and for the first time he smiled as he put a cigarette in his long holder.

It was then he said, with some vehemence, that he could see no reason to hurry about the recognition of Franco, that he would let him "stew in his juice for a while," and that he would like me to remain in Washington for some time. He was leaving the next day for Warm Springs, and later, when recognition was accorded, I learned from two members of the Cabinet that on leaving he had given instructions that nothing be done until after his return.

When I saw Sumner Welles he reiterated what the President had said about doing nothing for the time.

6

The night of the day I saw Roosevelt, I was with Senator Key Pittman, an old friend, chairman of the Foreign Relations Committee, and author of the embargo, from nine o'clock until dawn alone in his house. When I entered, after shaking hands, he walked over to a table for a cigarette, saying over his shoulder: "I am afraid we made a mistake in Spain." He then added that in the beginning he thought the embargo good in that it would keep other nations out, and localize the war. I agreed, but added that when, two or three weeks later, it was notorious that the Axis powers were sending arms, ammunition, and even armies to Franco, the embargo on military material for the defense of the legal government might well have been lifted and Spain given her rights under international law; and that the material would have been carried in other than American vessels.

A few days later I was standing beside Mr. Messersmith at a reception given me by Senator Guffey, when Sol Bloom, chairman of the Foreign Affairs Committee of the House, approached and asked if I would appear before his committee and give it my impressions about Spain. To my astonishment, Messersmith said he hoped I would. I thereupon accepted. The committee met in secret session and there was a full attendance. I talked frankly for more than an hour, receiving the closest and most courteous attention, and, at the close, questions were asked and answered. When asked if I thought the embargo had contributed to the Fascist triumph, I replied that it unquestionably had. The only question I refused to answer was whether I thought the Franco regime should be recognized. I evaded by saying that this was a matter for the State Department and the President. At the conclusion I was warmly cheered, and I had the feeling that the committee was sympathetic to my view.

Thus the President had said we had made a mistake.

Senator Pittman, author of the embargo, had said we had made a mistake.

The House committee was sympathetic.

But it was too late.

It was very clear, however, that the recognition of Franco had been determined upon. Mr. Dunn, on whose political judgment as to western Europe Mr. Hull leaned, was clearly impatient for an immediate recognition. Seeing no object in lingering longer in Washington, I told Mr. Welles that but for the fact that we had heavy investments in Spain that might suffer through Fascist resentment, I would never favor the recognition, but since the recognition was clearly indicated, I thought there should be three conditions in according it:

(1) That there would be a positive pledge that there would be no interference with American interests in Spain.

(2) That there would be a positive pledge that there would be no reprisals, political executions, and persecutions of the defeated democrats.

(3) That the imprisoned loyalists should be given their freedom.

Mr. Welles said:

"We have these assurances."

Just whence these assurances came, and through what intermediary outside Spain, he did not say. It was not until after the appearance of Mr. Hull's *Memoirs* that I learned that it was Mr. Bullitt who negotiated with the Franco agents in Paris for the recognition, and that no pledge was made against reprisals, executions, and imprisonments. Mr. Hull reports that "in the full flush of victory, the Franco government was not inclined to make any promise worth having." And so, with that perfectly clear, we accorded recognition to Franco, and the "full flush of victory" was to last for at least ten years.

I told Mr. Welles that I would leave at once, close the embassy in Saint-Jean-de-Luz, and go to Madrid to supervise the packing of my belongings.

"I wish you would not go to Madrid," he said.

Astonished, I asked with some feeling if it were possible we were recognizing a government so contemptuous of international usage that an American Ambassador dare not go to Madrid to collect his property in an American Embassy. Mr. Welles, who seemed embarrassed, replied that it was the Italians he feared. "Very well," I said. "I acted as intermediary in the exchange of military prisoners at the request of Franco and succeeded in releasing quite a number of Italian aviators, and have a fulsome letter of appreciation from the Italian Ambassador. Perhaps I can get a *salvoconducto* from the Italian Embassy." Mr. Welles looked at me reproachfully and said nothing.

7

I returned to Saint-Jean-de-Luz to close the embassy. I found Colonel Behn, of the International Telephone and Telegraph Company there, champing at the bit because Franco refused him permission to cross the border into Spain; and Mr. Caldwell, his manager in Madrid, was not permitted to enter the American telephone plant where German technicians were at work for a very long time.

So that part of the "pledge" someone had given the department had already been repudiated.

No prisoners were released, many held for execution, and thousands of others were being thrown into prison.

So that part of the "pledge" was ignored.

The firing squad was working all the time and would continue to work for some years, mowing down democrats and republicans.

So that part of the pledge was worthless.

Whoever gave the pledge was manifestly dishonest or he had acted without authority; and whoever accepted it manifestly had too much faith in the word of a Fascist.

8

In Paris I was informed by our embassy there as I was passing through, en route home, that Dr. Negrín, the Prime Minister of the overthrown government, was in the city and would send a car to take me to his lodgings. I found him living on the top floor of an apartment house at 24 Avenue Charles Floquet. He was serene and not outwardly embittered as he described the closing scenes. He appeared honestly puzzled when he asked me why the great democracies had been so grimly determined to tie the hands of the government they recognized as legal in its fight against the Axis. It was an embarrassing question I could not answer.

I found the frontier at Hendaye more closely guarded than ever, and the Franco cheer leaders in Biarritz were becoming thoughtful and subdued. Soon the German Nazi officers would swagger in to take possession of their pleasant villas, and the owners would precipitately retreat before these "defenders of order." I found the Franco press, "in the first flush of victory," screaming its derision of the "moribund and degenerate democracies"; and Queipo de Llano, bidding farewell to the departing German and Italian soldiers, was fervently assuring them that the Spanish Fascists "never would forget or cease to support the German and Italian comrades"—and they kept the pledge throughout the World War that almost immediately followed.

En route to Paris, at Bayonne, some Basque refugee children from a camp near by boarded the train with a nurse to present candy to my daughter, flowers to my wife, and a book on the Basques to me, for the little I had been able to do for them. On Christmas Day they had serenaded us with carols at my villa at Chantaco.

In Paris I called on José Aguirre, the noble, scholarly, and devout Catholic President of the Basques, and found him with Leizaola, his Minister of Justice, who had acted with such humanity on the fall of Bilbao. Aguirre was sad, but confident of the resurrection of his people and the ultimate vindication of their principles and their faith.

Leizaola and Ernest Hemingway were at the boat train to see me off.

So ended my six years as Ambassador to Spain.

Index

About the Author

CLAUDE G. BOWERS *was United States Ambassador to Spain from 1933 until 1939 when he resigned. In the same year he was appointed Ambassador to Chile where he served for fourteen years.*

Before this he had been a distinguished newspaperman in Indiana and New York where he was editorial writer on the Evening World. *In 1928, he was keynote speaker and chairman of the Democratic National Convention. In addition to diplomacy, newspaper work and politics, he has written ten books of political history, including such notable works as* The Tragic Era, Jefferson and Hamilton, *and* Party Battles of the Jackson Period.